Insights into Autonomy and Technology in Language Teaching

Technology and autonomy share a common mission in language education, that is, to transform language education into learner-centered learning across boundaries. With this shared mission, technology and autonomy are closely intertwined, shaping the role of each other in language education. The two, if in harmony and mutually supportive, may work in synergy and reinforce each other in achieving the goal. Drawing on the literature and research findings from relevant research fields, including educational technology, educational psychology, adult and workplace learning, and language education, this book gives an overview of the relationship of technology with learner and teacher autonomy. It discusses how technology both benefits and constrains autonomy, and how a positive interaction between the two could be fostered. It underscores a critical perspective in understanding their relationships and a holistic approach to boosting a positive reciprocal relationship between the two.

Chun Lai is an Associate Professor at the Faculty of Education, the University of Hong Kong. Her research interests include self-directed language learning with technology beyond the classroom, technology-enhanced language learning and teacher technology integration.

Language Teaching Insights Series
Series Editors: David Nunan & Glenn Stockwell

Burston & Arispe: *Mobile-Assisted Language Learning and Advanced-level Second Language Acquisition*

Eginli: *Insights into Emotional Well-Being of Language Teachers*

Farrell: *Insights into Professional Development in Language Teaching*

Horwitz: *Becoming a Language Teacher (2nd ed.)*

Jitpaisarnwattana & Reinders: *Insights into Language MOOCs*

Khezrlou: *Insights into Task-Based Language Teaching*

Lai: *Insights into Autonomy and Technology in Language Teaching*

Leis: *Insights into Flipped Classrooms*

Mohebbi (Ed.): *Insights into Teaching and Learning Writing*

Son: *Insights into Digital Literacy and Language Teaching*

Tanaka-Ellis: *Insights into Teaching and Learning with Technology*

More information about titles in this series can be found at
https://www.castledown.com/academic-books/book-series/language-teaching-insights/

Insights into Autonomy and Technology in Language Teaching

Chun Lai
The University of Hong Kong

Melbourne – London – Tokyo – New York

4th Floor, Silverstream House, 45 Fitzroy Street Fitzrovia, London W1T 6EB, United Kingdom
Level 9, 440 Collins Street, Melbourne, Victoria 3000, Australia
2nd Floor Daiya Building, 2-2-15 Hamamatsu-cho, Minato-ku, Tokyo 105-0013, Japan
447 Broadway, 2nd Floor #393, New York NY, 10013, United States

First published 2023 by Castledown Publishers, London

Information on this title:
www.castledown.com/academic-books/view-title/?reference=9781914291111

DOI: 10.29140/9781914291111

Insights into Autonomy and Technology in Language Teaching

© Chun Lai, 2023

All rights reserved. This publication is copyright. Subject to statutory exception and to the provisions of relevant collective licencing agreements, no reproduction, transmission, or storage of any part of this publication by any means, electronic, mechanical, photocopying, recording or otherwise may take place without prior written permission from the author.

Typeset by Castledown Design, Melbourne
ISBN: 978-1-914291-11-1 (Paperback)
ISBN: 978-1-914291-12-8 (Digital)

Castledown Publishers takes no responsibility for the accuracy of URLs for external or third-party internet websites referred to in this publication. No responsibility is taken for the accuracy or appropriateness of information found in any of these websites.

Contents

List of figures	ix
Introduction	1
Autonomy and language education	1
Enhancing learning effectiveness	2
Fulfilling learning needs	2
Defining the purpose of learning	3
Technology and language education	3
Redefining the goals of language education	3
Expanding the temporal and spatial dimension of language learning	4
Reshaping the consumption and production of language	5
Autonomy and technology	6
Technology shaping the exercise and development of autonomy	6
Autonomy influencing the efficacy of technology	8
In situ interplay of autonomy and technology	9
PART I LEARNER AUTONOMY AND TECHNOLOGY	**11**
1 Learner Autonomy and Technology: An Introduction	**13**
Learner autonomy	13
Definition of learner autonomy	14
Support of learner autonomy	16
Technology and learner autonomy	19
Technology shaping the evolving understanding of learner autonomy	19
Technology interacting with learner autonomy	22
2 Technology as a Facilitator of Learner Autonomy	**23**
Contribution of technology to the technical dimension of learner autonomy	23
Technology expanding autonomy in in-class learning	24
Technology boosting autonomy outside the classroom	32
Technology bridging autonomy inside and outside the classroom	38
Contribution of technology to the psychological dimension of learner autonomy	42
Contribution of technology to the political dimension of learner autonomy	46
3 Technology as a Constraint on Learner Autonomy	**50**

Constraints at the student level   51
  Digital capacity   51
  Self-regulation skills   53
  Digital habits   53
  Living circumstances   55
Constraints at the material level   55
  "Abundance" challenges   55
  Experience constraints   56
  Design constraints   59
  Unintended consequences   59
Constraints at the institutional level   60
  School culture   60
  Conventional practices   61
  Literacy practices   63
Constraints at the social/structural level   64
  Economic resources   64
  Political resources   66
  Cultural resources   68
Constraints at the ideological level   69
  Ideology in technology design   69
  Ideology in technology use   70
A synthetic framework of the constraints   72

4 Factors that Influence Technology and Learner Autonomy   74

Learner internal factors   75
  Beliefs   75
  Motivational factors   78
  Learner characteristics factors   83
  Self-efficacy   86
  Skills   88
Learning situation factors   93
  Nature of learning situations   94
  Instructional support   97
Environmental factors   100
  Cultural artifacts   101
  Societal discourse   103
  Social resources   104
A framework of factors that influence learner autonomy with technology   107

5 Facilitating the Interaction between Learner Autonomy and Technology   109

Designing an autonomy-amplifying technology-enhanced learning experience   109
  Nature of an autonomy-amplifying learning experience   109

Design elements of an autonomy-amplifying learning experience 117
Developing interventions that enhance learner autonomy with technology 120
   Boosting self-directed learning 121
   Strengthening language learning autonomy 123
A framework of supporting learner autonomy with technology 140

PART II TEACHER AUTONOMY AND TECHNOLOGY 143

6 Teacher Autonomy and Technology: An Introduction 145

Teacher autonomy in language education 145
   Teacher autonomy in professional work 145
   Teacher autonomy in professional learning 147
   Intersection of teacher autonomy and learner autonomy 151
   Development of teacher autonomy 152
Teacher autonomy and technology 153
   Influence of teacher autonomy on technology integration 153
   Influence of technology on teacher autonomy 155

7 The Impact of Technology on Teacher Autonomy 158

Technology as a facilitator of teacher autonomy 158
   Facilitating teacher autonomy in professional work 158
   Facilitating teacher autonomy in professional learning 163
Technology as a constraint on teacher autonomy 173
   Constraints at the individual level 173
   Constraints at the structural level 177

8 Fostering Teacher Autonomy with Technology – The What 183

Factors that influence teacher professional work with technology 183
   Teacher internal factors 184
   Teacher external factors 201
   Moderating factors 206
Factors that influence teacher professional learning with technology 210
   Factors that influence the individual aspects of learning online 210
   Factors that influence the social aspects of learning online 215

9 Fostering Teacher Autonomy with Technology – The How 218

Key principles of adult learning 218
Facilitating formal professional learning 219
   Interest-driven job-embedded learning 220
   Sustained authentic experience-focused learning 223
   Collaborative learning 225
   Reflective learning 228
Facilitating informal professional learning 230
   School cultures that support informal learning 230

Professional development programs that encourage informal learning	231
Mechanisms for promoting teacher autonomy with technology	232

Conclusion: Critical and Holistic Perspectives — 234

A critical perspective of the relationship	234
A holistic perspective of the relationship	236
Concluding remarks	238
References	*239*
Index	*299*

List of figures

Figure 1 Facilitating the technical dimension of learner autonomy — 42
Figure 2 Facilitating effect of technology on learner autonomy — 48
Figure 3 Constraining effects of technology on learner autonomy — 72
Figure 4 Factors that shape learner autonomy with technology — 107
Figure 5 A framework of supporting learner autonomy with technology — 140
Figure 6 The impact of technology on teacher autonomy — 182
Figure 7 Factors that influence teacher autonomy with technology in professional work — 208
Figure 8 Factors that influence teacher autonomy with technology for professional learning — 216
Figure 9 Facilitating mechanisms of professional learning in support of teacher autonomy with technology — 232
Figure 10 A critical view of the relationship between technology and autonomy — 235
Figure 11 A holistic view of the relationship between technology and autonomy — 237

Introduction

Autonomy and language education

The concept of personal autonomy originated in the Enlightenment period, and was coined by the 18th century German philosopher Immanuel Kant to refer to human potential to make individual rational decisions that also respect other people's autonomy (Schmenk, 2005). This concept was brought up by philosophers who argued against the prevailing absolutism of the French enlightenment that advocated using a common set of criteria to evaluate all societies and individuals. These philosophers underscored the prime importance of individual uniqueness, and advocated the promotion of autonomy, namely individuals take responsibility for their own acts (Dickson, 1995). Thus, personal autonomy has carried political and cultural connotations right from the beginning. Since then, fostering personal autonomy, the capacity to think and act independently against dominance and manipulation, has become an educational aim in many Western countries, and later, worldwide.

Holec (1981) introduced the concept of autonomy into language education and coined the term "learner autonomy" to refer to learners' capacity to take charge of their language learning. The focus on learner autonomy as a goal of language education brings increased attention to teacher autonomy, as the former depends on the latter (Little, 1995).

As teaching and learning are social activities, autonomy is inherently a relational concept, that is, individuals in relation to the environments. Ballou (1998) defined autonomy both "as the quality or stage of being self-governing" and as "the capacity of an agent to determine its own actions through independent choice within a system of principles and laws to which the agent is dedicated" (p. 105). Thus, autonomy is both a governance issue and a capacity issue. Benson (1997) conceptualized three manifestations of learner autonomy in language learning: technical, psychological, and political. According to Benson, the technical version of learner autonomy refers to the act of learning that is free of institutional constraints and without the intervention of a teacher; the psychological version of learner autonomy refers to the capacity (both attitudes and abilities) to take responsibility for learning; and the political version of learner autonomy refers to control over the processes and content of learning. Although Benson devised the three versions of learner autonomy in the context of language learning, it could be applied to the discussion on teacher autonomy as well.

Fostering autonomous behaviors in language teaching and learning is essential. "Feeling free and volitional in one's actions" is a basic psychological need, and this need nourishes our intrinsic motivation that fuels proactive behaviors (Deci, 1995, p. 2). Autonomous individuals are both motivated (i.e., taking responsibility for their own actions) and reflective (i.e., constantly reflecting on and adjusting their self-management of actions). These characteristics contribute to the effectiveness and efficiency of teaching and learning (Little & Dam, 1998). Learner autonomy is deemed an essential aspect of language education (Benson, 2011; Littlewood, 2004), and three lines of arguments have been presented in favor of autonomy in language education.

Enhancing learning effectiveness

The first line of argument is the learning effectiveness argument. The link between learner autonomy and language development is substantiated by the analysis of characteristics of good language learners (Rubin, 1975). Good language learners exhibit a clear understanding of the best ways of learning and are cognitive and effectively active in the learning process. Language learning is facilitated when learners assume a greater share of responsibility for learning (Dickson, 1995). Learner autonomy is significantly and positively associated with language performance, with correlation coefficients ranging from 0.24 to 0.41 reported in research studies across different cultural contexts (Deng, 2007; Ghorbandordinejad & Ahmadabad, 2016; Myartawan, Latief & Suharmanto, 2013; Şakrak-Ekin & Balcikanli, 2019). That is to say, learners with higher language proficiency are found to exhibit significantly higher levels of learner autonomy (Abadi & Baradaran, 2013).

Fulfilling learning needs

The second line of argument is the language development needs argument. Language development demands frequent and varied language exposure and language use experiences. Relying solely on the learning experience inside the classroom is not sufficient to fulfill the necessary conditions for language development (Richards, 2015). Take vocabulary learning as an example. Language learners need a large vocabulary size for the comprehension of English: 3,000-word families (i.e., a base word with its inflections and derivatives) for initial comprehension of television programs and movies; 5,000-word families for books and magazines; 6,000-7,000-word families for comprehension of conversation; and 8,000-9,000-word families for novels and newspapers (Schmitt, 2004; Webb & Nation, 2013). A knowledge of 10,000-word families is needed for fluent use of English in a variety of contexts (Hazenberg & Hulstun, 1996). Classroom experience alone is inadequate to develop the vocabulary size and the depth of vocabulary knowledge needed to function in

English, and scholars deem it crucial to extend vocabulary learning beyond the classroom (Nation, 2015; Schmitt, 2014; Webb & Nation, 2017). Thus, it is important for learners to exercise autonomy in creating and utilizing the language learning opportunities beyond the classroom to extend, expand and enrich their language learning experience.

Defining the purpose of learning

The third line of argument is the language learning purpose argument. Developing autonomous individuals, individuals who are independent and free-thinking, meets the needs of the modern world. The constant update of knowledge and evolving societal needs make it more reasonable to define the goal of education "as a long-term aptitude development effort that seeks to foster human preparedness for later stages of life" (Jiménez Raya & Fernández, 2002, p. 62). The ultimate purpose of learning a language is to proffer learners with linguistic resources and the concomitant scope of action in life. Thus, developing learner autonomy in making informed decisions on linguistic choices (the languages to learn, the competencies to achieve for each language, and the intensity of learning investment) is essential (Benson & Lamb, 2020). The key to the realization of learner autonomy in the classroom setting is the shift of control from teachers to students, and this shift relies on the degree of teachers' own autonomy in instruction (Little, 1995). Hence, teacher autonomy is indispensable in facilitating learner autonomy (Breen & Mann, 1997; Little, 1995). Teacher autonomy in pursuing personal professional learning also brings exposure to innovative pedagogical ideas, fosters an open mindset about teaching, and broadens teachers' horizons. Such experiences increase teachers' willingness and capacity for autonomy-supportive behaviors inside the classroom. Thus, autonomy—both learner autonomy and teacher autonomy—is a critical aspect of language education.

Technology and language education

Redefining the goals of language education

Communicative competence based on linguistic resources has long been deemed as the paramount goal of language education. However, technology expands the semiotic scopes for communication, and hence brings in new dimensions that question the primacy of linguistic competence as the goal of language education. Kern (2021) highlighted that technology introduces "a complexified view of literacy that goes well beyond the skills of encoding and decoding print" (p. 134) and pluralizes literacy since literacy practices take on different forms and serve different purposes in different technological and non-technological spaces. Technology also transforms the nature of literacy into "sociocultural practices for relationships, identity construction and positioning" (Kim, 2018, p. 41).

Writing education scholars like Polio (2019) hence point out that technology challenges the epistemological foundation of L2 writing by shifting writing from an individual activity into a collaborative, multimodal, and remixing activity. This shift questions the legitimacy of the conventional practice of placing language as the central focus of writing instruction. Consequently, Guikema and Williams (2014) argued that developing digital literacies is a fundamental goal of language education, and that "it is therefore critical that digital literacies be integrated throughout foreign/second language education" (p. 3).

Technology enables a globally connected world where multilingual and multimodal communication practices are commonplace, and hence provides "translanguaging spaces" that supports "everyday flexible multilingual practices of the individual" (Li, 2011; Li & Lin, 2019, p. 209). It makes multilingualism a reality for all language learners, including foreign language learners. This reality challenges the monolingual view of language learners and urges a renewed view of language use as the coordination of cognitive, semiotic, and linguistic resources. Scholars like Li (2018) argue that the purpose of language learning needs to be reoriented towards achieving and supporting multilingualism. Consequently, developing language learners' competence in fluid and adaptive coordination of linguistic and semiotic modes in communication situations to achieve effective meaning making becomes an essential goal relevant to all language learners.

Expanding the temporal and spatial dimension of language learning

The exponential growth of access to technology and the concomitant proliferation and accelerated mobility of spaces for language learning spark interest in the spatial theory in language education (Benson, 2022; Lamb & Murray, 2018). Spaces are the language-bearing resources (people, things, and information) that are brought together in certain ways at particular moments in time (Benson, 2022). Technology not only expands spaces for language learning that are not constrained by physical boundaries, but also brings experiences of learning that are diversified and different from that of language learning via physical interaction (Chun, Kern & Smith, 2016). The diversification of learning experience is essential to fulfilling learners' affective, cognitive, and social needs for language learning (Lai, 2015). The diversified spaces for learning mediated by technology also augment self-initiated out-of-class learning, which plays a significant and unique role in language learning. For instance, Peters (2018) found that in-class instruction explained 7% of the variation in vocabulary size among secondary and university language learners, but out-of-class language experience accounted for an additional 13% of the variation. Brevik (2019) revealed that the higher frequency of playing online games, watching TV series, and engaging in social media exchanges in English than in Norwegian contributed to a group of 11th graders' 20th percentile and below performance in Norwegian reading and 60th percentile and above performance in English reading in national reading tests. Experiences in diversified spaces afforded by technology may also influence students' in-class learning. Lamb and Arisandy (2020) found that diversified language experience beyond the classroom correlates positively with learners' in-class English learning motivation and their attitudes towards English classes.

Language learning demands intensive time investment, which makes a sole reliance on the limited in-class time for language development unrealistic (Reinders, 2020). Technology proffers ubiquitous learning as a potential solution to fulfilling the time demand. Ubiquitous learning aided by mobile devices enables anytime and anywhere access to language resources. Mobile technologies allow access to learning resources and support not only at any time learners prefer but also at the right time and right place when learners need them (Ogata & Yano, 2004).

Reshaping the consumption and production of language

Technology influences learners' interaction with texts. Take research on learners' interactional behaviors with online reading as an example. Reading pure texts online is found to have a negative effect on reading comprehension when compared with reading the same texts on paper, with an average effect size of between -0.21 and -0.25 (Clinton, 2019; Delgado *et al.*, 2018). This negative effect is particularly salient for the comprehension of expository texts, and it becomes even stronger as readers' technological experience increases (Clinton, 2019; Delgado *et al.*, 2018). However, texts that actively utilize multimodal features, such as audio narration, to enrich the presentation are found to benefit reading comprehension and vocabulary learning, with an average effect size of over 1.0 (Abraham, 2008). E-textbooks are further found to boost the reading behaviors of low-performance student groups, including boys, reluctant readers, and children from lower socio-economic status (Tveit & Mangen, 2014).

Technology also reshapes the production of language. It makes possible the production of multimodal texts and new forms of narratives, such as branching stories (Kern, 2021). Multimodal composition bridges learners' multimodal experiences with L2 writing, "expand(s) the repertoire of resources for text construction" (Hafner, 2015, p. 486), provides opportunities for composing "identity texts," increases learners' willingness for creative language use, and influences students' self-positioning in relation to writing and concomitant investment in English writing (Christiansen & Koelzer, 2016; Elola & Oskoz, 2017; Jiang, 2018). Technology also changes the nature of writing by making collaborative writing a common practice. The co-working space mediated by technology allows learners to engage in collaborative meaning negotiation, co-construction of metacognitive knowledge about writing and language, and co-development of writing and language skills (Storch, 2019). Collaborative writing is found to have a large effect on both the quality of the written texts and that of subsequent individual composing, with an average effect size of 0.73 and 0.94 respectively (Elabdali, 2021). Moreover, the ease of publishing mediated by technology makes language learners change from the conventional consumer role to the role of producer, publisher, and social participant (Kern, 2021).

Since technology is integral to the goals and process of language learning and language use, it closely intertwines with autonomy in language teaching and learning.

Autonomy and technology

Technology shaping the exercise and development of autonomy

Technology serves as a tool and resource, and a medium and space for the exercise and development of autonomy. In either role, technology is a double-edged sword, both facilitating and constraining autonomy. Technology is learner-defined, and its autonomy-supportive potential is determined by how learners perceive, position, and utilize it for autonomous action.

Technology as tool and resource

Technology provides the tools and resources for the exercise of autonomy for learning. These tools and resources enable independent and social learning. Individuals, both learners and teachers, don't need to depend on institutional provision to engage in learning. Technology frees individuals from the time and space constraints of institutionalized learning and enables individuals to engage in ubiquitous learning anytime and anywhere. Technology also facilitates autonomy supportive pedagogies, since it provides pedagogical tools and resources to support learning experiences that cater to different learning goals and needs. Thus, it enables the redefinition of the role of teachers and learners and makes it easier for teachers to shift the control and responsibility of learning onto learners (Jiménez Raya & Fernández, 2002).

However, although technology provides self-instructional tools and resources that enable independent learning, "self-instructional modes of learning may even inhibit autonomy" (Benson, 2001, p. 9), especially when the self-instructional materials are highly structured or when individuals delegate the control over learning to these resources. Moreover, learners and teachers need fundamental understanding of the affordances and constraints of individual tools so as to use the tools and resources adaptively and creatively for autonomous actions to meet individual needs. Individuals also need relevant technical, cognitive, social and affective skills to match individual tools and resources with the desired learning and teaching purposes and use the tools in effective ways to achieve the intended learning and teaching purposes. Technology brings not only tools and resources but also structural and managerial demands for the reconfiguration of teacher-student role inside the classroom. Consequently, teachers' capacities in relevant structural and managerial management determine whether they can utilize the tools and resources to exercise teaching autonomy. When these capacities are lacking, what technology brings to the classroom might be chaos. Moreover, the lack of easy access to technological resources may deprive some learners and teachers of the opportunities for autonomous action or lessen its scope (Reinders & Hubbard, 2013).

Technology as medium and space

Technology provides the medium and space for the development of autonomy. Technological platforms afford constructivist principles, which are essential conditions for the development of learner autonomy. Blin (2004) conceptualized technology as mediating tools for language learning activities. Activities on a particular technological platform, individual or collective, allow teachers and learners to recreate procedures, tools and rules and social structure of the language environment and facilitate subsequent internalization of new tools or rules, which contributes to the transformation of the learning environment and of the individuals who participate in the activity. Empirical studies have shown that creative and collaborative activities on technological platforms enhance learner ownership and autonomy (e.g., Hafner & Miller, 2011; Lan, 2018). Technology provides spaces for learning, spaces with unique and diversified affordances for actions and relations. The diversified affordances may fuel autonomy for learning. Moreover, technology forms constitutive spaces that can be orchestrated along with physical spaces to construct personalized learning ecology that transcends beyond formal learning contexts (Godwin-Jones, 2019). Technology is also found to provide the medium for critical analysis of modes and meaning-making online, which enhances learners' multimodal communicative competence and multi-literacy skills for the exercise of autonomy in online spaces (e.g., Fuchs *et al.*, 2012). Technology has also been used to foster self-regulated learning, an important psychological antecedent of learner autonomy (Azevedo *et al.*, 2019). Multimedia and hypermedia environments are conducive to self-regulation (Azevedo, 2014; Mayer, 2014). Moreover, adaptive computer-assisted learning systems can detect and monitor learner's self-regulation process during the learning process, and use the information collected to provide timely and adaptive scaffolding to support individual learners' self-regulated learning process (Azevedo *et al.*, 2019). Thus, technology could serve as not only a medium and space for autonomy-supportive learning experience but also a medium and space for the enhancement of essential knowledge and skills for learner autonomy.

However, technology is not self-determining on its own. Whether its autonomy-supportive potential can be realized relies crucially on how individuals interact with it. Whether learners and teachers have the capacity to perceive and act on the affordances of individual technological spaces and to develop effective and reciprocal interactions across spaces may further constrain the medium and space role of technology in developing learner autonomy. Moreover, the lack of supportive features on the technological platforms that encourage the exercise and development of learner autonomy (e.g., encourage learners to plan, monitor and reflect on their learning process) may limit the potential of learners' experience on the platforms for learner autonomy development (Bernacki, Aguilar & Byrnes, 2011; Reinders & Hubbard, 2013). Failing to create supportive structures to facilitate the potential (e.g., no mechanisms to support quality collaboration during collaborative work on technological platforms) may also inhibit individuals from utilizing the potential of technology to develop learner autonomy.

Autonomy influencing the efficacy of technology

Learners' willingness and capacity for autonomous action shape the learning efficacy of technology. For instance, self-regulation is an important prerequisite propensity for effective interaction with technological platforms. Self-regulatory ability, or the lack thereof, has been identified as a major determinant of the effectiveness of computer-based learning environments (Zimmerman, 1990). Learners with higher levels of self-regulation tend to spend more time coordinating the different learning resources on a technological platform and use a higher percentage of effective learning strategies when interacting with the technological platform than peers who have lower levels of self-regulation (Bernacki *et al.*, 2011). Moreover, learners with high levels of self-regulation tend to apply task strategies more flexibly and adopt more flexible learning paths when interacting with massively online open courses (MOOCs). They are also more likely to adapt their behavior according to personal objectives and ongoing needs and use the courses as one source of informal learning, whereas low self-regulators approached MOOCs more as formal learning opportunities (Alonso-Mencía *et al.*, 2020). Granting learner control on E-learning systems, especially control over time and pace and control over navigation and design, is found to have a direct positive effect on cognitive learning outcomes (test scores, perceived learning performance and enhanced learning transfer). Control in general, irrespective of the dimensions of control, is associated with positive emotional reactions towards the e-learning course (Sorgenfrei & Smolnik, 2016). Studies have further found that building supportive elements for autonomy in online activities may enhance learning from the online experience. For instance, Flowers, Kelsen, and Cvitkovic (2019) found that building elements of learner autonomy, such as individual goal setting, planning and reflection, in online intercultural exchange activities led to greater gains in cross-cultural interactional confidence.

But at the same time, autonomy in technological environments may sometimes overwhelm learners with information overload or lead to disorientation. High dropout rates and diminished abilities to focus have also been reported to accompany learning experience on technological platforms that grant learner control (Mayer, 2011; Salomon & Almog, 1998). In such cases, the situational freedom of autonomy may not necessarily contribute to positive learning. Jang, Reeve, and Deci (2010) argued that both autonomy support and structure, antagonistic as they are, contribute uniquely to learning: autonomy support contributes to students' autonomous motives and supports volitional endorsement of learning behaviors, whereas structure keeps students on task and help them manage their learning behavior and avoid chaos. Van Loon, Ros, and Martens (2012) found that a digital learning task that only provided autonomy support did not induce positive learning outcomes. Instead, a digital learning task that combined autonomy support with structure had a positive effect on both intrinsic motivation and learning outcomes. Thus, autonomy may shape the effects of technological experience for better or for worse.

In situ interplay of autonomy and technology

The dialectical relationship between autonomy and technology is situated in the nexus of relations with other factors and may vary across contexts. Studies have found that the relationship of autonomy and learning behaviors and outcomes with technology may be moderated by other factors. For instance, Sorgenfrei and Smolnik (2016) conceptualized that the relationship between learner control and cognitive and affective outcomes on e-learning systems is moderated by individual differences in the willingness and capacity to make rational choices to control their learning process and by environmental factors such as learning task and course characteristics and learning conditions. Lai (2019a) found that learners' belief systems shaped not only what technologies they selectively utilized but also how they interacted with specific technological resources for self-directed learning beyond the classroom. Studies have further found that human factors may moderate the relationship between autonomy intervention and learning gains on technological platforms (Wong *et al.*, 2019). For instance, examining the efficacy of two types of self-regulation prompts (reasoning-based self-explanation and predicting-based self-explanation) on students' interaction on a computer-based environment, Yeh and colleagues (2010) found that the effects varied in response to the levels of prior knowledge. Learners with lower prior knowledge gained more from reasoning-based prompts, whereas learners with higher prior knowledge benefited more from the predicting-based prompts. Chen and Huang (2014) found that integrating self-regulation strategies in online reading enhanced male learners' reading annotation abilities but not their reading comprehension performance, whereas the opposite was observed for female learners.

Thus, technology and autonomy are closely intertwined, and the relationship between autonomy and technology is a dialectical one. In this book, I will explore how the dialectical relationship between autonomy and technology manifests in the domains of learner autonomy and teacher autonomy. Two premises form the basis of the exploration:

1) Technology is not neutral and may both benefit and constrain autonomy. The same goes for the effects of autonomy on learning with technology. Thus, a critical view towards the relationship between the two is needed
2) The relationship between technology and autonomy needs to be understood in relation to various inter-playing factors. Thus, a holistic view is needed to understand the relationship between the two

This book adopts a critical and holistic perspective to illustrate the dialectical relationship between technology and autonomy in situ.

PART I

LEARNER AUTONOMY AND TECHNOLOGY

1
Learner Autonomy and Technology: An Introduction

Learner autonomy

Henri Holec introduced the notion of autonomy to the field of language education out of his work with adult language learners in a language resource center, the Centre de Recherches et d'Applications Pédagogiques en langues (CRAPEL), in the 70s. Autonomy in language teaching and learning has drawn considerable attention since then. Various arguments have been put forth that underscore the importance of autonomy for language education. Some arguments focus on the political and educational significance of autonomy. Holec (1981) advocated learner autonomy for its significance in achieving the aim of adult education, i.e., to instill a sense of liberation among individuals and support their development as producers of society who "act more responsibly in running the affairs of the society in which he lives" (p. 1). Jiménez Raya and colleagues (2017) further added that learner autonomy is "central in considerations of how education can become more inclusive and empowering for learners and teachers" (p. 11), and that "a focus on autonomy in education is intrinsic to such significant values as democracy, liberty, justice, rights and some versions of equality" (p. 12). Learner autonomy could trigger teachers' critical reflection on their prevailing beliefs about teaching and learning and is the key to achieving democratic teaching and learning (Benson & Lamb, 2021; Jiménez Raya *et al.*, 2017). In addition to this political argument for learner autonomy, Little (1991) further introduced the psychological and social arguments for learner autonomy. According to Little (1991), learning only takes place when individuals can integrate what is offered with the sum of his prior experience, and personal constructs (prior knowledge, interest, and commitment, learning needs and purposes, and emotions) determine what individuals may acquire from a learning event. Thus, a sufficient degree of autonomy is fundamental to the psychology of human learning. Little (1991) further argued that language acquisition is inherently autonomous as it arises from individuals' initiatives to meet the communicative needs in a variety of social contexts and to achieve the social freedom to interact with people they desire. These varied arguments for learner autonomy have made learner autonomy a focal issue in language education and research for decades.

Definition of learner autonomy

Given that personal autonomy entails both the governance dimension and the capacity dimension, definitions of learner autonomy in the language education profession have revolved around these two dimensions.

Some scholars define learner autonomy as an ability or a capacity. For example, Holec (1981) defined it as "the ability to take charge of one's learning" (p. 3). Little (1991) and Dam *et al.* (1990) underscored that learner autonomy can be transformed into reality when properly nurtured and defined it as a capacity: "a capacity—for detachment, critical reflection, decision-making and independent action" (Little, 1991, p. 4), and "a capacity and willingness to act independently and in cooperation with others, as a social, responsible person" (Dam *et al.*, 1990, p. 102). Murray (2014) and Lewis (2013) brought to the fore the sociality aspect of learner autonomy and conceptualized it as the "social-interactive" ability to communicate and collaborate, and to engage in cross-cultural interactions. Benson (2009) argued that it is more than an ability, and entails a composite of "abilities, attitudes or dispositions" (p. 18) to take control over content, learning management and cognitive processing (Benson, 2011). Murray *et al.* (2014) further added the connotation of control over spaces to the definition, that is, "having the possibility to exercise one's agency within the space" (p. 99). Jiménez Raya *et al.* (2017) expanded the definition further and charged it with an educational mission: "the competence to develop as a self-determined, socially responsible and critically aware participant in (and beyond) educational environments, within a vision of education as (inter)personal empowerment and social transformation" (p. 17). They further argued that this competence is a composite that "involves attitudinal dispositions, knowledge and abilities" (p. 17). Thus, their definition highlights the relational and critical dimension of learner autonomy, emphasizing the social role of learner autonomy in challenging the status quo and achieving social transformation. Lamb and Vodicka (2018) developed this critical aspect further to highlight the "socio-spatial dimension of learner autonomy" (p. 21) and stressed that collective autonomy creates spaces for social (re)construction to challenge and counter the monolingual hegemony, especially among ethnic minorities. The whole set of ability-capacity-competence conceptualizations of learner autonomy diverges in whether they regard learner autonomy as innate or something to be acquired through experience. For instance, Holec (1981) regarded learner autonomy as something that must be acquired – "not inborn but must be acquired either by 'natural' means or (as most often happens) by formal learning, that is, in a systematic, deliberate way" (p. 3). In contrast, Little and colleagues took learner autonomy as a part of biologically determined human constitution – "a universal human capacity and drive" (Little *et al.*, 2017, p. 12), and argued that to support language learner autonomy is to help learners harness this inborn capacity in language learning (Little, 1991; Little *et al.*, 2017). These definitions also differ in their conceptualization of whether learner autonomy resides at the individual cognitive plane or at the social interactive plane. Holec (1981) stressed the individual cognitive aspect of learner autonomy, defining learner autonomy as individual learners' independent learning with resources, whereas Dam *et al.* (1990) and Little & Thorne (2017) highlighted the social interactive aspect of learner autonomy, featuring the dialogic, peer-oriented views of autonomy. Among the scholars who underscore the social dimension of learner autonomy, disagreements exist in the conceptualization of the social aspect in relation to learner autonomy. Some highlight the role of social spaces in the development of learner autonomy and argue that learner autonomy is developed not in isolation but through collaboration with others (Dam et al, 1990; Little, 1991). Some underscore the role of social spaces in the exercise of learner autonomy, stressing that the social spaces may afford and constrain the exercise of learner autonomy (Lewis, 2013; Murray, 2014). Still others emphasize the entanglement of learner autonomy with power flows and social identities and draw attention to the activist role of collective autonomy in social transformation (Lamb & Vodicka, 2018).

Other scholars have defined learner autonomy not as an ability, but as a situation or a state. For instance, Dickinson (1987) defined autonomy as "the situation in which the learner is totally responsible for all the decisions concerned with his learning and the implementation of those decisions" (p. 11). Allwright (1990) defined learner autonomy as a state of "optimal equilibrium between dependence and self-sufficiency" (p. 1). To them, learner autonomy exists in the interaction of the individual capacity and dispositions with the structural affordance. According to Deci and Ryan (1985), learners often come to learning situations with the psychological needs for autonomy, which is conditioned on learners' competence and human relationships in the learning situations. The degree of autonomy learners can exercise is a function of the interplay of the resource infrastructure and the social and discursive configurations of a learning space with the individual factors such as dispositions, goals in learning, individual values and beliefs (Dang, 2012; Oxford, 2008; Nunan, 1996). As Bensons (2009) rightly pointed out, learner autonomy exists in the dialectic interaction between the individual and the social, discursive, and resource realities of the context within which the individuals reside. This relational nature is reflected in Macaro's (1997) definition of learner autonomy: "an ability which is learnt through knowing how to make decisions about the self as well as being allowed to make those decisions" (p. 168).

Thus, existing definitions of learner autonomy suggest that learner autonomy is a multidimensional concept. The different conceptualizations of autonomy draw attention to the different aspects of learner autonomy:

both the capacity and situational freedom aspects and their interplay; and both the individual cognitive and social interactive aspects and their interaction. Existing literature also emphasizes the different purposes of learner autonomy. A narrow focus on one purpose of learner autonomy, for example, the psychological aspect of autonomy (i.e., constructing learner-centered learning experience), without considering the other dimensions, namely, the political mission of learner autonomy (i.e., questioning the purpose and structural condition of the learning experience), may lead to passive submission to the dominant ideology of learning and deprive learners of their autonomy (Benson, 1996). The multidimensionality of learner autonomy calls for a holistic approach to researching and supporting learner autonomy. Despite the different orientations, these definitions all agree that learner autonomy is malleable: autonomy rests on a continuum of degree, and can be developed, discovered, amplified, or maintained (the terms used to describe its malleability vary in different conceptualizations of learner autonomy) (Breen & Mann, 1997; Nunan, 1997; Little & Thorne, 2017).

Support of learner autonomy

What to support?

Scholars have identified three types of autonomy that are pertinent to language learning: general/personal autonomy, language autonomy and learner autonomy (Germain & Netten, 2004). General/personal autonomy is a psychological predisposition that drives human volitional behaviors. Language autonomy is the freedom and ability to use any language or combination languages to express oneself, connect with others, perform varied discursive roles, and fulfill a multitude of social functions (Benson, 2012; Macaro, 2008). Learner autonomy is the organizational (technical skills in planning and managing time and spaces), procedural (informational and methodological skills in locating and coordinating resources), and cognitive (the skill to manage the social, cognitive, metacognitive, and psycho-affective dimensions of learning) skill sets needed to engage in effective learning (Albero, 2003; Stefanou *et al.*, 2004). The relationship between the three dimensions of autonomy has been conceptualized differently. Some scholars postulate a sequential relationship. For instance, Germain and Netten (2004) hypothesized that language autonomy leads to learner autonomy and ultimately to general/personal autonomy. Little (2013) and Dam (2013) conceptualized the opposite, where the support of personal and learner autonomy triggers language autonomy. Other scholars elaborate on a concentric overlapping relationship among the three. For instance, Benson (2012) construed that personal autonomy entails learner autonomy, which encompasses language learner autonomy. In contrast, Toffoli and Perrot (2017) conceptualized a dialectic and dynamic relationship among the three, where different types of autonomy interact with one another bi-directionally.

Notwithstanding the varied conceptualization of the relationship of thereof, scholars agree upon these three as the core goals of autonomy in language education. They reinterpret the three types of autonomy in the language education context as *Autonomy as Person*, *Autonomy as Language User* and *Autonomy as Language Learner* (Benson, 2012; Macaro, 1997). *Autonomy as Person* underscores personal empowerment and autonomy in life through language learning. It emphasizes raising critical awareness of the social functions of language and how language(s) can be used for "(inter)personal empowerment and social transformation" (Jiménez Raya *et al.*, 2017), and to enhance "cultural capital, identity and future desires" (Oxford, 2015; Palfreyman, 2014). *Autonomy as Language User* refers to creative language use. It emphasizes the use of situation-appropriate communication strategies that not only facilitate communication but also increase learning and life opportunities. These strategies include but are not limited to help-seeking strategies, cross-cultural skills and strategies to establish and augment social connections, and strategies to choose, use and coordinate multiple languages and semiotic devices flexibly to fulfill communication purposes (Lewis, 2014; Macaro, 2008; O'Leary, 2014). *Autonomy as Language Learner* involves the control over and the management of not only the learning objectives, contents, resources, process and strategies but also the socio-emotional aspects of learning (Benson, 2011; Costa & Kallick, 2008; Oxford, 2015). All the three goals of language learning autonomy need to be targeted when developing initiatives to support learner autonomy.

How to support?

Different conceptualizations of learner autonomy determine different ways to support learner autonomy.

Scholars who believe that learner autonomy is abilities or competences to be acquired emphasize the provision of a strategy repertoire to assist the exercise of learner autonomy. The facilitation can be achieved through either "natural means" or "a systematic, deliberate way" (Holec, 1981). Kohonen (1992) proposed a natural approach to foster learner autonomy. His model highlights experiential learning augmented by constant critical analysis of and reflection on learning experiences to develop explicit metalinguistic and metacognitive awareness of learning. These reflective practices can assume the form of personal journals or diaries, portfolios, case studies, and visualizations and imaginative activities. Through cycles of experience and reflection, learners develop personal awareness (e.g., self-concept, self esteem, and identity), task awareness (e.g., using and constructing communication skills in context) and learning process awareness (e.g., monitoring, reflection, and self-assessment). The awareness development is situated in teachers' professional awareness, the culture of the learning institution, and social interaction with other learners. In contrast, Nunan (1997) suggested a deliberate approach to develop learner autonomy. His model features five levels of autonomy implementation to facilitate individuals' independent interaction with learning resources: explicating the pedagogical goals in the learning materials, selecting individual goals from a range of alternatives, modifying, and adapting the goals of learning experience and associated tasks, creating their own goals and associated tasks, and transcending beyond the classroom to make use of the resources in the wild. Thus, these scholars highlight providing learners with experience where they take control of learning and supporting the experience with resources and strategies.

Scholars who believe that learner autonomy is an inborn capacity learners bring with them to the learning situations regard the development of learner autonomy as a process of "amplifying" or "focusing" (e.g., Little & Thorne, 2017). Instead of supporting strategy and skill development, these scholars emphasize creating learning environments that may amplify learner autonomy. To them, learning situations in favor of learner autonomy are those that validate and actively build on "the vast semiospheres that [learners] have created over the entirety of their lives that relate to learning, doing, knowing, being, social identities, being experts, being passionate enthusiasts, etc." (Little & Thorne, 2017, p. 24). They believe that language is the medium of learner agency, and learner autonomy development and language proficiency development are closely intertwined and integrated (Little, 1991). It is important that "learners' life experience and social identities are made relevant in the learning process and what they are learning could be immediately applied to benefit and extend their life" (Little & Thorne, 2017, p. 24). In such environments, teachers' roles are twofold: 1) to develop proficiency in language use through learning experiences co-created with students, comprising individual and collective target language use, and learning around things relevant to their larger life, that enables students to harness inherent learner agency; and 2) to develop proficiency in language learning through giving students responsibilities for decision making and evaluative reflection of learning (Little *et al.*, 2017). Consequently, Dam (2008) emphasized creating a classroom learning environment that promotes interaction and negotiation between the instructor and learners and among the learners, and guiding learners through the process of the planning, implementation, and evaluation of the metacognitive, cognitive, social, and affective dimensions of learning. Little and Thorne (2017) further suggested building in "structured unpredictability" – unpredictable learning experience with support (p. 17), that allows and invites learners to define their learning experience in the seemingly structured learning activities. Little and Thorne further provided examples of how structured unpredictability can be constructed. For instance, teachers can structure learning experience around learners' interests in personal life that they bring with them to class, and help them share, curate, and further pursue their personal interests in the new language with teacher and peer support. Teachers can also provide "rewilding" (p. 26) experience in "intense contextualization" (p. 21), where learners carry out communicative tasks in the target language in the real world and bring the experience and associated artefacts into the classroom for mediation and expansion. Thus, these scholars underscore immersing learners in autonomy-inducing but mediated second language (L2) use and learning experience and guiding them to monitor the learning process.

Reconciling the strategy-vs-environment debate, Littlewood (1997) pointed out that these two approaches are both needed as they contribute uniquely to different goals of learner autonomy. Developing learners' communication and learning strategies assists the development of autonomy as a communicator and autonomy as a learner. Engaging students in independent work and facilitating them to construct personal learning contexts contributes to the development of autonomy as a learner and autonomy as a person. Pedagogical experiences that validate and tap into linguistic creativity and that encourage and support the expression of personal meanings benefit the development of autonomy as a communicator and autonomy as a person.

In summary, learner autonomy and language learning are mutually benefiting and intertwine with each other (Little, 2007). On the one hand, learner autonomy is not only integral to effective language learning but also an ultimate goal of language learning. On the other hand, language learning enhances the potential of autonomy, both as competence and as situational freedom. The manifestation and support of learner autonomy is subject to the configurations and demands of the language learning situations.

Technology and learner autonomy

Technology has been closely interwoven with the evolving academic discourses around learner autonomy since its onset. It shapes the evolving understanding of what learner autonomy entails, how learner autonomy can be supported, and the position of learner autonomy in language education. At the same time, technology also interacts with learner autonomy, and the nature of the interaction shapes how their roles get enacted in language learning.

Technology shaping the evolving understanding of learner autonomy

Technology and the conceptualization of learner autonomy

When Holec first introduced the notion of learner autonomy in the 70s, it was situated in the context of self-access centers, where learners have access to language resources mediated by stand-alone technology. The nature of technology at that time shaped his emphasis on "the individual-cognitive-organizational dimension" of learner autonomy (Little & Thorne, 2017, p. 12). With the advancement and popularization of expressive and connective technological platforms, academic discourses on learner autonomy have shifted towards a greater emphasis on the relational account and the social dimension of learner autonomy (Lewis *et al.*, 2017; Murray, 2014).

Autonomy is contextual and "assumes different shapes in different environments" (Lewis *et al.*, 2017, p. 3; Little & Thorne, 2017). Technology expands the environments where language learning and use can take place, and the exercise of learner autonomy in these different environments demands different sets of competence and different configurations and balance of dependency and self-sufficiency. Moreover, every technological space has its affordances and constraints, and consequently "the ability to convert constraints into affordances" and to coordinate the affordances across different online and offline learning environments becomes an essential facet of learner autonomy (Lewis *et al.*, 2017, p. 3). Thus, technology adds new dimensions to what learner autonomy entails. These dimensions are particularly relevant in the context of informal learning, which is characterized by the omnipresence of technology (Sockett & Tofolli, 2012). The enhanced opportunities for language exposure and use in informal learning contexts have elevated learners' role as language users and social actors (Sockett & Toffoli, 2012). Previous conceptualizations of learner autonomy that focus primarily on the management of language learning process and much less on issues related to language use and language socialization have hence become outdated. As Illés (2012) pointed out, technology shifts the major obstacle to language learning from the lack of language exposure to "the problem of plenty" (p. 506). This change calls for distinguishing language learning and language use when conceptualizing learner autonomy and demands greater attention to learner autonomy with regard to making informed choices about language use (Benson & Lamb, 2020). Illés (2012) hence redefines learner autonomy as "the capacity to become competent speakers of the target language who are able to exploit the linguistic and other resources at their disposal effectively and creatively" (p. 509). The exploitation of resources involves an enhanced awareness and effective coordination of learning resources and opportunities across formal and informal learning spaces (Lai, 2015; Kashiwa & Benson, 2018). In Benson and Lamb's (2020) words,

> Autonomy may be less about controlling learning processes and more about being aware of learning resources in the environment and being able to use those resources productively … To some extent, autonomy is a matter of learners working out how the resources of the classroom can complement the resources that are available to them outside the classroom and fitting them together in a way that

benefits their learning. Pedagogy for autonomy could be about helping learners to do that. (p. 83)

Technology not only expands language use and socialization opportunities, but also increases linguistic diversity in the online spaces students have access to, since it connects people from all around the world. Benson and Lamb (2020) further pointed out that the boosted multilingualism redefines what "choice" entails in learner autonomy. It broadens the scope from the choice over learning materials, process and strategies to the choice over the languages, the competence level and the dimensions of competence to strive for in each language, and "ways of learning, practicing and using the languages" (p. 80).

Technology and the support of learner autonomy

The evolution of technology has changed how educators operationalize the support of learner autonomy. In the 70s, prior to the advent of the Internet, self-access centers that are equipped with abundant material and human resources are deemed a viable route leading to learner autonomy. The advent of the Internet and the permeation of personal computers and mobile devices have shifted the support mechanism away from providing conventional resources and spaces towards developing support programs and applications that feature advising and assisting students in harnessing the resources available to suit personal needs (Everhard, 2016; Mynard & Kato, 2022). Advising sessions are characterized by "structured awareness raising," where learners are guided on exploring personal motivation and interests in relation to learning goals, discovering, and experimenting with different resources and strategies, evaluating the learning gains and reflecting on the process, and becoming aware of and managing emotions arising in the learning process (Kato & Mynard, 2016).

Technology and the scale of the learner autonomy movement

In the past decades, initiatives on supporting learner autonomy are often institutionalized, constrained either inside the state-of-the-art self-access facilities, mostly in universities, or inside the classroom through learner strategy training or pedagogical moves such as portfolio, logbooks and reflective journals, and learner-centered assessment. These initiatives have primarily taken place in the formal or non-formal education contexts. The popularization of personal computers and electronic devices has brought learner autonomy to the informal learning contexts. Initiatives like holes-in-the-wall in India (Mitra, 2013) and hand-held device initiative in Jakarta (Lamb, 2013) have made the exercise of learning autonomy possible for the impoverished and underprivileged populations in the remote mountain areas (Everhard, 2016).

Technology interacting with learner autonomy

Technology and learner autonomy share a common mission in language education, i.e., to transform language education from the centrality of teacher-centered activities in the formal learning contexts to the validation of learner-led everyday technological and literacy practices in informal learning contexts (Reinders & White, 2016). These two, if in harmony and mutually supportive, may work in synergy and reinforce each other in achieving the goal.

At the same time, the interaction of technology and learner autonomy is full of tension (Reinders & Hubbard, 2013). The tension originates in the fact that technology is not neutral but rather a double-edged sword. On the one hand, technology provides the impetus, the freedom, the tool and the venue for the exercise of learner autonomy (Benson, 2013). On the other hand, technology, with its inherent openness and ambiguity, brings a set of knowledge and skill requirements that may bring challenges to the exercise of learner autonomy and even introduce inequality in the development of learner autonomy. Moreover, learner autonomy determines how learners may position technology in relation to language learning and shapes the concomitant learning experience in and gains from technology-mediated learning environments (Bouchard, 2009, 2012). Thus, the interaction between technology and learner autonomy is quite intricate and deserves in-depth exploration and discussion, which is the aim of Part I.

2
Technology as a Facilitator of Learner Autonomy

Benson (1997) underscored three dimensions of learner autonomy: the technical dimension, the psychological dimension, and the political dimension. The technical dimension refers to learners' act of engaging in autonomous learning without the intervention of teachers. The psychological dimension refers to learners' attitudes and abilities to conduct autonomous learning. The political dimension refers to learners' self-governance of the structural conditions and norms of learning. In the chapter, I discuss the facilitative role of technology on learner autonomy along these three dimensions.

Contribution of technology to the technical dimension of learner autonomy

The technical dimension of learner autonomy is closely linked to the concept of situational freedom and space for autonomy. Situational freedom refers to "the scope of external constraints on the movements of actors" (Levine, 1981, p. 230), and it shapes the possibility and scale of autonomous action. Technology has the potential to increase situational freedom by providing resources and expanding spaces for language learning and use. Space is a composite of the human and non-human objects gathered at particular moments of time, the nexus of social relationships, and the ongoing interactions among humans and between human and non-human objects (Benson, 2022; Murray, 2014). Different spaces offer different resources, different forms of organization, different nature of relationships, and different levels of situational freedom. Technology is both spaces for learning (e.g., an online news platform for informational or leisure reading) and constituent objects and resources in spaces (e.g., a translation app for a conversation on the street with a native speaker). Thus, it provides resources and spaces that free people of constraints in language use (e.g., allowing anonymous interaction; enabling more equal discourse; forming communities for sharing), minimizes the time and spatial constraints in language learning. Since scholars speak of language learning environment as a continuous landscape of in-class and out-of-class settings (Benson, 2022; Lai, 2015), it makes sense to discuss how technology expands the space and situational freedom for learner autonomy in these two settings.

Technology expanding autonomy in in-class learning

Technology can facilitate autonomy-supportive pedagogies, extend class activities beyond the physical and temporal boundaries of the classroom, and enable collective learning experiences. All these affordances may enhance learner autonomy in class activities.

Facilitating autonomy supportive pedagogies

Self-determination theory provides a key frame of reference for understanding students' autonomous motivation in the academic context. According to this theory, whether learners would autonomously engage in learning depends on whether the social environment is structured in ways that support their basic psychological needs for autonomy, competence, and relatedness (Ryan & Deci, 2000). The need for autonomy refers to "the experience of behavior as volitional and reflectively self-endorsed" (Niemiec & Ryan, 2009, p. 135). Inviting students to pursue personal interests, providing students with personally meaningful choices, enabling learner voices, and allowing for self-paced learning are the key to support this psychological need (Reeve & Cheon, 2021; Reeve & Jang, 2006). The need for competence refers to "the experience of behavior as effectively enacted," and this need can be supported by providing challenging tasks that are differentiated and supported with appropriate tools and feedback (Niemiec & Ryan, 2009, p. 135). The need for relatedness refers to the experience of feeling connected with others and having a sense of belonging. This psychological need can be supported by encouraging cooperation and teamwork, prioritizing individual needs, and having learners feel respected and valued by others (Bechter et al., 2019). Autonomy supportive teaching can contribute to the three psychological needs and drive autonomous learning behaviors.

Andragogy is the philosophical umbrella for autonomy supportive teaching. Knowles (1980) defined andragogy as a learner- and learning-centered approach to teaching and learning. According to Knowles, andragogy satisfies the essential conditions for adult learning: 1) an explicit understanding of the rationale for a learning arrangement and an awareness of the immediate value of learning; 2) experiential learning experience and experience of learning as problem solving; and 3) the development of a self-concept of being an independent person. To promote andragogy, Knowles (1980) highlights the necessity of being responsive to learner needs and interests, involving learners in goal setting based on personal interests and needs, and designing learning experiences in support of these goals. He also underscores the development of a cooperative learning environment. Although Knowles proposed the concept of andragogy in the context of adult learning, the principles apply to learners of all ages (Halupa, 2015; Merriam, 2001). Andragogy is the underlying principle behind student-centered learning practices that supports learner autonomy. In these student-centered practices, students co-design and co-regulate their learning experience (Bechter et al., 2019).

Technology provides tools and spaces for creating learning experiences that are connected to learners' personal interests and needs (Larsen-Freeman & Anderson, 2011). How to adapt learning to learners of different levels and accommodate different paces of learning have been a longstanding struggle in education. Technology may address this struggle by enabling the personalization of learning even inside the classroom (Escueta et al., 2017). Computer-assisted learning programs enable students to work on individual problems and engage in customized practice, provide timely feedback and guidance along the way, and visualize student performance data to help teachers adjust instruction to meet students' learning needs. The choices provided in these programs accord students control over the learning path and pace when completing instructor-created classroom learning experiences (Blaschke, 2019). A meta-analysis study conducted by Ma et al. (2014) reported a moderate positive effect of intelligent tutoring systems on learning (0.36 based on fixed-effect model and 0.41 based on random-effect model). Their analysis further revealed that intelligent tutoring systems have a greater effect on learning when compared with large-group human instruction (effect size: 0.44), with individual non-adaptive computer-based instruction (effect size: 0.57), and with individual textbook or workbook (effect size: 0.36). Focusing specifically on the effects of supplemental use of adaptive reading systems, Shamir et al. (2020) found that adaptive reading systems had positive effects on literacy development and the positive effects lasted for extended periods of time. Research has further revealed that even individual tools can help boost student choice and voice. For instance, audience response tools and systems (e.g., Mentimeter, Socrative and GoSoapBox), sharing platforms (e.g., Padlet and Voicethread) and participation platforms (e.g., Twitter and Today's Meet) enable teachers to collect student voices and use them to adapt subsequent learning experiences on the go. Technological tools can also increase student control during learning activities. For instance, De La Fuente (2014) found that giving students individual devices to listen to the same passage and answer the same set of listening comprehension questions within the same timeframe led to better performance in both bottom-up and top-down comprehension than letting the teacher control the play of the passage. The research showed that just by giving students control over the pace of an activity, technology can help enhance task performance.

Technology also provides tools and resources to support students to play a more active role in learning and boost their self-efficacy for autonomous learning. A typical example is concordance. Concordance enables learners to become active researchers in data-driven learning on lexis and grammar. The use of concordance is found to have an effect size of 1.80 on vocabulary and grammar learning (Boulton & Cobb, 2017). Various annotation tools can boost learners' confidence in autonomous learning. For instance, audio narration facilitates vocabulary learning and models fluent reading, and can even benefit advanced readers, since it helps to slow down the content and engage students to listen to every single word (Dalton, 2014; Grover & Hannegan, 2012). Text-to-speech and read-aloud tools positively influence the reading comprehension of learners with reading disabilities, with an effect size of 0.35 (Wood et al., 2018). CALL glossing has a positive effect on reading comprehension (effect size ranging from 0.73 to 1.44) and on vocabulary learning (effect size ranging from 0.46 to 1.40) as reported in a second-order meta-analysis study (Plonsky & Ziegler, 2016). Technology is also a key tool to support autonomy supportive practices such as differentiated instruction (Karatza, 2019). Technology provides multi-sensory and multimedia resources and gives easy access to references and feedback that not only support students' autonomous learning but also allow teachers to differentiate instruction to cater to students' diversified needs and interests.

Having a sense of belonging and relatedness is essential for internalizing regulation (Deci & Ryan, 2002), and providing an environment that allows and supports learners to negotiate new roles within the 'social context' of classroom learning is key to foster learner autonomy. Technology can create online learning and collaboration spaces where learners can exercise collective autonomy and have their voices heard and valued by others. Bloch (2007) shared the story a Somali immigrant student, where participating in the class blog made him able to overcome his weakness in academic forms of written English and utilize vernacular spoken English to voice his thoughts and reflect on his readings freely and critically. The student took advantage of the unique discourse features on blogs to interact actively with peers and engage with their arguments. Having his voice heard and respected in the class blogs enhanced his investment in English use. Sun and Chang (2012) also reported how seven L2 graduate students co-constructed knowledge about academic writing and reflected on language learning skills in a blogging environment. They argued that the blogging site provided multiple methods of online social support and enabled students to establish a learning community. Alm (2006) further pointed out that Web 2.0 tools can enhance learners' relatedness and boost autonomous learning motivation. Emulating the liberating affordance of globalized online spaces and engaging learners in literacy activities in unstructured online spaces provide a viable approach to support learner autonomy. Akbari et al. (2015) compared the learning experience of two groups of language learners: one group via 20 sessions of face-to-face meetings in a classroom and the other group via online teaching sessions and conversations and interactive activities with peers on Facebook. They found that students in the Facebook group exhibited greater learning gains than students in the face-to-face group, and that the Facebook group also showed significantly greater perception of autonomy, competence and relatedness. Perceived relatedness contributed the most to the observed differences in learning gains across the two groups. Meeting the psychological needs of relatedness may further contribute to self-regulation in online learning (e.g., Zhou et al., 2021).

Empowering learners as creative language users

Technology provides multimodal resources that enable learners to combine different semiotic resources to make meaning, construct knowledge, and project identities (Belcher, 2017). To put in Kress's (2000) words, "the work of the text maker is taken as transformative of the resources and of the maker of the text. It gives agency of a real kind to the text maker" (p. 340). Integrating into language classrooms digital multimodal forms of communication that students are immersed in daily life helps "tap into [students'] interest in using digital media, accept their lived experiences, and invite them to use their funds of knowledge in multiliteracies" (Pirbhai-Illich, 2010, p. 257). The validation and embracement of the funds of knowledge students bring with them to the learning context may enhance students' learning motivation and autonomy, enable them to negotiate and construct new identities as multimodal designer, empower them in class participation and prepare them for their digital future (Hafner, 2015; Jiang & Luk, 2016). Hafner and Miller (2011) engaged their university students in a collaborative multimodal scientific documentary creation project and found that students invested heavily in the project and exhibited strong enthusiasm for taking control over many aspects of the creation and learning process. They independently explored relevant resources online and practiced English when creating the videos, provided peer feedback, and worked as a team to monitor each other's learning, and reviewed and evaluated the record of their language production to reflect on learning. The authors concluded that the digital video creation project in globalized online spaces provided students with opportunities to exercise learner autonomy within the structured language learning context. This is particularly beneficial to marginalized or disadvantaged students. Pacheco et al. (2019) introduced a digital multimodal project to their Vietnam and Spanish immigrant students at a middle school, where the students were instructed to integrate multiple languages and modes into their digital products. The researchers found that the project enabled their participants to leverage heritage languages and cultures as linguistic and cultural capitals to achieve positive social transformation at the school. Jiang et al. (2020) also introduced collaborative digital multimodal projects to a group of EFL university students in China. Focusing on the learning experience of an ethnic minority student in the class, they found that, despite lacking confidence and playing "invisible" in her English class out of a phobia of English, the student exhibited changed investment in English since the initiation of the digital multimodal project. She developed a positive identity of an English user who can use English to do things, actively utilizing her ethnic knowledge as a resource in her multimodal work, asserting her ethnic identity that was invisible in class, and serving as a cultural broker for her classmates. The authors concluded that "DMC plays an empowering role by both giving voice to minority students and providing space for them to dialogue with the ideological structure that traditionally devalues/ignores ethnic cultures" (p. 971).

Empowerment not only comes from the validation of learners' funds of knowledge, but also derives from the action of creation (Blau & Shamir-Inbal, 2017). Lan (2018) pointed out that creation per se is an autonomous process of discovering, solving problems and reflecting ideas. Yeh and Lan (2018) provided 29 fifth graders with a 3D virtual learning platform, where students could engage in voice- and text-based chat and construct their own 3D virtual contexts by manipulating the virtual objects from a database. They found that the creation activities increased students' motivation and willingness to use English to do things in the virtual world. Lee (2011) further found that a creative writing task, blogging, developed learner autonomy by fostering self-expression and self-management, and boosted learner investment in the task.

Moreover, social participation enabled by web 2.0 tools also empowers learners on "their potential with the resources of production and the resources of dissemination" (Kress, 2003, p. 23). Being able to share one's creation with a real audience, make an impact and create values for others are drivers of autonomous action and continued investment. Wang and Jiang (2021) shared a one-year writing intervention with WeChat moments. They assigned students randomly to two conditions in class writing: one group posted writing entries on WeChat moments and the other group submitted their writings to the teacher in the paper version. They found that the WeChat group not only showed significantly higher writing performance, but also reported a higher level of autonomy. The participants attributed the heightened autonomy in the WeChat condition to perceived personal relevance and meaningfulness of the tasks: having a wider range of audiences for writing strengthened the sense of authorship and being able to interact with others on the moments changed the nature of the task from a writing task to a sharing activity. For marginalized populations, ethnic minorities in particular, the characteristics of social media interactions as low-risk and nonthreatening language use and social practices, capital-enhancing social connections, and transcultural and plurilingual identity construction and performance afford empowering acculturation experience. Lai (2019b) found that engagement with the mainstream social media was positively associated with ethnic minority students' bicultural orientation identity and bicultural competence, which predicted students' motivation for learning the mainstream language. As a follow-up initiative, Lai and colleagues integrated mainstream social media materials into the Chinese-as-a-second-language class for a group of secondary school ethnic minority students at the beginner-high level in Hong Kong. One class was provided with social media materials aligned with topics covered in the class and was supported in consuming these materials for information seeking purposes and producing relevant information in Chinese to share on the mainstream social media. The other class was also given the same social media materials but engaged more in reading comprehension and drill and practice around these materials. The social media intervention lasted one year and took up one third of the instructional time in this course. The class with social media participation activities integrated showed significantly greater gains in ideal L2 Chinese self, and greater, despite non-significant, gains in motivation for Chinese language learning. The teachers also reported observing greater initiative among the students in venturing out into the digital wild to seek information to share with classmates.

Expanding the time and space for autonomous action

Technology, especially mobile devices, gives learners increased mobility of time, space and learning experience to create ubiquitous learning experience and personalized learning ecologies that facilitate autonomous learning (Bachmair & Pachler, 2014; Kukulska-Hulme et al., 2017). Meta-analysis studies of mobile assisted language learning have revealed an effect size of 0.51-0.72 for language learning in general (Cho et al., 2018; Sung et al., 2015; Chen et al., 2020) and a weighted effect size of 1.005 for vocabulary in specific (Lin & Lin, 2019). Mobile technology has been used to transcend the constraints of time and space in students' classroom learning. Language educators have used mobile short message service (SMS) or multimedia message service (MMS) to deliver mini-lessons or learning materials at spaced intervals to increase students' repeated exposure to learning resources beyond the classroom. Mobile devices have also been used to enhance social connectivity and facilitate information sharing (Lin & Lin, 2019). Context-aware MALL applications have been used to gather information from the environment through sensors, and support situated learning so as to create real-world and place-based learning. For instance, during a field trip to the zoo, Chang (2018) utilized the location-awareness function of mobile devices to deliver individualized learning materials based on individual students' specific locations in the zoo to support their vocabulary learning. Mobile devices have also been used to create augmented reality experiences that overlay virtual multimedia objects on a physical object. Marker-based AR applications enable learners to scan text or image or concrete objects to retrieve multimedia illustrations, hyperlinks, social media feeds, in-situ assistance (Godwin-Jones, 2016). GPS-based AR applications have also been used to create place-based collaborative problem-solving experiences for students. For instance, Holden and Sykes (2011) created a location-based mobile game for Spanish pragmatics learning. The game threaded different components of the learning experience: in-class learning and reflection activities around Spanish pragmatics; independent gameplay with non-playing characters to obtain relevant information; a site visit to different locations of a Spanish-speaking neighborhood to learn about historical accounts and contemporary life; and interact with Spanish-speaking inhabitants to solve the game narrative around a murder. Similarly, Thorne and colleagues (2015) created a sci-fi AR game that immerse learners in a narrative that the earth is undergoing severe environmental problems and the players are sent back to the year of 2015 as agents to learn about green technology. Carrying the AR app around the university campus, the players receive multimodal AR information in English to help them accomplish various tasks when reaching certain spots on the campus. Examples of the tasks include verbal recording of observations, video clip creation, written reports and oral presentations. These are only a few examples of how mobile devices have been used to create ubiquitous and situated learning experiences for learners.

Another epitome of technological application that transcends the constraints of time and space is the concept of flipped learning. In flipped learning, instructional materials, usually in the form of short videos, learning management systems and Web 2.0 applications, are given to students to study independently or collaboratively prior to class. Students then come to class to engage in in-depth discussions and higher-order thinking tasks to consolidate learning (Chen Hsieh, Wu & Marek, 2017). In this design, time and space for autonomous action is largely expanded. When classroom learning is flipped, students can enjoy extra opportunities to study the learning materials and construct an initial understanding of the content, which may reduce cognitive load during in-class collaborative activities around the content. Thus, flipped learning enables learning to take place in multiple interactive learning communities and through various channels, which provides more potential for student control over their learning process (Zhu, 2021). Based essentially on active learning and learner responsibility for learning, the flipped learning mode may make students independent and reflective learners (Enfield, 2013). Meta-analysis studies of flipped learning have revealed an effect size of 0.99 on learning outcomes (Vitta & Al-Hoorie, 2020). Researchers have further revealed that flipped learning not only enhances learning but also increases the likelihood of students becoming active learners (Chen Hsieh et al., 2017; Turan & Akdag-Cimen, 2019). Tsai (2021) conducted a quasi-experimental study to compare students' learning autonomy in flipped and non-flipped learning conditions. The flipped learning group was given PPT and pre-recorded mini lectures together with TED talks and YouTube videos to study prior to the class, work on worksheets and group discussion and presentation during class, and complete online assessment such as quizzes and journals after class. The non-flipped group attended traditional lectures and completed the materials and assessments on the learning management system. The researcher found that students in the flipped group showed significantly greater improvement in self-management of learning than students in the control group, exhibiting greater engagement with the learning resources that were provided for pre- and after-class activities.

Enabling the exercise of collective autonomy

One major affordance of technology is to create and facilitate collaborative learning experience beyond the classroom. Collaborative work brings social modes of regulation. Hadwin and Oshige (2011) conceptualized that three types of regulation may co-exist in collaborative work: self-regulation, co-regulation, and socially shared regulation. Self-regulation refers to individual metacognitive control of the cognitive, behavioral, motivation and emotional conditions of learning through the iterative process of planning, monitoring, adjusting and reflection, which may be promoted through prompting, modeling, or feedback in collaborative work. Socially shared regulation refers to the synergetic communal metacognitive control of the various conditions of the collective activity through which the co-constructed goals are achieved. Co-regulation refers to the distributed regulatory resources within the group and the interaction around regulation. Requesting and sharing of regulatory resources among individual learners may support or thwart the shift of regulatory ownership to individual or shared regulation. Technology may provide a space that fosters collective autonomy.

Hafner and Miller (2011) engaged their university EFL learners on a collaborative digital video project. This project emulated learners' digital experience in unstructured informal learning environments and tapped into learners' funds of knowledge. The researchers observed the occurrence of co-regulation that facilitated the shift of regulatory ownership to individuals and group, reporting instances of learners working as a team to monitor each other's learning and instances of peer teaching to raise awareness of important aspects of the learning process. Tseng et al. (2020) reported on a research project on students' use of a 3D virtual environment for vocabulary learning under different conditions: teacher-controlled exploration, individual exploration and pair exploration. The researchers found that their elementary school participants in the paired exploration condition outperformed those in the individual exploration and teacher-controlled exploration condition in both immediate and delayed vocabulary posttests. However, there were no significant differences between the individual exploration condition and the teacher-controlled exploration condition. The researchers reasoned that co-regulation in the paired exploration condition fostered positive interdependence and mutual accountability. They concluded that collective autonomy is more advantageous than individual autonomy.

Working together in online collaborative spaces can help learners become more autonomous. Two examples of classroom initiatives that capitalize on the power of collective autonomy are collaborative writing and tele-collaboration. Computer-based collaborative writing enables learners to co-regulate their writing process. Bhowmik and Hilman (2018) found that collaborative peer writing enhanced learners' self-awareness of their strengths and weaknesses in writing. Li et al. (2021) examined a group of university students' performance in wiki-based collaborative literature circle activities. The researchers found that students exhibited a high level of socially shared regulation during wiki-based collaborative literature circle. Shared regulatory behaviors significantly predicted students' engagement in the collaborative literacy circle activities and learning outcome. Engaging a group of student teacher trainees from Hong Kong in a tele-collaboration project with language learners from UK, US, Germany, and Poland to analyze web resources and social networking tools for language teaching, Fuchs et al. (2012) found that the collaborative, experiential work developed a critical understanding of the digital tools among the student teachers and enhanced their autonomy for making use of these tools for teaching. Lenkaitis (2020) applied the concept of tele-collaboration to a group of learners from the same university and organized Zoom-based interpersonal interaction tasks around the topics covered in class. They found that "virtual co-presence' enhanced learners' autonomous engagement with each other to practice L2 skills beyond class time.

Technology boosting autonomy outside the classroom

Language learning involves the accumulation of extensive experience across varied settings. Out-of-class language learning is critical to language development in that it not only comprises an important space for authentic language exposure and use, but also plays an essential role in maintaining learners' motivation for learning (Benson, 2011; Richards, 2015). Autonomous language learning beyond the classroom is particularly important, given that in-class learning is rather constrained in fulfilling the amount and diversity of language use experience needed for language development (Richards, 2015). Moreover, learning beyond the classroom is a necessity if we are to transform language learning from a process of acquiring a linguistic tool/skill to a process of engaging with the world (Godwin-Jones, 2020). As Warner and Dupuy (2018) put it, "If FL [foreign language] education is to take learners seriously as legitimate users of the language, scholars and instructors must consider the different ways in which their students could imagine engaging with the world beyond the context of classroom" (p. 124). Technology provides learning spaces, venues, medium and supportive tools for such experiences (Godwin-Jones, 2020; Luckin, 2010; Lai, 2018). Researchers argue that technology drives the shift of language learning landscape. Ito and colleagues (2020) observed that technology catalyzes the changing landscape of learning opportunities. They argued that, with the mediation of technology, learners can pursue personal interests and create their personal ecology of connected learning, taking advantage of the opportunities for learning in varied settings and the mentoring relationships distributed therein. Godwin-Jones (2018) concurred with this observation and argued:

> Evidence is accumulating that a major shift is underway in the ways that second language (L2) development is taking place. Increasingly, especially among young people, that process is occurring outside of institutional settings, predominantly through the use of online networks and media. (p. 8)

Autonomous use of technology for language learning beyond the classroom is positively associated with learners' language gains (Cole & Vanderplank, 2016; Lai et al., 2015; Sylvén & Sundqvist, 2012; Sundqvist & Wikström, 2015). It also relates positively to affective outcomes, such as enjoyment of and confidence in language learning, and willingness to communicate (Lai et al., 2015; Leona et al., 2021). Peters and colleagues (2019) compared the vocabulary size of a group of Flemish English-as-Foreign language learners in their 3rd year of English learning with a group of French-as-Foreign language learners in their 6th year of French learning and found that the English language learners exhibited greater vocabulary size than the French language learners. To understand the reason behind the observed differences, the researchers found that the English language learners had significantly greater exposure to English language media (audio-visual input with and without subtitles and written media) and English online media (online gaming and language websites) than to French language media. Thus, despite the shorter duration of in-class learning, English language learners demonstrated greater vocabulary size. Similar studies have shown that access to online media in the language contributes more to language development than in-class learning experience (Brevik, 2019; Peters, 2018). These studies attest to the significance of autonomous engagement with technological resources beyond the classroom for language development.

Informal learning is "intentional or tacit learning in which we engage either individually or collectively without direct reliance on a teacher or an externally organized curriculum" (Livingston, 2006, p. 204). Learning in the digital wild beyond the classroom is agentic in nature and has the following characteristics: 1) It is unstructured; 2) It is driven by personal interest and choice and embedded in valued meaningful everyday activities or shared practices; and 3) It is contextual and relational, and learners are part of the context (Hager, 2012; Rogoff et al., 2016). Technology may create favorable conditions for learning and facilitate learners to exercise agency to reap the immense learning opportunities in the informal learning context.

Bringing structure to unstructured learning experiences

A key characteristic of informal language learning is the absence of supportive structure (Godwin-Jones, 2018). However, even adult language learners, especially learners of lower language proficiency levels, may struggle with the lack of structure in the informal learning contexts. Lai (2015) interviewed a group of university foreign language learners on their selection and use of out-of-class language learning resources. These learners reported a strong preference for out-of-class learning resources containing learning support. They reported not incorporating into their out-of-class learning resources that lacked structure and supporting mechanisms.

Technological platforms, such as instruction-oriented social networking sites and grammar websites, instructional apps, such as vocabulary apps and reading apps, and instruction-oriented social media channels, such as instructional channels on YouTube or Facebook, provide structured learning materials that learners can incorporate into their informal learning journey to complement the predominantly meaning-focused experience in the digital wild. Lai et al. (2018) found this type of technological experience is rather dominant in Hong Kong foreign language learners' informal learning experience beyond the classroom. Preference for this type of technological experience is also reported in other research contexts (Lamb & Arisandy, 2020; Trinder, 2017). Participants in Lai and colleagues' (2018) study reported that instruction-oriented technological experience, although perceived boring, was regarded as beneficial to language learning since it provided useful support to help overcome the learning difficulties encountered in the informal learning experience. Moreover, assistive technologies, such as online dictionaries, dictionary apps, Google translation and translation apps, were actively used to trouble shoot language problems and facilitate comprehension during various informal technological experiences.

Language learning social networking sites (LLSNSs), such as Duolingo, Busuu, and Polyglotclub, and massively online open language learning courses (MOOCs) provide structured learning materials for personal tutoring. These sites are gaining popularity (Chik & Ho, 2017). In his survey with 4095 language learners who used the Busuu app for language learning on their own, Rosell-Aguilar (2018) found that 40.2% of the learners used the app to complement other informal language learning resources and experiences such as websites, books and online videos, and 35.8% of them used the app as the only resources for their autonomous language learning. Thus, learners relied on structured materials quite heavily in their autonomous language learning beyond the classroom. Chik and Ho (2017) followed the learning trajectories of three adult experienced language learners who embarked on the learning of a new language in the digital wild. They reported that all the learners started their learning journey with online platforms that provided structured learning materials, and then gradually supplemented these non-formal learning resources with informal learning materials from pop cultural media. However, after a period of exploration with informal materials and experiences, all of them went back to a greater reliance on the structured non-formal materials. The reason for the renewed preference for non-formal and structured materials was reflected in one participant's interview quote: "when you have to source your own learning material, you end up learning things randomly, with no structure. For example, I remember learning Italian from food packaging five years ago. I might have learned something that's beyond my level without knowing the basics" (p. 167). They also attributed their heavy reliance on non-formal materials to the "continuity of learning" (p. 167) and "a logical progression along a given curriculum" (p. 168) embedded in these materials. Thus, structured materials provided by technology help to balance, support and complement the learning experience in the digital wild to create the "structured unpredictability" ideal for learner autonomy (Little & Throne, 2017).

Enabling pursuit of interest and daily activity engagement in L2

Barron (2006) highlighted that interest drives learners to agentically construct personalized learning ecology across formal and informal contexts and perpetuates sustained efforts in informal learning. Interest determines the sustainable life course of a person, and resolving life-centered problems of personal interest is a key purpose of autonomous engagement in informal learning (Akkerman & Bakker, 2019; Morris, 2019). Enjoyment and interest are found to be an important consideration in language learners' selective engagement in out-of-class experience (Chan, 2016; Lai & Zheng, 2018). For example, Pill (2001) asked her adult learners to brainstorm the reasons for not choosing certain out-of-class learning activities, 24 reasons listed by the learners had something to do with the activity not being part of their personal life.

With the omnipresence of technology in everyday life, quite a portion of daily life activities are mediated by technology these days. Technology makes it possible for language learners to pursue their personal interest in a language he/she is learning and connect with people and culture in that language. In effect, Lai et al. (2018) found that using technology to seek information and entertainment was a dominant type of informal learning experiences that Chinese university foreign language learners engaged in. For example, Fanfiction and video blogs provide opportunities for self-expression and publishing, and they can also be virtual landscapes where second language learners aggregate to pursue personal interests (Sauro,

2020; Codreanu & Combe, 2020). In addition to enhanced ease of access, technology also proffers affordances like anonymity, masked identity, and democratic and non-threatening socialization that may boost learners' willingness of and confidence in pursuing personal interests in such places. For instance, Knight et al. (2020) pointed out that digital and online games allow for "low-risk practice in simulated conditions with and through multiple player identities" and attract second language learners to pursue their interests while learning the language incidentally (p. 105). Reinhardt (2019) pinpointed that social media hold a few affordances to facilitate second language learners' participation in social communication in the target language: Interaction on social media allows identity-masking and contains reduced social cues, which affords low-risk and nonthreatening language and social practices. It is community-based and contains distributed power and resources, which facilitates equal-status communication with common goals and brings capital-enhancing social connections and emotional bonding (Sykes, Oskoz & Throne, 2008; Wang & Vásquez, 2012). These affordances encourage L2 learners to perform daily life activities on the target language social media, such as seeking information and socialization, despite a deficiency in the target language. Lai and colleagues (2020) gave accounts of how a group of ethnic minority students in Hong Kong utilized multilingual resources to access the local Chinese and their culture on everyday social media to obtain social and cultural capital that are essential to their acculturation into the mainstream society.

Moreover, the multimodal nature of technological resources and the manipulability of the materials (e.g., speech rate adjustment; pause and replay) make the process of interest pursuit in non-native language well supported and more enjoyable. In effect, language learners often rely on the subtitles of TV shows, movies, and online videos to help grasp the content. They also pause videos to check dictionaries on unknown words that are critical to the comprehension of the content. Aragon and Davis (2019) studied the fanfiction behaviors of a group of adolescents and concluded that these online interest communities provide immense opportunities of informal mentoring that supports learners' development of writing skills. Valero-Porras and Cassany (2015) shared the story of how online dictionaries and translators and 24-hour feedback and support from a scanlation community helped Shiro, a Spanish-speaking girl with beginning-level proficiency in English, participate actively in translating manga from English into Spanish on this site. Gameplay and simulations also contain supportive mechanisms. Some scholars highlight that cognitive support from the within-game interaction with non-player characters (NPCs) allows for the practice of high-stake speech acts without offending real people (Sykes et al., 2008). Others underscore that affiliative bond among players on shared affinity spaces and mutual support and assistance from experienced players that are prevalent in the gaming culture provide valuable emotional support to learners' interest pursuit in a new language (Thorne & Black, 2007).

Providing contexts for the construction of language learning ecology

Informal learning is highly contextual and relational. It is contextual in that learning in different informal contexts is subject to the characteristics of the discursive, social, and material resources in the context. It is relational in that learning in different informal contexts is related and subject to the influence of these contexts. Thus, a holistic view towards learners' interaction with various elements within the context and related contexts is important (Jackson, 2013; Rogoff et al., 2016). Technologies and informal learning network technologies provide important contexts for informal language learning and open up opportunities for learners to construct their own language learning ecology (Lai, 2018).

Language learners are found to actively utilize technological resources and tools to construct their personalized language learning ecology (Cabot, 2014; Lai, 2015). Moreover, learners use technology in a selective and coordinated way to construct their language learning experience. Lai (2015) provided accounts on how a group of Hong Kong university foreign language learners used technology selectively outside the classroom to complement their in-class learning experience. The students searched for additional information associated with class topics outside the classroom and incorporated in-class technological activities and related online resources to their out-of-school learning experience. Their selection and construction of out-of-class experiences with technological resources were shaped by their appraisals of the affordances and constraints of in-class learning. Tracing six French upper secondary students' construction of English learning ecologies over time, Cabot (2014) found that learners' selective use of technological resources was shaped by their changing perceptions of the norms of use, the content and the functionalities of the technological resources. Research has also revealed that learners coordinate different technologies and utilize the unique affordances of these technologies to construct language learning experience. For instance, in Lai and colleagues' (2022) dairy and interview study with a group of university English language learners in China, participants reported using an average of five technological resources for out-of-class language learning. The participants' accounts abounded in instances of selective and coordinated engagement with different technological tools. One participant, An, reported that he "watched TV shows to pick up colloquial expression, listened to TED talks for exposure to different ways of thinking, thus paying less attention to language; and listened to songs for pure relaxation." They further found that how participants interacted with technological resources depended on their perception of the affordances of the resources. One participant, Jan, regarded the words appearing in online news as common expressions and hence positioned online news as a valuable resource for obtaining useful information about word usage. Consequently, when reading online news, she paid special attention to how the words were used in particular contexts. In contrast, she positioned vocabulary app as a means to support systematic study of English vocabulary through repeated access, and hence would not pay attention to the exemplary sentences provided in the app. Instead, she made a deliberate effort to constantly review words learned in previous days.

Democratizing access to and use of L2

Systematic exclusion of the disadvantaged groups from access to English language education has been widely reported in the existing literature (e.g., Coleman, 2011; Lamb, 2011). The exclusion originates not only in the inaccessibility of the material resources, but also in the inhibitive discursive characteristics of the social context. Lamb (2013) shared the story of a rural Indonesian girl who felt compelled to conceal her English proficiency and abstain from using English in the local context to avoid appearing "arrogant" and "putting [her]self above everyone else." The limited opportunities to access and use English, the limited provision of English at school, and parents' inability to provide concrete study help and their fatalistic attitudes towards their children's future all constrain rural and disadvantaged learners' agency in English learning.

The diffusion of technology—particularly cheap mobile technologies—has the potential to liberate learners from these constraints. Rural participants in Lamb's (2013) study reported how mobile and internet platforms helped activate and legitimate their ideal English L2 selves despite constraints in their immediate social milieu. In Lamb's (2013) words, "because of its capacity to reach across national borders, [online] social networking appears to legitimate the use of English when in more local domains it may be considered pretentious" (p. 25). Smith et al. (2018) referred to this as "democratizing effect on access to English" (p. 12). Sockett and Tofollio (2020) also noted how technology has enabled naturalistic acquisition of English through extramural activities for youngsters, and how the concomitant democratization of access to English has increased French young learners' English language skills in general. Technology facilitates the democratization of access to English not only through giving equal access to resources, but also through making language variants that are alive in different communities accessible to learners. Canagarajah (1999) argued that by making diverse language variants available, it democratizes English learning from a narrow focus on the formal and institutionalized variants that are featured in the textbook. Online spaces abound in multilingualism and multimodality, which enriches the semiotic resources that language learners can rely on for self-expression and communication and liberates learners from being constrained by their limited linguistic capacity in the target language.

Technology bridging autonomy inside and outside the classroom

Barron (2006) called attention to the intersection or the bi-directional flow of formal and informal learning. According to her learning ecology perspective, learning can take place across the boundaries of in-school and out-of-class contexts. Learning experience in formal and informal learning contexts can trigger and reinforce each other (Greenhow & Robelia, 2009). Similar arguments for bridging formal and informal learning also abound in the language education field. Language researchers argue for the complementarity of in-class and out-of-class language learning experience. For instance, university foreign language learners in Lai's (2015) study reported that in-class learning experience primarily helped them acquire the basics of the language and kept them focused and persevere in learning the language. Whereas out-of-class learning experience helped maintain motivation and interest in learning, gave a stronger sense of how the language is actually used, brought a sense of accomplishment and boosted self-efficacy, and connected them to peer learners and the target culture. Thus, in-class and out-of-class learning experience contribute uniquely and complementarily to language learning. Godwin-Jones (2019) further pointed out that out-of-class technological experience helped expose learners to "sophisticated pragmatic and critical reading capabilities" that are often not available in formal learning contexts (Chern & Dooley, 2014, p. 114). Another line of argument in support of the intersection is the "equitable multilingualism" turn of second language learning. Scholars argue against benchmarking second language learners with standardized forms of language and "native-speaker" norms, and advocate validating the linguistic repertoires that learners bring with them to the learning context (Ortega, 2019). Hafner et al. (2015) pinpointed that school-based language use often focuses on standardized forms, whereas multilingual and translingual language use abounds in out-of-class contexts. Thus, how language learning inside the classroom might interplay with multilingualism in out-of-school language use context deserves attention. Moreover, Wagner's (2019) sociological approach to language learning holds that "learning is bound to participation in the life world and therefore to the personal history of each learner" (p. 254). Thus,

> Classrooms need to feed on the everyday practices of the students. Classroom organization needs to have a close relevance for students' activities in the life world and accept the obligation to help students to establish life world relations. (Wagner, 2019, p. 255)

Arguments from different perspectives hence converge on the call for attention to the interface of and bi-directional flow between in-class and out-of-class learning experiences. Technology is very much in presence in these arguments, playing an important role in bridging in-class and out-of-class learning.

On the one hand, technology provides important tools and resources for the creation of learner-defined personalized learning environment that supports lifelong and informal learning and facilitates heutagogical approaches to learning, which emphasizes supporting learners as active agents in learning (Hase & Kenyon, 2000). In Greenhow and Lewin's (2016) words,

> Technology has the potential to disrupt the boundaries between sites where learning takes place. It can empower learners through greater agency, opportunities to participate in networked communities and access to a wide range of resources to support knowledge building and collaboration. (p. 13)

Technology, like social media, enables learners to expand upon and grow their personalized learning environment and networks to include the broader local and global communities throughout their lifetimes. For instance, technology allows learners to connect with and follow experts within fields of interest and share resources and discoveries of inquiry with peers who share similar interests (Blaschke, 2019). Personalized learning environments and networks mediated by technologies integrate formal and informal learning (Dabbagh & Kitsantas, 2012). Deliberate incorporation of these networks and experiences in the instructional contexts to create heutagogical environments can help foster self-directed lifelong and "lifewide" learners who engage in sustained learning across life span and bridge and connect life experiences across time and space (Blaschke, 2019). Another epitome of heutagogy in technological spaces is connectivist MOOC (cMOOC). In connectivist MOOC courses, learners are provided with a pool of self-study materials. They are supported to chart out their own learning trajectories with these learning materials and form communities to co-explore and co-construct knowledge and understanding through sharing resources and experiences, exchanging languages, and serving as tutors for one another. In Reinders and White's (2016) words, technology "is enabling a wider range of pedagogies in more locations that are less formal and that give more control to learners" (p. 150).

On the other hand, technology provides essential resources and experiences for the realization of usage-based experiential pedagogies. Learners' experience in the digital wilds makes up an essential aspect of their daily life experience and needs. Researchers have proposed various ways to enrich in-class learning with relevant out-of-class digital resources and experiences. Trinder (2017) recommended asking students "to find and share digital resources (news articles, forum comments, videos, etc.) that relate to content/topics on the curriculum, to post them on learning management systems or in closed Facebook groups, and to comment on the contributions of others" (p. 140). Hafner et al. (2015) advocated going further to engage students in critical analysis of these resources. According to them, inviting students to bring examples of their new media communication artefacts and experience, such as remixing, interaction on social media, and online gaming sites, to classroom and engage them to apply discourse analytical techniques to analyze these artefacts can be a powerful bridging activity that helps develop learners' metalinguistic knowledge and metacognitive awareness of online interaction. Godwin-Jones (2018) shared a project where the instructor engaged intermediate-level students to curate and evaluate authentic audiovisual materials (e.g., videos, music) and online materials (e.g., blog, websites) in the target language to enhance their digital literacy and enrich sources for language learning. The instructor then invited some students to be co-designers of student learning experience by transforming some of the materials that received the highest peer ratings into interactive learning materials and sharing these materials as open educational resources.

In addition to facilitating the permeation and coordination of in-class and out-of-class learning experience, technology also helps augment the bond between in-class and out-of-class learning. Meta-analysis studies have shown that technology-enhanced language learning experience not only strengthens learners' engagement in the immediate learning situation but also boosts their long-term language learning motivation in general (Golonka et al., 2014; Macaro et al., 2012). Thus, technology sustains learning investment across boundaries. Lamb and Arisandy (2020) surveyed a group of Indonesian university English language learners on their out-of-class learning experience to examine how the out-of-class experience related to learners' motivation for in-class English learning. The researchers found that learners' out-of-class learning experience was largely technology-mediated. The out-of-class learning experience, regardless of whether it was entertainment-oriented, socialization-oriented or self-instruction-oriented, correlated positively with these learners' motivated efforts in English learning and English ideal L2 self, i.e., their projected future self-concept in relation to English. More importantly, they found that out-of-class learning experience—self-instruction-oriented and socialization-oriented experiences in particular—correlated positively with these students' attitudes to in-class English learning. The study suggests that technology-mediated out-of-class experience may motivate in-class learning. Integrating technological experiences into in-class learning helps prepare learners for language use beyond the classroom, and hence build a "psychological 'bridge' between what happens in the class and what learners are doing outside" (Lamb & Arisandy, 2020, p. 24). The scaffolded exercise of agency and supported trial and error in discovering and exploiting online resources in the instructional context can "ensure that learners are not demotivated by disturbing communicative encounters or excessive linguistic difficulties" in the digital wild (Lamb & Arisandy, 2020, p. 26), which contributes positively to self-initiated and sustained engagement in out-of-class learning.

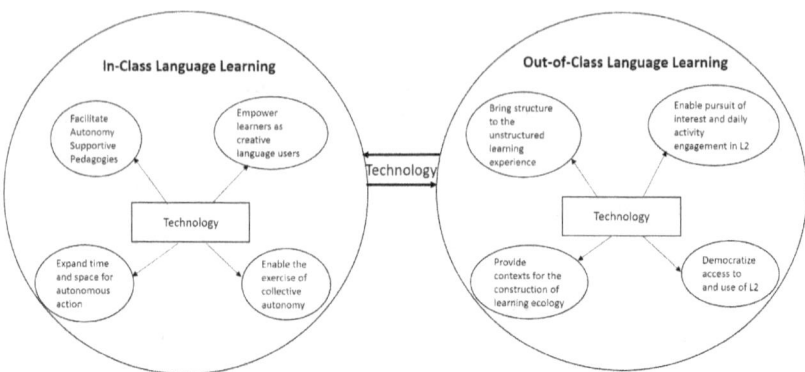

Figure 1 *Facilitating the technical dimension of learner autonomy*

In general, scholars perceive technology as a boost to the porous and slippery nature of learning across boundaries (Dabbagh & Kitsantas, 2012). Technology enhances the fluidity of learning experience across time and space, connecting informal and formal learning seamlessly (Goodyear, 2021; Sangrà et al., 2019). Greenhow and Lewin (2016) further argued that rather than bridging formal and informal learning, technology, like social media, is inherently a learning space that carries varying formal and informal learning attributes, and hence a natural cement of formal and informal learning.

Figure 1 summarizes how technology boosts situational freedom and space for autonomy, that is, the technical dimension of learner autonomy.

Contribution of technology to the psychological dimension of learner autonomy

In addition to amplifying and supporting the exercise of learner autonomy, technology can also enhance learners' capacity for autonomy, i.e., the psychological dimension of learner autonomy. Markauskaite and Goodyear (2017) regarded the ability to "configure an epistemic environment" as an essential competence for autonomy as a lifelong learner. According to Goodyear (2021), this competence involves "assembling tools, artefacts and other resources so that they come efficiently to hand during learning/knowledge-making activities" (p. 1601), and technology is constitutive "epistemic devices" that form an essential part of this capacity (p. 1599).

Mobile technologies have been used to deliver timely and adaptive interventions to support learner capacity for autonomy. For instance, Goh et al. (2012) took advantage of the ubiquitous nature of mobile devices to deliver persuasive short messaging service (SMS) over 12 weeks to a group of students to boost self-regulation in learning. The weekly messages contain self-regulated learning strategies and reminders and encouragement of participation in various learning opportunities and assignments. The researchers found that the SMS messages significantly increased students' ability to manage their time and effort in learning. Students who received the SMS reminders showed greater improvement in the utilization of cognitive, meta-cognitive and resource management strategies. Zheng et al. (2018) integrated a mobile self-regulated learning intervention in a reading task, where students were guided to make a brief evaluation of the reading task and strategies, then set goals, make plans, and select strategies, and finally conduct self-evaluation and self-reflection. The researchers found that the group who went through the intervention showed greater self-regulated learning skills than the control group who read the four reading passages without self-regulation intervention. Ko et al. (2015) further utilized social power to enhance self-regulation. They developed a group-based intervention app to improve self-regulation of individual behaviors and limit smartphone use. The app engaged participants in setting goals on smartphone usage and visualized their actual behaviors against the objectives to enhance self-monitoring. It also induced social learning and competition by engaging the participants to share their practices and strategies with others and displaying the statistics of individual behaviors across group members. The researchers found that this group-based app helped control the participants' smartphone use and enhanced the participants' level of disturbance management. Moreover, training materials are also hosted online as open educational resources for flexible manipulation. For instance, Luo (2020) reported a study where she incorporated a MOOC course on general learning techniques (e.g., strategies against procrastination and cramming, spaced repetitions, chunking tasks, etc.) into her Spanish classes. The researcher found that after four 30-minute training sessions using the MOOC course, learners utilized more effective learning techniques in their interaction with the online learning platforms and showed greater course achievement, and the positive effects lasted beyond the training period. Broadbent et al. (2020) further combined online strategy training with a mobile app-based learning diary. Students were prompted to fill out on a mobile app the intended SRL strategies prior to each study session and the actual use of SRL strategies after the session. These students also received online training on goal setting and time management, strategies to deal with distractions and procrastination, frame of reflection and self-motivation. Examining the changes in students' engagement in self-regulated learning, the researchers found that the online training condition surpassed the control condition with no training, whereas mobile learning diary alone did not show significant difference from the control condition. Instead, the combined use of mobile diary entry and online training led to the most improvement in SRL strategy use, manifested in greater utilization of cognitive, metacognitive and resource management strategy. Thus, technology can serve as intervention conveyors to enhance learners' capacity for learner autonomy.

Pedagogical agents or visualization tools have been embedded in technological platforms to enhance learners' capacity for autonomous actions on the platforms. Reviewing the literature on flipped learning, Rasheed et al. (2020) reported various technology-mediated strategies to enhance self-regulation in flipped learning. These strategies include the use of learning analytics with feedback to support students to identify strategies that can increase performance (Silva et al., 2018), the use of instant response system to facilitate social comparison and collective learning to improve students' self-regulation initiatives on the use of the self-study materials (Chen & Hwang, 2019), and the use of Intelligent Tutoring System (ITS) to provide cognitive strategies and support students' help-seeking during task performance (Mohamed & Lamia, 2018). These measures have all found to enhance self-regulation in flipped learning. Karaoğlan Yilmaz et al. (2018) also reported on a study where a pedagogical agent was embedded in a Flipped Classroom to provide metacognitive support. The agent prompted questions to engage students in planning learning before studying the pre-class self-study materials, remind them of cognitive strategies to utilize, and cue them to self-monitor while studying the materials and reflect on the learning experience. The researchers reported that students who received support from the pedagogic agent exhibited significantly higher levels of self-regulation skills than those who did not. MOOCs is another field where researchers have experimented with different ways of technology-mediated interventions to enhance learners' self-regulation during the course so as to reduce attrition rates and enhance learning effectiveness (Littlejohn et al., 2016). Different assistive tools have been built into MOOCs to enhance learner autonomy. Davis, Chen, Jivet, Hauff, and Houben (2017) used the Learning Tracker prototype widget to provide personalized social comparison feedback, where learners' learning behaviors and successful learners' behaviors were visualized and contrasted so that learners could learn from successful peers and strengthen strategy application in learning. The feedback system included three key features: 1) feedback framing that provided an interpretive progress summary of a student's self-regulated learning in the course, 2) an interactive visualizer where the student can explore the comparative data of his/her performance against the average graduates across different metrics of task completion, and 3) plan-ahead prompts where average graduates' task completion behaviors in the upcoming week were provided to enable learners to plan ahead. They found that this assistive tool helped increase students' course completion rate and caused desirable changes in learner engagement in the course. However, they found that the feedback system only improved the performance of learners who were already highly educated. Other assistive tools researchers embed in

MOOC courses to enhance learner autonomy include ProSOLO software that tracks students' learning processes and course competencies to enhance self-monitoring (Dawson Joksimović et al., 2015), prompts of study tips with recommended learning strategies (Kizilcec et al., 2017), and learning analytical tools that provide guidance on personalized learning strategies (Nawrot & Doucet, 2014).

In addition to enhancing learner's competence to control and manage different aspects of learning, technology also boost learners' competence for "(inter)personal empowerment and social transformation," which is considered an essential aspect of learner autonomy (Jiménez Raya et al., 2017, p. 17). Technology affords the potential to empower learners and transform both individuals and societies, especially for disadvantaged learners such as immigrants. Lam (2000) reported the story of a teenage second language learner of English, Almon, who moved to the United States with his family at the age of 12. He was classified as a low-achieving student at school and was assigned to remedial courses. However, building a fan page for his idol singer to complete an assignment of an introductory web design course led him to regular engagement with an international network of fellow fans on instant messengers or email. He exhibited fluent use of English and projected himself as a successful and confident English user in these interactions. Thus, these technology-mediated communication situations facilitated personal empowerment, which may have lasting effects on his autonomy in English language learning and use. Black (2006) documented engagement on Fanfiction sites for a few years of a girl named Nanako who immigrated to Canada at age 11, observing that participation in fanfiction sites "provided her with a supportive social context for foregrounding and backgrounding different aspects of her identity according to her comfort level and the situation" (pp. 180-181). The enhanced opportunities to perform varied identities in virtual spaces were also echoed in Lai and colleagues' (2020) research findings on a group of Hong Kong ethnic minority students' social media engagement. They found that these students took advantage of masked identity on social media to reach out to the mainstream people and culture and use Chinese to perform identities they were deprived of in daily life. The researchers also documented instances where ethnic minorities' technological experiences contributed to social transformation. The potential power of social media for social transformation was reflected in the story of one participant who stood up against people's habitual practices of blindly suspecting ethnic minorities for criminal cases by posting rebuttal comments to challenge their stereotypical views. It was also exemplified in the story of another participant who, upon learning more about the poverty issue in Hong Kong through social media news, was inspired to commit her future self to addressing the poverty issue in Hong Kong. Thus, technology may drive learner agency to achieve both individual and social transformation.

Contribution of technology to the political dimension of learner autonomy

Ligas (2021) pointed out that language education is to enhance learners' linguistic repertoire and communication techniques and tools to help them orient themselves in their community and exercise active citizenship to increase the development of the community. Thus, learner autonomy carries a strong political connotation of freeing oneself from structural constraints. Technology can contribute to the political dimension of learner autonomy by promoting democracy in language learning. It helps liberate students in their learning actions, induce reflective thinking about the purpose and focus of language learning, and facilitate the fight against monolingual hegemony in language teaching and learning.

Navarro and Thornton (2011) argued that self-directed language learning with technology beyond the classroom alleviates some contextual constraints for learning and allows learners more control over choices of learning actions. In such learning situations, learners can enact their language learning beliefs without constraints, and are more likely to exhibit learning actions that align with their learning beliefs. In addition to providing more freedom for the enactment of learning beliefs, technological experience also frees learners of normative beliefs about language learning. For instance, Başaran and Cabaroğlu (2014) found that 14 weeks of in-class pair or group activities around podcast episodes changed a group of Turkish language learners' language learning beliefs. The podcast experience increased students' confidence in English listening and speaking, freed them from a narrow focus on grammar study, and shifted them towards a stronger belief in learning through naturalistic approaches and through interacting with native speakers of English. Moreover, these learners' intrinsic motivation for English learning increased, and their English learning was driven more by the desire to socialize with native speakers of English and learn about their cultures. Lai (2019a) also gave an account of an English language learner, who used to believe in rote memorization as a useful strategy for vocabulary learning and relied on digital flash cards to support vocabulary learning. However, the learner soon found that this technological experience was not very helpful in retaining the vocabulary, which made her shift belief towards a more holistic approach to vocabulary learning. Thus, when she started to learn her third language, German, she incorporated a large amount of authentic digital materials even at the early stage of German learning. Another participant shared that processing online Japanese songs during her Japanese class led to changes in her belief in learning the basics of a language before using it for authentic purposes. She recounted that this technological experience boosted her confidence in the ability to handle authentic materials and made her realize that it was possible and necessary to use the language for authentic purposes, such as listening to songs in the target language for entertainment, even in the early stage of language learning. Similarly, Lyu and Lai (2022a) showed how some participants broadened their views of language learning as a result of their experience on Lang-8, a blog-based language learning-oriented tandem social networking site. They found that receiving comments from native-speaking peers, who showed interest in the contents they blogged and who neither criticized nor laughed at their language errors, made some participants begin to accept their own "imperfect language." They started to shift from a belief of equating errors to embarrassment and as something that needs to be avoided toward the belief that errors were opportunities for learning. Consequently, they no longer treated blogging merely as a venue for writing practice, but rather as a venue of self-expression and opportunities for social communication.

Technology also affords translanguaging spaces, where people can creatively and critically integrate and orchestrate multilingual, multimodal, and multi-sensory repertoires across linguistic, spatial, and temporal boundaries to interact, socialize and co-produce meanings (Li, 2011). Such spaces also allow the multilinguals to "bring together different dimensions of their personal history, experience and environment; their attitude, belief and ideology; their cognitive and physical capacity, into one coordinated and meaningful performance" (Ho & Tai, 2021, p. 3), and empower them to "challenge language and modal hierarchies" and liberate their multilingual identities beyond linguistic or national boundaries (Li, 2011, p. 1223; Oliver & Nguyen, 2017). Ho and Tai (2021) analyzed two online English teaching YouTube videos and associated comments and revealed that YouTube enabled the two teachers to orchestrate different semiotic resources fluidly, including registers, styles, language varieties, gestures, attire, music, background settings, to create an interactive translanguaging space. The commenting function enabled the viewers and the two teachers to position and reposition themselves, negotiate, contest, and reverse the traditional "teacher-student" relationship and challenge conventional power structure. Lai and colleagues (2020) also shared the account of how the multilingual practice on social media spaces enabled marginalized ethnic minority adolescents in Hong Kong to perform the Hong Konger identity that they were often denied of in daily life. Oliver and Nguyen (2017) examined the Facebook posts of seven Australian Aboriginal youth, and found that this virtual space facilitated their unconstrained, creative, and flexible use of aboriginal language and English as well as visual and graphic signs to construct multiple identities and project different social roles and positions, and to include or exclude others from their interactions. Larsen-Freeman (2019) defined learner agency as "optimizing conditions for one's own learning and choosing to deploy one's semiotic resources to position oneself as one would wish in a multilingual world" (pp. 70-71). Sultana and Dovchin (2021) revealed that trans-semiotizing across different lan-

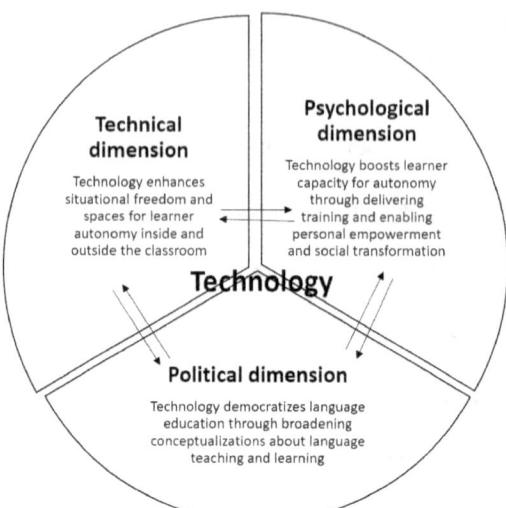

Figure 2 *Facilitating effects of technology on learner autonomy*

guages, emojis and pictures afforded in social media interactions boosted university language learners' agency to learn English as a foreign language beyond the classroom. Chen et al. (2022) examined teacher-student interaction in an online CLIL course with a social media chat group for synchronous learner support. The researchers documented the trans-semiotizing interaction between the teacher and students in the chat group, and how those trans-semiotizing practices increased learners' perceptions of learning opportunities. Teachers' strategic deployment of trans-semiotic resources and learners' perceptions and utilization of the potentials of trans-semiotic resources to negotiate power helped to liberate learner agency in the learning process.

Thus, technology has an important role to play in facilitating learner autonomy. The facilitation can manifest in multiple dimensions. Figure 2 synthesizes the facilitative role of technology in promoting the technical, psychological, and political dimensions of learner autonomy.

Figure 2 suggests that technology can play a multitude of roles in boosting different aspects of learner autonomy, and the promotion of one dimension of learner autonomy may contribute positively to the other dimensions. Thus, a synergic approach is needed to maximize the facilitative role of technology for learner autonomy. Existing literature on technology and learner autonomy in language education has focused predominantly on the technical dimension, as evidenced in the increasing volume of research studies on the link between technology and the exercise of learner autonomy inside and outside the classroom. The links between technology and the psychological and the political dimension of learner autonomy were insufficiently discussed. Across all three dimensions, greater attention to the interaction between in-class and out-of-class learner autonomy is needed. Moreover, how using technology to facilitate one dimension of learner autonomy may shape the other dimensions of learner autonomy also deserves attention.

3
Technology as a Constraint on Learner Autonomy

> *Digital Technology is hardly the benign, neutral presence in education that we are often assured it to be.* – Selwyn (2015, p. 248)

> *How a given technological artifact might manifest is largely dependent on how it is storied into existence.* – Lynch (2015, p. 145)

Sproull and Kiesler (1991) distinguished two types of effects associated with technology: first-level effects and second-level effects. First-level effects refer to "the planned efficiency gains or productivity gains that justify an investment in new technology" (p. 4). Second-level effects refer to the unintended or unanticipated outcomes incurred by the utilization of technology. According to them, the unintended effects might arise because, when technology is deployed in particular settings, "people pay attention to different things, have contact with different people, and depend on one another differently" (p. 4). Scholars point out that research on technology and education has focused narrowly on first-level effects, keeping second-level effects largely ignored and unmapped (Bigum, Bulfin, & Johnson, 2015; Selwyn, 2015). Moreover, Selwyn (2015) argued that existing research is busy with presenting tidy applied research findings on the efficacy of practical applications of technology for teaching and learning and set its eyes on "developing more efficient ways of 'doing technology'" (p. 248). This tradition of research has treated technology as already-made things that have some determinable effects on learning. This deterministic view largely ignores the fact that technology may be deployed in ways that are not educationally desirable. Technology use is a social phenomenon, and social phenomena are interconnected and are always messy. Technology may be employed in a "flawed" way due to the strategic interest of various parties involved in the social phenomena. Thus, a critical perspective needs to be adopted to "make sense of technology and education as a set of profoundly political processes and practices that are framed in terms of issues of power, control, conflict and resistance" (Selwyn, 2015, p. 252). Scholars advocate abandoning the "technoromantic rhetoric or theology of IT in education," and the technologically determinist lens that fixated on "impact," "effect," "progress," and "cause." They argue that the taken-for-granted assumptions of technology-as-savior and technology-as-boosters need to be problematized and challenged to seek "a more balanced and realistic assessment of its strengths and shortcoming" (Beynon & Mackay, 1988, p. 245; Johnson, 2015; Selwyn, 2012). In effect, Burbules and Callister (1999) pointed out that the positive and negative consequences of technology are inseparable: "The very same decisions that give rise to one set of effects give rise to the others" (p. 108). They proposed a post-technocratic view of technology, where the focus is not to weigh risks and promises against each other, but to see both anticipated and unintended consequences as fundamentally inseparable and an inherent part of technology. They hence call for taking both aspects into consideration when conceptualizing the utilization of technology and understanding its impact. Similarly, when discussing the relationship between technology and learner autonomy, Littlemore (2001) argued that "the increasing opportunities offered by new technologies do not necessarily make these technologies automatically favorable to learner autonomy" (p. 42). Thus, scholars like Lynch (2015) and Selwyn (2012) point out that greater attention needs to be given to the complex social milieu of technology and education, i.e., the social, cultural, political, ideological, and economic aspects of technology use that are often ignored in existing literature, and to how technology is relational and subject to never-ending negotiation, re-negotiation and re-contextualization. As Newfeld and Delcore (2018) argued, the relationship between technology and education needs to be examined in the situatedness of technology use. The situatedness may manifest in an array of nested layers: the student level, the material level, the institutional level, the social level, and the ideological level. Thus, following this critical perspective, I examine and elaborate on the forces that constrain the relationship between technology and learner autonomy at each level.

Constraints at the student level

Digital capacity

To utilize the potential of technology for autonomous action, students need to have relevant digital capacity. Despite the argument that this generation of learners grow up with digital technologies and may, by default, possess sophisticated digital skills to use digital tools effectively and efficiently (e.g., Prensky, 2001), evidence is mounting to suggest that the digital native argument is a myth.

On the one hand, students are found to put technology to use for purposes other than learning. Researchers have documented that this generation of learners is immersed in the technological world for entertainment and socialization but engage much less frequently in using technology for learning and creative work (Kennedy & Fox, 2013; Margaryan, Littlejohn, & Vojt, 2011). Kennedy and Fox (2013) pointed out that students are using technology primarily for "personal empowerment and entertainment, but [are] not always digitally literate in using technology to support their learning. This is particularly evident when it comes to student use of technology as consumers of content rather than creators of content specifically for academic purposes" (p. 76). Consequently, intervention studies that focus on increasing technology accessibility have revealed either no significant impact on students' academic achievement or negative impact (Escueta, Quan, Nickow, & Oreopoulos, 2017). For instance, intervention studies in Romania, where households were provided with subsidized computers, and in the Netherlands, where schools were subsidized on computer and software procurement, have both reported a negative impact on students' academic outcomes. Researchers attributed the negative impact partly to the fact that students utilized the newly added accessibility not for learning but for gaming instead (Leuven et al., 2007; Malamud & Pop-Eleches, 2011).

On the other hand, students may lack relevant technological and digital literacy to engage effectively with technology for learning (Kirschner & De Bruyckere, 2017). Generic digital skills include three dimensions: theoretical knowledge, operational skills, and evaluation skills. Gui and Argentin (2011) assessed the digital skills of 980 third-year high school students in Italy. They found that, despite having good operational skills, these students performed poorly on evaluation skills, skills that determine the appropriateness and efficacy of selective use of technology. In addition to generic skills, the (non)presence of knowledge and skills to perceive and act on the affordances of technology also shapes the extent to which students can exercise agency to engage in self-directed language learning with technology. Van Lier (2007) highlighted the mediated nature of agency: "language learning-as-agency involves learning to perceive affordances (relationships of possibility) within multimodal communicative events" (p. 53). Research has frequently reported that students are unaware of the embedded functions and tools within digital platforms that facilitate language skill development, lack the ability to perceive, critically evaluate, and act on the affordances on and across different technological platforms, and lack the socio-emotional skills to engage effectively in online interactions and benefit from the interactions (Stockwell & Hubbard, 2013; Shadiev & Yang, 2020; White & Bown, 2020). To quote a university participant in Lai, Yeung and Hu's (2016) study, "I have been immersed in the Internet world and am very versatile in using the tools. However, I still haven't figured out how to use them for Japanese learning. But I'm very interested." Relevant knowledge and skills determine the degree to which learners perceive the use of technology for autonomous language learning as compatible with one's beliefs and goals for language learning. Knowledge and skills also determine the repertoire of activities learners voluntarily engage in beyond the classroom (Fuchs et al., 2012; Lai, 2013; Toffoli & Perrot, 2017). Fathali and Okada

(2017) found that perceived competence was the strongest determinant of students' engagement in self-directed use of technology beyond the classroom.

Self-regulation skills

Not only are generic digital skills and language-learning-specific knowledge and skills important, students' abilities for self-regulation and self-direction are also essential for their engagement in autonomous language learning with technology. Yen et al. (2016) examined students' learning experience in online courses with an open design (i.e., open learning environments with multiple Web 2.0 tools). They revealed that goal setting, environmental structuring, task strategies, time management, help seeking, and self-evaluation predicted the sense of control and level of self-regulation in students' creation of personal learning environments. All these self-regulation factors, except for environmental structuring, were significant determinants of the level of initiatives these students took in managing personalized learning trajectories in the courses. When learners lack self-regulation, they may encounter cognitive overload and distractions, which constrain their abilities to utilize the freedom and control afforded in technological platforms (Devolder et al., 2012). For instance, Escueta and colleagues (2020) pointed out that, despite delivering quality online learning materials to learners at fingers' tip, MOOCs also suffer from very low completion rates. They further pinpointed that the low completion rates are largely due to procrastination and students' deficiency in effective time management. Studying the impact of self-regulation (metacognitive self-regulation and time management), digital tool literacy and information literacy together, Lim and Newby (2021) found that metacognitive self-regulating capability and digital tool literacy were influential predictors of students' willingness and positive attitudes towards utilizing various web 2.0 tools to construct self-directed personal learning environments. Regarding autonomous use of technology for language learning, researchers found that students' willingness to seek language learning and use opportunities and their resilience against boredom and procrastination influence the extent to which they engage in autonomous language learning with technology (Kormos & Csizér, 2014). Research in different contexts have revealed that although language learners are positive about assuming responsibilities for organizing and controlling learning experience beyond the classroom, their enthusiasm is often hampered by perceived lack of self-management skills in setting learning goals and managing distractions on the internet (Castellano et al., 2011; Lai, 2015).

Digital habits

Students' digital use characteristics and digital habits may also constrain autonomous use of digital tools for language learning. Students' immersive experience with technology shapes certain learner characteristics, including the preference for multimodal materials and constant connectivity, the mixing of work and play and the use of leisure time for effortful pursuits, the expectation of technology being a part of the learning landscape, and the tendency to multitask and process information in nonlinear fashion (Ito, 2013; Prensky, 2001; Rosen, 2010). These characteristics bring benefits, but at the same time pose potential risks to self-regulated learning, such as the observed inability to persevere when facing boredom and to manage digital distraction (Credé & Kuncel, 2008). Thompson (2013) pointed out that students' "get in, get the answer, get out" approach to learning from the Web may constrain them from taking full advantages of the affordances of the web for learning.

Students' habitual engagement with a small set of technologies may also constrain autonomous learning with technology. For instance, surveying 337 first-year Japanese university students, Gobel and Kano (2014) identified that students used a narrow set of technologies to engage primarily in communication-related activities. In Australian context, Kennedy et al.'s (2010) found that only 14% of the university students they surveyed used a wide variety of technologies. Most of the students were restricted in not only the range of technologies but also the technological features (basic mobile phone features) they utilized. Similarly, Thompson (2013) surveyed 388 students from a university in the US and found that many technologies that have educational potential, such as blogs, were used infrequently or not at all by the majority of the participants. Instead, rapid communication technology and web resources were the technological activities most students frequented. They further found that the frequency of engagement in rapid communication technology associated negatively with productive learning behaviors, such as persistence in short-term boredom, the ability to control multitasking and listen attentively to lecture and staying on task when studying with friends.

In addition, learners are found to limit the dimension of technology use for learning. Research on self-directed use of technology for language learning beyond the classroom reveals that students' technological experience primarily centers on receptive activities (Lai, 2018). Lai et al. (2018) examined university learners' out-of-class technological experience for language learning and revealed that students engaged more in using technology for instructional purposes and for entertainment and information seeking purposes, but less for socialization purposes. The limited use of technology for socialization has something to do with the clear line learners draw between technology use for personal life and for learning (Stockwell, 2010). For instance, Liu and Yu (2013) reported that some English learners resisted taking part in Facebook projects, requesting joining the projects via an alternative non-private account.

Living circumstances

The assemblage of social obligations and material resources is found to further constrain learners' autonomous action with technology. Selwyn (2007) pointed out that students juggle in-between multiple expected social roles such as learners, socialites, volunteers, and future employees, and these roles may sometimes conflict with one another. The multitude of roles makes students very often approach their study in a pragmatic and tactical manner. They may prioritize assessment over learning performance and make the strategic decision of not to use technology extensively in the learning process. Moreover, the set of technological tools that students have access to may constrain whether and how they put a particular technological device to use for learning (Neufeld & Delcore, 2018). For instance, Lai and Zheng (2018) reported how a group of university foreign language learners in Hong Kong selectively used mobile phones and laptops for different dimensions of self-directed out-of-class language learning experiences: Students used mobile phones primarily for social communication and instant help on language comprehension and use, used laptops primarily for surfing online and watching videos, and used mobile phones and laptops equally for listening, casual reading and vocabulary and grammar study. They further found that the selective use of different technological devices was related to how these students positioned the tools in their life: Students associated mobile phones more with daily life and leisure, and associated laptops more with serious study and learning.

Thus, autonomous learning with technology might be constrained by students' lack of relevant knowledge and skills, unfavorable digital habits, and pragmatic approach to technology use due to one's socio-material circumstances.

Constraints at the material level

"Abundance" challenges

Technology develops very quickly and is constantly updating. The rapid proliferation of new technologies may outpace educators' ability to evaluate their educational potential. As Escueta and colleague (2020) pointed out, "while most agree that ed-tech can be helpful under some circumstances, researchers and educators are far from a consensus on what types of ed-tech are most worth investing in and in which contexts" (p. 898). The constantly updating technological field may overwhelm students. Reviewing various technological tools that can support language skill development, Blake (2016) commented that "new technological features are not intuitively clear, even to the younger generation of students" (p. 134). He thus cautioned that students may find themselves challenged to take full advantage of the changing array of affordances offered by the constantly updated new technologies.

An associated issue with the proliferation of technological innovations is the massive, very often overwhelming, information, tools, and resources available online. Commenting on information flooding online, Postman remarked: "Information … now… comes indiscriminately, directed at no one in particular, disconnected from usefulness; we are glutted with information, drowning in information, have no control over tie, don't know what to do with it." The information overload creates the situation where "humans are left without agency against a barrage of relentless information" (Tillberg-Webb & Strobel, 2013, p. 329). Facing the wide array of tools and resources, learners encounter difficulty in selecting and orchestrating the immense resources to construct their learning ecology. For instance, university foreign language learners in Lai et al.'s (2016) study expressed difficulty locating appropriate and trustworthy resources (e.g., "I don't know which website is most useful or fits me better. I have great difficulty selecting the appropriate resources"; "When I searched for podcasts in Korean on Google, I simply chose the sites according to chronological order. I usually chose the first one or two. I'm not sure about my ability to select the most appropriate resources") and evaluating the accuracy of the information and language usage they encountered online. The challenges may discourage students from utilizing technological resources for autonomous language learning, which was reflected in one participant's comment: "I may not be able to locate good websites, which may discourage me from using online resources at all." Even in the case where educators provide a set of technological tools to facilitate the construction of personalized learning environments, students may still find themselves at a loss concerning what to choose for what learning purposes. For instance, Fini (2009) reported that students in a MOOC course felt overwhelmed by the tools provided in the course and had difficulty constructing an effective multi-tool personal knowledge environment.

Thus, the constant innovation and the rich choices of tools and resources brought by technology, while presenting new potentials for language teaching and learning, may pose high demands that hinder students from taking full advantage of technological resources for autonomous language learning.

Experience constraints

Notwithstanding the fast development, technological tools and platforms per se have inherent constraints that may suppress learner autonomy. Jones and Hafner (2012) argued that "all tools bring with them different kinds of affordances and constraints. The way McLuhan puts it, while new technologies extend certain parts of us, they amputate other parts" (p. 3). Reinders and Hubbard (2013) presented a list of technological constraints that may lead to non-utilization or misappropriation of technological affordances, hence curbing learner autonomy in language learning. Reinders and Hubbard categorized the constraints into organizational constraints, that is, constraints related to access and delivery of technological features and mediated materials, and pedagogical constraints, in other words, constraints related to the types of experience learners can construct on and with technological platforms. Examples of pedagogical constraints include the narrow range of language repeatedly used on CMC, the limited range of situations of language use online, distractions induced by multimedia materials, and the poor quality of the feedback provided on and via technological platforms.

Features and functions of technological tools may further condition how learners position the tools in autonomous learning and put them into use. Take mobile devices as an example. The small keyboard and display screen of mobile phones may induce a high cognitive burden that discourages students from using it for learning. The limited network speed and memory and the low display resolution may further constrain the types of activities students may engage with mobile phones (Li & Hegelheimer, 2013; Stockwell, 2007). Students also report that it is too hard to concentrate in mobile learning mode, and thus refrain from using mobile phones for study purposes (Stockwell, 2008). Lai and Zheng (2018) found that, despite the acclaimed advantage of mobile devices for facilitating ubiquitous learning, university foreign language learners chose not to use mobile devices to enhance the authenticity of language learning because of the small screen and slow internet speed. They found it tiring to process audiovisual and textual resources (e.g., videos, lengthy texts) on mobile devices, and the small screens also made it hard to concentrate (e.g., "very difficult to concentrate for a long time," "when the screen is larger, I feel more concentrated"). Thus, these learners used mobile devices predominantly for socialization and for tasks that were quick and not taxing.

Another example is social media. Social media has been acclaimed for being community-based, socialization-oriented, and identity-masking with reduced social cues (Reinhardt, 2019). These features lend themselves to language learning because they proffer low-risk and nonthreatening language and social practices, capital-enhancing social connection, and transcultural and plurilingual identity construction and performance (Reinhardt, 2019; Wang & Vásquez, 2012). However, Fuchs (2014) argued that social media are "the outcome of social relations between human beings" (p. 12), and thus have both "positive potentials and negative realities" (p. 15). According to her, learners' social media participation might be interfered with by forces of power in contemporary society. Social media are the spaces where economic (i.e., material and financial resources), political (i.e., rules of governing), coercive (i.e., physical forces) and symbolic (i.e., information and communication) powers in society manifest themselves. The power struggles within social media intricately interweave with those in the physical world to shape its role in society and in students' learning. For instance, studies have found that, while providing resources and spaces to facilitate acculturation, social media may lack "key contextual cultural signifiers" to convey complex cultural meanings, and hence may increase cross-cultural misunderstanding (Veronis et al., 2018). Lai et al.'s (2020) interview study with 31 Hong Kong ethnic minority secondary school students revealed that, despite increased opportunities for interaction with local Chinese on social media, some participants chose to shun away from interacting with local Chinese to minimize potential miscommunications caused by the lack of social cues and the lack of opportunities for negotiation of meaning. The multilingual nature of social media further made some of them avoid using Chinese when interacting on social media, thus limiting the potential of social media interaction for language learning. To add structure and support to interaction on social media, educators have also tried to combine the features of social media with tutorial materials to create social networking language learning sites, such as Livemocha. However, Lin, Warschauer, and Blake (2016) found that, due to the lack of supervision on these sites, most users quit after a few months and ignored the persistent language errors they made during social media interaction.

Moreover, technological features determine its context of use, which may constrain its potential for learner autonomy. For instance, Lai and Zheng (2018) found that the contexts where mobile devices are normally used—on the go, full of distraction, and of short duration—discouraged learners from using mobile devices to do more complicated tasks that demanded greater attentional resources. Instead, they used the mobile phone for casual reading, short posting and quick tasks such as "checking dictionaries," "posting short passages," and "surfing on Twitter and Instagram." The researchers concluded that technological features and the "tempo-spatial circumstances and sociocultural contexts of the use" constrained learners' selective use of the mobile phone for autonomous language learning beyond the classroom. Moreover, technology does not stand alone but rather co-exists with other technological artefacts and non-technological artefacts in one's learning environments (Hamilton, 2013; Lai, 2018). Each artefact carries its material, discursive, and social affordances, and constraints. Thus, the relationship of a given technological platform with learner autonomy is shaped by other artefacts that co-exist. For instance, Lyu and Lai (2022b) traced a group of language learners' use of a social networking language learning site—Lang-8—and found that these learners did not use the social networking features and associated affordances on this site. These learners felt that the lack of public posts made it hard to start conversations, the non-presence of emoji and meme on the site made the conversation dull and not interesting, and the asynchronous nature of interaction on this technological platform made it difficult to sustain in-depth conversations.

Consequently, these learners turned to other communication technologies that were more facilitative of social networking, such as Skype and WeChat, to socialize with peers they met on this site. Thus, the potential of Lang-8 for social interaction was suppressed by the other technological tools that learners had access to.

Design constraints

The quality of the materials and activities mediated by technology may also curb learner autonomy. Kukulska-Hulme (2005) remarked that since mobile applications are not designed specifically for learning, students may not embrace them as useful learning resources. The low quality of the instructional videos is found to be a major challenge to the implementation of flipped learning (Akçayır & Akçayır, 2018; Zainuddin & Halili, 2016). Banyard et al. (2006) pointed out that tasks on technological platforms, if designed poorly, may "create limiting systems that inhibit SRL [self-regulated learning]" (p. 483). Examples of poorly designed tasks that may suppress learner autonomy include repetitive and pointless tasks such as the non-selective and unstructured search of the Internet, tasks that contain too many barriers that challenge learner self-esteem and efficacy beliefs, and tasks that proffer low levels of personalization. Buchem et al. (2014) pinpointed that learner control provided in most computer-delivered instructional environments is quite superficial, primarily in the form of choices over topic, pace, task sequencing, difficulty level and content display. The limited choices may constrain learner autonomy. They argued that control over learning goals and outcomes, over tasks, resources and tools, and over social interaction and collaboration need to be built in to support autonomy in personalized learning.

Unintended consequences

Moreover, unintended consequences are an inherent aspect of technology. As Diamond (2005) put it, "New technologies, whether or not they succeed in solving the problem that they were designed to solve, regularly create unanticipated new problems" (p. 505). Convenience has always been a major reason that drives learners' embracement of online learning. However, notwithstanding its various advantages for learning, convenience may bring online cheating and a less rigorous school experience, and generate self-gratification and laziness in learning (Serdyukov, 2017).

Ubiquity and persistent presence of information via mobile devices and on social media enable accessing information and learning any time and any place, but may at the same time lend to addiction or excessive use and lead to adverse effect on academic performance, such as school burnout and lack of engagement (Salmela-Aro et al., 2017), and poor cognitive functioning, such as a deficiency in attention control and concentration (Hawi & Samaha, 2016; Wilmer et al., 2017). Selwyn (2016) surveyed 1658 university students on the aspects of digital technologies that they found to be "particularly unhelpful" and/or "not useful." The likelihood of causing procrastination and diverting attention from work, especially by social media and smartphones, and "the unbounded nature of the internet" appeared at the top of the list (p. 1011). They further listed that the social nature of the internet caused co-procrastination with peers, and the inconsistent design of online systems and applications incurred difficulties and ongoing hindrances.

In addition, researchers have also noted the persistence nature of the online world, despite making learning ubiquitous, causes the prevalence of digital addiction, i.e., the prolonged and excess use and dependence on digital devices and digital worlds. Digital addiction has detrimental effects on students' capacities to take responsibilities for and engage actively in learning, leading to withdrawal behaviors and low self-control (Wilcox & Stephen, 2013; Yildiz, 2021). For instance, Yildiz (2021) found that digital addiction is significantly and negatively associated with high school students' abilities to acquire knowledge through inquiry and self-confidence in learning through inquiry. Wang et al. (2021) further identified five categories of stress that technology may bring: techno-overload (i.e., increased learning demands in technological platforms drive learners to learn faster and longer); techno-invasion (i.e., technology-mediated learning makes learners connected all the time and hence invading into their personal life); techno-complexity (i.e., technological materials increase the difficulty of students' work); techno-insecurity (i.e., technology induces the sense of insecurity because of the need to learn and relearn skills); and techno-uncertainty (i.e., technology disrupts learning plans and creating ambiguous learning expectations). They found that techno-complexity, techno-insecurity and techno-uncertainty were significant predictors of university learners' technology burnout (i.e., feeling overwhelmed by technology-enhanced learning), which associated negatively with learner agency, persistence and self-regulation in using technology for learning.

Thus, the characteristics of technological tools, the design of technological materials and tasks, the circumstances of technology use, and the unintended consequences of technology may constrain autonomous learning with technology.

Constraints at the institutional level

School culture

School culture is a major factor that shapes technology use both inside and outside the classroom. The (non)presence of expectations and support at school directly influences technology integration in the instructional context. The lack of school culture in support of technology integration may suppress teachers' intention of technology integration, which constrains the utilization of technological affordances for learner autonomy inside the classroom.

Moreover, whether there is a class culture to support students' use of technology for learning determines students' likelihood of engaging in self-directed use of technology for learning. For instance, Lai (2015) identified three types of teacher behaviors that significantly predicted the frequency of language learners' self-initiated and self-directed technological experience for language learning beyond the classroom. She found that teacher affective support, such as encouragement and recognition of the utilization of technological resources beyond the classroom for language learning, predicted students' perceived usefulness of this learning behavior, which associated positively with the frequency of learner engagement in this behavior. The participants in her study reported treating everyday technological resources more seriously and approaching them with greater consciousness for learning because of teacher encouragement. Both teacher capacity support in terms of technological resource recommendation and cognitive and metacognitive tips on interacting with technological resources and teacher behavior support in the form of incorporating technological tools and resources in class instruction and learning assignments were significant predictors of students' perceived availability of facilitation and self-efficacy in the learning behavior. The participants shared that capacity and behavior support from teachers increased their attention to the language while processing technological materials and boosted their confidence in engaging with these materials and activities despite limited language proficiency, which contributed to their engagement in self-directed out-of-class language learning with technology. Hoi and Mu (2021) further identified that teacher orientation (i.e., encouragement, recommendation, and strategy sharing) was a more significant predictor than teacher behavior (i.e., integration of technology in instruction and assignment) of Vietnamese students' intention to adopt MALL resources for language learning.

Conventional practices

In his seminal article "Computer Meets Classroom – Classroom Wins," Cuban (1993) attributed the "snail-like pace" of technological progress at school to the fact that what teachers can do and cannot do is constrained by the dominant views of what proper schooling entails. According to Cuban, the cultural beliefs "such as that teaching is telling, learning is listening, knowledge is subject matter taught by teachers and books, and the teacher-student relationship is crucial to any learning" (p. 192) are deeply rooted at schools and determine what is permissible and supported in the terrain. Moreover, the century old practices of "self-contained classrooms separating teachers from one another, a curriculum divided into segments of knowledge and skills distributed grade by grade to students, and a schedule that brings students and teachers together to work for brief periods of time" (p. 192) are difficult to alter. Consequently, technology may be tailored to "mirror millennia-old cultural beliefs" and "reinforce existing practices" (p. 193), especially in the higher grade levels where disciplinary subjects reign and teacher-centered learning dominates. Lynch (2015) pointed out that the effect of technology is indeterminate and depends on the social context where it is put into use and argued that "this indeterminacy is a double-edged sword" (p. 145). On the one hand, the indeterminacy of technology enhances its adaptability and brings potential for innovative practices in learning and teaching; on the other hand, the (re)contextualization of technology in usage is subject to the risk of "domestication" (Cuban, 1986) or "schooling" (cf. Illich, 1971). Technology usage may be inflicted with "familiar power relations and patterns of success" (p. 145) and "schooled notions of suitable and appropriate behaviors and learnings" (Lynch, 2015, p. 151).

Institutionalized structures and processes emanated from authoritative figures may constrain or discourage learners' transformative practices with technology (Bigum, 2012). Take the filtering and surveillance practices at school as an example. Online information filtering and surveillance are common practices at school to protect student privacy. However, by controlling the types of materials and resources that students can access, schools may constrain the scope of learner autonomy inside the classroom (Banyard et al., 2006). Belz (2002) further identified that simple institutional elements, such as differences in computer access, academic calendars, and accreditation systems, shaped the degree of learner agency in a tele-collaborative pen-pal project. Ideological conflicts with school conventions may also make innovative practices fail. For instance, Lamy (2013) shared how a blogging project that engaged university students to discuss assignment marks failed due to the lack of school cultural in favor of open discussions of assignment marks. Initiatives that incorporate social media as adjunct learning opportunities often encounter resistance from students because the culture of social media interaction counters the ideology of formal instruction. The following comment from Lamy (2013) elaborated on the conflict:

> The culture of SN is characterized by casual frequentation, then teacher-fronted invitations to join in prescribed talk or tasks may be experienced as going counter to SN practices and may thereby induce more restricted forms of interaction such as answering the teacher or halting the interaction altogether. (p. 235)

Moreover, formal conservative curriculum and conventionalized assessment practices at school decree what counts as legitimate, appropriate, and meritorious practices, and may constrain autonomy in learning. Godwin-Jones (2019) reported how the initiatives of providing a repertoire of multimodal materials for students to choose from or inviting students to discover on their own were thwarted by the fact that instruction in formal instruction was centered on the use of a traditional print textbook. Banyard et al. (2006) further pointed out that there is a mismatch between what is assessed in traditional modes of assessment and the skills students develop through technology use. They argued that when those skills are not featured in the assessment, the benefits of self-regulation would get lost. Even worse, students may choose to avoid self-regulation to achieve high grades in the assessments. To put it in their words, "broadband technology provides the opportunity for developing self-regulation skills, but the assessment process does not give the opportunity to use these and in fact may discriminate against them" (p. 485). Researching Chinese university EFL learners' out-of-class English learning experience, Zhan and Andrews (2014) revealed that standard tests such as College English Test (CET-4) shaped these students' predominant attention to vocabulary and grammar rules and the use of a narrowed set of learning materials during out-of-class learning. Moreover, Hafner, Chik, and Jones (2015) pointed out that, despite increasing advocacy for integrating digital literacies into language curriculum, language and literacy standards in conventional assessment remain a roadblock. To put it in their words, "until such high-stakes examinations are altered, many teachers are likely to continue to perceive digital literacies as more of an add-on than an integral part of the curriculum" (p. 5).

Literacy practices

The mismatch between valued language practices at school and students' everyday literacy practices may further constrain learner autonomy with technology. Luke (2004) put forth the "home-school mismatch hypothesis" to capture the contrast between the monotonous school literacy practices and children's creative practices outside school. Koutsogiannis (2015) further pointed out that literacy practices inside the school are characterized by hierarchical learner-authority structure and the use of static texts. In contrast, literacy practices outside the school are often multimodal, involve remixing and mashing, and reflect fluid novice-expert relations.

Despite the wide range of literacy practices that children participate in, not all literacies are granted equal status by institutions, which constrains learners' autonomy over their literacy practices at school. Hafner et al. (2015) identified yet another aspect of disconnection between language learners' in-class experiences and out-of-class experiences:

> School-based language use tends to focus on standardized forms (e.g., standard English) and use so-called "native-speaker" norms as its taken-for-granted benchmarks. In contrast, language use in online spaces is more fluid, often drawing on a form of global English, which may be mixed with other codes. (p. 3)

They argued that translingual practices valued in online spaces support a sense of expressivity unimaginable inside the classroom, since it "allows [learners] to creatively express themselves by drawing on resources from a range of languages" (p. 3). However, when such translingual practices are denied a legitimate status in in-class language use, learner autonomy is largely constrained.

Thus, school culture regarding technology use, and the school's ideology, conventional teaching practices, and legitimate literacy practices may curb learner autonomy with technology.

Constraints at the social/structural level

"Social world is constituted of historically established structures that at any given point in time confront actors as external and constraining" (Klein & Kleinman, 2002, p. 35). Structures imply formal and informal, explicit, and implicit resource distributions, capacities, and incapacities. One's structural location determines the extent to which he/she may benefit from a certain experience, and "social setting shapes technologies as much as vice versa" (Williams & Edge, 1996, p. 875). Warschauer and colleagues (2004) underscored "the social embeddedness of technology," and highlighted that "technology does not exist outside of a social structure, exerting an independent force on it, but rather that the technological and social realms are highly intertwined and continuously cocreate each other in myriad ways" (p. 585). Thus, technology use and its impact are subject to the influence of social structure. At the core of the social structure is resource accessibility. There are different types of resources, including economic resources, political resources, and cultural resources.

Economic resources

The influence of economic resources on learner autonomy with technology has been widely examined and confirmed. Escueta et al. (2017) pinpointed that educational transformation of technology is constrained by the deep and persistent inequality in society. Citing that 98% of children from families with annual household income exceeding $100,000 have access to computer at home, as compared to only 67% among children from families with income lower than $25,000, Escueta and colleagues argued that there is inequality in digital access. Similar digital divide in reliable power source and internet connectivity in different regions of the world has also been reported (ITU, 2015; World Bank, 2013). Escueta et al. (2017) further pointed out that this inequality also exists in children's access to guidance and support for productive technology use. From this perspective, educational technology that demands guidance and support may amplify and aggravate existing economic inequalities. They cited MOOCs as an example: Although MOOCs provide disadvantaged individuals with opportunities to access free and high-quality educational materials and thus may potentially "democratize education," this potential remains largely unrealized as it is found that enrollment and success rates in those courses are highly skewed towards the advantaged populations. They attributed the low enrollment and success rates among the disadvantaged to the lack of relevant skills, guidance, and support. This phenomenon was also reported in Hansen and Reich's (2015) study, where students with greater socioeconomic resources were found to be more likely to earn a certificate from MOOC courses. They lamented that MOOCs may "exacerbate rather than reduce disparities in educational outcomes related to socioeconomic status" (p. 1245). Similarly, Kizilcec et al. (2017) observed that social inequality has come to be reflected in the online world. In their study, learners from less-developed countries reported greater concern about being perceived negatively on MOOCs because of their nationalities, and "suffer[ed] from cognitive burden of wrestling with feeling unwelcome while trying to learn and therefore, underperform" (p. 251).

Social inequality in technology use goes beyond the issue of accessibility to technological resources and support, but is also reflected in the different nature of technology practices that learners of different socioeconomic status engage in. Neufeld and Delcore (2018) gave a vivid account of how, when given the opportunity of acquiring digital devices, students from higher socioeconomic conditions made the purchase decision more to enrich their own ICT assemblage, whereas students from lower socioeconomic backgrounds made the purchase decision more to enrich their family's ICT assemblage at the sacrifice of individual needs. Koutsogiannis (2007) also reported that children from privileged social groups used word processing at home to prepare school assignments more frequently than children from less privileged social groups. Koutsogiannis (2015) further pointed out that different home literacy practices of children from different socioeconomic backgrounds lead to different opportunities and abilities to realize various types of "rescaling" (i.e., to shift comfortably from vernacular digital literacy practices to school-rewarded literacy practices). Moreover, Kormos, and Kiddle (2013) found that there were significant differences in the independent use of technology in language learning and independent selection and use of resources for language learning among Chilean secondary school English language learners of different socioeconomic backgrounds. Students from high class and upper-middle class engaged significantly more frequently in seeking resources and using technology for language learning on their own. Ghorbani and Golparvar (2020) further revealed that socioeconomic status was a significant determinant of a group of university English language learners' self-initiated adoption of technological resources for language learning. The researchers attributed the close association between the two to the possibility that learners from higher socioeconomic status may have higher language learning motivation, self-regulation skills, and computer self-efficacy (Butler, 2014; Kormos & Kiddle, 2013).

Van Dijk (2012) thus concluded four areas of digital divide because of socioeconomic factors: 1) motivation to use digital technologies; 2) physical access and permission to use digital tools and contents; 3) digital skills including technical, informational, and strategic skills; and 4) different usage in terms of variety and frequency.

Political resources

Political resources carried by the language may influence learner autonomy. It is widely acknowledged that English carries great linguistic power. This power comes from its scale of spread around the world, its functionality of providing access to important scientific and technological information, its role of mediating cross-cultural domains of knowledge and interaction, and its material values as a tool for mobility, economic gains, and social status (Kachru, 1988). English is the most popular language online as of 2020, and is the language used by 60.4% of the top 10 million websites (Bhutada, 2021). The political power of English may incentivize learner autonomy with digital resources in English while suppress learner autonomy in other languages. For instance, Brevik (2019) reported on a group of Norwegian teenagers who exhibited high performance in English reading but poor Norwegian reading performance. The researcher found that these kids' higher reading proficiency in English (their L2) could be attributed to the significantly greater amount of time they spent surfing, gaming, and socialization online in English than in their native language, Norwegian. According to these teenagers, the preference for English materials was due to greater availability and diversity of English online materials that aligned with their daily life interests. Similarly, Peters and colleagues (2019) compared Belgian secondary school students and university students' vocabulary size in French (one of their official languages that was introduced at an earlier age in school) and in English (their L2 that was introduced later in secondary school education). They found that all the student groups showed greater vocabulary size in English than in French, despite much less in-class instruction time. They found students had greater exposure to English in daily life, from a young age onward, because of the omnipresence of English in Flemish society through music, TV and online. The larger amount of self-directed access to English in the informal learning contexts contributed to the observed greater vocabulary size.

Political resources are also at play in technological spaces and how they operate. Take social media as an example. Content developers on social media often push personalized content to individuals based on a wide range of demographic and personal categories and individuals' browsing and purchasing history. Delivering personalized information and content has the potential of making learning adaptive. However, selecting information and content for the learners and forcing it upon them is a political act in itself, since it makes learners vulnerable to external control and, to a large extent, constrains learner autonomy. Another salient example is how media are used by those in power to regulate others' thinking and behavior, which Tillberg-Webb and Strobel (2013) referred to as "medium determinism."

Moreover, political resources also intertwine with economic resources to amplify learner autonomy with technology for some and constrain that for others. Students' digital identity and practices are often shaped by their experiences at school and at home, which subsequently determine the nature of interaction with technology and how they navigate technological ecosystems in daily life (Neufeld & Delcore, 2018). Power is in the hands of institutions and teachers, whose technological practices may constrain students' agency. Teachers who teach at schools with a high proportion of students from low-income families are found to adopt more didactic rather than constructivist pedagogical approaches, leaving limited room for learner autonomy (Campbell et al., 2003). For instance, Becker (2000) found that low-SES students used computers more in math and English courses where the applications were primarily computer-based drills; whereas high-SES students used computers more in science course for simulation and research. Hester (2002) also reported similar findings: students at high SES schools reported engaging in more critical thinking activities with computer than their counterparts at low SES schools. Goode (2010) concluded from the existing literature that there is strong evidence that low-income students receive less access to high quality technology-related curricula. Thus, school technological practices may be shaped by and in return exacerbate existing inequalities in school and society (Warschauer et al., 2004). Warschauer and colleagues (2004) found that the difference showed up in not only in-class learning experience but also students' out-of-class learning experience. Similar to other researchers, they found that, despite having equivalent infrastructure of Internet-connected computers per student, high-SES schools engaged more in using computer for research and analysis, but low-SES schools used computers more for visual presentations. Teachers at high-SES schools also spent less class time on helping students familiarize themselves with software programs, but more on supporting students to master important academic materials with the assistance of technology. Moreover, teachers from high-SES schools also assigned more homework that involved computer use since home computers were more readily available among their students. The researchers further identified that the observed differences across the two types of schools was due to the fact that low-SES schools had limited investment in professional development and technical support, lacked support networks that would make technology workable and effective, and had the stronger challenges and pressure from high-stakes testing. Thus, technological experience students experience at school may constrain the diversity and sophistication of some students' technological practices both inside and outside the classroom.

Cultural resources

Technology embodies cultural values, and digital resources are embedded with cultural biases (Munro, 2018). Learners who are not from the predominant culture may not benefit from, or even be disadvantaged by multimodal resources. For instance, Thompson and Ku (2005) examined the experience of a few Chinese international students in an online course. These students reported not enjoying nor benefiting from the open discourse and the delayed feedback on discussion forums in online classes. Their culturally ingrained practices of seeking the correct answers and giving conservative critiques made them perceive some of their American peers' imaginative or provocative posts as irrelevant and hence unable to benefit from the interaction online. They were further troubled by the prescribed role of instructors as facilitators rather than authoritative opinion providers, feeling disappointed at having less direct instruction and lecturing from the instructors. Similarly, Chen et al. (2019) investigated the home mobile practices of six immigrant families from different cultural backgrounds, including China, Mexico, Japan and Cambodia. They found different mobile practices across cultural backgrounds. Whereas Mexican parents mainly used their mobile phones for communication and modeled operational-level digital skills, Chinese, Japanese, and Cambodian parents displayed more advanced content-related digital use and modeled information, content-creation and strategic skills. Chinese and Cambodia parents engaged in shared activities with their children after school; while Mexican parents did not engage their children in technology-related activities after school. The researchers concluded that children from different cultural backgrounds acquired different technology-based funds of knowledge at home due to the social stratification in their parents' mobile practices. Thus, the cultural milieu and associated technological funds of knowledge learners are acculturated into at home may shape whether their learner autonomy with technology gets amplified or constrained. Technology also brings rich multimodal resources that may potentially facilitate the exercise of learner autonomy. However, mode is "a socially shaped and culturally given semiotic resource," and the same semiotic resource may carry different connotations in different cultures (Kress, 2010, p. 79). Thus, it is important to "consider the social shaping and consequent cultural distinctiveness of semiotic resources" (Kress, 2010, p. 68). Given that "multimodal texts are culturally grounded" (p. 83), Fuchs et al. (2012) argued that lacking relevant multimodal competence may constrain online learner autonomy.

Cultural values shape human identity, purpose, and ways of thinking and behaviors (Markus & Kitayama, 1991). Hence, cultural values intertwine with individuals' preference for and use of information technology (Leidner & Kayworth, 2006). Lai et al. (2016) examined the relationship of a group of university students' espoused cultural values with their engagement in self-directed use of technology for language learning beyond the classroom. They found that learners' long-term orientation, collectivistic orientation and power distance were significant determinants of their technology use for language learning. Language learners who focused on long-term learning benefits, who held collectivistic orientation of thinking and behaving and who believed in high power distance were more likely to engage in self-directed use of technology for language learning beyond the classroom. Moreover, uncertainty avoidance positively moderated the impact of social influence on learner' intention for technology use. For learners who were more likely to avoid uncertain and ambiguous situations, the more they perceived social pressure in their surroundings for technology use, the more likely they were to engage in self-directed technology use for language learning. Thus, cultural values that learners espouse may shape the degree to which they engage in self-directed use of technology for language learning beyond the classroom.

Hence, differences in economic, political, and cultural resources determine the scale and nature of learners' autonomous action with technology.

Constraints at the ideological level

Ideology in technology design

Sewlyn (2007) pointed out that decision making around the use of technology is not a technical one but an ideological one. The ideological influence resides in the design, deployment, and use of technology.

In his paper, "It's not about the tool, it's about the ideology," Armory (2007) argued that learning technology standards, such as the concept of Reusable Learning Objects (RLOs) and the Sharable Content Object Reference Model (SCORM), are "driven by fundamentalist totalitarian instruction ideologies" (p. 661) that treat knowledge as something that can be dissembled into discrete objects and (re)assembled like LEGO blocks to build structures. These reusable learning objects (RLOs) are designed in alignment with SCORM and get implemented in Open-Source Learning Management Systems (LMS) with prescribed instructional sequences. This design approach helps to construct large-scale cost-effective learning environments, but at the same time dictates learning requirements and outcomes. Students are to learn from the standard content via technological artifacts. Similarly, LMS, with its emphasis on content and user management components, very often reciprocates teachers' conservative ideologies. This ideology emphasizes that absolute truth is passed on from expert to students and shapes the "panopticon" use of technology to replicate the past. Technological resources designed under such ideologies "perpetuate conservative hegemonic practices that are maintained through surveillance and automation" (p. 663). Thus, ROLs, SCORM and LMS work together to reinforce the *learning from technology* ideology and the associated constraining power relationship that restrains learner autonomy with technology. Armory pinpointed that those ideologies "appear to be the overarching constraining element limiting educational transformation" of technology and curbing "liberalism in learning" (p. 666). Similarly, Friesen (2012) pointed out that learning management systems like WebCT or Moodle are often developed as a result of individual or community projects of faculty and instructional designers. Consequently, these systems often conform to the interests and structures of educational institutions and reinforce existing functions and identities at such institutions.

Moreover, the development of digital technologies often involves commercial IT firms, who may "prioritize the most 'profitable' subject areas and forms of knowledge," which may actually constrain learner autonomy with technology (Munro, 2018, p. 9). As Selwyn (2011) put it, digital technologies may support "a greater volume of learning opportunities … these are often homogenous and interchangeable," since the provision is often constrained by "poplar and profitable areas of study" (pp. 100–101). Take social media as an example. Social media and online search engines often adjust their content delivery and online addressing based on the demographic and personal categories of the user. Such practices may reproduce existing social inequality and reinforce subsequent inequality in learner autonomy with technology. As Friesen (2008) put it, "the personalization and localization provided by sites and services like Google and Amazon can be understood as powerful ideological and broadly identity-forming tools" (p. 11).

Ideology in technology use

Ideological influence also exists in the context where technology use is situated in. Amory (2012) pointed out that "epistemic beliefs embedded with many education practices foster the neo-liberal dream of power, commercialization and profit making" (p. 42). According to him, neoliberalism is a product of history, which emphasizes disenfranchising race groups, perpetuating gender exclusivity and supporting fundamentalist beliefs. A neo-liberal reconceptualization of education features market principles and efficiency. Students are viewed as the clients to be served with "quality" choices that are ensured through monitoring, control, and quality assurance (Ball, 1998). Under this vision, traditional hierarchies of class and race are maintained, and "learning can be subjected to surveillance to support conveyer-belt driven instructional ideologies" (Amory, 2012, p. 51). Under the drive for marketization and efficiency in neoliberalism ideology, technology use in the education sector is often tainted with "market-orientated framing," which constrains technology deployment and use to replicate and promote content-driven pedagogical models and automate administrative tasks, and to facilitate competition among universities and schools, reducing dropouts and ensuring comparability of results (Munro, 2018, p. 15). This managerial and efficiency-driven technology deployment and use is rather constraining to learner autonomy and is limited in achieving liberalism in education.

An associated neoliberal meta-narrative is the discourse around knowledge-based economy and "academic capitalism" and the repositioning of university's social roles: Universities are shifted from their elitist origins to the "entrepreneurial" and "managerial" roles as workplaces that efficiently produce skilled workers who are "information-literate" and "tech savvy" for knowledge economies (Selwyn, 2007). Selwyn (2007) further pointed out that, under this ideology, students are given limited forms of technology use that focus more on the operational level. This form of use "can be seen as mitigating against the more novel, expansive, creative, and unstructured forms of technology use believed by many education technologists as lying at the heart of empowering the individual user and learner" (Selwyn, 2007, p. 86). What accompanies the managerial role of schools is the "technology-based effectiveness" mentality. Under this mentality, technology is merely used to automate and enhance efficiency of existing practices and becomes "a product of the wider 'game' of high education and the strategic interests of those who play it" (p. 90), rather than to transform education into "fluid sites of learner-centered discovery" (p. 88).

Neo-liberalism puts emphasis on student needs and interests, depicting learners as autonomous, individualistic, self-regulated and rational subject, and conceptualizes technology and digital learning in ways that would support personal responsibility, self-management, and autonomy (Munro, 2018). Nonetheless, Moltó Egea (2014) criticized that under this ideology, learners are still viewed as "the normative 'subject of education'" (p. 281) to be trained to perform effectively and proactively towards one's own personal destiny that is independent of the social and relational influences, and technology is to reinforce the "educability" of the subjects. Moltó Egea argued that technology-mediated personalized learning systems fosters a false sense of learner autonomy, a restraining one that is reduced to the technical dimension. Instead, Moltó Egea argued for the importance "to consider instead which other desirable qualities of human beings we could discover from this fragmented, technologically rich world" (p. 281), and emphasized guiding learners to explore new possibilities technologies provide to make sense of themselves and the world.

Thus, ideological forces behind the design and the use of technological resources position learners and teachers in particular ways in the teaching and learning experience, which may constrain learner autonomy with technology.

A synthetic framework of the constraints

Examining the relationship between technology and learner autonomy from a critical perspective reveals tensions between the two at various

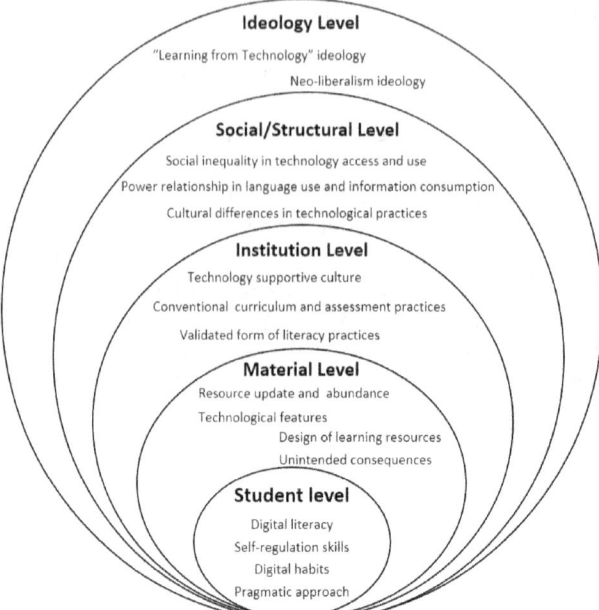

Figure 3 *Constraining effects of technology on learner autonomy*

levels. Figure 3 summarizes the different levels of constraining forces and their relationship in a concentric manner. These forces are not independent, but rather may interact with one another.

Forces in the inner layers are embedded in the outer layers, and factors in the outer layers may aggravate the potential constraining influence of factors in the inner layers. For instance, material-level factors (e.g., constant technology update and the concomitant overwhelming abundance of resources) amplify the influence of student-level factors (e.g., digital literacy) in shaping learner autonomous action with technology, since the constraining factors at the material level make student-level factors even more crucial in determining the possibility for autonomous action. Similarly, constraining forces at the ideology level (e.g., neo-liberalism ideology) may exacerbate the negative influences of forces at the social/structural level (e.g., gaps in technology use in high- and low-SES schools), as these ideological forces exert greater demands on school teachers' capacities to break the constraints and innovate. In return, the resolution of factors in the inner layers may help ameliorate the constraining influences of factors in the outer layers. For instance, validating out-of-school literacy practices at school (an institutional-level factor) may mitigate the negative impact of school-level divide in technology practices (a social/structural-level factor) on learner autonomy with technology, since it brings in additional funds of knowledge that empower learners and teachers to overcome the hurdles of resource accessibility at school. Similarly, designing technological resources, even drill and practice items, in a constructivist manner (a material-level factor) may help minimize the constraining influence of conventional teaching practices (an institutional-level factor) on learner autonomy with technology, since it provides transformative learning experience that may counter conventional teaching practices and induce changes in thinking and belief about teaching and learning.

The framework of constraining forces on learner autonomy with technology reminds us that the much-acclaimed liberating role of technology for learner autonomy should not be taken for granted, and needs to be treated with caution. Any initiatives to foster a positive interaction between technology and learner autonomy need to keep these tensions in mind. Moreover, the concentric relationship among forces at different layers reminds us that fixating on factors at one particular layer only is insufficient. Instead, a holistic view of the potential constraining forces needs to be adopted when developing interventions on and researching learner autonomy with technology.

4
Factors that Influence Technology and Learner Autonomy

Although scholars debate on whether learner autonomy is an inborn psychological trait or a capacity to be acquired and developed, it is generally agreed that learner autonomy is malleable, either to be "developed" in Holec's term (1981) or 'amplified' and 'focused' in Little and Thorne's term (2017). The proposition that learner autonomy is subject to the influence of internal and external factors is elaborated in Everhard-Theophilidou's (2012) definition of autonomy:

> Autonomy is a way of being and a sense of self which is achieved through acquiring the ability to cooperatively make decisions about one's own learning and that of others and which is exercised by being allowed to make and execute those decisions through access to both internal and external resources. The degree of autonomy achieved and exercised varies according to the disposition and predisposition of the learners in terms of affect, motivation, commitment, engagement, interaction, cooperativeness, ownership, reflection and uptake, and fluctuates according to circumstances. (cited in Everhard, 2016, p. 558)

Similarly, Nunan (1996) highlighted that the degree of autonomy is dependent on both individual factors (e.g., personality, learning goals and prior educational experience) and contextual factors (e.g., the ideology and philosophy of a culture or community). Synthesizing existing theorization on self-direction, Song and Hill (2007) pointed out that self-directed learning has been theorized as a personal attribute, a process, and the design characteristics of the learning environment. From the personal attribute perspective, the degree of self-direction is subject to the influence of individual characteristics. From the process perspective, the degree of self-direction depends on the nature and structure of specific learning situations. And from the environment perspective, the degree of self-direction is susceptible to the (non)presence of the culture and support mechanisms for learner control. Thus, in this chapter, I will discuss the influencing factors on technology and learner autonomy primarily from the three aspects: learner internal factors, learning situation and environment factors.

Learner internal factors

Fishbein and Ajzen (1975) proposed a behavioral model that conceptualizes the factors that shape volitional behavior. According to them, beliefs (i.e., thinking, the cognitive domain) and attitudes (i.e., feeling, the affective domain) interact with each other to give rise to conation or desire. Self-efficacy is integral to the model since "self-efficacy beliefs determine how people feel, think, motivate themselves and behave" (Bandura, 1994, p. 1). Mercer (2011) further added actual skills and abilities into the equation. Mercer argued that self-directed language learning behaviors are contingent upon "a learner's sense of agency involving their belief systems, and the control parameters of motivation, affect, metacognitive/self-regulatory skills, as well as actual abilities and the affordances, actual and perceived in specific settings" (p. 9).

Beliefs

Belief factors that mediate the relationship of technology and learner autonomy include both language learning-related beliefs, such as beliefs about knowledge, the learning approaches, process and strategies, and technology-related beliefs, such as perceived affordance of technology and perceived usefulness of the technological behavior.

Language learning-related beliefs

Learners' epistemological beliefs about the nature of the language and language learning process and their beliefs about approaches to language learning are two major facets of language learning-related beliefs that mediate the relationship between technology and learner autonomy.

Epistemological beliefs, i.e., beliefs about the nature of knowledge, are found to associate closely with self-directedness in learning. Research studies have shown that students with more sophisticated epistemological beliefs, such as belief in learning efforts rather than innate ability, belief in the complexity and uncertainty of knowledge and the defiance of authority/expert knowledge, are more likely to engage in self-directed learning (Choi & Park, 2013; Paulsen & Feldman, 2005). Not only beliefs about the nature of knowledge but also beliefs about the learning process are determinant factors of autonomous learning behaviors. How learners perceive the purpose of language learning may shape their perception and engagement in autonomous language learning with technology. Zheng et al. (2016) found that learners who took language learning as a means of constructing integrated linguistic and cultural understanding and of gaining new perspectives in life were more positive towards self-regulating English language learning online than those who believed in learning English for good grades. The former were more likely to engage actively in self-regulating online English learning, whereas the latter were less likely to set goals, plan and adjust task strategies and engage in time management and self-evaluation while learning online. The researchers attributed students' test-oriented conception of learning to the test-centered culture in English language education in China. Moreover, Cheng and Lee (2018) found that learners who reported studying language for the purpose of improving academic results and acquiring knowledge were less motivated to engage in self-directed language learning with technology. In contrast, learners who set the purpose of language learning as preparing for future life needs and socializing with native speakers showed greater motivation for volitional technology use for language learning. Moreover, students' conceptions of learning also associate closely with their volitional behaviors with technology. Yokoyama and Miwa (2018) revealed that conception of learning as personal development positively predicted active learning behaviors, whereas conception of learning as duty and memorization negatively predicted active learning behaviors.

Researchers have further identified that beliefs of language learning approaches and strategies also shape how learners select and appropriate technological resources for language learning. Surveying and interviewing a group of university English language learners, Lai and Gu (2011) found that learners who believed in learning English through actively seeking language use opportunities in daily life were more likely to engage in self-regulated use of technology to support language learning, using technology to expand learning resources and commit to English learning goals in particular. In contrast, belief in learning English through drilling and practicing on the linguistic system had no association with learners' use of technology to self-regulate learning. Lai (2019a) examined the relationship between learning beliefs and learner autonomy with technology in greater depth. She identified five dimensions of language learning belief: sequential vs. holistic approach (i.e., whether language learning and language use take place sequentially or simultaneously); levels of ambiguity avoidance (i.e., level of risk taking in language use); primacy of accuracy (i.e., the importance of accuracy in language use); long-term vs. short-term orientations (i.e., the degree of orienting towards immediate visible outcomes); and individual vs. collective learning orientations (i.e., the degree of preference for social learning). Interviewing twenty foreign language learners at a university in Hong Kong, Lai found that the level of ambiguity avoidance and the direction of goal orientations shaped these learners' selective engagement with technological resources. Learners with a low level of tolerance of ambiguity tended to engage with a narrow set of instruction-oriented resources such as language drill apps, grammar websites and listening training materials. Learners who believed in short-term learning goals tended to select only technological resources that aligned with the contents covered in class. Moreover, learners' belief in the primacy of accuracy and sequential approach to language learning influenced the cognitive strategies they used when interacting with technological resources. Learners who believed in the importance of accuracy and in sequential approach to language learning exhibited more serious learning attitudes, paying greater attention to language forms and taking notes while processing technological resources.

Technology-related beliefs

Technology-related beliefs entail learners' attitudinal beliefs about the use of technology for autonomous language learning and beliefs about the affordances of particular technologies.

Attitudinal beliefs about technology refer to both perceptions of the value of technology use for learning and affective feelings towards it. Attitudinal beliefs are one of the key components in the theory of planned behavior (Ajzen, 1985). According to this theory, human behavioral intentions are predicted by three key components: the attitudinal component, the perceived behavioral control component, and the social influence component. Perceived usefulness and attitudes to technology use are key constructs in the attitudinal component. These two constructs have been found to be robust predictors of individuals' intentions of technology use for learning (Lai et al., 2012; Šumak et al., 2010). Surveying undergraduate EFL learners in Hong Kong, Lai (2013) found that perceived usefulness was a dominant predictor of self-initiated, self-directed use of technology for language learning beyond the classroom. Perceived usefulness mediated the influence of language belief factors, social influence factors, and motivational factors on learner autonomy with technology. Lai et al. (2022) also documented that Chinese EFL learners' overall attitudes towards the use of mobile technologies for language learning significantly predicted their intention for mobile learning. Lee et al. (2015) focused specifically on one attitudinal factor, perceived enjoyment. They examined 544 first-year undergraduate students' autonomous use of internet-based learning media on a course portal, including lecture notes, video recordings of past sessions, and chat room. They found that perceived usefulness and perceive enjoyment were the two significant predictors of students' continued intention for regular use of the internet-based portal. Similarly, Karimi (2016) found that learners' belief in the usefulness of mobile learning for language learning was a significant predictor of UK undergraduate students' volitional adoption of m-learning in formal learning contexts, but not in informal learning contexts. The researcher further introduced another attitudinal factor – perceived playfulness, defined as curiosity and enjoyment about the learning task and the degree of focused attention during the task. The researcher found that perceived playfulness of m-learning was a significant predictor of voluntary m-learning in both contexts. The above studies suggest that attitudinal beliefs shape the extent to which learners utilize technology for learning.

In contrast, learners' perception of the affordances and constraints of technology is often found to influence how learners interact with technology. There have been various accounts of how learners may use the same technological resource in different manners, depending on how they position the technology. For instance, Lai and Zheng (2018) examined a group of undergraduate EFL learners' self-directed use of mobile devices for language learning. Learners reported frequent use of mobile devices to personalize their learning experience, but limited use of mobile devices to enhance the authenticity of learning and for socialization purposes. The greater use of mobile devices for personalization purposes was shaped by these learners' perceived affordances of mobile devices for language learning, namely extending learning across time and space and providing instant help. The limited use of mobile devices for socialization in English was because they felt that mobile-mediated virtual communication in a second language was detrimental to their daily life social networking. Learners further perceived some limitations of the technical features of mobile phones, including small screens and slow connections, regarded the characteristics of the circumstances of mobile phone use as being casual, noisy and of short duration. Due to the perceived affordances and constraints of mobile phone, these learners selectively used mobile phone and laptop for different learning purposes: they associated mobile phones with casual learning and simpler tasks, but associated laptop with serious learning and more challenging tasks. Similarly, examining a group of adult learners' interaction on the blog-based instructional social networking site, Lang 8, Lyu and Lai (2022a) revealed that these learners perceived this platform differently: some perceived it just as a language learning platform, while others perceived it as both a language learning platform and a social networking platform. Consequently, these two groups of learners engaged with peer feedback on this platform differently. Those who positioned the platform merely as a language learning platform tended to attend to and respond to only instruction-related feedback and used the platform as a venue to seek help on linguistic forms. In contrast, those who positioned the platform for both language learning and social networking purposes engaged with both error correction feedback and socialization-oriented feedback.

Motivational factors

Motivation, as one of "the most important factors affecting the speed, intensity, direction and persistence of human behavior" (Fırat et al., 2018, p. 63), is an important individual factor that influences learner autonomy with technology. Examining a set of factors that influence the frequency of language learners' self-directed language learning with technology beyond the classroom, Lai (2013) found that language learning motivation was a major individual construct that drove self-directed technology use for language learning, and its effect was both a direct one and indirect one via perceived usefulness and self-regulation skills. Existing research has examined the influence of motivational factors drawn from different motivational frameworks.

Motivational factors in self-determination theory

Self-determination theory (SDT) is an oft-adopted motivational framework to examine self-direction in learning. SDT underscores that human beings have a natural tendency to internalize external regulations into self-regulations to achieve personal psychological growth and well-being (Ryan & Deci, 2000; Deci & Ryan, 2002). This macro-theory consists of two sub-theories: cognitive evaluation theory that conceptualizes the driving forces of intrinsic motivation, and organismic integration theory that stipulates different forms of extrinsic motivation and the facilitative or hindering conditions for extrinsic motivation. According to cognitive evaluation theory, three psychological conditions are drivers of intrinsic motivation: the need for autonomy (i.e., the desire to engage in activities of one's choosing), the need for competency (i.e., the desire for effective interaction to achieve the desired outcomes), and the need for relatedness (i.e., the desire to feel connected with others). This theory further hypothesized that extrinsic motivation may have negative effects on intrinsic motivation. Organismic integration theory specifies different forms of extrinsic motivation, including external regulation (i.e., the locus of causality of the behavior is external to the learner), introjected regulation (i.e., learners display a level of regulation but not fully accepting it as one's own), identified regulation (i.e., learners value the behavior and identify with the behavior as a part of the self) and integrated regulation (i.e., learners fully integrate the behavior as a coherent sense of the self). According to this theory, the first two types of extrinsic motivation are controlling motivations, which have a locus of causality external to learners and undermines intrinsic motivation. The latter two types are autonomous motivations with a sense of behaviors stemming from inside, contributing to intrinsic motivation. SDT underscores that self-regulatory process is influenced by self-determination, and learners who endorse a strong self-determined motivation are more likely to self-regulate their learning (Vansteenkiste et al., 2004; Zimmerman & Schunk, 2011).

The three drivers of intrinsic motivation have been consistently found to be significant predictors of learner technology use. For instance, Nikou and Economides (2017) adopted the self-determination framework of motivation to examine the motivational factors that influenced 140 high school students' intention to use mobile-based assessment. Perceived autonomy and relatedness significantly predicted perceived usefulness of mobile-assisted assessment, whereas perceived autonomy, competence, and relatedness predicted perceived ease of use. Both perceived usefulness and perceived ease of use were significant determinants of students' intention to use the mobile-assisted assessment. Fathali and Okada (2017) examined a group of Japanese English learners' self-directed reading practices with technological resources outside their general English classes, and found that perceived autonomy, perceived competence, and perceived relatedness were significant predictors of their intention to continue self-directed technology-enhanced reading practices beyond the classroom, with competence and autonomy being the more significant determinants. The three factors explained 43% of the variance in technology-enhanced out-of-class learning. In a follow-up study, Fathali and Okada (2018) further combined self-determination components with attitudinal factors on technology use to understand how these factors predicted technology-based out-of-class language learning. They found that these factors explained 58% of the variance in Japanese undergraduate students' intention for autonomous technology-enhanced language learning beyond the classroom. Among the three basic psychological needs factors, perceived competence was the most significant predictor and determined both perceived usefulness and perceived ease of use, which further predicted learners' intention for autonomous learning with technology. In contrast, perceived autonomy and perceived relatedness were related to perceived ease of use only.

Extrinsic motivation factors are reported to exert differential effects on autonomous technology use. Lee et al. (2015) examined the motivational factors that influenced a group of American undergraduate students' use of an online knowledge sharing system, Qboard. They found that autonomy, relatedness, and competence were significant predictors of performance expectancy, an indicator of extrinsic motivation, and autonomy and relatedness significantly predicted perceived enjoyment, an indicator of intrinsic motivation. Performance expectancy and perceived enjoyment contributed positively to their use of Qboard. They further found that providing controlled extrinsic motivation, such as awarding gift certificates and football tickets for using the Qboard, undermined the students' intrinsic motivation for using Qboard, but autonomous extrinsic motivation, such as "Hall of Fame" that acknowledged those who posted the most useful and interesting message, did not have an undermining effect. Zhou (2016) further found that autonomous extrinsic motivation was a significant antecedent of perceived behavioral control, subjective norms, and attitudes of using MOOCs, whereas controlled extrinsic motivation served as the antecedent for subjective norms only.

Motivational factors in expectancy-value framework

In addition to self-determination theory, expectancy-value framework has also been adopted to understand the relevant motivational factors that mediate the relationship between learner autonomy and technology. According to Expectancy-Value theory (Wigfield & Eccles, 2000; Eccles & Wigfield, 2002), learners' expectancies for success and their subjective task values, including attainment value, intrinsic value, utility value and cost, directly influence their behavioral choices and efforts. Attainment value is the perceived importance of doing well in a task. Intrinsic value is learners' personal enjoyment of doing a task. Utility value is the perceived usefulness and value of a task for future goals. Cost is the perceived competition with other goals.

Among these constructs, intrinsic value has been drawing the most attention. For instance, Bonney et al. (2008) found that intrinsic value in language learning was the best predictor of a group of high school foreign language learners' self-regulated extracurricular learning activities. Similarly, Bai and Wang (2020) found that intrinsic value in English learning was a significant determinant of a group of Hong Kong primary school students' self-regulation in English language learning, including effort regulation, goal setting and planning. Focusing on primary school Chinese as foreign language (CFL) learners, Chai et al. (2016) found that intrinsic value in Chinese language learning suppressed the influence of learner self-efficacy in predicting learners' self-directed learning with technology.

Utility value has also been widely researched. Lai (2013) revealed that task value belief with regard to English learning was a major factor that drove self-initiated use of technology use for language learning, when efficacy and social influence factors were controlled for. Li and Zheng (2018) examined the relationship of 299 seventh grade students' task value and self-regulated learning in a one-to-one computing environment. They measured students' intrinsic value, utility value and perceived emotional and resource cost of using a one-on-one environment for learning and examined how these subjective value variables influence students' engagement in self-regulated learning behaviors in this environment. They found that both intrinsic value and utility value were significant predictors of self-regulation. Moreover, the three subjective task value constructs mediated the influence of students' self-efficacy on self-regulation.

Motivational factors in L2 motivational self-system framework

In language education, the L2 motivational self-system framework has often been adopted to operationalize language learning motivation. According to Dörnyei (2009) who devised this framework, motivation is individuals' drive to close the gap between aspired self and actual self in relation to the L2. Thus, learners' future self-image as a L2 speaker is the motivational source for learning. Dörnyei (2009) proposed two types of L2 selves: the ideal L2 self and the ought-to L2 self. The ideal L2 self is one's internalized aspired future self in work and life in relation to the L2, and the ought-to L2 self is the externally sourced self-image that one feels he/she needs to possess to avoid negative consequences. Both types of L2 selves determine individuals' motivated effort in language learning.

Zheng and colleagues (2018) adopted this motivational model to examine the relationship between L2 motivation and university English language learners' online self-regulated English learning. They found that the ideal L2 self had a positive association with these learners' online self-regulation. In contrast, they found the ought-to L2 self had a negative association with self-regulation. Specifically, learners with a strong ought-to L2 self were less likely to be proactive in seeking help and were reluctant to accept others' support. Similarly, Kormos and Csizér (2014) found that language learners' ideal L2 self and intended efforts in English learning predicted their self-regulation capacities, which determined their engagement in independent use of technology for language learning. The relationships were consistent across secondary school learners, university students, and young adult language learners.

Goal orientations

There are two learning goal orientations in language learning literature: integrative orientation (i.e., learning for the goal of belonging to the L2 community) and instrumental orientation (i.e., learning for instrumental values). Educational psychology literature also introduces two general learning goal orientations: mastery goal orientation (i.e., learning for the sake of mastery) and performance goal orientation (i.e., learning for the sake of outperforming others). Research has found that learners' goal orientations directly influence their intention for autonomous action with technology. Tseng et al. (2019) examined how these four learning goal orientations relate to learners' intention to use mobile devices for language learning. They found that although all four learning goal orientations were significant predictors of a group of Taiwan EFL learners' intention for mobile-assisted language learning, integrative orientation and mastery orientation were the most significant determinants, with the former having a stronger effect than the latter. The authors hence argued that learners' decision making in relation to autonomous language learning with mobile devices was more likely a process of identification with the target language community than a process of individual valuation of language learning. However, the influence of instrumental learning goals manifested differently in Kormos and Csizér's (2014) study. In their study, instrumental orientations played a more significant role. They found that instrumental learning orientation goals that underscore the utilitarian values of English learning significantly predicted learners' ideal L2 self and their concomitant intended efforts in English learning for all three groups of English learners. However, the international posture goals that highlight the international status of English directly predicted ideal L2 self for secondary school students only. For university students and adult language learners, this link was mediated by instrumental learning orientation goals.

Learner characteristics factors

Existing literature has identified a set of psychological factors that mediate the relationship between learner autonomy and technology.

Anxiety

Anxiety, an affective variable, has been identified as a factor that mediates the relationship between technology and learner autonomy. Both anxiety in language use and that in technology use are relevant. Anxiety in English learning is found to be a significant predictor of Chinese EFL learners' autonomy in English learning (e.g., Cheng et al., 2018). Savaskan (2017) compared the learner autonomy for English learning across Turkey learners with high foreign language classroom anxiety and those with low anxiety and found a significant difference across the two groups. Specifically, learners with high anxiety were less likely to engage in autonomous learning both inside and outside the classroom.

Researchers have further found that anxiety in technology use also influences learners' technology adoption. The more an individual feels anxious over the use of computer, the more likelihood he/she would perceive the use of computer as complicated and difficult (Raaij & Schepers, 2008). Baki et al's (2018) meta-analysis of factors that determine e-learning adoption revealed that anxiety was a significant negative predictor of learners' perceived ease of use in adopting e-learning systems.

Grit

Grit is a psychological trait variable that has been linked to autonomous language learning with technology. Grit refers to the passion for and persistence in achieving long-term goals. It includes both consistency of interest and perseverance of effort (Duckworth et al., 2007). Thus, grit is often associated with a higher degree of self-control.

Wolters and Hussain (2015) investigated the relationship between grit and self-regulated learning among a group of university students and found that grit—in particular perseverance of effort—is a significant predictor of all indicators of self-regulated learning. Pasha-Zaidi et al. (2019) further found that grit was a significant predictor of perceived task value, self-efficacy, and self-regulation in learning among university students in Turkey, UAE and USA, and it was consistently the most influential factor of self-regulation across the three cultural contexts. Kooken et al. (2021) examined the dynamic interaction between self-regulation, emotion, and grit during students' interaction with intelligent tutoring system. They found that grit in the forethought phase of self-regulation predicted success in the performance phase, and that grit also mediated the influence of emotion, such as frustration or confidence, on learners' mastery level during the performance phase. Thus, grit may intertwine closely with learners' autonomous actions on and with technological environments.

Growth mindset

Another psychological variable that is related to learner initiative and responsibility is growth mindset. Growth mindset is the belief that ability is malleable and can be increased through efforts (Dweck, 2006). People with growth mindset have more autonomous motivations, and exhibit greater grit, persistence, and resilience, which relate to self-regulation in learning.

In their meta-analysis study on the relationship between growth mindset and self-regulation, Burnette et al. (2013) found the growth mindset associated positively with persistence in learning and planning, monitoring and regulation of the learning process. They further found that grit significantly predicted goal setting, operating, and monitoring. Focusing on language learning in specific, Bai and Wang (2020) found that growth mindset in English learning was a strong motivational factor that predicted their Hong Kong primary school participants' monitoring, effort regulation, goal setting and planning in English learning. The predictive power of growth mindset was found to be even stronger than that of self-efficacy for these Asian EFL learners.

Personal innovativeness

Personal innovativeness, defined as learners' willingness to try new things, is another learner characteristics factor that associates with learners' self-directed use of technology for learning. Personal innovativeness is a key determinant of technology adoption in Rogers' (1995) innovation diffusion theory and is associated with an open attitude to change and reduced level of anxiety about technology use (He & Zhu, 2017).

In their meta-analysis of the key determinants of e-learning, Zhao and colleagues (2021) found that personal innovativeness was a robust predictor of individuals' e-learning adoption. More importantly, the link between personal innovativeness and intention for e-learning adoption remained despite cultural variations. He and Zhu (2017) also found that personal innovativeness was the strongest predictor of university learners' digital informal learning after controlling for the learners' digital competence and their attitudes towards digital informal learning. Huang et al. (2012) found that resistance to change negatively predicted a group of Taiwanese university students' perceived English learning through using electronic dictionaries. Huang and colleagues further revealed the working mechanism of personal innovativeness. They found that Taiwanese language learners with higher personal innovativeness were more likely to perceive the use of mobile devices for language learning as useful and playful, which in turn predicted their volitional intention to adopt mobile devices for language learning. Moreover, Karimi (2016) found that the influence of personal innovativeness differed across learning contexts. Specifically, personal innovativeness was a key determinant of UK undergraduate students' adoption of mobile devices for self-directed learning in the informal learning contexts, but not a significant determinant in the formal learning contexts.

Gender

In addition to these psychological and personal trait variables, the influences of other learner characteristics factors like gender have also drawn research attention. Previous studies have reported that male students express more positive attitudes towards technology than female students, leading to the claim of "technological gender gap" (Canada & Brusca, 1993; Li & Kirkup, 2007).

This technological gender gap has been verified in some studies that examined language learners' autonomous learning with technology. For instance, Gokcearslan (2017) found that male students manifested significantly higher levels of perceived usefulness, perceived ease of use, and attitudes towards the use of tablets for language learning and expressed significantly stronger intentions to adopt tablets for language learning. Accordingly, male learners exhibited higher levels of self-directed learning with technology than female learners, although the difference was not statistically significant. Similarly, Kuznetsova and Soomro (2019) found that male students engaged more frequently in Web 2.0 practices beyond the classroom to learn a foreign language than female students.

However, with the permeation of technology in daily life, researchers suspect that the gender difference may dwindle. Cai et al. (2017) conducted a meta-analysis of 50 papers published from 1997 to 2014 on gender differences in technology adoption. They revealed that gender difference in attitudes towards technology remains: Males showed stronger beliefs about the societal usefulness of technology use and held stronger self-efficacy towards technology use. Gender differences in technology-related cognition and beliefs, such as perceived societal usefulness, increased when compared with the meta-analysis findings two decades ago. However, there is a reduction in the scale of gender difference in learners' affective responses to technology use, such as anxiety, and in their computer self-efficacy. Findings on non-significant gender difference in university language learner's self-directed use of technology for language learning have been reported in Hong Kong and Indonesian context (Lee et al., 2016; Subekti, 2021). In contrast, other studies have reported that female learners exhibit a significantly higher level of ICT tool use for self-directed learning than male learners, and researchers attributed the finding to the higher levels of self-directed learning readiness among female students (Asfar & Zainuddin, 2015; Slater et al., 2017).

Despite the inconclusive findings on the (non)existence of gender difference in levels of engagement in autonomous language learning with technology, studies have reported differences in how male and female learners interact with technology for language learning. For instance, Dincer (2020) found that university male learners engaged in more "watching" behaviors in out-of-class English learning, whereas female learners engaged more frequently in behaviors that involve "writing" skills. Similarly, other research has found that boys are frequent gamers, whereas girls report a significantly higher frequency of watching movies or TV series with subtitles, listening to music and reading on the Internet (Muñoz, 2020; Sundqvist & Sylvén, 2014). Cabot (2014) further revealed that boys and girls showed different evolution trajectories in the out-of-class digital activities they engaged over time: Girls engaged more in playful-artefact-dominated activities when in primary schools but shifted towards greater engagement in expressive-artefact-dominated activities when in secondary schools. A reverse pattern was observed among boys, i.e., they shifted from an expressive past to a playful present.

Age

Age is another learner factor that is found to mediate the relationship between learner autonomy and technology. Lee et al. (2017) found that the older university English learners reported a higher level of readiness for and desire to use technology for self-directed language learning than their younger counterparts. Older adolescents and adults are found to exhibit a higher frequency of engagement with Internet activities and talking online, and a greater variety of online activities than younger adolescents (Muñoz, 2020; Sundqvist & Sylvén, 2016). Peters (2018) further found that the types of English language media that learners engaged with evolved over time: the 16-year-old learners played computer games more frequently, whereas the 19-year-old learners watched non-subtitled TV programmes and movies more often.

In addition to shaping the type of autonomous technological activities learners selectively engage in, age is also found to shape learners' affective factors when interacting with technology. For instance, Lee and Lee (2020) found that age was not a significant predictor of Korean university language learners' willingness to communicate inside and outside the classroom but was a significant negative predictor of their willingness to communicate in the digital settings. Younger students were more willing to communicate in L2 in digital contexts.

Thus, learner autonomy with technology is subject to the influence of a suite of psychological and personal trait factors and demographic factors.

Self-efficacy

Self-efficacy, learners' perception of their ability to achieve a desired goal, is a significant factor that influences the relationship between learner autonomy and technology. When learners are confident about a learning situation, they are more likely to take responsibility for the learning process, view themselves as proactive learners, and use self-regulated learning strategies in the process (Zimmerman & Bandura, 1994; Zimmerman & Kitsantas, 2005). Self-efficacy has a positive association with performance-approach goal orientation and a negative association with performance-avoidance goal orientation, and hence positively predicts learner persistence and effort expenditure in problem solving and learning (Greene & Azevedo, 2007; Liem et al., 2008). In effect, the relationship between self-efficacy and self-regulated learning is a reciprocal one as they may reinforce each other over time (Song et al., 2016). Two types of self-efficacy may play a role in influencing learner autonomy with technology: self-efficacy in language learning and self-efficacy in technology use.

Self-efficacy in language learning

Greater self-efficacy in learning a language may give learners more confidence in taking control over learning. Bai and Wang (2020) found that self-efficacy in English learning positively predicted a group of Hong Kong primary school students' learning monitoring, effort regulation and goal setting and planning in English language learning. Similarly, An and colleagues (2021) examined the influence of Chinese undergraduate EFL learners' self-efficacy in English skills and enjoyment of English learning on their self-regulated English learning with technology. They found that self-efficacy had a direct and significant effect on students' self-directed use of technology for motivational regulation, goal setting and learning evaluation, and social strategy regulation. They further found that self-efficacy in English speaking was the most significant predictor of students' use of a variety of technology-based self-regulation strategies. In the context of South Korea, Kim et al. (2015) clustered a group of Korean EFL learners into high, medium and low self-efficacy groups, and found that the learners with medium and high self-efficacy levels used significantly more self-regulated learning strategies than those with low self-efficacy levels. Moreover, they found that learners with medium and high self-efficacy levels were disproportionately female and had longer language learning experience.

Self-efficacy in technology use

Self-efficacy in technology use has proven to be a robust predictor of technology adoption in various meta-analysis studies (Baki et al., 2018; Cai et al., 2017). Pan (2020) found that technological self-efficacy was a significant and strong predictor of a group of Chinese English language learners' attitudes towards self-directed English learning with technology. This influence was primarily mediated by English learning motivation. Honarzad and Rassaei (2019) came to similar findings when examining Iranian EFL learners' technology-based out-of-class language learning, where technology self-efficacy was found to be a significant predictor of learners' engagement in self-directed language learning with technology.

Sumuer (2018) examined different types of self-efficacy that influenced 153 Turkey undergraduate students' self-directed learning with technology, including online communication self-efficacy (i.e., confidence in online communication) and computer self-efficacy (i.e., comfort level with and confidence in effective use of computers). The researcher found that both online communication self-efficacy and computer self-efficacy influenced learners' self-directed learning with technology positively.

A factor that is closely associated with self-efficacy is learners' prior technological experience. Relevant prior knowledge and experience in the context of learner autonomy and technology include learners' technological experience and domain-specific knowledge. Learners with greater technological experience often report higher levels of self-regulation (Samruayruen et al., 2013). Rashid and Asghar (2016) examined the relationship between overall technology use and self-directed learning among 761 Saudi Arabian undergraduates at a university. They found that there was a positive association between overall technology use and learners' self-directed learning. Specifically, learners' technological experience with email, smartphone, Internet and social media positively predicted levels of self-directed learning. Technological experience provides opportunities for collective autonomy and hence may enhance students' autonomous learning. A typical example is social networking tools, where opportunities for collaborative learning abound. Hamid et al. (2015) found that students who were frequent users of social technologies were versatile in discovering new knowledge both independently and collaboratively. Moreover, technological experience may also shape learners' self-efficacy in autonomous action for good or for worse. The foreign language learners in Lai's study (2015) shared that technological experience teachers brought to class boosted their confidence in the ability to process technology-mediated authentic resources, which led to self-initiated use of similar resources on their own. However, if the technological experience did not go well, it may discourage learners from incorporating it into their learning resource repertoire. This is exemplified in the story of a French language learner in Lai's (2019a) study. Her teacher introduced an online newspaper and a regular news-sharing oral activity in her French class. However, without teacher support to facilitate their interaction with the online news, the learner found the experience very challenging and not beneficial and quit using this resource immediately after the class was over.

Skills

The skills that are essential to learner autonomy with technology include both generic skills, such as digital literacy and self-regulation skills, and domain-specific skills, such as language skills and skills to use technology for language learning.

Generic skills – self-regulation skills

Decades of research on self-regulated learning have shown that possessing self-regulated learning skills is essential to successful learning in computer-based learning environments (Azevedo & Witherspoon, 2009; Bannert et al., 2009). Self-regulation capacities have been often reported as a significant determinant of autonomous language learning with technology. Lai et al. (2022) found that self-regulation skills both directly influenced a group of Chinese undergraduate students' use of mobile technologies for self-directed language learning and moderated the link between the intention of use and the actual use. Moreover, self-regulation positively predicts computer self-efficacy, which contributes to learner autonomy with technology (Lai, 2013; Chen & Hsu, 2020). Surveying 638 English language learners in Hungary, Kormos and Csizér (2014) found that self-regulation strategies mediated the relationship between motivational factors and autonomous use of resources for language learning. They further found that different dimensions of self-regulation capacities associated differently with autonomous language learning. Students' opportunity control capacity (i.e., willingness and proactive attitudes to seek opportunities for English language learning and use), satiation capacity (the capacity to overcome boredom in English language learning), and time-management control capacity were all significant determinants of students' self-directed use of traditional learning resources beyond the classroom. However, only the opportunity control capacity significantly predicted their self-directed use of technological resources for English learning. García Botero et al. (2019) focused on students' use of a mobile app, Duolingo, and found that learners struggled with sustained use of the app for out-of-class learning. Their limited use of the app was constrained by their abilities to effectively self-monitor and manage their learning experience. Thus, self-regulation skills are important determinants of learner autonomy with technology.

Research has further revealed that self-regulation skills may mediate the relationship between learners' autonomous learning behavior with technology and learning outcomes. For instance, Hromalik and Koszalka (2018) examined the learning experience of a group of community college novice Spanish language learners in the online Spanish class. They found that students who had higher performance in this course demonstrated greater time management, persevered in using the word cards they created to support learning and were reflective and constantly adjusted their methods of learning to improve learning outcomes. Moreover, Tseng and colleagues (2019) found that the intention to adopt mobile devices for language learning did not significantly predict a group of university EFL learners' reading and listening performance. Instead, its influence on the two language competences was mediated by learners' self-regulation behaviors.

Self-regulation skills may also moderate the link between psychological factors and learners' intention for autonomous action in technological environments. For instance, Lai et al. (2022) found that self-regulation skills positively moderated the link between their behavioral intention and their actual technology use behavior. Namely, the higher learners' self-regulation skills are, the more likely their intention for technology use may turn into actual technology use behavior. Moreover, Huang (2014) found that self-regulation helped buffer the negative influence of resistance to change on autonomous mobile learning: learners' resistance to change related negatively to their mobile English learning satisfaction for learners with low learning management skills, while the negative association was not significant for learners with high learning management skills. The link between satisfaction with mobile-assisted language learning and intention for continued use was stronger for learners with higher learning management skills. Moreover, these two groups of learners valued different aspects of technological experience. For learners with higher learning management skills, playfulness of mobile devices was the most significant factor in determining learner satisfaction of language learning experience with mobile devices and the concomitant continued intention for mobile-assisted language learning. In contrast, for learners with lower learning management skills, the perceived usefulness of mobile devices was a more important determinant.

Generic skills – digital literacy

In addition to self-regulation capacities, learners' digital competencies and 21st century skills also relate to learner autonomy with technology. Karatas and Arpaci (2021) found that learners' 21st century skills, i.e., learning and innovation skills, life and career skills, and information, media and technology skills, positively predicted a group of pre-service teachers' readiness for online learning. Furthermore, digital literacy, "the awareness, attitude and ability of individuals to appropriately use digital tools and facilities to identify, access, manage, integrate, evaluate, analyse and synthesize digital resources, construct new knowledge, create media expression, and communicate with others" (Martin, 2006, p. 155), was also found to be a significant predictor of senior adults' use of mobile apps for language learning in Puebla and colleagues' (2021) study. Kara (2022) found that digital literacy influenced undergraduate learners' engagement in online learning, and this link was mediated by learners' self-directed learning readiness and motivation. Examining the over-time development of undergraduate students' digital literacy and their self-regulated learning skills in using daily life technologies to create personalized learning environments in a business course, Perera Muthupltotage and Gardner (2018) revealed that digital literacy components influenced self-regulated learning sub-processes. Specifically, technical literacy (i.e., the technical and operational skills to use digital technologies for learning) and cognitive literacy (i.e., critical thinking with regard to information and tool usage) had significant impacts on almost all subprocesses of self-regulated learning. In contrast, social emotional literacy was associated with goal setting, assistance seeking and environment structuring only. Technical literacy was the strongest determinant of setting achievable learning goals, taking responsibility for learning actions and reorganizing physical and social environments to make them compatible with goals. Cognitive literacy had the strongest impact on learning strategy utilization and (re)construction of physical and social environment. Social and emotional literacy showed the highest association with help-seeking behaviors. The analysis also suggested potential reciprocal interaction between digital literacy and self-regulated learning over time.

Domain-specific skills – skills related to technology use for language learning

Besides these general skills, what is equally important is the skills essential for effective interaction in technological worlds using the target language. Chen et al. (2021) highlighted the importance of critical literacy skills. They used PISA 2018 data to examine the relationship of extramural social media use – chatting, participating in social networks, and browsing for fun, with adolescents' digital reading literacy, and found a small positive effect of social media use on digital reading literacy. The researchers reasoned that whether autonomous experience online contributes to language development depends crucially on learners' critical evaluation skills in processing information retrieved on social media, and hence advocated the importance of developing learners' critical meta-literacy skills. Socio-emotional skills have also been identified as essential to effective communication online. Bandura (1997), in his socio-cognitive model of self-regulated learning, highlighted the importance of socio-emotional factors in a learning situation. According to the model, learners' emotional experience is mediated by the interaction of learners' self-efficacy and beliefs about task value with their encounter in the learning environment, and emotions evoked in return influence cognition and learning strategies. Bandura further highlighted the importance of collective agency in enhancing self-efficacy and the concomitant persistence against challenges and setbacks. Activities in online spaces are often collaborative in nature, and effective engagement in such spaces depends crucially on learners' socio-emotional skills. Peeters and Ludwig (2017) pointed out that autonomy in online collaborative spaces is indispensable of social mediation – sharing resources, artefacts and experiences and acknowledging peers' sharing, and supporting each other motivationally. Moreover, the execution of learner autonomy is inherently a process of negotiating the "relationship of possibility" between learners and the affordances of technological spaces, and negotiating shared interests, entities, and spaces among learners (De Moraes Garcia et al., 2017). Thus, learners' social and emotional competencies play an essential role in the execution of autonomy in technological environments (Lewis, 2014; O'Leary, 2014).

Learners' ability to perceive, utilize and orchestrate the affordances of different technological resources and tools for language learning is also essential. Fathali and Okada (2017) revealed that learners' perceived competence of learning English beyond the class using technology was the strongest determinant of their engagement, or lack thereof, in self-directed technology use beyond the classroom. Each technology has its own configuration of codes of behaviors and communication pragmatics. Thus, learners' capacities to perceive the affordances of technologies and make choices on the semiotic channels and resources available to them are essential to self-directed learning (Bouchard, 2009). Limited self-management skills in managing distractions on the internet and lack of competence to select appropriate technological resources and use them effectively for language learning have been reported to induce hesitancy in autonomous language learning with technology beyond the classroom, despite positive perceptions of task values and willingness to take responsibilities for learning (Castellano et al., 2011; Cabot, 2014; Lai, 2015; Lai et al. 2016). Moreover, abilities to deal with the "intimidating and overwhelming" learning experience in informal contexts are equally important (Davis, 2013, p. 93). These skills include a level of familiarity with the culture and conventions of social behaviors and interactions in different online environments, and the strategies to deal with the conversational patterns and discourse features in these environments (Davis, 2013; Sykes, et al., 2010).

Domain-specific skills – language skills

Learners' knowledge in the disciplinary field is another essential domain-specific factor. Research on self-regulated learning has found that learners with high prior knowledge are more likely to use planning and monitoring strategies to activate prior knowledge and compare prior knowledge with the knowledge provided in the learning environments to actively construct personal understanding. In contrast, learners with low prior knowledge rely more on surface-level strategies, such as note taking and summarizing, to learn the given knowledge in technological environments (Moos & Azevedo, 2008). Moos and Azevedo attributed the limited utilization of self-regulatory processes among learners with low prior knowledge to the fact that self-regulatory processes and the needed disciplinary knowledge compete for the limited working memory capacity available. Moreover, learners with low prior knowledge are challenged in their abilities to make accurate judgement and monitoring of their learning, which leads to poor decisions on control strategies and adjustive behaviors (Ehrlinger et al., 2008).

In the context of autonomous language learning with technology, language skills are essential. Ünal et al. (2017) reported that, as their proficiency level increased, learners perceived autonomous out-of-class tasks more positively and held a stronger belief in the effectiveness of learner autonomy in language learning. Language proficiency level significantly predicts learners' self-regulation levels (Nikoopour & Khoshroudi, 2021). Language proficiency level influences the types of technological resources that learners find comfortable and beneficial. For instance, Luef et al. (2019) found that their German and African participants' language proficiency level was positively associated with the number of language learning apps they downloaded and used. Moreover, learners with higher proficiency level tended to use more varied and social-oriented apps. Language proficiency also shapes learners' experience in technological environments (Godwin-Jones, 2019). For instance, Chen et al. (2020) found that despite having no significant difference in motivation for, anxiety over and willingness to use Google Assistant, learners of different proficiency levels had different experience with this intelligent personal assistant. Students of high language proficiency considered themselves better understood by Google Assistant and were more likely to keep the interaction going when facing communication breakdown. Language proficiency may further influence learner gains from autonomous learning with technology. As revealed in De Vos and colleagues' (2018) meta-analysis findings, language learners with higher proficiency levels are more versatile in deriving word meaning from context and hence benefit significantly more from incidental vocabulary meaning with meaning-focused input. Yudintseva (2015) further pointed out that learners of different proficiency levels may benefit differently from different technological resources: Unlike learners of higher proficiency levels, learners of beginning proficiency levels showed a low level of willingness to communicate in a target language when playing MMORPGs and were not able to improve vocabulary knowledge significantly from such experience. In contrast, beginning language learners benefited more from serious games and synthetic immersive environments.

In all, existing literature has researched the influence of learner factors on learner autonomy with technology extensively and has generated a rich list of learner internal factors that may interact with one another to shape autonomous language learning with technology both inside and outside the classroom.

Learning situation factors

Learner autonomy is situation specific. Learners may display different levels of autonomy in different situations, given the unique assemblage of temporal, spatial and relational parameters in each situation (Benson, 2009; Murray, 2014). In Murray's (1999) words, learners may be "autonomous in one area while dependent in another" (p. 301). The structure and relevance of the learning experience, and the amount of support and the degree of control learners have are reported to be important factors that influence learner autonomy in technological environments (Loyens et al., 2008).

Nature of learning situations

Structure in learning situations

Research has shown that the structure of learning tasks may influence learners' self-regulation in task completion and in learning. Highly structured tasks may constrain learners' exercise of self-determination (Pintrich & Schunk, 1996). At the same time, open learning tasks without structure may be too demanding, hence discouraging self-direction in learning. Lodewyk et al. (2009) revealed that ill-structured tasks and well-structured tasks induce unique self-regulated learning responses among students, and thus may need to be balanced when structuring meaningful learning experience for students. Moreover, they found that task effects varied for different learners: While learners with high prior knowledge showed greater use of self-regulatory processes when doing ill-structured tasks than when tackling well-structured tasks, learners with low prior knowledge exhibited the opposite pattern. Namely, learners with low prior knowledge utilized fewer self-regulatory strategies during ill-structured tasks. Completion of ill-structured tasks demands learners to set sub-goals on their own, which students with low prior knowledge might find challenging. Failing to set sub-goals may suppress these students' use of advanced planning and deep-level learning strategies. Thus, the researchers argued for a combination of tasks with varied degrees of structure. This point was echoed in Schmid and Petko's (2019) research findings. They examined two approaches to realize personalized learning with technology at school: adopting an open teaching method where students use technology to work on autonomous learning activities or introducing digital choice and voice on the learning content, schedule, and procedure in existing teaching method. They found that open teaching methods significantly predicted students' self-reported digital skills and their beliefs about the usefulness of ICT in learning. In contrast, digital choice and voice was not a significant predictor. The researchers thus argued that it is important to integrate slots of open self-directed learning into structured teaching at school to strike a balance of structure and openness in learning experience. These studies suggest that structure in tasks influences learners' self-regulation in learning.

Researchers further found that structured tasks and open tasks contribute to different aspects of learner autonomy. Lee (2016) examined a group of beginning Spanish language learners' perception of the relationship between different types of online tasks and autonomous learning. These learners perceive teacher-designed structured blog entry tasks as scaffolding independent work in content creation with clear instructions, whereas unstructured tasks gave them freedom in co-constructing conceptual understanding through social interaction. Thus, the researcher argued that these two types of tasks contributed differently to learner autonomy.

Perceived meaning in learning situations

Perceived meaning is a significant predictor of motivated behavior and learning goal pursuit (Rosenberg et al., 2019; Seifert and O'Keefe, 2001). Thus, perceived meaning in tasks determines learners' motivational investment and self-regulation of the experience. Moxnes (2000) identified two conditions that determine perceived meaning of a learning task: 1) to what extent the learning task is related to one's previous experience; and 2) to what extent the learning task leads to a goal that is desirable. Perceived meaning in a learning task is closely related to the purposes and aspirations in one's life. Promoting perceived meaning in a learning situation is indispensable to the close connection of the task with students' unique interests and needs. When learners' interests, preferences and values are satisfied, learners may perceive autonomy in the learning task (Deci & Ryan, 2002).

Interest may strengthen self-regulatory resources during task performance by focusing attention and enhancing perseverance towards a learning task. Interest also activates exploratory behaviors and shapes repeated and frequent engagement with a particular activity (Renninger & Hidi, 2015). Barron and Martin (2016) found that interest drives people to actively appropriate and create opportunities to engage in self-propelled, self-sustaining learning across temporal and spatial boundaries. Personal interest has been found to be the main drive behind people's self-directed appropriation of internet-based tools and resources to create online personal learning networks (Cheng, 2014; Morrison & McCutheon, 2019). Hennis et al. (2017) proposed an interest-driven pedagogical design framework to boost autonomy and engagement among at-risk migrant youth. The framework highlights designing learning experience that starts with and centers on learners' interests, and hence makes the learning experience personally relevant and meaningful. The scholars highlighted four types of interest: personal interests and values that pertain to one's personal identity, interest to belong to a certain social group, professional or academic interest, and interest in societal issues. Carrying out a digital video project with university undergraduate students in Hong Kong, Hafner and Miller (2011) found that the possibility of writing for a real audience and selecting personally meaningful content boosted these English language learners' agency in a digital video project.

Learner control in learning situations

Learner control is an essential component of learner autonomy. There are controversial findings on the effects of learner control in learning situation on student learning experience: positive findings include boosted learning effort and metacognitive activities (Hannafin & Land, 1997); and negative findings include disorientation, distraction, and cognitive overload (Granger & Levine, 2010; Scheiter & Gerjets, 2007). Thus, learner control may boost or curb learner autonomy, depending on the types and levels of learner control in the learning situation (Sorgenfrei and Smolnik, 2016).

You and Kang (2014) examined the relationship between perceived control and self-regulated learning among a group of Korean undergraduate students who were taking an online course. They found that perceived control predicted self-regulated learning both directly and indirectly via emotional variables such as boredom, anxiety and enjoyment. Bansal and colleague (2020) compared a group of medical students' perception of learning experience that was designed with a pedagogical approach (teacher-centric), andragogical approach (problem-driven, teacher-facilitated) and heutagogical approach (student self-determined). Students reported heutagogy and andragogy most positively because these approaches "allow them to choose their own method of innate learning, giving them feelings of maximum participation in their own learning" (p. 305). Thus, learner control is associated positively with perceived situational freedom. Fishman (2014) further revealed that self-responsibility mediated the link between perceived control and self-regulated learning. The more learners believe that they have control over the learning environment to achieve desired learning goals, the more likely they may feel a sense of internal obligation to produce the desired outcomes and hence engage in self-regulating their learning process. Sorgenfrei and Smolnik (2016) identified five dimensions of learner control: control over time and pace; control over location of learning; control over the navigation and design; control over interaction; and control over content and task selection. They found that the five dimensions of learner control had differential effects on the learning process and cognitive and affective learning outcomes. They further pointed out that perceived control was a stronger determinant of learning process than the actual degree of control afforded in the learning situation.

Perceived playfulness of learning situations

Perceived playfulness, the extent to which learners feel curious about the interaction and find the interaction intrinsically enjoyable during a task, may further shape learner autonomy with technology. Wang et al. (2021) found that perceived playfulness of online learning predicted students' intention to take part in online learning. Similarly, Karimi (2016) found that perceived playfulness was a significant predictor of undergraduate students' m-learning adoption in both formal learning context (i.e., to access learning material provided by tutors) and informal learning contexts (i.e., to access resources available online to support their learning). Huang et al. (2021) further revealed that perceived playfulness also influenced Taiwanese English language learners' intention for continued use of mobile devices for English learning. The association was both directly and indirectly via self-management of learning.

Thus, the nature of the learning tasks plays an important role in shaping learner autonomy with technology. The influence of the nature of learning tasks is relative and intertwines with that of learner factors.

Instructional support

The presence of instructional support, or lack thereof, may facilitate or constrain learner autonomy in technological environments. For instance, Nikou and Economides (2017) found that optimal levels of challenge and availability of immediate feedback directly and significantly predicted perceived autonomy and perceive competence in using mobile-assisted assessment. They further revealed that technological features that facilitate interaction among students, with the instructor and with the content, and technological features that support collaboration, such as sharing of knowledge and experiences, were significant positive determinants of perceived relatedness. Thus, elements of instructional support in technological environments may mediate learner autonomy with technological resources.

Support for language processing

Support for language processing is an important aspect of instructional support that determines learning gains from autonomous engagement with technology. Researchers have examined the influence of support-on-the-go that facilitates language processing, such as glossing and annotations. They found that computer glossing is an important element of instructional support in the context of digital reading. According to a second-order meta-analysis conducted by Plonsky and Ziegler (2016), computer glossing has a strong positive effect on learners' performance during digital reading, with an effect size between 0.46 and 1.44. Computer glossing also has a strong positive effect on learners' immediate and delayed incidental vocabulary learning from digital reading, with an effect size of 1.40 and 1.25 respectively (Abraham, 2008). Moreover, text-to-speech and other read-aloud tools positively influence the reading comprehension of learners with reading disabilities, with an effect size of 0.35 (Wood et al., 2018). Moreover, different aspects of glossing and annotation tools that support language processing have differential impacts on learning. For instance, multiple glosses that complement textual annotation with visual ones have a larger, positive effect on learners' vocabulary acquisition than single-mode glossing with text annotation only, with an effect size of 0.83 (Vahedi et al., 2016). Audio narration is found to be beneficial for incidental vocabulary learning via digital reading (Dalton, 2014). Similarly, bi-modal and tri-modal input, such as captions on audio-visual materials, is beneficial to listening comprehension, vocabulary acquisition, grammar learning and pronunciation (e.g., Long, 2020).

Researchers have also examined the effects of adaptive and situated support on language processing and language use. For instance, research has reported the effects of providing context-aware ubiquitous learning support on vocabulary learning via mobile-assisted language learning. Context-aware information is based on four types of information: learners' location, current learning time, learners' vocabulary ability and leisure time available to the learners. Comparing the vocabulary gains among the students who used a mobile personalized English vocabulary learning system with or without the context-aware service, Chen and Li (2010) found that 10th graders who used the learning system with the context-aware English vocabulary materials on 12 campus locations at a high school showed significantly greater gains than those who used the learning system without the context-aware feature.

Support for self-regulation

The availability and forms of support for learners' self-regulatory capacity are also found to influence autonomous learning with technology. The inclusion of self-regulation scaffolds has a positive effect on learner performance in computer-based learning environments (effect size =0.44) (Zheng, 2016). Zheng et al. (2018) compared students' reading performance on two mobile reading systems, one with prompts that engaged students in self-regulation during reading and the other without any self-regulation prompts. The researchers found that students who received the self-regulation support showed better reading performance and greater improvement in self-regulated learning abilities than those who did not receive the support. Thus, supports on self-regulation impact not only students' autonomous engagement with technological resources but also their learning gains from the interaction.

Hannafin and colleagues (1999) categorized four types of instructional support or scaffolding. Conceptual scaffolds are the scaffold that guide learners on concepts to consider when tackling the pre-defined problem or task (e.g., to stimulate the recall of specific concepts). Metacognitive scaffolds provide different ways to think about a problem and different strategies that could be utilized (i.e., to induce the use of cognitive and metacognitive strategies). Procedural scaffolds are those that guide learners in using the features available in the learning situation (i.e., to promote the use of certain procedures, techniques and operations in learning). Strategic scaffolds are guides on how to approach a problem or task (Azevedo & Hadwin, 2005; Bannert & Reimann, 2012). Yelland and Masters (2007) further added technical and affective scaffolding to the list. Technical scaffolding underscores the features within the technological environment that mediate learning, and affective scaffolding underscores the features that support learners to focus on and persist with the learning task. As for the form of delivery, scaffolding can be static, with a fixed set of scaffolding materials or dynamic/adaptive in response to learners' performance. The scaffolds can either be embedded in the technological system or initiated by learners. The tools that are used to deliver scaffolding are often in the form of prompts, scripts or pedagogical agents.

How scaffolds are delivered may influence their effects on learning in technological environments (Devolder et al., 2012). For instance, Simon and Klein (2007) found that when students were required to use the embedded scaffolds, they produced more organized notebooks than those who were given the scaffolds as optional support. Moreno and colleagues (2001) found that spoken scaffolds led to significantly higher learning gains than written scaffolds. Vogel and colleagues (2016) further pointed out that learning with scripts had a large positive effect on collaboration skills, and scripting is particularly effective when combined with content specific tools such as worked examples and concept maps. They further found that both micro scripts that used sentence openers to prompt students' content generation, reflection and discussion, and macro scripts that guided the general orchestration of activities and processes provided useful scaffolding for learning in the technological environments. In the context of collaborative technological activities, Näykki and colleagues (2017) highlighted that both socio-cognitive monitoring scripts and socio-emotional monitoring scripts are essential in supporting students' successful collaborative learning with technology. Moreover, grading scaffolds that gradually shift the control over the learning process to learners may be more beneficial in enhancing self-regulation and learning gains (Devolder et al., 2012).

Support for task implementation

Whether technological activities are to be conducted individually or collaboratively may mediate learner autonomy in technological environments. In their meta-analysis on the role of collaboration in computer-supported learning settings across different disciplines, Chen et al. (2018) found that collaborative learning in computer-supported settings has a significant positive effect on learning when compared with computer-supported learning done in non-collaborative manner. Specifically, they found that collaborative learning had an effect size of 0.42 on knowledge acquisition, 0.64 on skill development and 0.38 on learners' overall perception of the learning experience. Similarly, meta-analyses on the impact of mobile devices on language learning and augmented reality on education all reveal that collaborative approach has a greater effect on learning compared to other pedagogical approaches such as self-directed learning, inquiry-based learning and situated learning (Chen et al., 2020; Garzón et al., 2020). The greater learning benefits of collaborative learning could be attributed to the fact that collaboration reduces cognitive load. Li et al. (2021) examined English language learners' performance during a wiki-supported literature circle activity and found that collaborative engagement in this technological experience induced instances of socially shared regulation and co-regulation that helped enhance learner engagement during the activity. Liu et al. (2018) compared Taiwan 6th graders' performance in digital storytelling task in English in two conditions: groups of three versus independently. The researchers found that students who worked in groups exhibited greater gains in language knowledge and perception of language learning autonomy in addition to reduced anxiety and a higher level of happiness during the task.

Moreover, the (non)presence of expectations and guidance on task implementation may influence learners' self-directed learning experience in technological environments. Jang et al. (2010) conceptualized three dimensions of task implementation guidance: 1) explicit and detailed directions on expected behaviors during the experience; 2) a program of action to guide ongoing activity; and 3) constructive feedback to guide learner control over valued outcomes. Moreover, Kicken et al. (2008) pointed out that learners often face the challenge of selecting suitable tasks for self-directed learning, and thus it is essential to provide guidance on task selection. Corbalan et al. (2010) further proposed shared control as a way to get out of the self-directed learning conundrum, where learners make the final task selection based on a subset of optimal tasks suggested by the system.

Thus, the presence and non-presence of support on different aspects of learner experience may influence the nature of learners' self-directed learning in technological environments and the concomitant learning gains.

Environmental factors

Ben-Eliyahu and Bernacki (2015) argued that the social and cultural contexts where a learning event is situated may deplete or replenish learners' self-regulatory strength and capacity to learn. Highlighting the situational freedom aspect of learner autonomy, scholars like Benson (2009) and Hamilton (2013) have emphasized the influence of the environment on learner autonomy. Benson (2009) underscored that autonomy exists in the interaction between an individual and the social, discursive and resource realities of the context he/she resides in. Both the resources accessible in the environment and the social and discursive configurations and characteristics influence the degree of autonomy an individual may exercise. Gao (2010) noted the influence of significant others on a group of Chinese undergraduate students' strategic language learning behaviors in Hong Kong. He identified that the interaction of social resources (e.g., parents, teachers, and peers), societal discourse (e.g., the status and value of English) and cultural artifacts (e.g., examinations and availability of English resources) affected learners' choice of English learning strategies. In this subsection, I will present the empirical evidence on how these

Cultural artifacts

Culture is the shared motives, values, beliefs and identities of a community. Brookfield (1993) argued that self-direction is a part of cultural tradition. Thus, cultural artifacts unavoidably influence learners' autonomous engagement with technology. Culturally shaped technological practices, values, beliefs, and educational practices are cultural artifacts that shape the relationship between learner autonomy and technology.

Culturally shaped technological practices

Culturally shaped technological practices may amplify or constrain learner autonomy. Muñoz and Cadierno (2021) examined how the variation in English exposure and linguistic distance may influence language learners' out-of-class experience and language development from the experience. They recruited 14-15-year-olds from two countries with different linguistic and societal circumstances—Denmark and Spain. Denmark has a richer English environment than Spain (e.g., English television programs and films in Denmark are broadcast in English with L1 subtitles but in Spain they are dubbed into native languages). Danish is also closer to English, sharing 59.3% of cognates in comparison to only 24% of shared cognates in Spanish. The study found that the association between the weekly frequency of audiovisual material viewing with English subtitles and listening comprehension scores was positive for the Spanish group only, and that for the Danish group was a non-significant negative one. The difference was due to the fact that Danish learners had daily access to English through TV and films, and extra exposure to audiovisual materials with English subtitles did not contribute much to English ability. For Spanish learners who did not have daily access to English TV shows and films, exposure to audiovisual materials with English subtitles would contribute greatly to their listening comprehension abilities. Thus, the researchers concluded that cultural technological artifacts, in this case dubbed or undubbed TV, influenced learners' gains from their autonomous learning with technological resources beyond the classroom.

Culturally shaped values

Cultural values also mediate self-directed action. Guglielmino and Guglielmino (2006) found that self-directed learning readiness differed across countries with different cultural values in power distance and individualism. Acknowledging the heterogeneity of differences within a culture and avoiding reductionism in categorizing cultural differences, Lai and colleagues (2016) examined culturally shaped value beliefs at the individual level and explored how individual espoused cultural values, including long-term orientation, collectivism, power distance and uncertainty avoidance, shaped self-directed language learning with technology. They found that all the four individual espoused cultural values directly predicted Hong Kong university language learners' voluntary technology adoption in informal language learning contexts. Power distance also moderated the link between technology adoption intention and the actual frequency of technology use. Tarhini et al. (2017) also found that individual espoused cultural values moderated the associations of perceived usefulness, subjective norm, and perceived ease of use with university learners' behavioral intention of e-learning. Conducting a meta-analysis on the moderating role of culture in students' e-learning adoption, Zhao et al. (2021) found that culture was a significant moderator. Specifically, subjective norm and self-efficacy are better predictors of students' behavioral intention for e-learning adoption in the collectivistic culture than in the individualistic culture. Perceived usefulness was a more significant predictor of students' attitudes towards e-learning adoption in the individualistic culture. The researchers thus called for strengthening social influence when we design online learning platforms for students in collectivistic culture.

However, observing a group of Chinese undergraduates' active engagement in self-directed Tandem learning, Gieve and Clark (2005) argued that "what are apparently culturally determined dispositions towards a certain approach to learning can turn out to be quite flexible" (p. 261) and that these dispositions may change in response to specific situations. Lai (2019a) showed that individual espoused cultural value beliefs regarding language learning influenced whether and how language learners selected and used technological resources for self-directed language learning beyond the classroom. These beliefs further changed over time in response to learners' technological experience. Godwin-Jones (2019) further pointed out that with enhanced internationalization and permeation of technology, the claimed influence of cultural value beliefs on technology use, if any, may disappear since technology may shape and change culture. To put it in the words of Viberg and Grönlund (2013), "technology itself seems to be the most important cultural-shaping factors, more important than culture inherited from the physical environment" (p. 178).

Culturally shaped educational practices

Educational practices may also influence learner autonomy with technological resources. Frambach et al. (2012) compared self-directed learning during problem-based learning among Middle East, Hong Kong, and Dutch students. They found that Middle East students expressed more feelings of uncertainty in adjusting to self-directed learning due to the strong contrast between problem-based learning and their secondary school educational experience that was characterized by traditional, teacher-centered education. This difficulty was further compounded by the cultural belief in preserving tradition and being wary of innovations. These students tried to overcome the feelings of uncertainty through seeking advice and materials from senior students, a strategy that suppressed the opportunity to develop independence. Hong Kong students encountered challenge of another nature. They found co-construction of knowledge during tutorials was not helpful because they distrusted their peers' contributions and felt these discussions created uncertainty about 'truth'. The perceived challenge was shaped by their teacher-centered secondary school education experience and the hierarchical culture that values the "truth" from the experts and authoritative sources. In contrast, Dutch students had experienced more self-directed learning experience in secondary school, and thus had less difficulty adjusting to problem-based learning. Thus, educational practices across cultural contexts may shape learners' readiness for self-directed learning.

Chik (2018) reported the self-directed foreign language self-study experiences of three Hong Kong adults. When constructing their foreign language learning journeys in informal learning contexts with free online resources, these learners tended to "re-create a language classroom learning experience" (p. 50). They relied heavily on structured learning resources and materials from more reputable, credentialed sources, and resorted to memorization-oriented learning strategies, such as copying vocabularies for multiple times and creating notebooks of vocabulary glossaries when interacting with online resources. They even expressed the sense of "guilty pleasure" (p. 54) when using unstructured learning resources such as pop cultural resources. Godwin-Jones (2019) attributed this phenomenon to the "lingering influence of the school culture" (p. 12). These studies give a vivid account of how culturally shaped educational practices may influence how learners respond to self-directed learning with technology.

Societal discourse

Discursive resources related to learning

Discursive resources, the formal and informal discourses about proper ways of behaving and about teaching and learning that circulate in a community, may either encourage or discourage learners from investing in language learning (Palfreyman, 2014). Palfreyman (2014) shared the narrative of a female Emirati undergraduate student on her family's disapproval of her sister's initiative of chatting with online acquaintances of both genders to practice English. This self-directed learning behavior was constrained by the local social discourse that prohibits social interaction with opposite gender beyond the family setting. Similarly, Murray (2014) showed how discursive resources shaped a group of Japanese English language learners' autonomy in English learning. According to him, societal discourse on globalization and language learning in Japan highlights the necessity and importance of learning English for claiming one's place in a globalized world. However, this social discourse discouraged some of his Japanese students' motivation for English learning since they tended to associate English with activities in the international arena and failed to see the relevance of English to their daily lives in Japan. The lack of motivation discouraged these students from engaging actively in self-regulating their English learning. Murray hence pointed out that it is important to consider the influence of social discursive resources on autonomous action.

Moreover, societal discourses may influence learner autonomy through teachers' practices. Johnson et al. (2021) found that teacher belief about their students shaped the support they provided for learner autonomy. Specifically, teachers who believed that their students had strong motivation in learning tended to provide autonomy-supportive opportunities to their students, such as involving learners in classroom rule development, engaging them in goal setting and delegating the responsibilities for group projects. In contrast, teachers who did not believe in students' ability to make appropriate decisions on learning tasks were not likely to utilize autonomy-supportive pedagogies.

Thus, discursive resources related to teaching may directly and indirectly influence learner autonomy with technology.

Discursive resources related to technology use

Discursive resources regarding technology use for language learning may also mediate the relationship between learner autonomy and technology use. Subjective norm, learners' perception of how important others think about his/her technology use, is a consistent predictor of students' technology adoption for learning. Subjective norms both directly influence attitudinal factors associated with technology adoption and moderate the link between perceived behavioral control and behavioral intention for technology use (Baki et al., 2018; Huang et al., 2020). Lai (2013) found that subjective norms may influence university language students' self-directed use of technology for language learning beyond the classroom via perceived educational compatibility between technology use and language learning and the concomitant perceived usefulness of this autonomous action for language learning. Lai et al. (2022) also found that subjective norms were a significant predictor of university language learners' adoption of mobile technology for self-directed language learning.

Thus, societal discourses related both to learning and to technology use may exert influences on learners' engagement in autonomous language learning with technology.

Social resources

Social resources lie not only in learners' in-class learning experience but also in the support from teachers and learners' physical and online social network.

In-class learning experience

In-class learning experience may influence autonomous language learning with technology. Lai (2019a) gave an account of a language learner who exhibited differential engagement with technology beyond the class when learning French compared to Spanish. She used a wider range of technological resources for Spanish learning beyond the classroom, incorporating social networking and online learning platforms even in the early stage of learning, but a narrower set for French learning, primarily constrained to vocabulary apps, songs, and videos. The learner attributed the differences to the different in-class learning experiences in these two language classes. Her Spanish teacher integrated cultural artefacts such as stories, songs, and videos in class instruction, which stimulated the participant to explore further about Spanish language and culture through self-directed learning. In contrast, her French teacher's class was rather teacher-centered and lacked multimedia resources, which was dull and demotivating and failed to stimulate her interest in French.

Moreover, in-class learning experience also influences the impact of out-of-class technological experience on students' language development. For instance, Lai et al. (2015) found the more meaning-focused English activities her junior high school participants engaged in on their own beyond the class, the higher their English grades were and the greater confidence in English they exhibited. She concluded that in the context where in-class English learning experience is dominated by a heavy focus on the acquisition of language forms, the diversity of meaning-focused activities is an important quality indicator of learners' out-of-class language experience. Thus, in-class learning experience, as a social resource, influences not only learners' volitional engagement with technology but also how they may benefit from the experience.

Teacher support

Teacher support for self-directed learning is an important factor that shapes learners' self-directed learning with technology. Schweder and Raufelder (2019) examined the influence of teacher support on German secondary school students' self-directed learning behaviors in the school context. They found that teacher support positively and significantly predicted students' volition in self-directed learning. Teacher support also determined students' utilization of control strategies to monitor learning and their use of elaboration strategies to engage in deeper learning during self-directed learning. They further identified that teacher support in self-directed learning, through guiding, monitoring and providing feedback on students' goal setting and implementation, was beneficial regardless of students' gender and age. Lai (2015b) identified three types of teacher support that associated with a group of university foreign language learners' engagement in self-directed out-of-class technology use for language learning: affective support, capacity support and behavioral support. Affective support referred to teachers' encouragement and acknowledgement of the behavior. Capacity support was in the form of teacher recommendation of technological resources and provision of cognitive and metacognitive strategies of effective interaction with technological resources. Behavioral support referred to teachers' use of technological resources in class instruction and assignments. Lai found that these three types of teacher support influenced students' self-directed technological behaviors positively and differently: Affective support influenced technology use through perceived usefulness, whereas capacity support and behavior support influenced technology primarily through perceived facilitation in technology use and computer self-efficacy. Lai thus argued for the importance of raising teachers' awareness of the different types of support they need to provide to students to enhance students' self-directed use of technology for language learning beyond the classroom.

Physical and online social networks

Learners' social networks, both physical and online, influence their out-of-class language learning with technology. A social network refers to "a finite set or sets of actors and the relation of relations defined on them" (Wasserman & Faust, 1994, p. 20). Peer network is an important source that facilitates self-directed learning process. Friends and teachers are consistently reported as the primary sources of resources and ideas for different types of self-directed informal language learning with technology (Lai et al., 2018). Students who receive emotional support from peers are more likely to persist in autonomous language learning with technology (Cheng & Lee, 2018).

Peer interaction during task performance also enables the occurrence of socially shared regulation and co-regulation that may contribute to learners' development of self-regulation. For instance, Li et al. (2021) revealed that group work on wiki-based literature circle activity induced socially shared regulation, where group members collectively regulated their joint activity to achieve a shared goal. Socially shared regulation enhanced students' learning engagement during the task. Eliciting the account of two learners' out-of-class Japanese learning experience, Inaba (2020) found that social networks with shared interests that involved the target language served as an important impetus for these learners' autonomous engagement with the language. The presence of distributed mentoring in interest-based online communities is found to be an important factor that sustains learners' engagement in language use in these informal learning spaces (Aragon & Davis, 2019).

Thus, social resources both inside and outside the classroom, and both online and in the physical world, play a role in shaping learner autonomy with technology.

Chapter 4

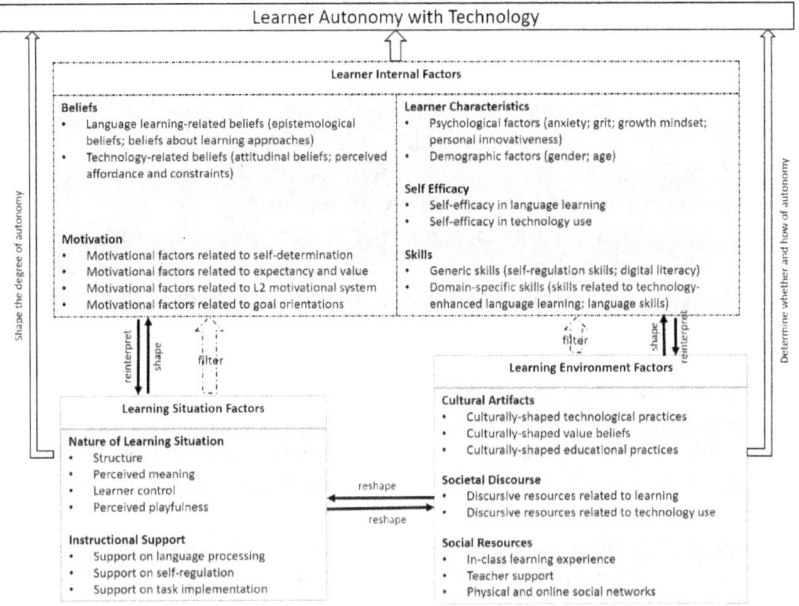

Figure 4 *Factors that shape learner autonomy with technology*

A framework of factors that influence learner autonomy with technology

Examining the literature on influencing factors of learner autonomy with technology, this chapter identifies a multitude of factors from the individual, learning situation, and learning environment domains. Learner internal factors contain several dimensions of individual factors that may shape the possibility and nature of learner autonomy with technology. These dimensions are not independent, but rather interact with one another, strengthening or offsetting each other's influence on the autonomous use of technology for learning. Learning situation and learning environment factors also contain multiple intertwining dimensions that are at play in influencing learner autonomy with technology. Figure 4 summarizes the list of factors.

Since autonomous language learning with technology is in essence an agentic action, which lies in the interaction of the individual and the structure. Accordingly, the influence of learning situation factors and learning environment factors are often mediated by learner internal factors, where learner internal factors filter the direction and degree of the influences of from learning situation and learning environment factors. Consequently, the influence of learning situation and learning environment factors is often relative, depending on the assemblage of learner internal factors. But at the same time, learning situation factors and learning environment factors may also directly influence learner autonomy with technology. Learning situation factors shape the degree of autonomy in technology use for language learning learners are able to and confident of exercising. Learning environment factors determine whether and how learners may exercise autonomy with technology for learning.

The three domains of influence also interact with one another. While learning situation and learning environment factors may shape learner internal factors, they are also subject to the (re)interpretation and (re)appropriation of learners. Thus, the same factor may manifest differently for different learners in shaping their decision making with regard to autonomous technology use for learning. There is also a bi-directional relationship between learning situation factors and learning environment factors. On the one hand, learning situation factors are situated in the learning environment and hence may be reshaped by factors in the learning environment under which the learning situation is carried out. For instance, the negative influence of the lack of instructional support in a learning situation may be mitigated by the availability of social resources. The potential positive influence of facilitative learning situation may be suppressed by the culturally shaped technological practices and societal discourses related to technology use. On the other hand, learning situation factors may also counter the influence of learning environment factors. Autonomy-supportive learning situations may provide discursive and social resources to ameliorate unfavorable learning environment factors. Autonomy-suppressive learning situations may put an extra demand on positive learning environment conditions and/or exacerbate the negative influence of unfavorable learning environments.

5
Facilitating the Interaction between Learner Autonomy and Technology

Learner autonomy and technology have a shared agenda, that is, to liberate and democratize education through breaking temporospatial boundaries and fighting against institutional, socio-cultural, and political fetters. However, the accomplishment of this shared goal depends crucially on the positive, reciprocal interaction between learner autonomy and technology. As elaborated in previous chapters, technology and learner autonomy may be mutually constraining. On the one hand, technological spaces, if designed in an autonomy-suppressive way, may impede learners' autonomous action in those spaces, while on the other hand, when learners lack essential skills related to learner autonomy, they may not capitalize on the technological affordances for autonomy. Thus, the absence of autonomy-amplifying elements in technology-enhanced platforms may limit their educational potential. The lack of opportunity and capacity to utilize technology may lose a powerful booster and an important space for autonomous action. Positive interaction between the two can be facilitated through the design of technology-enhanced learning experience that amplifies learner autonomy and through the development of learner capacity for autonomous action with technology.

Designing an autonomy-amplifying technology-enhanced learning experience

The design of autonomy-amplifying learning experience relies on two important considerations: 1) how to position technological experience in relation to the nexus of experiences that give learners exposure to the target language? And 2) what pedagogical design elements may amplify autonomy in technological experience?

Nature of an autonomy-amplifying learning experience

The design of a technology-enhanced learning experience starts with a clear conceptualization of the nature of the experience. The nature of the learning experience is shaped by how designers position the learning experience and the role of the learners.

Positioning the learning experience

Defining the nature of learning experience involves positioning the experience in relation to the nexus of relationships across different learning contexts. Autonomy-amplifying technology-enhanced learning experience needs to be positioned in ways that maximize and complement the strengths of different learning contexts. Scholars have argued for the importance of creating learning experience that connects students' classroom learning with everyday experiences. Wagner (2015, 2019) argued that the ultimate goal of language learning is to empower learners to use the language to participate in the wider life world and establish broader relations. Thus, to amplify learner autonomy in language learning, learning experience needs to work in concert to enable and support learners' everyday practices and social participation in the target language both in the physical and in the virtual world. Under this argument, the design of technology-enhanced learning experience needs to anchor around learners' immediate and future needs for language use in the life world.

Little and Thorne (2017) also argued that technology-enhanced learning experience needs to be designed to connect in-class and out-of-class learning so as to construct optimal environments for the inculcation of personal empowerment and societal transformation, which are key dimensions of learner autonomy. According to Little and Thorne, existing classroom learning that is primarily routine-based to achieve expected outcomes via foreseeable processes is not conducive to learner autonomy. The high level of predictability in in-class learning is quite different from learning that takes place in daily life. They thus argued for the necessity of "rewilding" and engineering learning experience that is characterized by structured unpredictability. Namely, they advocated constructing unpredictable experiences that are based on "intense contextualization" situated in the real world and provide rooms for the activation of funds of knowledge (e.g., ways of knowing, doing and being, social identities, life expertise, etc.) and personal interests, which may motivate and provide resources for a more active role in learning. Little and Thorne further suggested providing structure in the form of organizational procedures or teacher mediation and support to expand learners' communication repertoire and engender real-life episodes learnable, which increases extended efforts of exercising learner autonomy in informal learning contexts. Thus, various scholars have underscored the importance of augmenting the link across contexts when designing learning experience that amplifies learner autonomy. Connecting experience across contexts increases perceived relevance of learning and perceived resources for autonomous action, which boosts learner autonomy. A multitude of approaches have been proposed in current literature to create learning experiences that maximize and

A coordination and supplementation approach

Some scholars have recommended adopting a coordination and supplementation approach. The coordination and supplementation approach emphasizes coordinating the differential types of language skills in formal and informal contexts so that they would complement one another. For instance, previous literature has documented that voluntary language learning in informal contexts is characterized by a predominance of receptive activities, such as watching films, TV shows and/or short videos, listening to songs and the like. Given that learners' receptive skill muscles might be stronger due to the higher frequency of volitional engagement outside the classroom, Sockett and Toffoli (2020) argued that in-class learning might as well put a greater emphasis on speaking and/or writing activities:

> Since informal activities mostly involve listening and rarely involve speaking, it is reasonable to explore whether it is relevant to teach listening comprehension in today's English classroom and whether course design should instead allow more time for speaking or writing activities. (p. 479)

They hence suggested that when designing learning experience, listening, and reading activities can be assigned ahead of time as independent learning components that support subsequent teacher-facilitated speaking and writing activities inside the classroom.

Other scholars have suggested coordinating different types of language use experiences in formal and informal contexts in ways that the experiences can supplement one another. For instance, Lai et al. (2015) examined a group of middle school students in China on their out-of-class learning activities. They found that the total number of technological resources that these junior high school students utilized outside the classroom did not predict English grade. Instead, the total number of meaning-focused activities that learners engaged in was a significant determinant of both cognitive and affective outcomes. Thus, the more varied meaning-focused activities students engaged in, the higher their English course grades and confidence in and enjoyment of English learning were. The greater influence of engagement in meaning-focused activities could be attributed to the fact that the students' in-class learning experience was characterized by a heavy focus on language forms, and these meaning-focused activities beyond the classroom helped complement form-focused in-class learning. The authors hence concluded that

> When the in-class instruction is characterized by a heavy focus on language form, the degree to which the out-of-class learning activities focus on meaning and complement in-class learning experience is

indeed an important characteristic of quality out-of-class learning experience. (p. 293)

Similarly, Lee (2019) found that the quantity of out-of-class activities Korean university English language learners engaged in was a significant predictor of affective outcomes, such as confidence in and enjoyment of English learning. However, the diversity of out-of-class activities was a significant predictor of cognitive outcomes, such as TOEIC score, speaking proficiency and productive vocabulary size. Thus, these researchers advocated creating diversified activities that permeate in-class and out-of-class learning.

Learning experiences in formal and informal contexts also vary in terms of the level of structure, and researchers call for coordinating structured and unstructured learning activities. Little and Thorne (2017) advocated designing open learning activities that provide unexpected and contextualized learning experience, supplemented, and supported by structured learning inside the classroom. One example they provided was to bring in personal interest to add some degree of openness to structured learning experience inside the classroom: incorporate individual and collaborative learning experience that enables students to talk about their personal hobbies and interests at earlier stages of language learning; and support learners to work on projects of personal choice and interest at later stages. Hafner and Miller (2011) proposed yet another approach to design open learning experience, that is, to create a structured technological experience that emulates students' unstructured experience in the informal learning contexts and draw on their literacy practices in these contexts. They found that creating learning tasks that allowed learners to draw on daily life funds of knowledge, namely the digital tools and medium that learners were familiar in daily life, played an essential role in boosting learner autonomy. The researchers concluded that "a structured learning environment can be designed to emulate the kind of informal learning opportunities found in learners' unstructured learning environment" (p. 82). They regarded this as an effective approach for designing language courses that would amplify learner autonomy in the technology-enhanced learning environments.

Researchers also suggest coordinating different language user roles and different types of language practices in different learning contexts. Little and Thorne (2017) highlighted the importance of creating learning experience where learners are not just consumers of information and receivers of knowledge—the often-imposed roles inside the classroom—but also producers of knowledge. They advocated creating learning experience that boosts identities other than students, sharing an example of a project conducted with school-age children in rural Alaska. The children were sent to interview their tribal elders to collect and document traditional wisdom and practices, knowledge, and skills of fighting a global epidemic. By engaging the children in curating and promoting cultural funds of knowledge, the project enabled learners to assume the identity of knowledge producers, a role they were often denied of in conventional learning experience. Hafner et al. (2015) further drew our attention to the language used in different activities. They argued that language use at school focuses heavily on standardized forms of the language and native-speaker norms, which is different from the creative translingual and trans-semiotic language use that dominates online spaces. They hence suggested creating learning experience that tasks students with creative language use under teacher guidance to create multimodal and multilingual artifacts to share with the public.

An ethnographic approach

Another suggested design solution is to adopt an ethnographic approach, which underscores the roles of students in curating, sharing, evaluating, and transforming authentic online materials from the digital wilds for classroom use to expand access to and reflect on the multicultural and multilingual realities of language use in the real world (Godwin-Jones, 2020; Warner & Dupuy, 2018). This approach prompts learners to critically view and analyze their own and others' language use in everyday life under teachers' guidance. Thorne and Reinhardt (2008) advocated the inclusion of "bridging activities" that "combin[e] the best of the analytic traditions of schooling with the life experiences and future needs of today's foreign language students" (p. 562).

There have been various examples of how this ethnographic approach can be operationalized. To Thorne and Reinhardt (2008), an exemplary task would be to engage learners to apply discourse analysis techniques to analyze their own online communication samples on platforms like instant messengers, blogs, wikis and/or massive multiplayer online gaming. Similarly, Godwin-Jones (2018) shared the design of a learning project for university intermediate-level students. In this project, students were asked to curate authentic online materials that they found enjoyable, such as videos, music, and websites in the target language, and bring to class to share with peer learners. The teacher guided students to analyze and evaluate language use in these resources and rate these materials on the level of interest. The teacher then worked with students to transform some of the highly ranked materials into interactive learning materials and shared these materials as open educational resources. Little and Thorne (2017) further proposed sending students out to the real world with mobile devices to complete quests and working on the recorded interaction students bring back to the classroom to clarify language points and discuss communication strategies that may help in those communication scenarios.

By advocating usage-based experiential pedagogies that center on learners' socialization and real-life needs in daily life and work-related practices, this approach calls for revolutionizing the nature of in-class experience: "The classroom becomes a place of recollection, reflection and elaborated focus on what has happened or is happening in the world" (Eskildsen et al., 2019, p. 11; Wagner, 2019).

Positioning the role of learners

The nature of autonomy-amplifying learning experience is also defined by how learner roles are conceptualized. In the context of technology-enhanced language learning, different technological contexts induce different "relations between the abilities of organisms and features of the environment" (Chemero, 2003, p. 189). The introduction of any technological element may "transform the configuration of the learning environment, affecting how students respond to one another, altering the dimensions of affordances for learning, and influencing learners' use of language" (Hamilton, 2013, p. 217). Discussing the design of computer-supported collaborative learning experience, Tchounikine (2019) highlighted the importance of adopting the position of treating learners not just as "*a factor*" in learning tasks, but "*the actors*"—actors whose agentic actions redefine the nature of the tasks.

Thus, to design learning experience that amplifies learner autonomy, educators need to embed elements that help enhance learners' understanding of the affordances and constraints of different learning contexts. Tchounikine (2019) argued that it is important to empower learners to self-determine the media they want to use when designing learning experience. Three design principles are highlighted:

> Offering learners the possibility to select and inter-operate software applications;
> Offering learners the possibility to adapt software applications to their individual needs; and
> Offering learners relevant information and feedback to help them make informed decisions. (Tchounikine, 2019, p. 240)

Understanding the characteristics of different learning contexts per se is not sufficient, since individual's dispositions, material, and symbolic assets and positions in the learning contexts interact with the features of the learning contexts to determine individuals' practices and behaviors (Bennett & Maton, 2010). Heightened awareness of how individuals' habitus (e.g., dispositions, capacities, propensities to think, feel and act in certain ways) and capital (e.g., social, cultural, linguistic capital) interact with the contextual features across different learning contexts is fundamental to enabling informed decisions on selecting and utilizing technological resources for learning. This awareness is developed through conscious experiential learning and critical engagement with different technological contexts.

Learners' experiential and critical engagement across different learning contexts can be operationalized through creating heutagogical experience, self-determined learning (Blaschke, 2021). Heutagogy centers on the concept that "the learner serv[es] as the major agent in their own learning, which occurs, as a result of personal experience" (Hase & Kenyon, 2007, p. 112), and aims at "developing capability, self-reflection and metacognition (an understanding of one's own learning process)" and supporting learners to create their own networks of knowledge, learning and information (Blaschke & Hase, 2016, p. 27; Blaschke, 2019; Halupa, 2015). Different from pedagogy that focuses on content objectives and andragogy that focuses on competence, the focus of heutagogical approaches is learners' capability. Through focusing on the learning process rather than the content, heutagogy emphasizes supporting learner agency in the learning path and outcomes, developing self-efficacy and independence, reflection and metacognition development and non-linear path of learning (Blaschke, 2019). Thus, in Heutagogical educational environments, teachers are the "guide-on-the-side, providing mentoring and coaching for the student along the learning journey" (Blaschke, 2019, p. 77; Halupa, 2015) and creating "elements of exploration, creation, reflection, connection, assessment and sharing" in the learning experience (Blaschke, 2012; Blaschke & Hase, 2016). Blaschke (2021) elaborated on four principles of heutagogy. A key principle of heutagogy is to support learner agency and give learners the autonomy to make decisions on their own learning journey and processes. An associated principle is nonlinear learning where learners utilize avenues inside and outside the classroom and resort to collaboration and social connection to achieve their self-defined learning outcomes. Developing self-efficacy is another key principle, which underscores building scaffolding mechanisms to boost learner self-efficacy in carrying out a task and acquiring knowledge and skills. The last principle is utilizing reflection and activating meta-cognition to enhance analytical and critical thinking.

To realize heutagogy, the learning experience needs to provide learners opportunities and support to engage in self-directed inquiry-based learning on self-determined learning goals, using the resources recommended to explore and the venues and tools provided to organize information acquired. Learners are also given the opportunities to engage in individual and collaborative work for creative work with the information and understanding acquired. Henriksen et al. (2018) also concurred with the importance of engaging learners in "problem solving in situ and in practice," such as real-world problems meaningful to learners from their own interests, to help foster their creative habits of mind that is essential to learner autonomy in emerging settings. They further identified constant reflection in and on action as another important pillar of autonomy-amplifying learning experience. Blaschke and Halse (2016) further elaborated that reflections need to be on different aspects of learning, including understanding, learning process and approaches, and one's value systems and learning beliefs. Idros and colleagues (2010) shared an example of a heutagogical experience in language learning where a group of Malaysian learners were given a resource pool and online diagnostic tests that they could access at any time. Online diagnostic tests not only provided information on areas of weakness but also suggested remedial and enrichment learning tasks and materials from the resource pool. Learners thus can self-determine their own learning journeys to address individual areas of weaknesses. In addition, there were also project-based modules where learners teamed up with peers to work collaboratively on projects that utilize different language areas.

The element of collaboration is essential. Blaschke and Halse (2016) highlighted that venues for collaboration and for sharing learning process and strategies and sharing the information acquired are important to facilitate self-determined learning. Arguing from the perspective of Engeström's activity theory, Blin (2010) placed community and the rules and division of labor that govern the community and mediate individual and collective actions within the community at the center of a language learning activity system. Blin argued that tasks that involve collaborative production of tangible and re-usable artifacts that are useful within or beyond the community are more powerful in amplifying and developing learner autonomy than tasks that only aim at transforming individual learners into more competent language users. According to him, co-creating these artifacts enables not only the emergence of individual goals and autonomy but also the "convergent construction" of collective goals among participants in the community. Thus, he proposed a few principles in designing technology-rich language learning environments that amplify and focus learner autonomy. The central principle is to create *object-centered* language learning activities, and the most optimal objects are those that involve the creation of multimodal artifacts that can be re-used or re-mixed by self and others beyond a certain language course. Diversified yet converging ways of constructing the objects should be allowed and encouraged. He also argued for fostering a rich horizontal division of labor, where interdependence needs to be built in to ensure collaboration among learners. Moreover, learners need to be equipped with relevant skills and strategies that enable them to co-construct creative solutions to resolve potential breakdowns or problems induced by language or technological deficiency. The propositions by Blin (2010) could supplement the heutagogical experience by placing collaboration at the center of self-determined learning experience, guiding students to identify common interests and set communal goals on collaborative artifacts that align with the common interests and supporting co-inquiry based on common interests and convergent goals.

Thus, current literature suggests a few guiding principles for designing autonomy-supportive learning experience: 1) the learning experience needs to be connected with and supplement learners' experiences in different contexts, and enable learners to expand learning across contexts; 2) the learning experience needs to allow for and support self-defined learning journey and process; and 3) the learning experience needs to boost learners' metacognition and capacity for critical engagement in autonomous language learning across technological contexts.

Design elements of an autonomy-amplifying learning experience

Using these guiding principles to define the nature of the learning experience is a key step towards designing autonomy-amplifying learning. However, this step needs to be augmented by autonomy-supportive design elements. The literature on autonomy-supportive teaching further proposed some key design elements. Autonomy support refers to "nurturing and enhancing an individual's 'inner endorsement' of their engagement with educational activities" (Huggins, 2012, p. 21). Autonomy-supportive teaching is an instructional effort to support students' need for autonomy and enhance perceived locus of causality, volition, and choice (Deci & Ryan, 1987). Meta-analysis research reveals that teacher autonomy support has a small but significant effect on academic performance (effect size ranging from 0.16 in the K-12 context to 0.18 in the higher education context), a medium to large effect on intrinsic motivation (effect size ranging from 0.44 in the K-12 context to 0.30 in the higher education context), and a medium effect on academic engagement (effect size ranging from 0.37 in the K-12 context to 0.22-0.40 in the higher education context) (Okada, 2018; 2021). In addition, it has a large effect on learner's psychological need for autonomy, with an effect size of 0.50 (Okada, 2021), and associates positively with autonomous learning motivation (Ljubin-Golub et al., 2020) and with learners' personal goal set-up and agentic engagement (Benlahcene et al., 2021). Autonomy supportive practices are found to have a positive effect on learner autonomy among adults, with an effect size of 0.63 reported in the meta-analysis study of Su and Reeve (2011).

Autonomy support can be achieved through nurturing and developing inner motivational resources (e.g., personal interests, intrinsic goals, and self-endorsed values) when designing learning tasks and pitching the tasks to learners. It can also be achieved by providing explanatory rationales for the learning tasks and encouraging learners to make their own choices. Moreover, while implementing the tasks, relying on non-controlling and informational language, displaying patience in allowing self-paced learning, and acknowledging and accepting students' negative affect are also autonomy supportive (Reeve, 2016). At the core of autonomy-supportive instructional design is a respect for student perspective. Perspective taking manifests in adopting a student-focused way of organizing teaching and learning, making learning experience open to and actively embracing students' emerging interests, needs and preferences, and welcoming students' input and respecting students' way of doing things

(Reeve & Cheon, 2021). Moreover, the student focus needs to be backed up with an understanding tone, where students feel that their feelings and concerns are listened to and instructional adjustments are made to cater to their wants and preferences (Reeve, 2016). Reeve and Cheon (2021) argued that the ultimate goals of autonomy-supportive practices are twofold: 1) to support intrinsic motivation for learning and 2) to support learner internalization of the instructional expectations and arrangements. They further elaborated on some autonomy-satisfying design elements that could help achieve these two goals.

Offering choices that cater to students' thinking and wanting

Offering choice is the primary way to achieve autonomy satisfaction. Choices give learners the sense that behaviors originate from within themselves, and their interests, goals, and preferences play a role in determining the course of action. However, not all choices are autonomy supportive. Only the motivating and meaningful choices that nurture inner motivational resources, that is, choices that respect the students' perspective, are supportive of autonomy (Reeve & Cheon, 2021). To offer choices that respect this student perspective, various means to elicit students' thinking and wanting need to be built in when designing learning experience. Ongoing formative assessments are needed to assess students' reactions to, and invitations should be extended to students for suggestions on learning arrangements that could support individual learning. Moreover, it is necessary to involve students in decisions on optional content and assignment types and deadlines, learning pace and time to devote to each topic, and/or preferences regarding feedback (Huggins, 2012).

Autonomy-supportive choices should also provide authentic opportunities for learners to pursue their own interests and personal goals (Huggins, 2012; Reeve & Cheon, 2021). Interest optimizes self-regulatory resources and sustains continued investment in a behavior. Including materials and activities that are interesting to the students, directing students to venues and resource pools where they can find interesting things to explore and inviting learners to pursue personal interests are important design considerations. The emphasis on respecting personal interests is echoed among learner autonomy scholars. For instance, Benson (2016) highlighted that the exercise of choice and decision-making is key to autonomy-amplifying learning experience. He underscored the importance of scaffolding learners to set self-determined goals that align with individual interests and purposes. Moreover, learners need to be guided on selecting resources and activities that can help them achieve personal learning goals. Murray (2014) also underscored the importance of providing opportunities for learners to work with materials and carry out activities that they find interesting and appropriate. Murray further added the importance of utilizing the power of imagination in learning to foster students' future selves in relation to the language and broaden their personal goals and interests.

Using autonomy-supportive language

The use of autonomy-supportive language and the display of an understanding tone are equally important in helping learners internalize and identify with the values and utility of an activity (Reeve & Cheon, 2021). Autonomy-supportive language can be achieved through providing explanatory meaningful rationales that clearly articulate the academic standards that are expected of students in the task and explicate on the importance, benefits, and personal relevance of an activity. Providing a criterion-reference assessment with a clear explanation on the assessment rubrics and proffering feedback on the assessed work would be helpful, but such support needs to gradually fade to amplify autonomy over time (Huggins, 2012). Autonomy-supportive language is also characterized by verbal discourses that empathize with and legitimatize learners' negative feelings (e.g., "some people feel frustrated when they cannot get the perfect score on the quiz and those feelings are normal") and that direct learners towards volitional behaviors (e.g., "so what can we do to make sure we can get the perfect score next time?"). Moreover, autonomy-supportive language needs to rely primarily on invitational language that encourages student initiative. It is important to avoid evaluative and judgmental discourse (e.g., "you might consider …"). In addition, gestures like giving students the time and space to work at their own pace and preferred ways of learning, and guiding students to come up with answers rather than intervening right away are all examples of displaying patience.

Including supportive structure in the design

Researchers point out that structure might also be an important and inherent element of autonomy-supportive practices, at least in some Asian contexts. For instance, through their research with Japanese elementary students on their foreign language learning experiences, Oga-Baldwin and Nakata (2015) revealed that supportive structure, specifically clarity and direction in learning, strongly influenced these students' autonomy satisfaction and engagement. They argued that supportive structure might be a form of autonomy-supportive practice, at least in the Japanese context. Teacher autonomy support works best when combined with structured guidance (Jang et al., 2010), and the combination of the two is effective in fostering self-regulation (Hospel & Galand, 2016; Su & Reeve, 2011). Cheon et al. (2020) argued for the importance of providing structure in an autonomy-supportive way, communicating clear and concrete expectations, offering step-by-step guidance on learning progress, scaffolding progress, offering help, and providing constructive feedback. They found that when Korean teachers received training on how to support autonomy, provide structure, and provide structure in an autonomy-supportive way, their students reported greater perceived autonomy support and autonomy need satisfaction.

Adopting a differential approach to design elements

Different elements of autonomy-supportive practices have differential influences on learner autonomy. Smit et al. (2019) examined the efficacy of two different forms of autonomy-supportive communication styles—autonomy-supportive language and personal choice—in a Web-based computer-tailored health communication interventions on vegetable consumption. They found that featuring choices in communication had significant positive effects on perceived autonomy support and overall evaluation of the intervention, whereas autonomy-supportive language did not. Flunger et al. (2022) examined how four types of autonomy-supportive practices—offering choice, stimulating interests, providing rationale, and accepting frustration—related to students' intrinsic motivation in math and German classes. They found that all four autonomy-supportive practices associated positively with student motivation and engagement in both subject domains. However, different autonomy-supportive practices did associate differently with different aspects of motivation. For instance, stimulating interest was found to boost intrinsic motivation, utility value, and effort investment. However, providing choices related positively to intrinsic motivation only. The researchers concluded that "teachers should draw on a wide set of strategies to yield optimal outcomes for their students" (p. 9).

Researchers further found that autonomy support varies across contexts. For instance, Tripathi et al. (2018) found that autonomy-supportive instructions increased American corporate professionals' motivation for action but decreased their Indian counterparts' motivation. Indian corporate professionals were found to be motivated more by messages that invoke obligations. Moreover, autonomy supportive elements are found to make a greater difference in self-directed learning contexts. Schweder and Raufelder (2021) found that autonomy support was significantly and positively associated with control strategies and persistence in the self-directed learning environment, but the links were not significant in the teacher-directed learning environment. These research findings hence advocate a differentiated approach to selectively incorporating design elements in response to the educational contexts and instructional foci.

Developing interventions that enhance learner autonomy with technology

Immersing learners in autonomy-amplifying learning experience is one side of the coin. Since learner autonomy is malleable, developing interventions to enhance learner autonomy is the other side of the coin in fostering a positive interaction between technology and autonomy.

Boosting self-directed learning

Bouchard's (2009) framework of self-directed learning delineates four essential aspects: the psychological aspect (learners' incentives and self-efficacy), the economic aspect (learners' appraisal of the value of the action), the pedagogical aspect (learners' selection and use of activities), and the semiotics aspect (learners' ability to evaluate, orchestrate and use of the resources). The first two aspects are the affective and motivational dimension, and the latter two are the knowledge and skill dimension.

Boosting the affective and motivational dimension

The affective and motivational dimension includes both the intention and motivation to initiate a learning behavior (i.e., the entering motivation), and sustained interest in the behavioral intention (i.e., the maintenance of intention) (Garrison, 1997). Both types of motivation rely largely on having three basic psychological needs satisfied: 1) the need for autonomy (i.e., the need to be the initiator of actions and to obtain psychological freedom); 2) the need for competence (i.e., the need to experience a sense of confidence to achieve desired goals); and 3) the need for relatedness (i.e., the need of having a close and positive relationship with others and experiencing a sense of belonging) (Deci & Ryan, 1987).

Autonomy comes from the option of setting one's learning goals and making decisions on learning content and learning trajectory. It also comes from the internalized necessity and value of the actions (Hubbard, 2004; Lai, 2018). Moreover, learners need to see the whys behind and the value of the actions (Hubbard, 2004).

Competence comes from perceived possession of the mind-set, knowledge, and skills to pursue interest-driven authentic learning activities and to deal with the ambiguities and challenges inherent in those activities, and it also comes from perceive availability of institutional, social and discursive support (Kormos & Csizér, 2014). To boost competence, there needs to be opportunities and venues for sharing stories of self-directed learning behaviors from peers, and the inclusion of scaffolding mechanisms and buddy systems that provide support on resource and time management, cognitive and metacognitive management, and social and emotional management (Kizilcec, Pérez-Sanagustín & Maldonado, 2017; Saadatmand & Kumpulainen, 2012).

Relatedness comes from the feeling of being affiliated with a group of people who share common interests and who work together on common goals. To strengthen relatedness, it is important to establish communities of learners based on similar needs, interests, and learning preferences, and engage them to share resources and strategies and lend social and emotional support to one another (Littlejohn et al., 2016). Relatedness can also be enhanced through receiving informational feedback and positive regard from significant others who support learner autonomy, such as teachers, parents, and classmates (Lou et al., 2018).

Enhancing the knowledge and skill dimension

The knowledge and skill dimension involves both the resource component and the strategy component that are needed for autonomous language learning with technology (Lai, 2018).

Knowledge about online resources and how to use these resources effectively for learning do not come naturally to learners. Sharing information on the resources and providing explicit training on how various technological resources could be used effectively for language learning are much needed (Hubbard, 2013; Lai, Shum & Tian, 2016; Steel & Levy, 2013). Resources are multidimensional, including material resources (i.e., online tools and platforms), mental resources (i.e., technological and social skills and knowledge), social resources (i.e., social ties and relationships), cultural and discursive resources (i.e., beliefs and shared mentalities related to the behaviors), and temporal resources (i.e., time available for the behaviors) (Van Dijk, 2005). To obtain knowledge and skills related to the resource component, students need an understanding of the affordances of different online resources for language learning, the selection criteria for online resources, and the guiding principles of quality out-of-class learning experience (Beckman, Bennett & Lockyer, 2014; Lai et al., 2018; Lai et al., 2022). Students also need social and emotional support from learning communities, where they can receive information on resources obtained from various venues and ways to manage the resources (Ma, 2017).

The strategy component includes both cognitive and metacognitive strategies and social and communication strategies (Lawrence, 2013). The cognitive and metacognitive strategies contain both generic self-regulation skills and the specific skills of using technology for language learning (Benson, 2013; Lai, 2013). Generic self-regulation skills include the monitoring of various cognitive and metacognitive factor (goal setting, strategic planning, task appraisal, evaluation, and reflection), behavioral factor (effort management and help seeking), affective factor (self-efficacy, anxiety management) and environment factor (time and environment management, peer learning) at different phases of learning (Littlejohn et al., 2016; Pintrich, 2000). Language learning-specific skills include the abilities to comprehend and acquire language from authentic language exposure and experience, to view and interact with resources strategically to optimize incidental language learning (Hubbard, 2013; Reinders & White, 2010). These skills could be developed through scaffolding mechanisms like goal lists, templates and prompts, examples of strategy utilization, reflective assessments with metacognitive questions and feedback (Bernacki, Aguilar & Byrnes, 2011).

Strengthening language learning autonomy

Littlewood (1997) underscored the development of three aspects of language learning autonomy: 1) Autonomy as a learner, a dimension that highlights learners' control over the learning process and their flexible use of personal learning strategies. 2) Autonomy as a communicator, a dimension that underscores learners' capacity to engage in effective and creative language use. 3) Autonomy as a person, a dimension that values learners' capacity to use language to achieve personal autonomy in the creation of personal learning contexts and the expression of personal meanings.

Enhancing autonomy as a language learner – control over the learning process

Interventions on enhancing learner autonomy over the learning process have predominantly focused on increasing learners' self-regulation abilities. These interventions aim to make learners meta-cognitively, motivationally, and behaviorally active agents in the learning process. Self-regulated learning interventions have been found to have a moderate positive effect on self-regulation capacity of both K-12 students and university students, ranging from 0.32 to 0.68 as reported in several meta-analysis studies (Dignath & Büttner, 2008; Jasen et al., 2019; Theobald, 2021). Interventions have a greater effect on younger children and learners with low self-regulatory resources. Theobald (2021) further revealed that the effects of training on metacognitive strategies (planning, monitoring, reflection etc.) and resource management strategies (attention control, effort and persistence, time management and motivation regulation) were slightly larger than training on motivational outcomes (self-efficacy and value beliefs) and cognitive strategies (such as organization, elaboration, rehearsal strategies), 0.40 and 0.39 respectively in the former and 0.35 and 0.32 respectively in the latter. Examining the effects of self-regulated learning strategy training on second language learning, Ardasheva and colleagues (2017) reported a rather large effect on second language learning outcomes (0.8) and on self-regulated learning (0.9). Thus, interventions on self-regulated learning have the potential to enhance learner autonomy in the learning process.

According to Theobald (2021), existing literature has identified three types of training programs in enhancing self-regulated learning: feedback, cooperative learning, and learning protocols. The three types of training programs have differential effects. Feedback has larger effects on meta-cognitive strategies, resource management strategies, and motivational outcomes, such as self-efficacy and value beliefs. Cooperative learning has a greater effect on cognitive and metacognitive strategy use. And the effects of the provision of learning protocols are more salient on resource management strategies. In addition to the three types, explicit modeling and training is also an important strategy to enhance learner control over the learning process.

Explicit modeling and training on self-regulated learning

Explicit modeling and training on self-regulated learning can target discipline generic regulation strategies and/or discipline specific regulation strategies. Both are found to be beneficial. For instance, Luo (2020) supplemented her Spanish classes with a MOOC course that focused on developing learners' self-regulation in learning in general. The MOOC course focused on metacognitive and cognitive strategies in learning, including strategies against procrastination and cramming, spaced repetitions, and chunking tasks. The researcher found that receiving training on these discipline generic regulation strategies did enhance students' self-directed Spanish learning with online resources. García Botero et al. (2021) examined the effects of self-regulation training on a group of undergraduate language learners' self-directed use of Duolingo for French learning. For one group, they gave an introductory lesson on how to use the Duolingo application. For the other group, they included some explanations on self-regulation and its sub processes in learning and on how the sub processes were reflected in the Duolingo features and how these features could be utilized. This group of students also received reminder emails to complete weekly learning goals in the first few weeks. The group who received the self-regulation training were found to outperform their peers who did not receive self-regulation training on engagement in self-directed use of Duolingo beyond the classroom.

Other studies have examined the effects of discipline-specific training on learner's autonomous interaction with different technological resources. For instance, Gagen-Lanning (2015) trained a group of university ESL learners on cognitive and metacognitive strategies they could use when using TED talk videos for second language listening. The researcher found that, after the training, learners used more metacognitive strategies, such as pausing and rewinding, when interacting with TED talk videos, and that their ability to comprehend the videos also increased. Cross (2014) reported a case study where an advanced Japanese adult English language learner was guided, via weekly reflection meetings, on using meta-textual skills and metacognitive strategies when listening to podcasts for independent listening development outside the classroom. The learner's journal entries over the nine-week intervention indicated that her metacognitive capacities to interact with out-of-class podcast resources increased over time. Rashid et al. (2021) adopted Romeo and Hubbard's (2010) training framework and developed an eight-week training for a group of first-year undergraduate English language learners on the technical, pedagogical, and strategic aspects of mobile blog use outside the classroom. The researcher found that the training helped learners develop positive attitudes towards using personal blogs on smartphones to enhance English writing skills, and the quality of their writing increased over time too. Interventions have also been implemented to enhance students' self-directed language learning with technology beyond the classroom. For instance, Lai, Shum, and Tian (2016) conducted a 12-week training program that targeted at undergraduate English language learners' willingness and capacities to engage in out-of-class language learning with technological resources. Pedagogical rationales, resource selection strategies, and tactics for effective use of technological resources for language learning were weaved into the training that was structured around the self-regulation feedback loop of forethought, performance, and reflection. As a result of the training, students reported greater engagement in self-initiated out-of-class use of technology for language learning. They also reported more positive attitudes towards and greater confidence in making use of technological resources for language learning on their own.

Self-regulated learning prompts and feedback

Prompts and feedback involve the provision of information on goals, current performance, remedial action suggestions, and strategic hints on the monitoring and adjustment of learning strategies. Prompts and feedback can be embedded within technological platforms as fixed or adaptive scaffolds and can also be provided by teachers in learning advising sessions.

Platform embedded prompts and feedback. Bell (2017) identified that the delivery of self-regulated learning scaffolds can take three forms: 1) prompting strategies, 2) guiding strategies, and 3) cultivating strategies. Prompting strategies aim at activating self-regulation mechanisms during learning. Prompting strategies involve asking students to respond to given metacognitive prompting questions about self-regulatory activities (e.g., goals; learning strategies; progress towards goals) at specified intervals during task performance. Such strategies are found to work more effectively when learning is to take place for an extended period and when students have repeated exposure to prompts. Guiding strategies focus on augmenting learners' self-regulatory activity by providing prescriptive or evaluative information to guide learners' attention and effort allocation during task performance. Guiding strategies are often in the form of metacognitive scaffolding agents or templates that provide fixed or adaptive guidance on different aspects of the learning process prior to, during, or after task performance. Examples of adaptive guidance would be to provide learners with diagnostic and evaluative information on learner self-evaluation against specified performance standards and suggest remedial actions to help learners calibrate their progress. Cultivating strategies aim to advance learners' capacity to engage in self-regulated learning and often involve metacognitive strategy instruction either tailored to a specific learning context or targeting generic self-regulatory skills. Using self-questioning (e.g., "Are we getting closer to my goal?,"

"Why am I doing this?") to monitor one's performance is a common technique used. Hannafin and colleagues (1999) further categorized different types of self-regulated learning scaffolds regarding functionality: conceptual scaffolds (i.e., guidance on what to considered for a pre-defined problem), metacognitive scaffolds (i.e., guidance on the self-regulation of the problem-solving process), procedural scaffolds (i.e., guidance on how to use resources or perform tasks) and strategic scaffolds (i.e., guidance on techniques, methods or solution paths).

Scaffolds can be domain-general or domain-specific. In a meta-analysis study on self-regulated scaffolds, Zheng (2016) found that the use of both domain-specific and domain-general scaffolds generated a much greater effect than either domain-specific or domain-general only. Zheng further found that the provision of scaffolds that support the entire process of SRL generated greater effects than scaffolds that target individual SRL skills only. Yen et al. (2018) conceptualized a self-regulated digital learning framework. They proposed using a combination of domain-general and domain-specific prompts and feedback to support planning, monitoring, evaluating, applying strategies, and setting standards in the digital learning environments. In their framework, learning plans, learning records, and assessment scaffolds are to support domain-general self-regulation. Learning plan prompts goal setting and timetable scheduling, records and sharing remind learners of sub-learning goals and procedures, and assessment engages learners in confidence rating and reflection on the learning process and learning outcomes in reference to the standards/rubrics. Visualization scaffolds, prompts and pedagogical agents deliver domain-specific self-regulation. Visualization scaffolds use goal trees or procedural map to visualize the set of goals and procedures for planning and monitoring. Both fixed and adaptive prompts of rationales and directions, strategies and evaluation criteria can be delivered at appropriate moments. Pedagogical agents can be used to demonstrate SRL skills and provide pre-set or adaptive feedback to support SRL.

Existing literature contains varied examples of embedding prompts and feedback in technological platforms. Azevedo and Witherspoon (2009) shared an example of how scaffolds can be embedded in an online learning platform about the human circulatory system. An adaptive hypermedia-based ITS, MetaTutor, was embedded in the platform to detect, model and foster students' SRL during the learning process. MetaTutor contains four pedagogical agents, each on one aspect of SRL: Gavin the Guide, Pam the Planner, Sam the Strategizer, and Mary the Monitor. These agents provide feedback and scaffolding to enhance students' use of relevant SRL strategies during learning. Azevedo et al. (2019) further pointed out that adaptive and personalized feedback can be provided based on more sophisticated multimodal multichannel data collected in the learning process, such as eye-tracking data, videos of facial expressions of emotions, time-stamped log-file data, and electrodermal activity measured with wearable biosensors. Examples of using prompts and feedback on online language learning platforms also abound. For instance, Chen et al. (2014) embedded a self-monitor table menu in an online reading system. Learners were instructed to respond to the table menu, when first logging into the system, to schedule learning duration and learning units and set goals for performance, degree of effort and expected learning activities. In addition, the interface also provided a self-regulated radar plot with constantly updated information on learning duration, effort, reading rate, concentration level and understanding level.

Self-regulated learning scaffolds are found to benefit learning. Chang (2010) saw an increase in learners' motivation and general English proficiency as a result of embedding a self-monitoring strategy into the digital learning resources of a course. In a qualitative study, Andrade and Bunker (2010) observed noticeable improvements in L2 writing because of self-regulatory strategies, such as tracking their use of time. Li et al. (2021) designed a self-directed online reading environment that contained an e-book reader and an associated GOAL system. Learners' reading logs in the e-book reader were automatically synchronized in the GOAL system. Based on the collected data, SRL scaffolds were provided to students to help them take initiatives in setting SMART goals, monitoring the reading progress, and reflecting on strategy use. The researchers further found that self-directed learning (SDL) ability moderated the efficacy of the platform with SRL scaffolds: the Japanese junior high school EFL learners who perceived themselves as possessing high SDL abilities demonstrated significantly greater reading engagement and greater SDL behaviors especially in planning and monitoring. Researchers further found that the timing of the prompts also makes a difference. For instance, Thillmann et al. (2009) found that providing prompts during learning had a greater effect on learning than presenting the same prompts before the learning process started. Thus, self-regulation training interwoven into learning might be more beneficial (Bernacki et al., 2011).

Teacher-delivered prompts and feedback. Language advising is a process of helping learners develop language learner autonomy through support and feedback from human teachers. It involves one-on-one co-constructed supportive dialogues with language learners that start with learners' goals, interests and learning context and aim at enhancing learner autonomy (Karlsson, 2012; Kato & Mynard, 2016). The key focus is to promote deep-level reflective thinking on themselves as language learners and users and on their language process and progress. The dialogue revolves around three kinds of analysis: analysis of the learning content, analysis of the learning process and analysis of the premise that might lead to the reshaping of one's existing beliefs or assumptions (Mynard & Kato, 2022).

The purpose of language advising is to help learners develop conscious control over how they learn and achieve personal transformation in terms of challenging one's existing beliefs about learning (Kato & Mynard, 2016). According to Mynard and Kato (2022), advising sessions have both the pedagogical aim and the affective aim. The pedagogical aim is to help learners create and follow a self-determined learning plan. To achieve this aim, Kato and Mynard (2016) proposed four types of activities that are essential. One type of activity is to guide students to set their learning goals through engaging them to explore their motivations, dreams, and interests. Another type of activity is to guide students to discover and experiment with different resources and strategies that can help them achieve their learning goals. Still another type is to guide students on different ways to evaluate their learning gains. And the last type of activity is to guide the students to reflect on the learning process. The affective aim is to enhance learners' awareness of factors that influence motivation and affect and create action plans to manage motivation and affective factors (Yamashita, 2015). Affect management skills can be developed through completing low-risk challenges to help learners overcome language anxiety in a learning scenario, or through using interventions that incorporate positive emotions into learning (Mynard, 2020).

Advising may take different forms: real-time face-to-face or online individual advising sessions; asynchronous advising through messaging; or written feedback and guided reflection questions on learning journals (Mozzon-McPherson & Tassinari, 2020). Moreover, different tools can be used to activate and support the reflective process, including questionnaires, visuals, activity sheets, and games. Mynard (2020) introduced three types of tools: 1) cognitive tools (e.g., self-diagnostic tests or questionnaires on motivation, confidence or affect) that help learners see their progress towards goals and understand their learning process; 2) theoretical tools that enhance learners' knowledge of strategies and ways of learning and developing different language and linguistic skills and strategies to manage one's affect; and 3) practical tools, including plans, diaries, record sheets, and tools to share ideas and strategies with others. Kato and Mynard (2016) further pointed out that, although language advising is often provided by teachers, it may have additional value when provided by peers. According to them, peer advising could boost learners' self-coaching skills by providing advice and guidance on peers.

Self-regulated learning protocols

Learning protocols are the use of learning diaries, goal sheets, study logs and portfolios to engage students in regular self-evaluative reports on their use of self-regulated learning strategies. Learning protocols contribute to self-regulated learning primarily through enhancing self-monitoring techniques and are often used as tools in advising sessions. The protocols can be implemented in various forms.

Diary. Daily diary is a frequently used form. The use of daily diaries has been found to increase learners' self-regulation, self-efficacy and meta-cognitive skills and attitude (Dignath-van Ewijk et al., 2015). Broadbent et al. (2020) compared the effects of mobile-app learning diaries and online training on self-regulated learning. In the mobile app-based learning diary condition, prior to a study session, learners were prompted to plan the SRL strategies, such as planning, goal setting, task analysis, motivation and affect levels. They were prompted again to report on their actual use of SRL strategies during the session and again after the session. The online training condition consisted of three training sessions that was structured according to Zimmerman's forethought-performance-reflection model: the training on setting SMART goals during the Forethought phase, the training on strategies to deal with distractions, procrastination and other cognitive and metacognitive strategies at the Performance phase, and the training on attribution, self-motivation and rewarding in the Reflection phase. The researchers found that mobile app-based diary condition alone did not significantly outperform the control condition on the perception of SRL and actual SRL use. Rather, it was the combined use of mobile app-based diary and online training that was superior in effecting changes in both intended SRL use and actual SRL use and in inducing positive affect during learning.

Checklists. Learning protocols can also be provided in the form of checklists and question lists. Checklists engage learners to self-assess the quality of their learning processes. Self-assessment, such as performance log, self-assessment checklists, scripts, and questionnaires, was found to not only have a positive effect on self-regulated learning, with an effect size of 0.23, but also have a medium effect on inhibiting self-regulatory actions that are detrimental to learning (Panadero, Jonsson and Botella's metanalysis, 2017). Fukuda and colleagues (2019) developed an intervention that relied on self-questioning to enhance learners' self-coaching skills. The self-questioning protocol was developed based on Homma and Matsuse's WISDOM model. WISDOM model includes six components, including Will (set up concrete learning goals), Image (develop a concrete image of themselves as competent language users), Source (reflect on sources of motivation and success), Drive (devise a learning plan based on will, image, and source), Operation (consider concrete steps to carry out learning plan) and Maintenance (monitor and reflect on the learning process). Students worked on activities around one component of the WISDOM model for the first half of the class and then practiced self-questioning on the component and discussed with peers for the second half of the class. In addition, learners filled out weekly self-coaching skill worksheets with self-questions. The questions prompted learners to plan learning goals, learning activities to reach the goals, activities to be done each day, learning resources, motivation maintenance plans, progress assessment plans, potential sources of help, learning environment plan and motivational quote. The researchers found that developing students' self-coaching skills through filling out self-questioning worksheets helped to increase their Japanese university students' out-of-class English study time. Shelton-Strong (2018) engaged his Japanese university EFL learners to complete a self-assessment checklist on participation and communication, and then fill out subsequent personal learning goal worksheets. He found that building in mechanisms of self-assessment and personal learning goal setup enhanced autonomy in learning.

E-portfolio. E-portfolio is a method that has been adopted in language education to foster learner autonomy. E-portfolio engages students in formulating learning goals, self-assessing performance, and selecting future tasks. E-portfolio is found to enhance self-directed learning skills (Beckers et al., 2016). Beckers and colleagues (2016) further underscored that how e-portfolio is used is essential. E-portfolio was found to be most effective when it is integrated into the educational routine, and when regular coaching from teachers, feedback on past performance and guidance on future performance were available. The researchers further revealed that the design of e-portfolio also determined its effect. Thus, functionalities that support goal setting, task analysis, plan implementation and self-evaluation, and the mechanism of gradual fading of support and scaffolds need to be built in to optimize the effects of e-portfolio.

Self-regulation through cooperative learning

Cooperative learning involves pair or group work, where students share responsibilities, ideas, and thoughts. Hadwin and Oshige (2011) presented the socio-cognitive model of self-regulation, which argues that self-regulation originates in others, and that social context is at the core of the regulation process. In collaborative learning situations, two collective levels of regulation might be at play that facilitate self-regulated learning: Individuals may gradually appropriate self-regulated learning through collective sharing of regulatory resources and strategies on cognitions, emotions, behaviors and motivations, namely co-regulation, and through collectively regulating joint activities to achieve shared goals, namely socially shared regulation. Thus, collaborative work has the potential to enhance individuals' self-regulation skills. For instance, Li et al. (2021) examined the nature of social regulation mechanisms during a wiki-supported literature circle activity. They found that undergraduate EFL learners actively engaged in social regulation, with a greater proportion of shared regulation than co-regulation. Both co-regulation and shared regulation correlated positively with learners' engagement in the activity. However, they further pointed out that social regulation focused more on task understanding and time management, but not much on content-related regulation, which is key to the quality of collaborative work. Thus, support is needed to enhance the occurrence of and quality of social regulation in collaborative learning situations. Moreover, Sato (2020) compared the performance of a group of Chilean high school EFL learners' performance during communicative tasks across three conditions: paired communicative tasks with metacognitive instruction on collaborative interaction; paired communicative tasks only; and no paired communicative tasks. Training on three collaborative strategies was provided: appeal for help, clarification requests, and comprehension checks. The researcher found that students who received the training exhibited significantly greater use of relevant interactional strategies during task completion than those who did not receive the training.

To enhance social regulation during collaborative work, external collaborative regulation tools, such as group awareness and collaboration scripts, are essential.

Group awareness tools. Group awareness is to inform learners of group members' learning activities through visual display. Theophilou et al. (2021) proposed three types of group awareness: behavioral awareness (i.e., information about group members' performance and plan), cognitive awareness (i.e., knowledge, beliefs, and goals of group members), and social awareness (i.e., awareness of what group members are doing and act accordingly). Tracking and visualizing group members' performance has often been employed to support social comparison and collective learning. For instance, Davis et al. (2016) developed a learning tracker prototype widget that visualizes learners' own behaviors and successful learners' behaviors to enhance learners' self-regulation in MOOC. Lin et al. (2016) incorporated group awareness tools that raised learners' awareness of group members' learning goals and participation in training tasks and learning activities, their help-seeking behaviors, and their learning progress. They also included peer assistance tools that provided mechanisms for learners to motivate each other, seek help from team members and facilitate members who were facing learning barriers. The researchers found that students who had access to the group awareness and peer assistance tools performed significantly better in goal setting, planning, self-assessment and completion of the plans. These students also showed significantly greater improvement in overall SRL than those who did not have access to these scaffolds. Moreover, the scaffolds were found to be especially beneficial to low-SRL students.

Collaboration scripts. Collaboration scripts are another useful strategy to enhance social regulation and concomitant self-directed learning. For instance, Chen and Chiu (2016) explored the effects of embedding collaboration scripts in a multi-touch learning platform to facilitate collaborative work that was structured around the procedure of individual work, intragroup discussion, and subsequent intergroup sharing and feedback. The collaboration scripts prompted students to explain their ideas to partners and engage in discussions through reciprocal questioning. The researchers found that collaboration scripts had a significant effect on elementary school students' use of planning strategies. Students also exhibited a high level of control in learning. In addition, Rasheed and colleagues (2020) found that collaboration scripts that guide groups to value each members' contribution to encourage co-dependence and set limits on the discussion forum posts to reduce dominant behaviors from a single person helped facilitate group dynamic and promote prosocial behaviors.

In all, different SRL training mechanisms are facilitative of learner autonomy (Panadero et al., 2017; Theobald, 2021). The combined use of different training mechanisms yields the most optimal results, as evidenced in Boradbent and colleagues' (2020) study on mobile app-based diary and online training. Bannert and Reimann (2012) also found that the combination of a short training on SRL with SRL prompts embedded in the hypermedia environment had a greater effect than having access to SRL prompts only.

Enhancing autonomy as a language user – control over communication process

Illés (2012) pointed out that existing learner autonomy interventions have predominantly focused on equipping learners with the metacognition and metalanguage necessary for controlling learning process and argued that such interventions are insufficient to keep language learners abreast of the wide spread of language use in daily life and in informal learning contexts. She advocated greater attention to the communication process so as to foster "competent language users who can successfully cope with the demands of real-life communication under their own initiative" (p. 509) and who can utilize the various resources at disposal effectively and creatively for varied language use purposes.

To help learners assume the roles as competent language users, Illés (2012) proposed engaging learners in problem-solving tasks, exposing them to different varieties of the target language, and creating conditions for active participation in meaning-making and decision-making in language use through literature interpretation and translation or creative language use tasks such as designing blogs or websites. Godwin-Jones (2019) further stressed the importance of establishing and facilitating learners' lifelong personal connection with the language and supporting them to immerse in "interactions with specific target language communities with shared interests, passions, or professional or personal aspirations" (p. 16). Ushioda (2011) highlighted the significance of encouraging and supporting students to leverage his/her "transportable identities (e.g., as football fan, amateur photographers, and film buff)" (p. 204) and immerse themselves in out-of-class language use to perform these identities in the target language.

In addition to creating varied experiences of personally meaningful language use, Illés (2012) further stressed that essential skills need to be developed to support learners' identity as competent language users. According to her, the essential skills needed are "the ability to cope with the linguistic and schematic diversity, the fluidity, and the increased demand for negotiation that interaction in international contexts of use presents" (p. 509).

Developing media and information literacy

Media and information literacy is essential to meaningful engagement with media and information, and learners need to be equipped with relevant communication and media literacy before they can reap the benefits of online spaces for language learning (Sockett and Toffoli, 2012).

According to UNESCO Media and Information Literacy Curriculum for Teachers, media and information literacy include six components: 1) understanding the social roles of media and information; 2) understanding media content and uses; 3) effective information retrieval; 4) critical evaluation of information and its sources; 5) flexible and coordinated use of new and traditional media; and 6) understanding the socio-cultural context of media content. The Digital Competence Framework from the European Commission (DigComp 2.0) further highlighted the importance of using media and information for social participation, for self-empowerment and participatory citizenship, and featured safe use of information and media and the use of media and information for problem solving (Vuorikari et al., 2016). The most recent framework, the UNESCO DLGF framework, underscores seven competence areas: 1) the operation of digital devices and software; 2) the searching, filtering, evaluation and management of data, information and digital content; 3) effective communication and collaboration through digital technologies; 4) the development, remix and integration of digital contents; 5) the protection of data and privacy, social well-being and inclusion and environment; 6) the use of technological resources for problem solving; and 7) the use of digital technologies in one's professional field. Fedorov and Mikhaleva (2020) further highlighted the importance of sensitivity to cultural variations in information and media practices.

Existing literature has also suggested some important features of effective pedagogies for the development of media and information literacy among children and adolescents, namely collaborative, creative, and multimodal media production practices plus analytic, reflective and inquiry practices (Rasi et al., 2019). Researchers advocate engaging learners to analyze media texts of different types and genres and creating their own media texts (Fedorov & Mikhaleva, 2020). Brocca et al. (2020) conceptualized a didactic project that provide direct instructions on pragmalinguistic knowledge and support students to apply it to detect implicit messages in online texts. They argued that teaching lexico-grammatical structures for implicit encoding of meaning in sentences and presupposition and implicature features in different text types may enhance learners' ability to critically read information online.

Boosting social media literacy

Social media is a low-risk community-based participatory and socialization place for learners to perform their identity as competent language users. Social media affords opportunities to collaborate with like-minded peers in interest-based communities and venues to obtain crowd-sourced information in the target language. But at the same time, social media may incur potentially negative or harmful experiences, such as cyber bullying, information overload, and credibility of information from anonymous sources (Yeh & Swinehart, 2020). Thus, social media literacies are essential to safeguard learners' equal and successful participation in these environments (Hobbs, 2011; Jenkins et al., 2006), which does not come naturally with experience and needs to be supported with training (Yeh & Swinehart, 2020).

Vanwynsberghe and colleagues (2015) categorized two types of social media literacy: technical competence (the competence related to access, creation, navigation, organization and sharing of social media content), and cognitive competence (the competence related to the comprehension, evaluation, and critical analysis of social media content). Yeh and Swinehart (2020) further identified the third dimension of competence, i.e., sociocultural pragmatics of online environments (how language, interaction, and behavior changes in response to social and cultural contexts).

Interventions on social media literacy have started to emerge in the current literature. For instance, Taibi et al. (2020) shared initiatives of building functionalities on an innovative open-source social media platform, PixelFed, to help students become aware of working mechanisms behind social media—the use of content filter mechanisms in particular—with artificial intelligence algorithms so that students can use information on social media critically. Blattner and Fiori (2011) assigned a group of intermediate Spanish language learners to locate three Facebook groups whose content corresponded with the course themes related to Spanish culture. In addition to locating the groups, the learners were also asked to analyze the characteristics of greetings, leave-takings, and vocabulary selection on these groups to understand language use and identify culture elements. They found that students enhanced their sociopragmatic competence as a result of this awareness-raising task. Similarly, Pritchard (2013) implemented a learner preparation program that focused on functions of Facebook and use norms and strategies when using Facebook for language learning. The intervention consisted of four initial training sessions reinforced by repeated reminders. The researcher found that the intervention helped raise learners' awareness of the language learning potential of Facebook and enhanced their use of Facebook for communication and social capital development but failed to enhance their effective language learning strategies.

Supporting translanguaging and trans-semiotizing practices

Talking about the impact of multilingualism on learner autonomy, Benson and Lamb (2020) highlighted the importance of developing learners' flexible and coordinated use of the multiple linguistic and semiotic resources they have at disposal for meaning conveyance and identity projection. Benson and Lamb (2020) further stressed the importance of awareness: "Autonomy may be less about controlling learning processes and more about being aware of learning resources in the environment and being able to use those resources productively" (p. 83). To support this aspect of autonomy, Benson and Lamb advocated teachers' role in helping students become "aware of their plurilingual repertoires as a resource" (p. 84) and "learn how to utilize their own internal plurilingual resources, through learning to reflect on, analyze, hypothesize, test, and develop competence and confidence" (p. 85). Thus, immersing learners in multiliteracy and translanguaging and trans-semiotizing practices and engaging them in critical analysis of the practices are essential to supporting competent language use in online spaces.

Different initiatives have been reported in the existing literature. For instance, Fuchs et al. (2012) assigned various tasks to their participants, such as analyzing how modes featured on a web resource of their choice convey information and contrasting the modes across cultural contexts, collaborating on creating a joint multimodal product, and using technology tools for intercultural task design. They found that these experiential and exploratory practices helped enhance the participants' understanding of multimodal communicative competence. Similarly, Guth and Helm (2012) engaged Germany-Italy tele-collaborative partners in comparative analysis of cultural artefacts, such as parallel texts, class responses to questionnaires or the same news story in different online resources, and in co-creation of digital intercultural collage of images that represent a global citizen and intercultural communicator. They found that such tasks not only developed the participants' foreign language skills but also skills that are necessary for successful participation and collaboration in the online world. Yeh (2018) introduced the language learning affordances of a set of popular multimedia tools to a group of advanced EFL university students and engaged them to produce a digital multimodal video as the final project. Composing multimodal artifacts collaboratively was found to enhance students' awareness and grasp of how different modes might interplay with each other for meaning construction and how these varied semiotic resources could be combined to represent the cultural features they chose to present.

Enhancing autonomy as a person – autonomy for transformation

Jiménez Raya et al. (2017) defined learner autonomy as "the competence to develop as a self-determined, socially responsible and critically aware participant in (and beyond) educational environments, within a vision of education as (inter)personal empowerment and social transformation" (p. 17). This definition highlights learners' self-direction in learning and the utilization of plurilingual repertoires for personal and social good. These two dimensions align with Littlewood's (1997) concept of autonomy as a person, which entails learners' active engagement with language(s) for personal expression and social participation and active engagement in creating personal language learning contexts.

Supporting the construction of plurilingual repertoires – the experience dimension

To construct plurilingual repertoires for active engagement with language (s) for personal and social empowerment, learners need to first of all have opportunities to experience different languages. Benson and Lamb (2020) shared a high school experimental program that focused on enhancing learner autonomy through strengthening "the ideas of fluidity and choice" (p. 78). Students were first given 4-month taster programs on a variety of languages plus language awareness lessons on language diversity. They then selected a modern language to study. They were also given the opportunity to add a second modern language one year later. Through expanding learners' experience with different languages, they aim at enhancing learners' linguistic choices and helping them develop plurilingual repertoires.

In addition to helping learners make informed and flexible decisions on linguistic choices, it is equally important to "enable learners to become lifelong language learners with the knowledge, skills, and confidence to tackle any language they may find themselves needing or wanting to learn in the future" is essential (Benson & Lamb, 2020, p. 86). Benson and Lamb further shared an initiative that aimed to support learners' self-directed pursuit of multilingual repertoire. Under this initiative, learners were guided to choose a language they wished to learn, elaborate on the justification for learning the language, identify manageable targets in response to personal need, and locate resources and monitor their learning process. The teacher supported learners in compiling a learning portfolio to facilitate their learning process. Making the learning process explicit for students and raising their metacognitive awareness may help strengthen learners' capacities to construct plurilingual repertoires.

Supporting the construction of plurilingual repertoires – the identity dimension

Learners' self-concept and identity are critical to the construction of multilingual repertoires. When learners internalize a language as part of their future selves and visualize themselves as a future user of the language, their motivation for learning the language would get boosted (Munezane, 2013). Murray (2017) argued that, when learners don't perceive the language as part of their future, limited autonomous investment in the language is going to take place. He hence advocated supporting learners' imagination and identity construction in relation to target language(s). Thus, the starting point of learner autonomy is students' identities, and developing students' future selves in relation to the language(s) facilitates motivation and metacognitive development.

Fisher et al. (2020) argued that multilingual identity, i.e., the understanding of oneself as users of more than one language, is important. Multilingual identity boosts learners' effort investment in learning multiple languages and maintaining multilinguistic repertoires and enhances social cohesion in the mobile and diverse communities. An ideal multilingual self may enhance the strength of ideal L2 self in a language, add extra motivational energy to learning the language, and help resolve the inherent competitions and tensions among ideal L2 selves in multiple languages (Henry, 2017). Seeding an all-embracing multilingual identity in adolescence may provide the basis for developing the self-concept as a learner and user of languages.

Henry (2017) construed that, to support the development of multilingual identity, interventions should guide students to visualize oneself as being or becoming a multilingual in local and global contexts, explore being a multilingual in the wider society, and experience the critical and creative use of language resources in translanguaging. Forbes et al. (2021) proposed that three dimensions underlie multilingual identity – "learners' *experiences* of languages and language learning, their *evaluations* of languages and of themselves as language learners (and, by extension, others' evaluations of languages) and, by their *emotions* relating to language learning" (p. 435). They argued that evaluation and emotions are most likely to change under classroom interventions. Fisher et al. (2020) further proposed a framework of the participative construction of multilingual identity that engages learners "in the active and conscious process of considering their linguistic and multilingual identities and … become aware of the possibility of change in relation to these identifications" (p. 459). This framework consists of four stages. Stage 1 is to develop sociolinguistic knowledge and awareness of linguistic identities through engaging learners in meta-linguistic discussions on concepts like language, dialect, language varieties, linguistic landscapes in the world and in one's communities, and the meaning of "bilingual"/"multilingual." Learners are expected to develop an understanding of their own linguistic repertoires and those of people around them at this stage. Stage 2 focuses on the dialogic engagement around multilingual identity through reflection and knowledge building to reach an understanding of what multilingualism means for foreign language learning. Then the teacher guides students to relate the issue of multilingualism to oneself by reflecting on what this means for him/her and how the understanding may change their thinking and action. Stage 3 engages learners to re-conceptualize their identities, making explicit decisions to identify with specific languages or dialects as part of their linguistic repertoire. Stage 4 is to engage learners to contemplate changes in their future self possibilities and the concomitant time and effort investment in learning the language(s). Forbes et al. (2021) conducted an intervention study at secondary schools in England with the framework. They developed an identity-oriented pedagogy for language classroom based on the framework, which included three key elements: 1) cultivate learners' knowledge about the cognitive and social benefits of multilingualism; 2) raise learners' awareness of how multilingualism interacts with identity; and 3) encourage reflexivity and personal reflection. Intervention lessons on a range of multilingualism topics, including languages in different contexts and relationship of culture and language, with relevant materials and tasks in the target language were developed. Two intervention conditions were developed: in one condition, reflectiveness and reflexivity were encouraged through engaging learners to consider how the knowledge presented in these materials related to themselves as users and learners of multiple languages; in the other condition, they simply studied the materials. The researchers found that learners who received intervention on identity-focused activities that encouraged reflection and reflexivity showed significantly greater change in their multilingual identity than those who only studied the materials about multilingualism and those who did not receive any intervention at all.

Supporting the construction of personal learning contexts

Self-directed learning, especially in technology-mediated informal learning contexts, involves initiating and designing a personalized learning environment and trajectory and managing the learning process (Morris, 2019; Saks & Leijen, 2014). White and Bown (2020) proposed an informed consumer approach that aims at helping language learners to become informed consumers who play a proactive role in navigating and constructing personalized language learning ecology. The informed consumer approach highlights developing the framework and metalanguage of optimal language learning, immersing students in experimentation with different resources and choices, engaging students in critical evaluation of different language learning choices and opportunities in view of the framework and metalanguage of language learning, and helping students to make connections across experiences to achieve a coordinated view. Knowledge of useful resources and skills in selecting appropriate resources and using them effectively are much needed in helping learners construct personalized learning ecology (Hubbard, 2013; Lai et al., 2015; Steel & Levy, 2013).

Kicken et al. (2008) concurred that, in constructing personal learning contexts, learners often face the challenge of selecting suitable tasks and resources, and thus it is essential to provide guidance on task and resource selection. Such guidance includes providing students with some guiding principles in material selection. Examples of the principles are: narrow viewing of audiovisual resources that share the same topic or theme (e.g., TV series) is beneficial for vocabulary learning (Peters & Webb, 2018); collaborative game playing is more beneficial than playing games solo (Sundqvist, 2019); and dual attention to both meaning and language form when interacting with technological resources and the depth of lexical information attended to during interaction are important predictors of vocabulary development through technological experience (Lai et al., 2022). Kicken and colleagues (2008) further provided a framework on how to provide the guidance needed for learning resource selection. This model calls for three components: 1) a development portfolio. The portfolio provides students with an overview of their performance level based on system-generated and teacher- or peer-provided assessment of learners' previous task performance. The portfolio identifies the constituent skills that need improvement in reference to corresponding performance standards. The portfolio also guides students to systematically select learning tasks in response to the identified constituent skills and plan learning trajectories. 2) Task metadata. The task metadata contains information on the level of difficulty, available support, the corresponding performance standards, and the prerequisite knowledge, skills, and attitudes of each task. The task metadata can help students plan learning trajectories in their development portfolio. 3) Advice protocol. Advice protocol provides procedural or strategic advice in the form of feedback on learning goals in the development portfolio. Advice protocol also provides feed-forward information with suggestions on suitable learning tasks, modeling examples, and learning process self-monitoring worksheet. Support in the ISDL model follows a scaffolding principle with a gradual increase of learning tasks to choose from and a gradual decrease in the frequency and the level of details in the advice provision.

Moreover, the construction of personal learning contexts is often driven by the needs to fulfill personal needs and interests and to achieve personal growth. Personal interests drive the agentic utilization of learning opportunities in varied settings to create personal ecologies of connected learning across formal and informal contexts (Barron, 2006; Ito et al., 2020). Personal interest in a particular type of content in the L2 (e.g., pop culture or information of personal relevance) may drive learners' self-directed interaction with the relevant L2 online resources (Kormos & Csizér, 2014; Lai et al., 2018). Thus, interventions that support the construction of personal learning contexts may adopt an interest-driven, personalized approach to support learners in pursuing objects of personal interest in the language(s) (Lai, 2018; Littlejohn et al., 2016). Interest has three constitutive components: 1) affect (feelings), 2) value (perceived importance and personal connection) and 3) knowledge (prior knowledge and perceived competence). Affect is boosted by novel and challenging

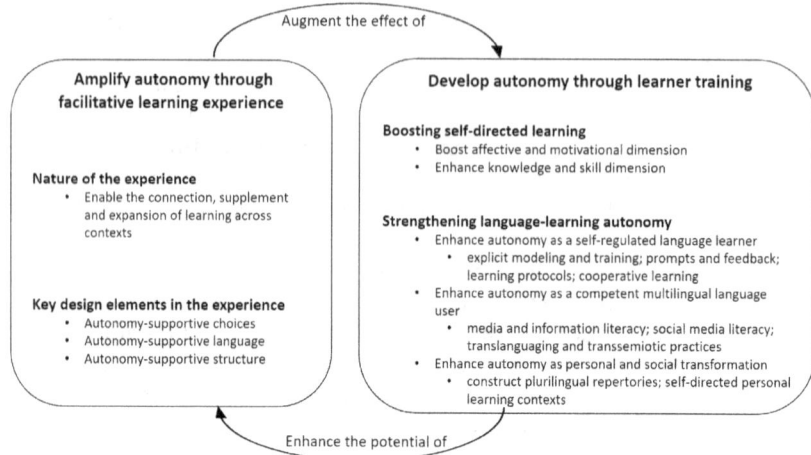

Figure 5 *A framework of supporting learner autonomy with technology*

but fulfilling experiences. Value is strengthened by linking the activity to daily life and underscoring personal relevance in a particular item. Knowledge concerns the coping-potential appraisal of skills, knowledge, and resources for the activity and is content-specific (O'Keefe & Linnenbrink-Garcia, 2014; Renninger & Hidi, 2015, 2019; Silvia, 2008). In the context of self-directed pursuit of personal interest in a target language, learners need the support on not only technological resources selection and use (Kormos & Csizér, 2014; Lai, Yeung & Hu, 2016; Lai et al., 2022), but also high-frequency vocabularies in the interest area. Thus, interventions may direct learners to identify an existing everyday interest object that they want to pursue in the target language and support them with relevant vocabulary learning materials and associated language processing and use strategies. Reflection probes, such as ICAN probes (a series of "I can ….." statements), can be used to strengthen personal connections with the interest object (Renninger & Hidi, 2015). In addition, joint activities and affinity-based mentorship that are important to maintain interest need to be included as well (Ito et al., 2020).

A framework of supporting learner autonomy with technology

Given that learner autonomy is both an innate trait that can be amplified or focused, and a capacity that can be developed, I elaborate on a framework that approaches the issue of facilitating learner autonomy with technology through these two aspects. Figure 5 illustrates the framework.

Learner autonomy with technology can be amplified through providing autonomy-supportive learning experience and can also be developed through providing learner training interventions. These two aspects of support are mutually reinforcing. Providing a facilitative learning experience that amplifies learner autonomy can enrich learners' autonomous learning experience, the propensities, capacities and metacognitive awareness ensued from which may increase learners' receptivity to learner autonomy training and bolster its effects. Providing training on learner autonomy can equip learners with relevant skills and strategies to boost the learning benefits from autonomy-amplifying learning experience and maximize its potential.

Both these two aspects of support are necessary in facilitating a positive interaction between learner autonomy and technology. The degree of support may vary for learners with different levels of self-regulation skills. For learners with low levels of self-regulation, learner training would be the core aspect of support needed, which may be further strengthened through autonomy-amplifying learning experience. For learners with high levels of self-regulation, providing autonomy-amplifying learning experience might be essential, which can be further bolstered by learner training.

PART II

TEACHER AUTONOMY AND TECHNOLOGY

6
Teacher Autonomy and Technology: An Introduction

Teacher autonomy in language education

The concept of teacher autonomy originates in discussions of professional autonomy. An oft-cited definition of professional autonomy is a worker's freedom to schedule work and determine the procedure to carry out the work (Hackman & Oldham, 1975). When this concept was introduced into the educational context, it was translated into "the ability to control daily schedules, to teach as one chooses, to have freedom to make decisions on instruction, and to generate ideas about curriculum" (Husband & Short, 1994, p. 60). Wilches (2007) expanded the concept further to highlight teacher autonomy in relation to the governing body: "Teacher autonomy can be conceptualized as a personal sense of freedom from interference or in terms of teachers' exercise of control over school matters' (p. 245). Smith and Erdoğan (2008) broadened the scope of control further to include the dimension of teacher control over learning. According to them, teacher autonomy is both the capacity and freedom for self-direction in professional work and the capacity and freedom for self-direction in professional learning.

Lamb (2008) pinpointed three constitutive elements of teacher autonomy: the capacity element, the freedom element, and the political element. The capacity element denotes that teacher autonomy is a technical action of engaging in autonomous behavior. The freedom element signifies that teacher autonomy is a social action and is situated in teachers' interaction with the context. The political element highlights that teacher autonomy entails the empowerment of the self and others. These elements can manifest in both teachers' professional work and professional learning.

Teacher autonomy in professional work

Teacher autonomy is defined as teachers' will and capacity to make key decisions concerning the content and conditions of work and the will and capacity to justify and develop practices (Lennert da Silva & Mølstad, 2020; Mausethagen & Mølstad, 2015; Werkme & Höstfält, 2014). Teacher autonomy correlates positively with work satisfaction, perceived self-efficacy, perceived positive work climate and transformative teaching practices, and associates negatively with teacher burnout (Huang, 2021; Parker, 2015; Wilches, 2007).

Conceptualizations of teacher autonomy in professional work

Teaching is a profession, and professional work involves a constant tradeoff between work practice and organizational constraints. Thus, teacher autonomy is often discussed in relation to others in the schooling context. Early conceptions of teacher autonomy highlight being independent of and resisting external influence, i.e., the aspect of "not depending on others for one's own (job) functioning and not being influenced by others" (Vangrieken, Grosemans, Dochy & Kyndt, 2017, p. 303). For instance, Little (1995) conceptualized teacher autonomy as a "sense of personal responsibility for their teaching, exercising via continuous reflection and analysis the highest possible degree of affective and cognitive control of the teaching process, and exploiting the freedom that this confers" (p. 179).

Later conceptions of teacher autonomy acknowledge that teachers and colleagues are very much connected, and that interdependence is an inherent part of the profession. These later conceptualizations highlight the aspect of making informed choices and underscore teacher agency in managing the interdependence. For instance, Aoki (2000) defined teacher autonomy as the capacity, freedom, and/or responsibility to make choices concerning one's own teaching. Benson (2010) also advocated understanding teacher autonomy in terms of the interaction between internal capacity and professional freedom. To him, "teacher autonomy can be understood both as a working condition that allows room for teachers' professional discretion and as the teacher's capacity to create this working condition within prevailing constraints" (Benson, 2010, p. 263). Wermke and Höstfält (2014) defined teacher autonomy as a capacity-determined scope of action to gain and maintain control over important aspects of pedagogical work in the classroom under school and sociocultural governance. Thus, teacher autonomy is a reaction to the tension between one's role as a professional practitioner in the classroom and one's dependence on the organizational and curricular structure.

Scope of teacher autonomy in professional work

Scholars have also focused on mapping the scope of teacher autonomy, namely, to identify dimensions of teacher professional work where teacher autonomy may manifest.

Since teachers' work is embedded in layered contexts, scholars like Frostenson (2015) and Wermke and Salokangas (2021) have argued that teacher autonomy in professional work can display both individually and collectively at varied levels: the classroom level, the school level and the profession level. In another word, teachers can exercise agency to take control of their individual professional practices and can also exercise agency to work together with others to (re)define the frames and conditions of their professional work. These scholars conceptualize three levels of teacher autonomy. The first level is the micro context of classroom where teachers work as individual professions. Frostenson (2015) referred to this level as "individual autonomy," and Wermke and Salokangas's (2021) labelled this level as the "classroom dimension." Thus, the first level is individual autonomy at the classroom teaching level. The second level of teacher autonomy is the context of school where teachers work as a member. Frostenson (2015) referred to this level as "staff or faculty" autonomy, and Wermke and Salokangas (2021) labelled it as the "school dimension" of teacher autonomy. This level is collective autonomy at the departmental or school practice level that involves relation to or cooperation with key stakeholders at the local school. The third level is the context of the teaching profession in general, namely the professional dimension of teacher autonomy. This level of teacher autonomy is also collective in nature, but at the teaching profession and policy level. It involves teachers' interaction with other actors in the education system, such as unions, textbook publishers, and education bureau.

Teacher autonomy has also been theorized to manifest in different job domains. Wermke and colleagues (2019) conceptualized four job domains for the exercise of teacher autonomy. The first domain is the pedagogical or educational practice domain. This domain entails pedagogical decisions related to lesson planning, instructional practices, and assessment, and consists of two sub-dimensions – curriculum autonomy and instructional autonomy (Pearson & Moomaw, 2006; Vangrieken et al., 2017). The second domain is the social domain, which involves the various social functions of teaching, such as disciplinary actions and student grouping. The third domain is the administrative domain, which involves the administrative work in relation to school functioning, such as timetabling, resource allocation and workspace arrangement. The fourth domain is the developmental domain, involving activities that steer the direction of schools on issues related to school development and teacher professional development.

Teacher autonomy in professional learning

Tort-Moloney (1997) is among the first scholars who drew the field's attention to the aspect of autonomy with regard to self-directed professional learning. She argued that an autonomous teacher is "one who is aware of why, when, where and how pedagogical skills can be acquired in the self-conscious awareness of teaching practice itself" (p. 51). Smith (2000) developed this idea further to highlight that professional learning is not just about developing pedagogical skills, but also about the acquisition of information and skills of all dimensions related to a teacher's professional work. He introduced the concept of "teacher-learner autonomy," and highlighted "teacher's autonomy as a learner" (p. 90), a learner who takes charge of learning, independently and/or in collaboration with others, to meet his professional development needs and purposes. Smith argued that this aspect of teacher autonomy is important because learning constitutes an important part of both becoming a teacher and succeeding as a teacher. The view was also concurred by McGrath (2000), who deemed teacher development an important strand of teacher autonomy. He referred to this as "teacher autonomy as self-directed professional development" (p. 100). Smith and Erdoğan (2008) further underscored the diversified sources and venues of teacher professional learning, defining teacher autonomy as "the ability to identify when, where, how and from what sources [teachers] (can and should) learn, including but not confined to the learning they can achieve via teaching" (p. 87). They argued that high autonomy in professional work does not necessarily indicate high autonomy in professional learning, and vice versa. Thus, these two aspects of teacher autonomy need to be differentiated and are both important dimensions of teacher autonomy. Concurring with them, Huang (2005) defined teacher autonomy as "teachers' willingness, capacity and freedom to take control of their own teaching and learning" (p. 206). In this definition, willingness, capacity, and freedom corresponds to the social-motivational, technical-psychological and critical-political dimensions of autonomy, and "'teaching' and 'learning' correspond to the two interrelated domains of teachers' classroom life: domain of teaching and domain of teacher-learning" (p. 206).

Formal and informal professional learning

There are two types of professional learning: formal learning and informal learning. Formal learning is often planned, structured, and facilitated by others, and informal learning is self-initiated deliberative, reactive or implicit acquisition of knowledge, skills or abilities through different sources including self, others and non-interpersonal sources (Lecat et al., 2019; Noe et al., 2013). The distinction between these two sources of learning is "agenda-based versus self-directed, and content-driven versus process-oriented" (Prestridge, 2019, p. 149). These two forms of learning are not dichotomous but rather lie on a continuum, and they are equally important elements of professional learning (Kyndt et al., 2016). Moreover, they intertwine with each other. For instance, in Dexter et al.'s (2016) study, 80% of their teacher participants who had taken part in a formal professional development program reported engaging in concomitant informal and non-formal professional learning. Moreover, the structural and cultural conditions for informal professional learning are also found to be influenced by leadership in the formal context (Howard et al., 2018).

These two types of professional learning experience hold differential impact on teacher learning. Attending formal training or workshops is associated with changes in instructional beliefs, but informal learning correlates positively with changes in instructional practices (Shirrel et al., 2019). Lantz-Andersson et al. (2018) found that formally organized communities and informally organized communities serve different professional learning needs, inducing different sharing practices and offering different emotional support. In formally organized communities, sharing practices are often characterized by the sharing of knowledge, personal experience and problem solving, whereas sharing in informally organized communities mainly involves the sharing of new ideas or applications and the filtering of the large amount of information available online. Although both formally organized and informally organized online communities provide emotional support for teachers, emotional support in formally organized communities often stimulates reflections on and adjustment of one's professional practices, and emotional support in informally organized communities is often associated with a sense of belonging to a competent and friendly community without hierarchy. Barton and Dexter (2020) further revealed that formal, informal, and independent teacher professional learning related differently to teachers' self-efficacy for technology integration in teaching. Formal professional development primarily served as verbal persuasion, and was constantly perceived as misaligned with teacher needs, lacking action orientation and being insufficient on its own. Seeking informal learning with peers who hold similar learning interests provided action-oriented verbal persuasion, enabled vicarious learning from peers and experts across school, and prompted reflection on personal experience with technology. In contrast, pursuing independent learning with online resources was reported to boost personal exploration with technology, and induced verbal persuasion or vicarious experiences from sources outside the school community.

Autonomy in informal professional learning

Teachers are found to show a high level of ownership of professional learning (Admiraal et al., 2016). Teacher autonomy in professional learning can manifest both in formal and informal learning contexts (Wermke, 2011). Informal learning is a professional learning context that is indispensable of autonomy.

Given that informal learning is by nature self-directed, researchers have examined the nature of informal learning that teachers engage in. Considering the attentional focus during learning, Eraut (2004) categorized informal workplace learning into three types, namely deliberative learning, reactive learning, and implicit learning. Deliberative learning refers to conscious learning that is driven by the need to complete a work-related goal and involves planning. Reactive learning is emergent conscious learning that takes place in the mid of action. Implicit learning is learning that individuals are unaware of. As for the source of informal learning, it may originate in both individual experience and interaction with others

(Billett, 2018; Noe et al., 2013). Kyndt and colleagues (2016) proposed a taxonomy of informal learning that focuses on the source of learning. In this taxonomy, there are seven categories of informal learning: 1) interaction and discussion with others, which constitutes two subcategories – collaboration and sharing; 2) learning from others without interaction, such as observations and feedback; 3) learning from doing, experiencing or experimenting; 4) consulting information sources; 5) reflection in and on action; 6) engaging in extracurricular activities; and 7) encountering difficulties. Lecat et al. (2019) further synthesized the source of teacher informal learning into three categories: the social source of learning, the non-interpersonal source of learning, and the inner source of learning. They identified different activities under each learning source. Under the social source of learning, there are activities like speaking to direct colleagues, talking to non-colleagues, listening to students, sharing with colleagues, and co-working with others. The non-interpersonal sources of learning include reading, visiting, watching films or documentaries, and observing. The inner sources of learning include reflecting, trial and error, learning by doing, and self-study.

Kyndt and colleague (2016) further revealed that teacher informal learning supports three areas of learning: subject knowledge; pedagogical knowledge and skills; and professional attitudes and identity. Informal learning can help both fill the gaps in subject knowledge and expand subject knowledge that has been discussed in formal education. Informal learning also facilitates, through collaboration and communication with others, the acquisition of teaching skills, new teaching methods, classroom management strategies and techniques. Moreover, informal learning boosts teachers' self-confidence and helps them gain a better understanding of students, themselves, and the implicit politics within school and the broader context. Informal learning is also associated positively with teacher competence development, employability competences and innovative work behavior (Lecat et al., 2018).

Differentiated autonomy in professional learning

Teachers at different stages of career development vary in autonomous engagement in formal and informal learning. Surveying 1939 mathematics and science teachers in German secondary schools, Richter et al. (2011) found that teachers' uptake of opportunities for professional learning showed a quadratic pattern. Teachers showed a low level of autonomous professional learning at the beginning stage of their careers, reached a peak mid-career, and then exhibited a decrease afterwards. Formal learning opportunities were taken up by mid-career teachers more often, whereas the utilization of informal learning opportunities varied depending on the specific type of activities. Specifically, with the increase of professional experience, teachers' consumption of professional literature increased, whereas learning through collaboration with colleagues decreased. Kyndt and colleagues (2016) also revealed that more experienced teachers engaged more in reading professional literature and less in experimentation, observation, or interactions with others when compared to novice teachers. The researchers generated a list of factors that influenced teachers' informal learning. Some factors were at the individual level, such as teachers' personality (e.g., proactivity, openness, extraversion); and some were at the contextual level, such as collegiality and good social and professional relationships, supportive and collaborative school culture, and time to learn. Moreover, teachers' self-directed learning is often driven by the problems they encounter in practice, but teachers at different career stages often attend to and are responsive to different problems. Beginning teachers' professional learning is also driven by issues like classroom management, teacher-student relationship, instructional and pedagogical skills, and school politics. Early career teachers are interested in administration tasks and self-impact enhancement, and their motivation is often intrinsic and mastery oriented. Mid-career teachers are often driven by the desire to increase impact on students' learning or the desire for career promotion. They are interested in experimenting with new teaching methods, expanding instructional repertoire, and integrating management into teaching. Late-career teachers are motivated more by their own interest in the subject and the learning climate (Louws et al., 2017).

Intersection of teacher autonomy and learner autonomy

Teacher autonomy and learner autonomy are inextricably interwoven. Researchers have presented various arguments for the link between the two.

According to Little (1995), teacher autonomy is a precondition for autonomy-supportive instructional practices and the concomitant development of learner autonomy. This argument is supported by empirical evidence. Roth and colleagues (2007) found a positive association between teachers' perceived autonomy in teaching and their engagement in autonomy supportive teaching, and between students' perceived autonomy support and their autonomous motivation for learning. Thus, teacher autonomy in teaching and learner autonomy in learning are related, and this relationship is mediated by teacher autonomy support. Little (1995) argued that "language teachers are more likely to succeed in promoting learner autonomy if their own education has encouraged them to be autonomous" (p. 180). One way to enhance teacher autonomy is to engage teachers in autonomous learning during initial teacher training. The experience of autonomous professional learning may help teachers develop a better understanding of the process of autonomous learning, and hence be more apt to the task of supporting learner autonomy (Vieira, 1997). Little (2000) further elaborated on the interconnection between teacher autonomy and learner autonomy:

In a paper published more than 10 years ago I argued that the development of learner autonomy depends on the development of teacher autonomy (Little, 1995). By this I meant two things: first, that it is unreasonable to expect teachers to foster the growth of autonomy in their learners if they themselves do not know what it is to be an autonomous learner; and secondly, that in determining the initiatives they take in the classroom, teachers must be able to exploit their professional skills autonomously, applying to their teaching those same reflective and self-managing processes that they apply to their learning. (p. 27)

Thus, teacher autonomy and learner autonomy may "develop simultaneously as teachers and learners engage in the construction of more democratic pedagogies" (Manzano Vázquez, 2018, p. 387).

Lamb (2008) put forth yet another line of argument for the interconnection between teacher autonomy and learner autonomy. According to Lamb, the fact that teacher autonomy is charged with a political agenda of empowering oneself and others for social transformation determines that teacher autonomy and learner autonomy have close affinity. Learners are a significant group of the others that teachers are charged to empower. Lamb (2008) further proposed a cyclical framework of teacher autonomy in relation to the development of learner autonomy. This framework highlights three dimensions: 1) teacher as (critical) reflective practitioner; 2) teachers as language or teaching-learner; and 3) teacher as innovator-learner in developing autonomy. Developing the three teacher roles to achieve the political dimension of autonomy is essential to strengthening the teacher autonomy-learner autonomy relationship:

1. The teacher learns how to (and has, or claims, the freedom to) develop autonomously as a professional, through critical reflection
2. The teacher has a commitment to empowering his/her learners by creating appropriate learning spaces and developing their capacity for autonomy
3. The teacher introduces interventions which support the principles and values which underpin their own and their learners' autonomy
(Lamb, 2008, p. 279)

Development of teacher autonomy

To develop teacher autonomy, researchers have pointed out the importance of providing opportunities for teachers to experience autonomy both in professional work and in professional learning (Jiménez Raya et al., 2017). A combination of pedagogical inquiry experience and critical reflection on the experience is essential to foster teacher autonomy. Jiménez Raya and Vieira (2011) argued that activities that aim at developing teacher autonomy should help teachers engage in constant critical analysis of how their pedagogical practices help or constrain the transformation of teaching and learning. These activities should guide teachers to uncover the explicit or implicit pedagogical beliefs and values behind their pedagogical practices, and reflect on the conceptual, practical, and social justifications for the practices. The activities should also enhance teachers' sensitivity to students' beliefs, priorities, values, and interests, and increase their engagement in analyzing whether their teaching practices support or constrain students' exercise and development of learner autonomy. Moreover, the activities should give teachers access to communities of practices that enable them to sustain individual and collaborative efforts towards the promotion of their own autonomy in teaching and learning and the promotion of learner autonomy.

Existing literature has revealed some effective approaches to developing teacher autonomy, including experiential activities, such as individual/collaborative exploration or action research that involves classroom implementation of autonomy-supportive pedagogies and techniques, and reflective practice through group discussions or the use of reflective tools such as learning diaries or portfolio (Huang, 2005; Manzano Vázquez, 2018). Jiménez Raya and colleagues (2017) further added case methods as a promising approach to developing teacher autonomy. Case method can either involve teachers in analyzing cases of others' practices or engage teachers in writing cases from their own experiences. At the core of case methods is problematizing dominant ideas and practices and stimulating teachers to explore autonomy-oriented teaching practices (Vieira, 2020).

Teacher autonomy and technology

Influence of teacher autonomy on technology integration

Autonomy, the perceived freedom and choice in action, is an essential component that shapes self-determined behaviors. Teacher autonomy is associated with instructional experimentation and innovativeness (Cribb & Gewirtz, 2007), and teacher's participation in professional learning activities (Kwakman, 2003).

Bolstering professional work with technology

Teacher autonomy is a significant predictor of teacher innovative behaviors (Buske, 2018; Clarke & Hollingsworth, 2002). For instance, Buske (2018) surveyed 896 teachers in Germany, and found that teacher autonomy in classroom practice decision making positively predicted teachers' innovativeness. Based on teacher responses to the OECD Teaching and Learning International Survey from 48 countries, Nguyen et al. (2021) found that teacher autonomy is a significant positive predictor of collective teacher innovativeness (i.e., teachers' perception of their school's receptivity and openness to new ideas and changes). Greater receptivity, openness and willingness to adopt change are associated with a greater likelihood of adopting technology to innovate teaching.

Since technology adoption demands a certain level of innovativeness, teacher autonomy is closely related to their use of technology in professional work. Scholars argue that teacher agency empowers teachers to explore instructional possibilities in technology, and hence associates positively with their classroom integration of ICT (Albion & Tondeur, 2018). The degree of autonomy teachers can exercise in a particular situation determines whether teachers would make the attempt to innovate teaching and learning with ICT (Digón-Regueiro et al., 2021). Becker (2000b) further found that when teachers perceived that they were not bound by constraints on how they should teach, they were more likely to exercise professional judgement and find ways to use ICT.

Teachers may value technology more when they have the freedom and knowledge to design instruction to foster student-directed learning (Chiu, 2022). Serın and Bozdağ (2020) examined the influence of different dimensions of teacher autonomy on teachers' attitudes towards the use of technology in education. They found that teaching process autonomy and professional communication autonomy were significant positive predictors of teachers' attitudes towards technology integration, and the two factors accounted for 30% of the variance in attitudes. Wu and Wu (2018) examined how a group of pre-service teachers' curriculum autonomy and general teaching autonomy related to their ICT competency. They identified a positive association between teacher autonomy and ICT competency. Specifically, curriculum autonomy and general teaching autonomy related positively with technology literacy.

Enhancing professional learning about technology

Teacher autonomy influences whether and how teachers engage in professional learning. De Brabander & Glastra (2018) proposed the Unified Model of Task-Specific Motivation to explain the motivational sources of autonomous action. According to this model, readiness for action is driven by affective and cognitive valences, which are influenced by four task-specific antecedents. The antecedents include individuals' appraisal of autonomy (i.e., both personal drive for action and freedom of action in the context), of competence (i.e., both personal competence and contextual conditions conducive to a successful performance), relatedness, and subjective norm. Thus, perceived autonomy may drive teachers' readiness to engage in autonomous learning with technology.

Louws et al. (2017) showed that perceived freedom for autonomous action influenced teachers' engagement in professional learning. They elicited 31 Dutch secondary school teachers' perception of their workplace conditions and their professional learning goals. They found that perceived approval of request for professional development and perceived support of autonomy on individual learning were important enablers of teachers' professional learning. In contrast, when teachers perceived not being involved in school decision making concerning professional development, they were less likely to engage in autonomous professional learning. De Brabander and Glastra (2021) examined how teacher autonomy influenced primary school teachers' motivation for professional development related to ICT use in instruction. They found that sense of personal autonomy (i.e., perception of volitional participation in the activity) had a strong positive effect on positive cognitive valence of learning about ICT, and directly contributed to teachers' readiness for learning about both the use of ICT to support student learning and the use of ICT to support teaching. Perceived freedom of action (i.e., perception of the extent to which the activity provided opportunities for free choice) influenced both perceived personal autonomy and perceived personal competence. The influence was stronger in the case of learning about learning-supportive ICT use when compared to learning about teaching-supportive ICT use. The researchers thus concluded that autonomy is a strong antecedent to teachers' motivation for professional learning on both types of ICT use, and needs to be given more attention when understanding teacher technology integration.

Influence of technology on teacher autonomy

Boosting autonomy in professional work

Technology provides tools and spaces for the exercise of autonomy in professional practices. It enables teachers to widen the context of teaching and learning beyond the time and spatial constraints of a physical classroom. It makes it possible for teachers to open their teaching and learning to a large, networked public audience, expand the teaching and learning resources to include a "hybridization of expertise," reshape their roles as facilitators, and implement constructivist pedagogies that are hard to realize without the help of technology (Manca & Ranieri, 2016; Greenhow et al., 2020, p. 6). Thus, technology serves as enabling tools of and spaces for autonomous action in professional work. Moreover, technology is found to be utilized by teachers to facilitate students' self-directed learning (Greenhow et al., 2020), helping realize the political aspect of teacher autonomy in terms of empowerment.

Facilitating autonomy in professional learning

Technology brings resources and venues for teacher professional learning. Teacher learning emerges in knowledge acquisition and participation (Sfard, 1998), and technology can expand both the sources of acquisition and venues for participation (Greenhow et al., 2020; Lantz-Andersson et al., 2018). As Galvin and Greenhow (2020) have pointed out, technology enables teachers to reclaim their professional learning and redefine the nature and direction of learning. Reviewing the research literature on teacher professional learning online, Maciá and Garcia (2016) revealed that, on informal online communities and networks, teachers are actively engaged in learning activities such as sharing and reflecting on experience, discussing individual questions, seeking help, sharing teaching resources and materials, and offering and receiving emotional support.

Moreover, technology expands teachers' interaction with a wider pool of expertise and knowledge. For instance, reviewing studies on social media and teacher learning, Greenhow and colleagues (2020) revealed that social media opens teachers' horizons to the wider networks of knowledge, and serves as convenient and adaptable troubleshooting spaces. Social media also expands teacher control. It not only supports teacher control over the sources, the time, the place and the approach to learning, but also provides a social venue that supports independent learning, strengthening a sense of belonging and proffering emotional regulation resources. Social media further enables collaborative inquiry and professional identity construction. Teacher informal learning on social media is found to address individual learning needs that are not easily addressed in formal training. Reviewing the literature on teacher online informal learning, Beach et al. (2021) synthesized four aspects of professional learning that technology contributes to: knowledge exchange, reflective practice with heightened awareness of one's professional needs, interests and goals, multifaceted formal and informal learning opportunities, and just-in-time support.

Supporting the development of autonomy

Technology provides tools and spaces for the development of teacher autonomy. Technology, such as digital portfolios, logs and digital forums, provides open learning spaces that support individual and collective reflection on practices. Technology affords convenient "written communication in virtual reality" that is logged and can be constantly referred to. The medium of interaction afforded by technology "might support reflectivity and metacognitive awareness" (Trebbi, 2008, p. 234). Thus, the multimodal channels of technology and the ease of keeping records of one's pedagogical practices may deepen critical reflection on teaching. Critical reflection on teaching practices contributes to enhanced awareness and understanding of one's pedagogical practices, which may fuel pedagogical transformation. Moreover, technology presents spaces for collaborative sharing and inquiry, which support collective experiential practices and contribute to the development of teacher autonomy.

Constraining autonomy in professional work and professional learning

At the same time, technology poses challenges to teacher autonomy. One source of challenge lies in the amount of time and energy investment needed to get familiarized with technology and be able to implement technology. The prerequisite time and effort investment might be overwhelming (Pan & Franklin, 2011). Second, the privacy and ethical boundaries of online interaction may also discourage teachers from utilizing the power of technology for teacher autonomy in professional learning (Kuo, Cheng & Yang, 2017). It is true that technology provides potential means for teachers to connect teaching and learning with the larger networked public and to broaden their social networking for both professional learning and professional work. However, concerns over privacy protection and ethical considerations may discourage teachers from utilizing the resources and networks made available by technology to exercise autonomy in teaching and learning. Third, the cultural norms of technology, social media as an example, may marginalize certain populations such as "women, people of color and other minoritized groups [who] are often harassed online" (Greenhow et al., 2020, p. 61). This may further hinder some populations from reaping the potential of technology for teacher autonomy. Moreover, there is also the concern over "miseducation" on technological platforms – issue of "mis- and disinformation," resulting from intentional or unconscious manipulation of information, establishment of norms online, and the content moderation or lack thereof (Greenhalgh, Krutka & Oltmann, 2021). Concerns over the possibility of miseducation online may discourage some teachers from integrating technology inside the classroom to enrich students' learning experience and discourage others from embracing the potential of technology for autonomous professional learning. Fourth, the dominant policy discourse on classroom technology integration, particularly student-centered technology use, may feed into social censure that hampers teacher autonomy in managing classroom teaching (Gao, 2018).

Thus, given the nature of teacher autonomy and the affordance and constraints of technology, a critical lens is needed when exploring their relationship. In the next chapter, I will elaborate on the harmony and tension between the two in both the context of professional work and the context of professional learning.

7
The Impact of Technology on Teacher Autonomy

Similar to the relationship between technology and learner autonomy, technology may both facilitate and constrain teacher autonomy in both professional work and professional learning.

Technology as a facilitator of teacher autonomy

According to Smith (2003), there are two constitutive domains of teacher autonomy: professional action and professional development. Under each domain, there are three dimensions: self-directed behavior, capacity for self-directed behavior, and freedom from control of self-directed behavior. In this section, I will explore the facilitative role of technology in teacher autonomy via this framework.

Facilitating teacher autonomy in professional work

Technology plays an important role in influencing teacher autonomy in professional work. It impacts not only the instructional aspects (e.g., pedagogical and curriculum practices) but also the interpersonal and administrative aspects (e.g., student-teacher relationship and school governing), the varied job domains where teachers can exercise autonomy (Wermke et al., 2019).

Supporting the instructional aspects of teacher autonomy

Facilitating innovative pedagogies

Technology lowers the hurdles of implementing innovative teaching pedagogies. ICT offers means to customize and expand teaching repertoires, strategies and methods (Bitner & Bitner, 2002; Sutherland et al., 2004). For instance, technological tools like microblogging (e.g., twitter) and student response systems (e.g., Mentimeter) enable ongoing elicitation and incorporation of student thoughts to enhance classroom interaction that centers around and builds on students' input (Major et al., 2018; Rasmussen & Hagen, 2015). Open educational resources allow teachers to construct personalized instruction (de los Arcos et al., 2016). Thus, technology broadens teachers' freedom of action, progressive pedagogical actions in particular. This technological potential was confirmed by teacher participants in Ertmer et al.'s study (2012), who reported that technology enabled them to align teaching practices with the beheld student-centered beliefs. According to these teachers, technology offered them the means to experiment and implement innovative and authentic classroom practices, such as a project-based approach. In their classrooms, technology served as tools for students to be active agents in learning: cognitive tools to solve real-life problems, and mind tools to represent understandings of a new and complex concept.

Technology may also transform teachers' conceptions of teaching and learning. Carhill-Poza (2017) shared how technology like iPads changed the teaching practices of teachers of English language learners at an urban high school. These teachers reported that technology stimulated school-wide conversations about supporting diverse learners and uplifting students as innovative users of technology inside and outside the classroom. They further shared that technology supported innovative classroom practices, including supporting student-directed research projects, differentiating content for learners of different English proficiency levels, and encouraging and enabling the validation of learners' first language as resources for learning. Carhill-Poza hence concluded that "using technology for teaching and learning develops our thinking rather than simply adding a set of technical skills" (p. 118). Similar examples of how technology may broaden and transform teachers' thinking about teaching and learning were presented in Hedberg's (2011) study on teachers' use of interactive whiteboards. Attending workshops on innovative ways of using interactive whiteboard and experiencing its use inside the classroom increased the teacher participants' strategic repertoire of in-class instruction. Hedberg featured one middle school math teacher, Stuart. Experimenting with an interactive whiteboard in his class made Stuart see more possibilities of class teaching. He started to shift away from whole class teaching towards activities that cater to individual kids, making regular use of learning stations to accommodate different learning styles and levels of achievement. Similarly, Dexter et al. (1999) also revealed that teachers felt that technological experience inside the classroom and reflections on the experience facilitated changes towards more student-centered progressive teaching practices.

Facilitating curriculum development

Technology also facilitates teacher participation in curriculum development. Textbooks are a major de-professionalizing factor and often lead to "the homogenization and standardization of teaching and learning processes" (Digón-Regueiro et al., 2021, p. 5). Over-reliance on textbooks may "stifle teachers' roles as classroom authorities and agents of change" and limit their methodological options (Scott & Husain, 2021, p. 235). Technology enables teachers to get rid of the fetter of textbooks and play an active role as designers of the curriculum. Matuk et al. (2015)

argued that when teaching materials are overly rigid in prescribed use, teachers are often confined by the embedded pedagogical orientations in the materials and may encounter difficulty adapting the materials to local use. Technology can provide flexible manipulable materials and authoring tools, log students' responses and make student thinking visible, and monitor students' ongoing learning performance and progress. Thus, it enables teachers to make curriculum customization decisions based on pedagogical orientations and student needs, free from constraining issues of practicality and feasibility. Burstein and colleagues (2014) introduced a web-based application that utilize natural language processing to generate the linguistic challenge profile of texts with information on spots that might be challenging so that teachers could use the information to adapt instructional materials for English language learners. The researchers found that this technological tool enhanced teachers' ability to design lessons that support English language learners' language development needs.

Technology also makes it easier for teachers to construct teaching materials. A typical example is open education resources. Open education resources save teachers from creating learning materials from scratch. Instead, teachers can easily locate other teachers' open education resources, re-use and re-purpose resources to meet instructional needs, and even co-create and remix resources with others (Beaven, 2013; Clements & Pawlowski, 2012). Open education resources empower teachers through supporting teacher sharing and collaboration, which enhances teacher autonomy in material development both at the individual and collective levels (Kasinathan, 2018). Beaven (2013) examined language teachers' use of the Languages Open Resources Online repository developed by the Open University, UK. The researcher found that language teachers actively adapted the OERs through making small modifications to resources to provide additional support to students and creating new resources based on inspirations garnered from these resources. Moreover, teachers are found to access social media sites such as Twitter and Pinterest to explore and locate instructional resources to address instructional needs (Opfer et al., 2016).

Supporting the social and administrative aspects of teacher autonomy

Facilitating student-teacher relationships

Positive teacher-student relationships make teachers more willing and confident to experiment with innovative pedagogies. Technology can boost student-teacher relationships through enhancing their interaction inside and outside the classroom. Carhill-Poza (2017) reported that by making multimodal learning materials accessible to English language learners anytime outside the classroom, teachers gained more time during class time to engage students in in-depth discussions and extended feedback loops, which helped redefine teacher-student relationships. Teachers also reported that technological tools like messaging and online course materials enabled increased interaction with students outside the classroom, which helped strengthen teacher-student bonding and elicit questions that were not likely to arise in class. Increased access to learning materials outside the classroom was also reported to induce changed teacher-student roles in classroom interactions, allowing "more student contributions and student-generated questions and topic-shifts" (p. 117). Hershkovitz et al. (2019) surveyed 300 5th-12th graders in Israel on their interaction with teachers on WhatsApp outside the classroom and found that WhatsApp interaction fostered close student-teacher relationships and promoted a positive classroom environment. Students reported greater satisfaction with their relationship with teachers and with the support they got from teachers when they interacted more with teachers on WhatsApp. And WhatsApp communication was also negatively associated with perceived conflict with the teacher. The researchers further found that WhatsApp out-of-class interaction with teachers had a unique contribution to positive classroom environment.

Technology can also boost positive student-teacher interaction through raising teachers' meta-awareness of their behaviors inside the classroom. Scholars have conceptualized various ways of visualizing teachers' classroom behaviors. Chen and colleagues (2015) developed a Classroom Discourse Analyzer (CDA) to visualize classroom discourse. The Analyzer uses multiple sources (e.g., video, transcripts) and representations (e.g., words, turn-taking patterns) to capture the complexity of classroom discourse data and visualize the talk moves. A series of studies conducted by Chen and his colleagues revealed that viewing the CDA on classroom teaching videos helped enhance beliefs about the importance of classroom talk, boost self-efficacy in directing positive interaction, and bolster abilities to use academically productive talk moves and reduce teacher dominance in classroom discourse (Chen, 2020; Chen & Chan, 2022). Alzoubi and colleagues (2021) argued that technology, such as feedback dashboards, can help provide scalable and sustainable automated observation and feedback on pedagogical strategies, which serves as powerful tools to trigger teachers' reflection on teaching strategies inside the classroom. They thus developed an automated feedback system, TEACHActive, to encourage evidence-based implementation of active learning strategies. The system visualizes classroom behaviors based on analytics on indicators captured via EduSense, including visual features (e.g., hand raise gesture detection) and audio features (e.g., speech detection). The system further provides reflective prompts to engage teachers in goal setting based on visualization of their in-class activities and in consciously monitoring their progress and pedagogical behavioral changes. An and colleagues (2020) also shared the design of Dandelion Diagram, a synthesized heatmap technique to visualize classroom proxemics, that is, how teachers divide time and attention over students in different regions of the classroom. The heatmap is generated through tracking and displaying teachers' positioning and orientation, attention patterns, and mobility patterns. By making this implicit dimension of teaching explicit, these visualization tools can enhance teacher's reflection-in-action and their conscious use of classroom proxemics to exert a positive influence on learners. Research studies have shown that visualization tools can be used to not only induce changed classroom behaviors but also enhance teachers' participation in professional learning. For instance, Wang et al. (2019) developed a visualization-based group awareness tool, where individual and group behaviors and peer comments are visualized to facilitate group interaction during a lesson study activity. They found that this kind of tool had a positive effect on both the quantity and quality of teachers' engagement in interaction during lesson study.

Facilitating teacher involvement in education governance

Technology may increase teacher voice on educational issues. Take social media as an example. Fuchs (2014) commented that social media sites, such as Twitter, have a liberating role in making the common people heard and seen. Baker-Doyle (2021) argued that the connected world mediated by social media may amplify the impact of individual teachers' behavior. He shared the story of a middle school teacher in Philadelphia, Reed, who maintained a regular blog column on the Public School Notebook. Reed regularly tweeted to challenge the stereotypical deficit-oriented views towards disadvantaged students and school communities and to promote teacher-led professional development. Baker-Doyle regarded Reed as a representative of "the contemporary transformative teacher," who use "digital-era cultural tools such as 'making', 'hacking', and 'connecting' to design, organize, and lead collective efforts to grow teacher knowledge and agency" (p. 8). He further pointed out that Reed is

> … part of a new wave of teacher-led, networked social movements in education that are transforming the concept of the teacher from that of an isolated, passive, technical worker to a connected, sociopolitically active, knowledge-building agent of change, and, in turn, taking the lead in shaping the cultures and practices of contemporary teaching and learning. (p. 8)

Baker-Doyle argued that the connected technologies and associated participatory practices enable teachers to "take leadership roles in improving education from the ground up" (p. 9). These teachers use technologies to bring resources into under-resourced schools and create enriching experiences for disadvantaged students. Tomlinson (2020) also gave an account of amplified voice via enhanced connectedness through the story of Badass Teachers Association in the U.S., a nonprofit advocacy organization that is active in elevating the voices of people who are most affected by education policies. The organization works towards shaping narratives around public education through testifying about education policy at state capitals and the U.S. Department of Education and engaging in public education research. This organization started as a closed Facebook group where educators and public education supporters around the nation gathered to discuss the teaching profession. Thus, Tomlinson argued that social media provides a perfect venue for educators to "connect and amplify their voice in political spaces" (p. 134). Similarly, Niesz, and D'Amato (2021) argued that social media provides more opportunities for teachers to engage in education activism and boost their participation in public dialogue around education policy. Social media "amplify less powerful voices and provide increased visibility to counternarratives contesting the hegemonic narratives of the powerful" (p. 303). The researchers found that teacher activist groups on Twitter were active in organizing social movement activities, both offline and online, to lobby for changes in local school district issues, call for transparency in educational decision-making and advocate local school communities' rights in decision-making related to education.

Technology also provides a non-threatening platform for teachers to invest in new identities that encourage active roles in educational affairs. Fox and Bird (2017) pointed out that social media such as Twitter allow teachers to explore new identities and speak to a larger audience, which may enhance teachers' self-concept as change agents who can make their voices heard and influence their profession. Similarly, researchers find that technology provides a tool and space for teachers, especially novice teachers, to construct professional identities and claim their position at schools. Gu and Lai (2019) interviewed seven novice ESL teachers who had 2 to 3 years of teaching experience at government-subsidized secondary schools in Hong Kong. They found that these teachers used technology as an important tool to gain more teacher autonomy and present a more professional image to their students. Dvir and Schatz-Oppenheimer (2020) also provided an account of how technology helped some novice teachers in Israel to display leadership skills and offer assistances to other teachers. As a result, these novice teachers gained acknowledgement from peers on their technological strengths and cemented their social and professional position among staff members as technological experts.

Facilitating teacher autonomy in professional learning

Autonomy with regard to personal and social empowerment depends essentially on teachers' professional learning. Existing literature has suggested some noteworthy features of effective teacher professional learning, including "ongoing, sustained, collaborative learning" experience from peer teachers, external coaches or scholars (Nguyen, Pietsch and

Gümüş, 2021, p. 3). Moreover, personalized learning opportunities are essential, since teachers need support that is catered to the particularities of the historical and cultural practices in their respective teaching contexts (Phelps et al., 2011). Technology provides venues for teachers to seek sustained, personalized learning opportunities, namely any-time, self-generating, and on-demand professional learning (Simonson et al., 2011). It facilitates teacher autonomy in professional learning, both through serving as a tool or platform for formal professional development and through providing a venue for informal and non-formal professional learning.

Facilitating formal professional development

Various learning experiences can support adult development, including personal experience, vicarious learning and collaborative learning. These learning experiences form the core features of formal professional development for teachers. Technology can play important roles in constructing and enriching these learning experiences.

Providing mastery experience

Personal experience and experimentation are an important source of learning and an effective method for teacher professional development. Technology enables immersive experience that provides teachers with mastery experience of using technology to realize teacher autonomy in teaching. Teachers' first-hand experience with instructional use of technology is an important determinant of teachers' autonomous engagement with technology for teaching (Drent & Meelissen, 2008; Tondeur et al., 2017). Farjon et al. (2019) found that pre-service teachers' experience with technology use in teaching had a significant effect on their intention for technology integration in the future. Intentional and intensive experience with technology can not only help teachers gain relevant knowledge but also boost their motivation. Xie et al. (2017) developed a professional development program, which involved explicit discussion on the evaluation of content quality, pedagogy, technology use and alignment to standards, actual engagement in critical evaluation of digital content and resources, and the completion of monthly review tasks on online teaching, digital teaching, instructional design, content evaluation and project evaluation. Implementing this professional development program with over 150 in-service teachers across different schools, the researchers found that engagement in conscious and intensive digital content and resource evaluation significantly boosted teacher participants' technological, pedagogical, and content knowledge. Moreover, teachers' perceived ability towards digital content evaluation also increased significantly. Sullivan et al. (2018) shared a web-based cross-campus teacher training initiative that immersed university faculty and instructional support staff in hands-on discovery learning to explore innovative and effective ways of using freely available emerging technologies. Self-directed activities were designed in the online platform, where teachers studied, at their own pace and in their own time, learning materials related to the use of audio, video, ePortfolios, gamification, simulation, online collaboration and web-based instructional technology tools. The experiential learning was supplemented by an online social networking community, where the participants could share learning experiences and troubleshoot each other's questions. The participants felt that the training platform was effective in helping them make sense of the myriad of technologies that can be used for instruction. They reported immediate uptake and implementation of the technology integration ideas while participating in the training program. They further reported that the experience inspired them to continue searching for and experimenting with new technological solutions even after the training concluded.

Other researchers have engaged teacher participants in classroom action research on technology-enhanced teaching. Dawson (2012) found that action research projects in classroom technological practices induced in-service teachers' conceptual changes regarding the perceived benefits of technology for teaching and learning. Lai, Wang, and Huang (2022) examined how the emergency intensive hands-on experience with online teaching during the COVID-19 pandemic influenced mainland China K-12 teachers' technology integration. They revealed that, after this short period of intensive technological experience, significant factors that influenced teacher technology integration underwent change. The researchers found that the influence of teachers' technological, pedagogical, and content knowledge increased, but the effect of value belief decreased. This change suggested that immersive technological experience might have helped teachers see the power of technology for learning and raised awareness of the deficiency in their ability. The researchers also found that the relationship between pedagogical practices and technology use decreased as a result of the experience, which they attributed to the development of greater flexibility toward technology use ensued from the experience. Thus, technology may serve as a tool to foster enactive mastery that boosts teacher autonomy with technology.

Enabling vicarious learning

Vicarious learning is another venue for teacher professional development. Vicarious learning contributes to professional development in ways different from personal experience. For instance, Hu et al. (2021) argued that viewing modeling videos provides model resources for imitative learning and viewing videos of one's own teaching induces self-reflection and raises self-awareness in noticing and understanding students' ideas. Vicarious learning adds to knowledge derived from one's personal experience, and induces modification of performance expectancy in light of others' experiences (Sullivan et al., 2018). Vicarious learning may also influence teachers' professional identity (Steenekamp et al., 2018).

Technology has been used to deliver opportunities for vicarious learning across schools. For instance, Wang et al. (2004) examined the effect of vicarious learning on pre-service teachers' classroom technology integration. They developed an instructional CD-ROM with examples of technology practices of six K-12 teachers. The training content included a combination of classroom teaching video segments, lesson plans and student products, and guided pre-service teachers to analyze these cases to identify models of effective technology integration. The researchers found that pre-service teachers who underwent the vicarious learning experience exhibited a significantly greater increase in their self-efficacy in technology integration than those who did not. Similarly, Willis et al. (2016) found that repeated exposure to a curriculum with authentic situations of technology integration in teaching led to a significant increase in technology and teaching efficacy and positive beliefs on the impact of technology on teaching and learning among a group of pre-service teachers. Chylinski and Hanewald (2011) further found that studying materials, resources and activities designed by other teachers and working with others on team action research to explore instructional use of technology helped enhance teacher autonomy in CALL. All the above examples showed that technology can help construct varied vicarious learning experience to boost teacher autonomy with technology.

Supporting collaborative learning

Collaboration is a key social capital that contributes to teacher innovation. Collaborative learning experience, such as professional learning communities, can enhance professional capital conducive to teacher innovation and enable "vicarious learning through the experience of others" (Sullivan et al., 2018, p. 351; Vangrieken, Meredith, Packer & Kyndt, 2017). Collaboration fuels the exchange of ideas and skills and helps offset the risk of innovating. When there is a lack of social interaction and support, teachers may revert to old methods despite exhibiting the highest level of expertise (Coburn et al., 2013). Working collaboratively is a very effective form of professional learning, since it often revolves around teachers' own classroom practices and hence provides situated learning experience (Blitz, 2013; Prestridge & Main, 2018). Moreover, reflection, the key drive behind teacher development, is found not to be effective unless it is part of a collaborative process (Emo, 2015). Collaborative learning in the form of professional learning communities, where teachers share exploration of the possibilities of emerging ICT, is a form of professional learning that is particularly conducive to reaping the transformational power of technology for education. It is most adaptive and resilient to the fast changes in the technological terrain, keeping discussions up to date with the development of ICT. Alibion and Tondeur

(2018) argued that "the crowdsourcing facilitated by networked ICT can contribute to solution of the challenges it presents" (p. 390).

Technology facilitates collaborative professional learning by extending it beyond time and space. Existing literature has documented various advantages of online professional communities, including improving teachers' content and pedagogical knowledge, fostering social participation and pro-social commitment, and sustaining professional interaction and ongoing peer-to-peer support (Tseng & Kuo, 2014). The internet and mobile communication technologies enable hybrid professional learning with a combination of face-to-face and online interactions, and make it possible to draw on expertise from outside the school (Prestridge & Main, 2018). Discussions on online communities of common interests often lead to offline interaction among members (Kling & Courtright, 2003). Online professional learning communities supplemented with opportunities for face-to-face interaction, such as conferences, are found to yield more benefits to teachers than online communities alone (Matzat, 2013).

Online professional communities have been found to boost teacher autonomy with technology. For instance, Zhang et al. (2017) developed an online platform for teachers from different schools to collaboratively analyze lesson plans and video recordings of class teaching. Participant teachers perceived the process of providing feedback and improvement suggestions as beneficial to linking theory to practice. Reeves and colleagues (2015) also reported an online professional learning community initiative where a group of university teachers got together on a video communication platform to share app reviews, teach technology tools to their colleagues and brainstorm integration ideas. Participants perceived the online community as a sustaining support system that facilitated their active experimentation with technological tools inside the classroom. Similarly, Mitchell et al. (2019) shared a cross-institution blogging project on technology integration among elementary school pre-service teachers. The participant teachers were requested to blog in response to prompts that engaged them to share technology integration ideas in literacy instruction they observed or experienced in their university and field practicum schools, uncover similarities and differences, and discuss challenges and solutions. The participants reported that digital collaboration broadened their perspective and experience. As a result of the interaction in this online professional learning community, 80% of the participants implemented, during the teaching practicum, at least one technology integration idea they picked up from blog posts. These pre-service teachers also expressed eagerness to incorporate blogging in future literacy teaching practices.

Facilitating informal and non-formal professional learning

Reviewing past teacher professional development initiatives, Park and

Sung (2013) identified that existing one-off professional development events are inadequate to serve teachers' learning needs. Instead, a systematic, ongoing, and developmental approach is essential to effective professional learning (Liao et al., 2017). However, participation in continued teacher professional development is deterred by a few factors, including teacher time, training and coaching, administration, materials, equipment and facilities, travel and transportation and university tuition and conference fees (Odden et al., 2002). A lot of these factors are related to accessibility, logistics and cost. These deterring factors become insignificant in informal and non-formal professional learning contexts, especially when mediated by technology. In the section below, I will take a few technological resources and platforms as an example to illustrate how technology enables informal and non-formal professional learning experience that resolves these factors.

Massive Open Online Courses

Massive Open Online Courses, with their openness, massiveness, and new ways of engagement, provide opportunities for flexible learning across time and space. Bali (2014) listed some benefits of MOOCs for teacher professional development: 1) learning new knowledge and skills in a structured way; 2) accessing quality (mostly free) resources on topics of professional interest; and 3) obtaining peer sharing of teaching practices. Chen et al. (2020) further pointed out that MOOCs grant a high level of agency in professional learning. They argued that teacher learning is often driven by workplace problems and takes place in the process of solving emergent problems and sharing and collaborating with others. MOOCs give professionals greater agency in shaping learning to the demands at the workplace, and foster connections for further learning to tackle the complex and constantly updating situation in the workplace.

Research has shown that teachers do perceive MOOCs as valuable professional learning venues. Openness and flexibility of the course, and strong connection of course content with classroom reality are the main drivers of their participation in MOOCs (Lauriallard, 2016; Koutsodimou & Jimoyiannis, 2015). Existing literature has revealed a high participation rate among teachers on MOOCs, and teachers reported using MOOCs primarily to obtain specific job skills instead of gaining professional certification (Castaño-Muñoz et al., 2016; Garrid et al., 2016). MOOCs have been reported to boost teachers' use of technology inside the classroom, as research has shown that participation in MOOCs can reduce barriers to technology integration. For instance, Castaño-Muñoz et al. (2018) found that Spanish MOOC participants reported significantly less accessibility-induced, time-induced, employer-induced, and motivation-induced barriers to professional development on classroom ICT integration.

Teacher educators have utilized the affordances of MOOCs and constructed MOOCs on classroom technology integration to support teacher informal learning on instructional use of technology. Koukis and Jimoyiannis (2015) developed a MOOC course to support primary school teachers' use of Web-based tools for instruction. Cycles of individual engagement, peer interaction and collaborative creation activities were incorporated into the course. Teacher participants perceived the MOOC course positively and reported that it enhanced their knowledge and skills to integrate Web tools in the classroom. Similarly, secondary school Greek language teachers in Koukis and Jimoyiannis's (2019) study perceived that learning experience on a MOOC course about classroom use of Google Doc to create collaborative writing activities boosted their interest and confidence in using Google Doc to create collaborative writing activities in class instruction. The teachers reported that learning on the MOOC course was more effective than conventional teacher training programmes in inducing changed views about instructional practices in writing lessons and in fostering collaboration skills, which are important for continuous professional development. Chen et al. (2020) further pointed out that experience in MOOCs may spark off additional learning opportunities. They observed in-service teachers' participation in a MOOC course about flipped learning and found that some of them retook the course multiple times. What drove these teacher participants to revisit the MOOC course was the authentic need to seek knowledge to help improve teaching practice, solve problems in teaching, and alleviate challenges in teaching. More importantly, taking the MOOC course sparked off the formation of online and offline communities of inquiry and informal support groups with peers in the course around shared knowledge, interests, and practical concerns. The learning communities even traversed across different MOOCs to seek solutions to shared practical problems. The researchers concluded that MOOCs support sustained access to learning and carry the potential "to support networked professional learning as an alternative approach to teacher PD in the information-rich, networked society" (p. 17).

Social media tools

Social media interactions not only provide timely on-demand professional learning but also trigger active inquiry learning in one's instructional contexts. Podcasts and blogs from experts allow teachers to update their knowledge and skills in ICT integration very conveniently. Thus, social media adds to teachers' professional learning repertoire (Prestridge & Main, 2018). Teachers are found to use social media to share and acquire new practice ideas, information related to technology use in schools in particular, filter and curate new ideas and seek emotional and professional support (Lantz-Andersson et al., 2018). Moreover, social media interactions change teachers from passive receivers of content, as is often the case in professional development events, to content generators, and stimulate teachers to actively communicate, share, reflect on, and collaborate with like-minded peers (Prestridge & Main, 2018). Take blogs as an example. Blogs contribute to teachers' knowledge construction and the development of personalized teaching e-portfolios, which help teachers to accumulate instructional knowledge and "re-envisage their identity as public intellectuals" (Prestridge, 2019, p. 145).

Social media not only provides places where teachers can find, exchange, and discuss ideas and resources as both knowledge givers and receivers, but also helps teachers combat professional isolation, build networks and gain emotional support (Carpenter & Krutka, 2015; Galvin & Greenhow, 2020; van Bommel et al., 2020). The possibility for anonymous participation also helps teachers to overcome potential threats of self-disclosure of job-related emotions and frustrations and post thoughts and sentiments more freely (Carpenter & Staudt Willet, 2021). Social media tools, such as Facebook, enable teachers to expand networks and hence resolve issues of isolation and cost that have often precluded teachers' engagement in self-initiated professional learning. Enhancing connectivity and accessibility to information boosts teachers' autonomy in professional learning (Prestridge & Tondeur, 2015).

Researchers have documented teachers' use of social media for informal professional learning. Van Bommel et al. (2020) argued that social media spaces are venues where teachers share knowledge useful for teaching and hence are increasingly important sites for informal teacher development. They examined six large Facebook groups created by and for teachers in Sweden on the teaching of mathematics and Swedish. They found that 86% of the discussion threads contained professional knowledge, including knowledge of learners, curricular knowledge and pedagogical content knowledge. Moreover, 11% of the discussion treads contained instances of transformation, i.e., the emergence of new understanding. Similarly, Carpenter et al. (2019) found that teacher interactions on social media are often profession oriented. They analyzed 33,184 tweets from K-12 teacher Twitter accounts and found that U.S. teachers' Twitter use maintained a strong professional focus and education-related hashtags predominated in their tweets. The regular use of educational hashtags indicated that teachers primarily utilized Twitter as an open space to share educational resources and for discussions on education-related subjects. Moreover, social media spaces are found to satisfy diversified professional needs. Carpenter and Staudt Willet (2021) pointed out that most teachers' social media use for professional learning is self-directed and voluntary. They collected 42 months of activities on two teaching-related subreddits, r/Education and r/Teachers, to examine teachers' self-directed professional learning on Reddit. The researchers found that diverse topics were discussed or shared in these teaching-related affinity spaces, including research-based or emotional critiques of educational issues, hyperlinks to policy-related articles, and teacher life beyond classroom practice. Posts in these spaces were characterized by "sophisticated, reasoned discourse" and emotional support. Carpenter and Staudt Willet concluded that social media spaces provide a venue for teachers to process and make sense of emotional issues in teaching, engage in collective deliberation of educational matters, and voice their opinions on educational policy issues.

Researchers have also explored the use of social media to construct professional learning spaces for teachers. Goodyear et al. (2014) shared teacher professional learning on a social media-mediated online professional learning community dedicated to cooperative learning. The community connected seven physical education teachers with an external facilitator. The external facilitator set up a Facebook page to share resources and upload videos of teachers' cooperative learning, and facilitated teacher interaction through tweets, retweets and likes. The researchers found that social media served as a "boundary spanner," where participant teachers and the external facilitator developed "mutual engagement, shared repertoire and joint enterprise" (p.11). Social media also supported sustained interaction around teaching practices beyond normal working hours. The researchers further pointed out that the facilitator's social currency on social media, the large number of Twitter followers, strengthened the teachers' normative belief, and made them perceive the innovative teaching practices that they were pursuing as something right. Having their teaching practice retweeted by the external facilitator also provided an affirmation of their competence and helped them develop the identity as "star performers" and innovators. Prestridge (2017) also argued that social media enables professional reflection, investigation and constructive dialogue that are demand driven and follow free-flowing, self-directed learning pathways. He shared a year-long online professional development program, where teachers developed and implemented individual action research projects with ICT with the support of university mentors. Teachers shared their curriculum materials, blogged the progress of the projects, and commented on each other's reflections. Contents generated by participant teachers formed the "content" of the professional development programme. A series of Web 2.0 tools such as Google Groups, Skype and wall.fm, a social networking site, were used to support teachers' professional learning activities. Participant teachers reported changes in ICT beliefs and practices, a sense of belonging to a community. Prestridge concluded that "the content-free demand-driven model of online professional development enabled teachers to engage in ways that were responsive to their needs and interests and professional school contexts and sustained teachers' involvement to varying degrees without any face-to-face contact" (p. 100). She further pointed out that in such social media mediated self-directed learning interventions, important enablers of effective professional learning include the set-up of self-defined learning milestones and expectations, multiple levels of leadership that give the more confident and experienced teachers the responsibility of peer-mentoring, and the formation of special interest groups. Thus, social media spaces serve as teachers' broader learning ecologies.

The internet and mobile devices

Yurtseven Avci and colleagues (2019) reviewed existing literature on professional development concerning technology adoption and identified a list of key factors that characterize effective professional development. The key factors include situating learning on specific teaching areas with classroom implementation tips, providing opportunities for active on-site, task-driven participation with sustained dialogue and collaboration with peer teachers, making learning ongoing, tailoring learning to local or regional needs, and supporting learning with school-wide learning culture. To realize these essential conditions, teacher professional learning experience needs to be flexible and easily accessible and enables personalized learning. Thus, Internet-based resource pools on a variety of topics are essential to facilitate teacher informal learning on topics of personal interest and needs.

The internet and mobile devices enable convenient and easy access to professional learning materials at any time and any place. Beach (2017) examined teachers' self-directed use of an internet-based professional learning site with free learning resources, including exemplary preK-6 classroom technology integration, video clips of expert teachers on effective practices, lesson plans and student work exemplars. The participant teachers expressed strong enthusiasm for using the site for professional learning because of convenient access to ongoing and just-in-time support, which is not easily accessible through traditional face-to-face professional development events. The participants reported that accessing the websites stimulated them to actively reflect on their teaching performance and increased their self-efficacy. Huang et al. (2022) examined the association of five types of informal professional learning activities with teachers' technology integration. These activities included self-study of online materials, interaction with colleagues, interaction with stakeholders, interaction with students, and reflection. Surveying 1881 K-12 teachers in mainland China, the researchers found that self-study of online materials, such as searching online teaching resources and pop cultural resources that had implications for education, was the most significant predictor of teachers' intention for technology integration in teaching. It also had the greatest effects on perceived usefulness of technology for teaching and self-efficacy beliefs about technology integration. Lee and Kim (2016) further reported on a mobile platform for professional development. The platform includes video resources such as sample lessons from expert English teachers in regular classes and trouble-shooting tips from expert teachers. Korean in-service teacher participants reported using the mobile-based platform flexibly at home, at school and even at café stores, expanding the venue of teacher development beyond time and space boundaries.

Thus, existing literature has revealed various affordances of technology for formal and informal professional learning. As elaborated in previous chapters, technology is a double-edged sword, which incurs hidden and unintended consequences while bringing benefits for teaching and learning. The same is true for the relationship between technology and teacher autonomy. While facilitating it, technology also constrains teacher autonomy.

Technology as a constraint on teacher autonomy

Teacher agency in professional practices emerges in the interaction between the individual and the structure (Priestley et al., 2015). Thus, I will discuss how technology might constrain teacher autonomy at both the individual and structural level.

Constraints at the individual level

Teacher skills to integrate technology in teaching

> As new hardware and software appear in classrooms they bring new possibilities for learning and teaching and sometimes result in the disappearance of familiar capabilities and changes in the skillsets required by teachers and learners. (Albion & Tondeur, 2018, p. 387)

Teachers are expected to have not only the capacity to keep abreast of the wide array of technical skills needed to operate emerging technologies, but also the capacity to appropriate these technologies effectively for teaching and learning. Guzman and Nussbaum (2009) synthesized six domains of skillsets that teachers need to be equipped with. The first domain is the instrumental/technological domain, which highlights the ability to correctly use technology to support the instructional process and solve problems in the instructional context. The second domain is the pedagogical/curricular domain, which refers to the ability to systematically and logically articulate technology within the existing curriculum. The didactic/methodological domain is the third domain and entails the knowledge that would bolster the use of technology to facilitate classroom activities and generate a motivating and collaborative learning environment. The evaluative/investigative domain is the fourth domain, and underscores teachers' abilities to use technological tools to generate feedback on student learning. There is also the communication/relational domain, which includes the abilities to generate appropriate social environments that promote positive attitudes towards technology and facilitate effective interaction with students and among students in the technological environments. The last domain is the personal/attitudinal domain, and this domain highlights teachers' beliefs, emotions, experiences, and expectations that support the integration of technology to transform pedagogical practices. Guzman and Nussbaum argued that all these six domains of skillsets are essential for teachers' autonomous and effective engagement in technology integration. Almerich et al. (2016) synthesized the array of competencies into two major categories: pedagogical competence and technological competence. Pedagogical competence include four domains of knowledge and skills: 1) the use of technology to plan teaching and design curriculum materials; 2) the use of technology to create a rich learning environment; 3) the use of technology to take part in collaboration and communication in educational communities; and 4) the ability to resolve social, ethical, legal and human problems that may arise from technology use. Technological competence is knowledge and skills that allow teachers to master varied technological resources for teaching practice. This competence includes the handling of a computer and intranet, the operation of basic computer applications, the use of multimedia and presentational operations such as educational software, audiovisual media and authoring languages and systems, and the use of information and communication technologies to search, communicate and design.

Unfortunately, teachers are often found to lack essential technological and pedagogical skills. Surveying more than 1000 Spanish K-12 and university teachers, Almerich and colleagues (2016) found that teachers, regardless of whether they are in primary education, secondary education, or university sector, had limited ICT competence, especially with regard to pedagogical competences. Teachers showed a normal level of technological competence but utilized their pedagogical competences only occasionally. Among pedagogical competences, teachers exhibited the most frequent use of technology to plan teaching. However, they seldom considered using technology to create rich learning environments and to seek professional development and interaction in the education community. Suárez-Rodríguez et al. (2018) further found teachers' pedagogical competence was a significant predictor of their technology integration inside the classroom. However, teachers reported limited grasp of educational software, and limited pedagogical competence, especially regarding the use of technology for communicative, collaborative and creative use. Consequently, teachers exhibited limited use of technology in daily classroom practice. Analyzing survey responses from over 2000 teachers across 11 countries, Hämäläinen et al. (2021) also revealed that 42% of the teachers reported weak or very weak skills in using technology in work. There was a great variation in teachers' digital skills, despite an overall positive attitude towards technology use.

In addition to general instrumental skill-based technological and pedagogical competence, the demanded skill sets also include the competence of translating and reconfiguring technologies across domains and contexts, and "adapting and redefining technologies to specific contexts and value orientations" (Engen, 2019, p. 13). Technologies are often designed for the consumer market and for private use purposes. Thus, teachers are charged with the task of converting technologies from a device in the private, consumer domain to the public, education domain. Moreover, technologies carry with them unique cultural expectations and demands for social resources. Thus, to incorporate technology in specific instructional contexts, teachers need to use technologies in ways that fit within the framework of a school and convert them into something that could work in concert with other activities inside the classroom. Thus, a decisive competence is "an awareness and knowledge of the social and cultural aspects of digital technologies' role and transformative potential in the late modern society" and the knowledge of "how to design practices within a context that (often) has strict normative beliefs and orientations regarding what is and what is not appropriate" (Engen, 2019, p. 17).

Teacher skills to support learner use of technology

European DigiCompEdu Framework for Teachers highlights three dimensions of teacher competence (Vuorikari et al. 2016). The first dimension is educators' professional competences, which refers to the competence to use technology for professional engagement, such as professional collaboration, reflective practices, and digital professional development. The second dimension is educators' pedagogic competences, which emphasize the ability to select, create or modify, manage and share digital resources, and the ability to use technology to enrich teaching and learning, to engage in innovative assessment practices, and to empower learners by creating differentiated, personalized and inclusive learning experience and enhancing active learner engagement. These two dimensions correspond roughly with technological and pedagogical competence. However, the framework introduces an additional dimension, i.e., learners' competences. This dimension highlights teachers' competence in facilitating learners' digital competence, such as information and media literacy, communication, content creation, responsible use of technology and problem solving.

Informal learning is increasingly recognized as an important context for student development and technology is a major source of informal learning outside the classroom. Teachers are hence charged with the task of preparing and supporting learners to make appropriate and effective use of technology for self-directed learning beyond the classroom. Thus, the ability to use technology for learner empowerment is a crucial competence teachers need to possess. However, research has revealed that teachers lack this competence. Adopting the DigiCompEdu Framework to measure teachers' digital competence, Lucas et al. (2021) surveyed over 1000 Portuguese teachers and found that the majority of them were at the integrator or the explorer level, i.e., integrating available technologies meaningfully into the teaching process. However, the use of technology for learner empowerment was rather weak. Similar findings are reported in the Moroccan and English context (Benali et al., 2018; Ghomi & Redecker, 2019). Interviewing university students and teachers on perceptions of teacher role in supporting students' autonomous learning with technology beyond the classroom, Lai et al. (2016) found that students expected teachers to have greater involvement in supporting their informal learning by recommending technological resources and sharing metacognitive and cognitive strategies for effective use. However, teachers expected to play a minimal role due to the concern over their limited abilities to provide such support.

Teacher capacity for autonomous action with technology

In addition to the heavy demand for skill sets that may overwhelm teacher autonomy, features of technology may also limit teachers' self-efficacy and incentives for autonomous engagement with technology.

First, the huge amount of constantly updating information online may cripple teacher autonomy. It is estimated that by 2025, 463 Exabytes of data will be created online each day (Vázquez-Cano et al., 2022). Facing the overwhelming amount of information online, teachers may encounter difficulty locating the most relevant resources (Carpenter & Staudt Willet, 2021). Moreover, teaching resources and curriculum materials available online and circulated via social media platforms may lack quality (Sawyer et al., 2019). Mason and Kimmons (2018) further pointed out that, despite designing for educational purposes, not all open educational resources are of high quality. Infoxication (misinformation, disinformation, and fake news) is prevalent on the Internet, which imposes extra cognitive load in processing online information (Vázquez-Cano et al., 2022). Hence, the characteristics of technological resources impose demands on teachers' abilities to critically evaluate the quality and trustworthiness of these resources.

Second, the affordance of technology may turn into constraining forces. Take social media as an example. Social media, due to its connectivity, may induce social comparison. Social comparison may stimulate some into action but impair the self-efficacy of action for others. For instance, Carpenter et al. (2020) reported that viewing peers' Instagram posts induced unhealthy social comparison, and made some teachers feel inferior in their own teaching. Moreover, although social media allows for teachers' voice to be heard by the public and may bolster transformation in education policy and education, the same amplification and anonymity affordances of social media may activate self-censoring among the teachers. Teachers may restrict their social media posts to avoid potential negative reactions, controversies, critiques or even negative professional consequences (Carpenter & Staudt Willet, 2021; Trust & Prestridge, 2020).

Third, teachers may develop overreliance on technology, which deters their professionalism and autonomy. Bower and Sturman (2015) pointed out that surrounded by varied technologies, teachers may exhibit overreliance on technology, putting the affordances of technologies before pedagogical needs and practices. They may take technology as a one-size-fits-all panacea for issues in teaching and learning, and hence overuse technology inside the classroom. One example is data-driven decision making. When given student data collected by technological platforms, teachers may show too much reliance on "datafication to create one-dimensional profiles of students," while ignoring their expert insights into the unique qualities of students, by which their critical role as educational professionals is largely restrained (Kay et al., 2020, p. 234; Kumar et al., 2019). Kemp and colleague (2015) pointed out that overreliance on technology leads to dehumanization in classrooms: "Teaching has been ripped from the realm of human endeavors and morphed into a technological leviathan that is slowly usurping the soul of the profession" (p. 4). When teachers depend too much on technology and technology-mediated teaching materials, rapport with students may be hampered and personal connections with students may be eroded. Teachers may consequently feel constrained in utilizing their professional judgement of the collective and individual needs of students to create meaningful learning experience for their students and bolster learning (Alhumaid, 2019; Tomlinson, 2020).

Constraints at the structural level

Tondeur and colleagues (2008) argued that a primary focus on the individual level factors would orient towards "individual blame" rather than "system blame." Given the complex systemic nature of ICT integration, structural-level factors deserve attention. Scholars have categorized three levels of structural factors where constraints of technology on teacher autonomy may manifest: the macro-level, the meso-level, and the micro-level.

Structural constraints at the macro-level

The macro-level factors rest at the policy and social discourse level and are primarily about societal censure of professional practices. These factors include the social and economic conditions of teaching and schooling, inflexible prescribed curriculum, standardized testing and accountability, and commercial educational resources, such as textbooks (Buchanan, 2015).

> Educational reforms together with marketization of education and shifting sociocultural conditions in these contexts have made teachers increasingly vulnerable to societal censure of professional practices, which is likely to waken effective control of learning and teaching. (Gao, 2018, p. 31)

Societal censure creates a tightened regime of accountability that subjects teachers to critical public scrutiny and constrains their freedom in following instructional practices out of their own professional judgement.

Societal censure may come directly from educational policies and discourses that promote technology integration inside the classroom. For instance, Bladergroen and colleagues (2012) shared how a group of African teachers from under-resources schools felt constrained by the need to chasing the constantly updating government policy about classroom technology integration. They felt that ICT was forced upon them, and hence lacked the internal drive to self-educate themselves. The researchers further pointed out that the macro globalization discourse on the uplifting role of ICT in education and the deterministic view of technology as a panacea for learning regardless of the sociocultural contexts had worked together to silence these teachers from voicing negative views about technological integration initiatives.

The way technology initiatives are framed and promoted may further constrain teachers' autonomy. For instance, Chikuni et al. (2019) conducted critical discourse analysis on the policy landscape of open educational resources at universities in South Africa. They found that the predominant instrumental discourses around OER and deficient discourses around teachers' design abilities discouraged the faculty from re-appropriating OER created by others. The transformation discourse "subjugate the teacher's role in the learning environment or the presence of tutors to support learning" (p. 174). Similarly, Anwaruddin (2015) analyzed government initiatives on the use of ICT to improve English language education in Bangladesh. The initiatives were driven by an instrumental rationality and charged teacher professional development and open language learning programs with the role of transmitting packaged bits of information. Anwaruddin observed that this transmission-oriented initiative to ICT gave teachers a passive role and led to decisionism—"the inability to reflect upon and assess values and goals" (Edgar, 2005, p. 57). Teachers' reflectivity upon pedagogical practices and agency on modifying the official curricula to suit student needs were largely suppressed under such top-down hegemonic initiatives that put them in a subordinate subject position. Anwaruddin hence argued for the importance of developing critical consciousness towards technology use among teachers to "guard against the reification of transmission models of education" (p. 9). Thus, the lack of criticality in policy discourses and government initiatives in relation to technology integration may stifle and fetter teachers' critical and creative responses to technology integration.

Societal censure may also derive from the incompatibility between technology integration and the advocated educational practices in government policies. Gu and Lai (2019) found that the high-stake standardized examination system in Hong Kong rewarded mechanical drills.

However, ICT integration was often interactive and demanded time investment. High-stake exams and ICT integration thus competed with each other for the limited instructional time available. Accountability for standardized tests very often constrains teachers' autonomy in instructional practices (Buchanan, 2015). Similarly, Digón-Regueiro et al. (2021) examined the factors that influenced a primary school Spanish language teacher's classroom technology integration. The incompatibility of technology use with the overloaded Spanish curriculum and standardized external tests was listed as a primary factor that constrained her autonomy in integrating technology into Spanish teaching.

Societal censure may be misleading too. On the one hand, governmental and societal discourses may have difficulty catching up with the rapid change in technology. Albion and Tondeur (2018) argued that the fast pace of technological innovation makes it hard for centralized systems to evaluate the potential of emerging technologies and prescribe appropriate ways of using the technologies in varied contexts. According to them, "top-down solutions emanating from a centralized authority are unlikely to be able to respond as quickly as necessary to the highly contextualized needs of learners and teachers" (p. 390). In such contexts, mandating practices from institutions and centralized authorities may be even constraining. On the other hand, educational discourse and policies are shaped by a neoliberal imagination, where education is conceived as a commodity, whose quality is safeguarded by mandates, sanctions, grants, training and accountability. Under the neoliberal framework, technology is regarded as a silver bullet to resolve enduring problems in education (Burch & Miglani, 2018). The dominance of this technocentrism discourse stimulates the upsurge of various data-informed technological solutions that reduce teaching to "a calculated set of choices based on analysis of individual student preferences" (Burch & Miglani, 2018, p. 14). Most of these solutions are silent on the role of teachers, and teachers have little say over the content, flow, and design of these technological solutions. Teachers were hence reduced to coaches, facilitators, and data analysts (Ratner et al., 2019). Burch and Miglani (2018) observed that under such an educational discourse, Indian teachers struggled to make sense of their professional role and found themselves in a position of fighting for spaces of "real teaching" with technology.

Thus, societal censure in the form of educational policies and social discourses related to technology and education may stifle teachers' professionalism and autonomy.

Structural constraints at the meso-level

Structural constraints the meso-level lie in factors within educational organizations and schools, including predominant policies and cultures in educational communities and school leaderships.

Schools have clear normative orientations and rules that regulate the suitability of the kinds of technology and the types of technology use (Engen, 2019). When schools control the purchasing, access and use of technologies, teachers are left powerless in intended pedagogical use of technology (Barbour, 2012). Nikolopoulou (2020) examined a group of Greek secondary school teachers' perception of the use of mobile devices for instruction, and these teachers listed prohibitive legislation, such as the ban of mobile phones and tablets as schools, as a major inhibitive factor.

Schools vary in innovation capacity and contextual characteristics, and thus may interpret and translate ICT policies differently. Schools vary in the degree to which they involve teachers in the process of constructing school ICT policies. Vanderlinde et al. (2012) examined the implementation of ICT policy at Flemish schools and identified a substantial variation in the creation of school ICT policy. Some schools adopted an inclusive discussion-based approach that involved teachers in setting up school ICT policies. In contrast, other schools adopted a more hierarchical approach that did not allow teacher participation in decision making. The different approaches adopted across schools influenced teachers' autonomy in ICT uptake. When schools embrace technology in mission statement but produce ill-defined processes and procedures or fail to produce concrete directive policies and procedures, teachers may feel oppressed in agentic action (Keengwe et al., 2009). Moreover, the nature of the ICT policies constructed by schools may further constrain teachers' room for action. Sparrius (2020) examined school ICT policies from 100 UK schools and found that schools emphasized "regulatory compliance and asset protection, rather than pedagogical best practice" (p. 86). The restrictive nature of these policies subjugated teachers to surveillance, and punishments were to incur when teachers violated the policy. Moreover, these policies often were quite lengthy and had poor readability, which hindered teachers from perceiving the relevance and purpose of the policy to teaching practices. Furthermore, school ICT decision making was often driven primarily by security considerations rather than pedagogical practice needs. The marginalization of teachers' pedagogical concerns in school ICT policies may lead to the situation where "teachers seek to work around, rather than with, their IT departments" (p. 89).

In addition to school policies on technology integration, school culture with regard to curricular freedom and professional development may further stifle teacher autonomy. Discussing reasons behind the limited use of open educational resources among teachers, Mason and Kimmons (2018) argued when there is no trust for, encouragement of and support on changing approved instructional materials with open educational resources from the administrators, teachers often exhibited little incentive or knowledge to curate, adopt and adapt those resources for teaching. Moreover, centralized professional development is often the primary form of professional learning offered at most schools. However, this conventional form of professional development is slow to respond to teacher learning needs arising from the fast development of technology, and not flexible enough to cater to the professional learning needs in different contexts (Albion & Tondeur, 2018).

Structural constraints at the micro-level

The micro-level factors are at the relationship level, including relationships with colleagues and with students (Digón-Regueiro et al., 2021; Islam et al., 2019). Colleagues have a great impact on teacher attitudes towards an innovation. The influence resides in providing information to shape one's knowledge, reinforcing or changing one's affective state, and shaping and communicating the teaching climate of the department (McConnell et al., 2020). While peers may boost teacher autonomous engagement with innovations, they may also exert a negative influence on teachers' agentic actions (Ertmer & Ottenbreit-Leftwich, 2010). When teachers perceive negative departmental climate that disfavors a given innovation, teacher agency to enact the change might be stifled. Moreover, technology integration may carry the risk of disrupting established social norms and practices in a teaching context, and hence have negative implications on teachers' relationships with colleagues (Ertmer & Ottenbreit-Leftwich, 2010). This risk may discourage some teachers from integrating technology into teaching. For instance, Hazzan (2003) examined novice high school mathematics teachers' technology integration and found that these teachers perceived a negative undercurrent among the veteran teachers towards technology integration. This observation discouraged these novice teachers from adopting technology in teaching. Similarly, Gu and Lai (2019) shared how novice English language teachers might be marginalized by more experienced teachers who considered it unnecessary to integrate technology. As a result, these novice teachers chose neither to share and promote their ICT use, nor to engage their colleagues in conversations about technology integration. Some of them even hid in-class technological projects from colleagues.

Technology may not only threaten teachers' relationship with colleagues, but also challenge teacher-student relationships. The Greek secondary school teachers in Nikolopoulou's (2020) study expressed concerns about the noise and disruption in the class when mobile devices were used, and about students' irresponsible use of mobile technologies such as getting off-task and abusive use of tablet and phone. Those concerns served as a major drive behind their decisions to not use mobile technologies in instruction. Moreover, technology may take away teachers' personal sense of expertise, as students may know more about technology than them and have access to information about the subject matter via technology (Lam, 2000). Consequently, teachers express loss of control inside their classrooms, and exhibit hesitancy in integrating tech-

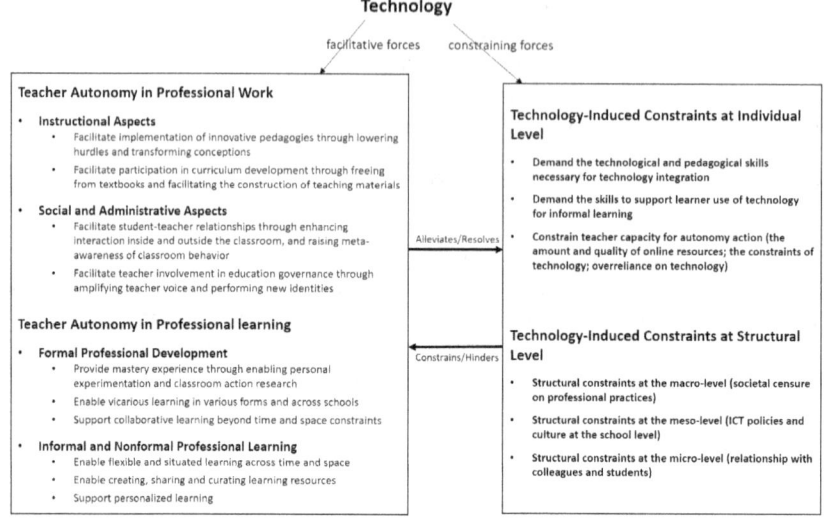

Figure 6 *The impact of technology on teacher autonomy*

nology into teaching (Lam 2000). Kyriacou and Zuin (2016) shared instances of how students used YouTube to challenge teacher authority through cyberbullying their teachers. These students recorded and posted online incidents that demean and ridicule teachers to challenge and undermine teacher authority. Cyberbullying is found to incur negative emotional, behavioral, and physiological impacts on teachers, including feeling uncertainty and reluctance to go to work (Kopecký & Szotkowski, 2017). Feeling belittled by their students made teachers resist integrating technology into teaching and learning.

Thus, technology brings both blessing and obstacles to teacher autonomy. Figure 6 summarizes the facilitative and constraining role of technology in teacher autonomy.

Technology has inherent affordances and constraints, which determines its simultaneous facilitative and constraining effects on teacher autonomy. On the one hand, the constraining forces may hinder or hamper teachers from utilizing technology to boost autonomy in professional work and in professional learning. On the other hand, the facilitative forces may help alleviate or resolve the constraints imposed by technology on teacher autonomy. Thus, to maximize the potential of technology for teacher autonomy, teacher educators need to, on the one hand, create the various conditions that facilitate the positive effects of technology on teacher autonomy and, on the other hand, help individual teachers develop technological and pedagogical skills and overcome the structural constraints so as to ward off the potential constraints that might be induced by technology.

8
Fostering Teacher Autonomy with Technology – The What

The basis of autonomous action is agency. According to Biesta and colleagues (2015) and Emirbayer and Mische (1998), teacher agency is shaped by the past, the present and the future dimensions of one's experience (Biesta et al., 2015; Emirbayer & Mische, 1998). The past dimension entails one's previous experience and dispositions formed out of the experience. The present dimension manifests in the interaction of existing resources and the configurations of reality. And the future dimension refers to one's future orientation and aspirations. These three dimensions suggest a set of factors that might shape teacher agency in utilizing technology for autonomous action. This chapter will elaborate on how these factors influence teacher autonomy with technology, and how these factors might be intervened to foster teacher autonomy with technology.

Factors that influence teacher professional work with technology

Decades of research have been dedicated to understanding factors that influence teacher technology integration. Several theoretical models are available in existing literature that capture the multitude of factors that may influence teacher technology integration.

Conceptualizing factors that influence an individual's intention for technology adoption in general, Venkatesh and colleagues (2003) synthesized the various theoretical frameworks that explain human volitional behavior and technology use behavior and devised the Unified Theory of Acceptance and Use of Technology (UTAUT) model. This model highlights that individual intention for technology adoption is shaped by four main constructs: performance expectancy, effort expectancy, social influence, and facilitating conditions. Performance expectancy is an individual's expectation of whether the intended behavior improves his/her work performance. Effort expectancy refers to an individual's expectation of the effort he/she needs to invest in the intended behavior. Social influence is the extent to which an individual feels that the intended behavior is the normative behavior expected of them from people who are important to them. Facilitating conditions refer to the extent of support an individual perceives to be available. According to Venkatesh and colleagues, these four constructs directly predict one's behavioral intention in technology adoption, which in turn determines one's actual technology usage. The four constructs entail factors that are both external and internal to an individual.

Following the same line of thinking and situating the discussion in the field of teacher technology adoption, Ertmer and colleagues proposed the Framework of Barriers to Teacher Technology Integration that comprises two types of barriers: the first-order/external barriers and the second-order/internal barriers (Ertmer, 1999; Ertmer & Ottenbreit-Leftwich, 2010). The first-order barriers are the availability of resources external to teachers, such as technological resources, instructional resources, and institutional support structure. The second-order barriers are factors intrinsic to teachers, including beliefs, knowledge, and skills (Ertmer, 1999; Hew & Brush, 2007; Kopcha, 2012). The second-order barriers are regarded as more influential, as they mediate the relationship of first-order barriers with teacher technology integration and reduce or magnify the inhibiting effects of first-order barriers to technology integration (Ertmer, 1999; Ertmer & Ottenbreit-Leftwich, 2010; Vongkulluksn et al., 2018).

In addition to these models that conceptualize both internal and external factors, two other influencing models focus specifically on internal factors. A dominating model of technology adoption, Technology Acceptance Model (TAM) by Davis (1989), elaborates on the internal factors of technology adoption: perceived usefulness, perceived ease of use, and attitudes to technology use. Perceived usefulness (i.e., how useful it is to use technology) and perceived ease of use (i.e., how easy it is to use technology) predict an individual's attitudes toward technology use, which determines behavioral intention for technology and subsequent actual use. Perceived usefulness also directly predicts behavioral intention. The Will, Skill, Tool, and Pedagogy (WSTP) Model of technology integration proposed by Knezek and colleagues (Knezek & Christensen, 2016) is another model that elaborates primarily on the influence of teacher internal factors. This model features four constructs that contribute to technology integration. Will is teachers' willingness of and positive attitudes towards technology integration in instruction. Tool is the availability, accessibility, and extent of technology use for instruction. Skill is teachers' ability, self-efficacy, and readiness to use technology. Pedagogy is a teacher's teaching style and the level of confidence they have in using technologies effectively to enhance student learning.

Despite the different foci, these models suggest an array of influencing factors that are both internal and external to teachers.

Teacher internal factors

Teacher internal factors can be categorized into three major dimensions:

the belief and attitude dimension, the knowledge and skill dimension, and the disposition dimension.

The belief and attitude dimension

The belief and attitude dimension entails how teachers view teaching and learning and view themselves. Teacher belief is "teachers' implicit assumptions about students, learning, classrooms and the subject matter to be taught" (Kagan, 1992, p. 66). Pajares (1992) expanded the scope of teacher belief further to refer to beliefs "about their work, their students, their subject matter and their roles and responsibilities" (p. 314). It includes factors like teachers' epistemological beliefs, pedagogical beliefs, motivational beliefs, and professional identity.

Epistemological beliefs

Research has found that epistemological beliefs are significant predictors of teacher technology integration. Epistemological beliefs refer to beliefs about the nature of knowledge and the nature of knowing (Conley et al., 2004; Hofer & Pintrich, 1997). According to Hofer and colleagues (e.g., Hofer & Pintrich, 1997), the nature of knowledge entails the structure of knowledge (i.e., whether knowledge is constituted of isolated elements or interrelated concepts) and certainty of knowledge (i.e., whether knowledge is certain and unchanging, or is uncertain and evolving). The nature of knowing refers to the source of knowledge (i.e., whether knowledge exists outside the individual, or is constructed inside a person) and justification of knowledge (i.e., whether knowledge is justified by authorities or gut feelings or is justified by integrating and balancing personal experimentation and multiple sources). These dimensions determine the level of sophistication in one's epistemological beliefs. Individuals who hold sophisticated epistemological beliefs tend to believe that knowledge consists of interrelated concepts and is constructed within individuals, and that knowledge is uncertain and constantly updating and needs to be justified through multiple sources of information.

Epistemological beliefs are closely associated with teachers' classroom practices and autonomy-supportive teaching (Depaepe et al., 2016; Roth & Weinstock, 2013). Existing research has revealed that sophisticated epistemological beliefs associate positively with teacher technology integration. For instance, Kartal et al. (2022) found that epistemological beliefs about the nature of knowing—the justification of knowledge in particular—significantly predicted pre-service teachers' perceived usefulness and perceived ease of use of technology use in teaching. Bahcivan et al. (2019) further found that pre-service teachers' sophisticated epistemological beliefs in knowledge and knowing predicted their educational technology integration competencies both directly and indirectly via constructivist conceptions of teaching. In contrast, naïve epistemological beliefs have a negative impact on teacher technology integration. Deng et al. (2014) found that Chinese high school teachers who held authority and expert knowledge as the truth were less likely to engage in constructivist use of technology for teaching. Moreover, epistemological beliefs associate differently with different types of technology integration. Examining factors that influenced a group of Chinese English language teachers' technology integration, Lai, Wang, and Huang (2022b) revealed that the belief that knowledge is constructed within individuals had a small but significant effect on the use of technology for content delivery and for learning enrichment. However, this epistemological belief had a negligible effect on the use of technology to boost the agentic role of students in learning.

Finding that epistemological beliefs underlay teacher conceptions of teaching and influenced their technology integration, Kim and colleagues (2013) argued that it is important to change teachers' epistemological beliefs so as to support technology integration. One suggested approach is collective reflection. Kim and colleagues (2013) suggested building a collaborative environment within and across schools to "guide and encourage the implementation of newer beliefs" and support the formulation of "collective beliefs" through engaging teachers to examine their existing beliefs, filter prior beliefs, and evaluate the alignment and conflict across beliefs (p. 83). Barr and Askell-Williams (2020) documented how teacher participation in a professional learning community changed their epistemological beliefs about self-regulated learning. Activities in the community were designed around 3R-EC Framework of epistemic reflexivity that consists of reflections on classroom practice, reflexive thinking and resolved action based on epistemic cognition. The training included six sessions, where teachers engaged in collaborative reflection on classroom practices and epistemic reflexivity, discussion of epistemic aims and processes to improve students' self-regulated learning, and documentation and discussion of lesson plans on the implementation of SRL instruction in their classrooms. Significant changes in epistemological beliefs among the teachers were observed in the study.

Conceptual change intervention is another suggested intervention to stimulate changes in epistemological beliefs. One effective conceptual change intervention approach is the use of augmented activation and refutational text (Guzzetti et al., 1993). Augmented activation is to focus attention on salient information in the provided readings that conflicts with one's own beliefs. Refutational text is the collection of scientific evidences that may lead people to rebut their current beliefs. Gill et al. (2004) found that the combined use of augmented activation and refutational text promoted changes in preservice teachers' epistemological beliefs about mathematics. Developing critical thinking towards assumptions and practices may also induce conceptual changes. This can be achieved through engaging people in critically analyzing problems and questioning their taken-for-granted understanding, such as inspecting and questioning the certainty of some scientific propositions (Kienhues et al., 2008).

Deniz (2011) presented yet another approach that led to changes in preservice elementary school teachers' epistemological beliefs about science. This approach involved explicit instructions on epistemological beliefs. A series of activities were arranged where teachers were asked to explicate their epistemological beliefs and provide justification for these beliefs. Then instruction was provided to promote sophisticated epistemological beliefs and simultaneously lower the status of naïve epistemological beliefs. Reflection activities and class discussions were threaded throughout the process to increase the metacognitive aspect of the instruction.

Pedagogical beliefs

Pedagogical beliefs refer to teachers' beliefs about teaching and learning (Tondeur, van Braak, Ertmer & Ottenbreit-Leftwich, 2017). Literature has identified two categories of pedagogical beliefs: teacher-centered beliefs and student-centered beliefs (Deng et al., 2014). Teacher-centered beliefs regard teachers as authoritative figures who construct a highly structured learning environment to deliver the subject content to the students. Student-centered beliefs respect student needs and interests and emphasize supporting students in constructing their own understanding. These two categories very often co-exist within individual teachers (Tondeur et al., 2017). According to Kagan (1992), pedagogical beliefs are the filter through which teachers screen new knowledge and experience for meaning and relevance. Thus, pedagogical beliefs intertwine closely with teachers' decision-making in relation to whether and how technology is to be integrated in teaching.

Existing literature has shown that teacher-centered pedagogical beliefs are often associated with negative perceptions of the instructional value of technology (Taimalu & Iuik, 2019; Tondeur et al., 2017). In contrast, student-centered pedagogical beliefs contribute positively and significantly to teachers' intention for instructional use of technology via perceived usefulness and perceived value of technology use (Liu, Lin & Zhang, 2017). Moreover, teacher pedagogical beliefs determine how teachers put technology into use. Student-centered pedagogical beliefs are reported to associate positively with teachers' likelihood of using technology in innovative ways beyond information delivery to experiment with new approaches to teaching and learning (Becker, 2000; Liu & Geertshuis, 2021; Tondeur et al., 2017). Student-centered pedagogical beliefs are also associated with more diversified ways of using technology (Tarling & Ng'ambi, 2016). However, teacher-centered pedagogical beliefs are linked to a more regulated and restricted manner of technology use to serve the instructional purpose of skill acquisition (Martin & Vallance, 2008). For instance, Lai and Jin (2021) found that student-centered pedagogical beliefs associated positively with the use of technology for content delivery, for learning enrichment and for the transformation of teaching and learning, whereas teacher-centered pedagogical beliefs predicted neither type of technology use. Moreover, research has shown that teachers who hold both strong student-centered pedagogical beliefs and strong teacher-centered beliefs are likely to exhibit the most frequent adoption of different types of ICT uses (e.g., Tondeur, 2020). Wu et al. (2022) also found that their Taiwanese high school teachers held both teacher-centered and learner-centered pedagogical beliefs to varying degrees. Cluster analysis of teachers' pedagogical beliefs classified teachers into three groups: learner-centered group (teachers who held strong learner-centered pedagogical beliefs and weak teacher-centered beliefs), double-emphasis group (teachers who held both strong learner-centered and strong teacher-centered pedagogical beliefs), and neutral group (teachers who held moderate learner-centered and teacher-centered beliefs). They found that teachers in different groups showed different levels of technological, pedagogical, and content knowledge: teachers in the double-emphasis group outperformed the other two groups in their TPACK for the implementation of video-based flipped learning.

Given the close connection of pedagogical beliefs with teacher technology integration, researchers have advocated greater attention to pedagogical beliefs in facilitating teacher technology integration. For one thing, it is important to introduce technology through pedagogical lenses. Teachers tend to find value in technology when its use aligns with their pedagogical lenses. Tondeur and colleagues (2017) suggested introducing technology in ways that align with teachers' pedagogical beliefs to increase the likelihood of technology integration. Most teachers simultaneously hold multiple pedagogical beliefs and may change their educational lenses depending on the instructional context (Levin & Wadmany, 2005). As Kopcha and colleagues (2020) pointed out, teacher technology use is driven primarily by what they believe to be possible and best for a certain instructional purpose. Thus, it is advisable to take a context-specific orientation when introducing technology, i.e., to introduce diversified and flexible use of technology in response to different instructional purposes, so that teachers can see the relevance of technology to their instructional practices.

For another, facilitating positive reciprocal interaction between technology use and pedagogical beliefs is also important. Reviewing existing qualitative studies on the relationship between pedagogical beliefs and teacher technology integration, Tondeur and colleagues (2017) pointed out that the relationship of technology and pedagogical beliefs is bi-directional: teacher beliefs enable technology integration on the one hand, and technology may stimulate changes in teaching approaches and beliefs on the other hand. Thus, driving a positive cyclical interaction between the two through immersing teachers in technological experience is a possible approach. Lai, Wang, and Huang (2022a) found that after experiencing a three-month emergent remote teaching during the COVID-19 pandemic, their Chinese K-12 teacher participants exhibited greater engagement in student-centered pedagogical practices and student-centered technology use. Moreover, the researchers found that, after this short-term emergent remote teaching, even teacher-centered pedagogical practices associated positively with both student-centered technology use and teacher-centered technology use. They reasoned that this immersive technological experience was characterized using varied technological activities to support student self-directed learning with online resources, which might have increased Chinese K-12 teachers' buy-in of and skills in alternative possibilities of technology use, and hence developed flexible mindset toward technology use. They thus argued that to promote diversified technology use among teachers, it is important to provide exposure to alternative ways of technology use and foster a flexible mindset toward technology use.

Motivational beliefs

Motivational beliefs refer to the beliefs that affect individuals' motivation for volitional technology integration.

Perceived usefulness and perceived ease of use. The Theory of Reasoned Behavior, the psychological theory that links beliefs to behavior, underscores that individuals' behavioral belief and outcome evaluation determine their attitudes towards a certain behavior. Based on this theoretical thesis, Davis (1989) developed the influential Technology Adoption Model, which conceptualized that perceived usefulness (beliefs about the usefulness of the behavior in enhancing job performance), and perceived ease of use (beliefs about the efforts needed in performing the behavior) are two important belief factors that shape individuals' motivation for technology adoption. The effects of these two belief variables are mediated by attitudes toward technology use.

There have been quite a lot of studies that examine how these motivational belief factors relate to teacher technology integration. Meta-analysis studies have proven these two belief factors as significant predictors of teachers' technology integration intention (Scherer & Teo, 2019; Šumak et al., 2011). For instance, Scherer et al. (2019) synthesized 114 relevant studies, and reported an overall moderate effect of perceived usefulness on integration intention ($\beta = 0.37$), and a significant relation between perceived usefulness and perceive ease of use ($\beta = 0.50$). Šumak et al. (2011) found that perceived usefulness and perceived ease of use significantly predicted intention for technology integration, and the effect sizes of these two factors were significantly greater for teachers than for students. Gamage and Tanwar (2018) further found that perceived usefulness was twice as important as perceived ease of use. These studies further revealed a significant effect of attitudes toward technology use on teacher intention for technology adoption, with its effect size ranging from 0.34 to 0.80, and on teachers' actual use of technology ($\beta =0.34$) (Scherer et al., 2019; Scherer & Teo, 2019; Šumak et al., 2011).

Value beliefs and competence beliefs. Cheng et al. (2020) argued that motivational constructs in Expectancy-Value Theory lay out the nuances of individuals' beliefs about the value and their competence of a certain behavior. According to Expectancy-Value Theory, individuals' choice behavior and persistence result from the interaction between beliefs about one's competence and the value of the behavior. There are four dimensions of value beliefs, namely intrinsic value (interest in the behavior), attainment value (importance of the behavior), utility value (usefulness of the behavior) and costs (effort/time needed for the behavior). Competence beliefs consist of two dimensions: ability beliefs and expectancy beliefs. Expectancy beliefs refer to individuals' beliefs about how well they will do on future tasks, and ability beliefs are individuals' perceptions of their current competence for the tasks. Cheng and Xie (2018) found that after controlling for personal characteristic variable, such as age, years of teaching, technology use, gender, educational qualifications and teaching contexts, value beliefs were a significant predictor of teachers' technology pedagogical content knowledge and also moderated the relationship of personal characteristics and teacher knowledge. They further found that value beliefs remained a significant predictor of teacher knowledge on technology integration even after a one-year professional development intervention on teacher knowledge. Based on the survey responses of a group of US middle and high school teachers, Cheng and colleagues (2020) found that intrinsic value beliefs (interest) and expectancy beliefs positively predicted the frequency of teacher technology integration. In contrast, perceived cost had a negative effect on technology integration. Attainment value predicted low-quality technology integration. Expectancy belief was the only factor that significantly predicted high-quality technology integration. Ability beliefs strongly predicted expectancy beliefs and the four dimensions of value beliefs, and its influence on technology integration was fully mediated by these belief factors. The authors argued that, since ability beliefs are a strong antecedent of other motivational beliefs, efforts should be made to nurture perceived technology integration competence.

The research evidences for the positive effect of self-efficacy beliefs on teacher technology integration is strong (Lai, Wang, and Huang, 2022b; Scherer et al. 2015). Despite the consistent findings on self-efficacy beliefs as a strong determinant, existing literature diverges on whether self-efficacy relates to teacher technology integration directly or indirectly via value beliefs. Backfisch et al. (2021) examined the nature of the relationship between self-efficacy beliefs and technology adoption with the survey responses from 524 in-service teachers. They found that self-efficacy not only directly influenced teacher technology use, but also influenced the frequency of technology use indirectly via utility beliefs. Moreover, efficacy beliefs are also found to influence teachers' continued intention to use online learning both directly and indirectly via reduced technostress (Chou & Chou, 2021).

Teacher identity

Identity is the self-imposed meanings of "who one is" (Beijaard et al., 2000). According to the Dynamic Systems Model of Role Identity (Kaplan & Garner, 2017), teacher identity is the personal version of teacher role that one construes in his/her lived context, and social-cultural role identity continuously emerges to frame experience and inform motivated action. Teacher identity in relation to professional roles determines teachers' willingness and ability to respond to changes and innovative teaching practices (Beijaard et al., 2000; Oyserman, 2009), and hence relates to teachers' intention for and nature of technology adoption. Chere-Masopha (2018) conceptualized three aspects of teacher professional identity: the personal landscape (i.e., teachers as individuals with personal skills and beliefs), the situational landscape (i.e., teachers as members of a school community), and the contextual landscape (i.e., teachers as members of the socio-cultural communities that one live in).

Personal identity. All three aspects of teacher professional identity have been reported to determine teachers' technology integration. For instance, Perrotta (2017) found that teachers' self-image as an open-minded innovator helped offset the unfavorable conditions in their work situations and overcome the challenges of missing or failing equipment and the heavy demand on personal investment in time and effort for technology use in teaching. In contrast, Gong and Lai (2018) revealed how a group of pre-service teachers' self- or socially imposed "novice" teacher identity made them powerless in pushing through innovative ideas and deterred them from embracing technology in teaching. These studies suggest that teacher professional identity in the personal landscape may shape their technology integration behaviors.

Situational identity. Other studies have shown that teacher professional identity at the situational level also plays a determining role in technology integration. Existing literature has identified three aspects of teacher professional identity in relation to disciplinary roles: 1) conceptions of roles regarding educational goals; 2) conceptions of roles in relation to instruction; and 3) conceptions of roles in relation to the professional knowledge base. In terms of professional identity with regard to educational goals, teachers' educator orientation, that is, broadly defined goals beyond the subject knowledge, is associated with learner-centered instructional approaches and greater engagement in student-centered technology use (Li et al., 2019). Concerning professional identity in relation to instruction, learner-centered instructional orientation is associated with innovative technology use beyond information delivery and more diversified use of technology (Li et al., 2019; Liu & Geertshuis, 2021; Tondeur et al., 2017). Teachers' orientation towards their professional knowledge base is closely related to their conception of teaching (Beijaard et al., 2000; Löfström et al. 2010). Lai and Jin (2021) examined the relation of these three types of discipline-specific professional identity with the nature of teacher technology integration among a group of in-service EFL teachers. They found that the broader educator identity orientation towards educational goals, pedagogical and didactic identity orientation towards professional knowledge base, and learner-centered identity orientation towards instruction were major determinants of technology use for content delivery and the sole determinants of technology use for learning enrichment and for transformation of teaching and learning. The researchers thus advocated fostering broader and learner-centric professional identity orientations to boost teacher technology use.

Social identity. Other researchers further brought in the social dimension of identity and examined the association of social identity with technology integration. Social identity refers to the sense of who one is and what one should do in response to their definition of "we" derived from perceived membership of social groups. The higher one's social identity is, the greater his/her tendency to perform the behaviors the group expects (Riley & Burke, 1995). Bock and colleagues (2005) found that individuals' adoption of a learning technology was driven by the desire to enhance one's image within the group. Social identity is empirically shown to have a direct effect on individuals' technology adoption intention and also positively moderate the influence of subjective norm on technology integration (Chu & Chen, 2016).

The above research findings advocate future professional development initiatives to feature intervention components on teacher professional identity. Effective professional development needs to provide opportunities for both changes in teachers' self-construal and gains in specific skills and content knowledge (Southerland et al., 2011). Garner and Kaplan (2019) argued that professional development should introduce information that challenges teachers' assumptions of the self and their work and help teachers to explore strategies to resolve the induced identity tensions. But at the same time, professional development needs to be sensitive to teachers' emotions and perceived safety and support them in exploring new possibilities for action and new assumptions about the self, the work practice and the context of work.

In the above section, I reviewed how various teacher belief factors relate to autonomous technology adoption. It needs to be born in mind that teacher beliefs are "a system of interrelated constructs rather than distinct, individual entities" (Kopcha et al., 2020, p. 742), and that different dimensions interact with one another to shape teacher behaviors (Pajares, 1992). Rokeach (1968) conceptualized the interaction of these dimensions on a central-peripheral continuum, with some, such as teachers' self-construal and epistemological beliefs, more proximal to teaching practice and others, such as beliefs about teaching and learning, more distant. For instance, Güneş and Bahçivan (2018) found that pre-service science teachers' sophisticated epistemological beliefs related positively to their constructivist conceptions of teaching. Teachers who believed that knowledge is uncertain and constantly updating and needs justification via multiple sources were more likely to hold constructivist conceptions of teaching. Constructivist conceptions of teaching contributed positively to their digital literacy skills. Lai and Jin (2021) identified that teachers' professional identity in relation to educational purposes and goals was at the more central position of the system and served as antecedents to professional identity with regard to professional knowledge base and with regard to instruction. Teachers' professional identity in relation to instruction mediated the effects of professional identity regarding educational purposes and professional knowledge base on teacher technology use. Thus, these teacher belief factors do not work in isolation, but rather interplay with one another to shape teacher autonomy with technology.

The knowledge and skill dimension

Knowledge and skills are an important cognitive dimension that determines teacher technology adoption. Wilson, Ritzhaupt and Cheng (2020) highlighted that knowledge and skill can be classified into two general categories: conceptual knowledge and practical knowledge. Conceptual knowledge is the knowledge and skill related to the intersection of technological, pedagogical, and content knowledge. Practical knowledge is the knowledge and skill related to technological knowledge and ICT or digital literacy. Practical knowledge also includes technology-related classroom management knowledge and skills (Hew & Brush, 2007).

TPACK

TPACK refers to teachers' technological pedagogical content knowledge that informs authentic technology integration. This construct captures the complex domain of knowledge, where three knowledge components (i.e., technology, pedagogy, and content) interplay with one another. According to Mishra and Koehler (2006), TPACK is a composite construct that consists of seven distinct components. The seven components include technological knowledge (knowledge of digital technologies), content knowledge (knowledge of the subject matter), pedagogical knowledge (knowledge of teaching methods and processes), pedagogical content knowledge (knowledge of using pedagogies effectively to teach content), technological content knowledge (knowledge of using technology effectively to present content), technological pedagogical knowledge (knowledge of using technology effectively in pedagogical activities), and TPACK (the ability to use technology to support pedagogical activities to teach subject content effectively).

TPACK has been found to be the strongest factor in predicting intention for technology adoption (Hsu et al., 2020). Studies have revealed that TPACK is a significant predictor of EFL teachers' technology integration in different research contexts, including Taiwan (Hsu, 2016), Thailand (Kwangsawad, 2016), China (Mei et al., 2018) and Iran (Taghizadeh & Hasani Yourdshahi, 2019). For instance, Raygan and Moradkhani (2020) examined the factors that influence Iranian EFL teachers' technology integration in English instruction and found that TPACK was a stronger predictor than attitudes toward technology use. Lai, Wang, and Huang (2022b) put first-order barriers (beliefs and TPACK) and second-order barriers (professional development and school culture) in one model to examine how these different barriers interacted with one another to influence the nature of technology integration. They found that TPACK directly predicted the use of technology for content delivery, for learning enrichment, and for the transformation of teaching and learning. The predictive power of TPACK was stronger in technology use for the enrichment of student learning experience and for the transformation of teaching and learning than in technology use for content delivery. Their findings are consistent with other research findings that TPACK is a significant predictor of teacher technology integration after controlling for other belief variables and school variables (Taimalu & Luik, 2019; Teo et al., 2019).

Given the significance of TPACK for teacher technology adoption, researcher have explored potential ways boost TPACK. Lai, Wang, and Huang (2022b) found that professional development and school culture significantly predicted TPACK, explaining 36% of its variation. They thus concluded that building school culture in favor of technology integration and providing technical and pedagogical support from formal and informal channels are important for the development of TPACK. In their synthetic review of research studies on TPACK interventions, Major and McDonald (2021) synthesized five types of interventions that facilitate the successful development of university instructors' TPACK: individual contextualized instructional consultations, train-the-trainer methods, online training courses, the provision of TPACK design scaffolds (e.g., lesson design formulas, TPACK activity designs) and long-term distributed training. In addition, existing research also suggests a series of intervention design features that are effective in developing TPACK. These design features include explicit discussion of TPACK framework, hands-on ICT-based teaching activity and design thinking, modeling from experienced teachers, engagement in collaborative lesson design, and the strengthening of value beliefs about technology use during professional development events (Cheng & Xie, 2018; Roussinos & Jimoyiannis, 2019; Taimalu & Luik, 2019). Focusing specifically on pre-service teachers, Tondeur et al. (2020) synthesized six key strategies that are found to facilitate pre-service teachers' technology integration. These six strategies include: 1) role modeling from teacher educators on exemplary TPACK practices; 2) reflections on the role, the opportunities and the risks of technology in education; 3) designing TPACK curriculum materials; 4) collaboration with peers on TPACK instructional design; 5) authentic experiences of applying TPACK knowledge in real technology experiences; and 6) provision of feedback informed by constant monitoring of ICT competence development through questionnaire, portfolio, observations. They found that the six strategies correlated significantly with TPACK even after controlling for pre-service teachers' general ICT attitudes.

Digital literacy

Digital literacy refers to the skills to use information and communication technologies creatively and critically. Digital literacy was found to be a significant predictor of pre-service teachers' effective use of technologies in science learning environments (Martinovic & Zhang, 2012). Scherer et al.'s (2019) meta-analytic study has revealed that computer self-efficacy had a significant effect on both perceived usefulness of technology integration ($\beta = 0.24$) and perceived ease of use ($\beta = 0.39$).

Nascimbeni (2018) highlighted two dimensions of digital literacy: the functional dimension and the critical dimension. The functional dimension refers to "the skills and competences that enable individuals to read, write and interact across a range of platforms, tools and media" and "a repertoire of digital literacy practices in specific social and cultural contexts" to maintain effective social, educational and/or professional relationships. The critical dimension is the understanding of the "non-neutral nature of digital tools and environments" and the ability to use technology critically for personal and social change (p. 4). The JISC Digital Capabilities Model elaborates on the two dimensions further to include a few components, including the foundational ICT proficiency, information, data and media literacies, digital learning and development literacies, competencies for digital creation, problem solving and innovation, and competencies for digital communication, collaboration, and participation. Digital identity and wellbeing are underlying issues in all these dimensions. Falloon (2020) introduced the teacher digital competence framework. This framework consists of curriculum competencies, personal-ethical competencies, and personal-professional competencies. Curriculum competencies refer to the capabilities and skills to use digital technologies for subject-based learning, including pedagogical and learning design competences, discipline knowledge competences, and technical and technological competences. It is about making informed decisions about digital technology selection and use in teaching, teaching about, with and through digital technology effectively, and using digital technology to support ubiquitous and transformative professional practices. Personal-ethical competencies refer to the capabilities and skills of considering the impact of digital technologies, exercising digital citizenship of sustainable, safe and ethical use of digital resources, managing personal presence and wellbeing, and assisting students to do so. Personal-professional competences refer to the capabilities and skills to effectively search, critically evaluate and organize, and creatively integrate information to solve problems in professional contexts, to seek and participate effectively in online environments and communities, and to commit to continuous professional learning.

Given the complexity and breadth of digital competences, scholars advocate a collaborative approach either within disciplines or across disciplines in teacher education programs (Falloon, 2020; Habowski & Mouza, 2014). Hobbs and Coiro (2018) highlighted three key design features in promoting digital literacy. The first design feature is to engage teachers to reflect on their motivation for advancing digital literacy and raise awareness of their motivational profiles towards digital literacy and the associated beliefs. The second design feature is to engage teachers in collaborative inquiry tasks, such as design studio, to enhance appreciation for and continued engagement in collaborative inquiry in respective working contexts. The third design feature is to foster a learner-centered, rather than machine-centered, approach to technology use and bolster criticality towards the impact of technology. Güneş and Bahçivan (2018) further identified that teachers' epistemological and teaching belief systems were antecedents to digital literacy. They found that constructivist teaching beliefs contributed the most to pre-service teachers' digital literacy, and thus suggested promoting constructivist conceptions of teaching in teacher education programs.

Teaching competence

In addition to knowledge and skills of designing and teaching in technology-enhanced learning environments, some general teaching competencies are also essential to teachers' autonomous engagement with technology in teaching practices. For instance, learning design skills are found to be essential to teacher technology integration, since the integration of innovative technologies often involves redesign of teaching (Alshammari et al., 2016). Moreover, classroom management skills are important. Classroom management is "the actions teachers take to create an environment that supports and facilitates both academic and social emotional learning" (Eversonte & Weinstein, 2006). Teachers' ability to manage the classroom and organize instruction is critical to the successful implementation of any teaching method. There are five dimensions of classroom management: the management of the physical structure of classroom, the planning of the teaching methods and principles that work best in the environment to achieve desired educational goals, the creation of time plan for classroom activities, the development and nurture of teacher-student relationships, and the prevention of misbehavior and reward for appropriate behavior (Başar, 2003). Technology integration requires changes in the instructional process, and different types and ways of using technology demands different classroom management approaches. For instance, technical issues may cause disruptions in teaching and engender negative student behaviors (Lim et al., 2005). Research has found that for new teachers who have less teaching experience, one major hurdle to technology adoption is classroom and time management (Lau & Sim, 2008; Osei et al., 2014). Developing competencies in classroom management in technological environments is thus an essential component of effective technology integration intervention programs (Varank & Ilhan, 2013).

The emotional dimension

Emotions have a filtering effect on beliefs about teaching, learning, and motivation (Mansfield & Volet, 2010). Emotions and adaptation behaviors bridge the gap between the disruption of routines and the creation of new routines or the re-establishment of old routines (Beaudry & Pinsonneault, 2010). Perrotta (2017) pointed out that most existing models of individual-level technology adoption rest solely on strong rationalistic assumptions, where individuals are perceived as "rational maximisers of interest and utility" (Green et al., 1994, p. 3). However, to Perrotta, technology integration is not a purely rational decision making but rather involves "an interplay of rationality and emotions in the complex dynamics that shape behavior" (p. 801). Thus, factors at the emotion dimension may also play a central role in influencing teachers' autonomous engagement with technology.

Anxiety

Anxiety includes terms such as worry, nervousness, uneasiness, apprehension, or fear. Through his meta-analysis study on the relationship between teacher anxiety and technology change, Henderson and Corry (2021) identified different sources of anxiety that are related to technology adoption. The sources include anxiety from identity change implied by the addition of technology, anxiety over students' perceptions of teacher expertise, and anxiety related to the worry of losing professional standing among peers and leaders.

Howard (2013) found teachers feared that the integration of technology might challenge their educator identity and the appropriateness of their current way of teaching. This fear triggered risk apprehension, and deterred teachers from incorporating technology into teaching. Bennett (2014) further found that teachers' fear of being perceived as incompetent with technology made them feel that technology integration may threaten their authority inside the classroom, which discouraged them from actively incorporating technology into teaching. Existing research further reveals that computer anxiety may have a greater impact on perceived ease of use and perceived usefulness than computer self-efficacy and associates negatively with teachers' satisfaction with e-solutions (Al-Busaidi & Al-Shihi, 2012; Chiu, 2017). Computer anxiety also negatively predicts teachers' attitudes toward educational technology (Agbatogun, 2010).

Scholars hence recommend paying attention to teacher computer self-efficacy and their risk perceptions in the effort to reduce teacher anxiety in technology adoption. Research reveals that instructional use of technology may combat anxiety. The experience of using technology and the concomitant computer self-efficacy is found to associate negatively with computer anxiety (Chiu & Churchill, 2016). Interventions in risk analysis are also important. Given that openness to technology is a predictor of how a person would assess risk (Howard, 2013), fostering an open mindset among teachers might help reduce anxiety as well.

Techno-stress

Techno-stress is an emotional factor that has been reported to influence teacher technology adoption. Techno-stress refers to the direct and indirect negative impact on attitudes, thoughts, behaviors, or psychology incurred by technology. Techno-stress is indicated by the degree of anxiety an individual feels when using technology. Techno-stress has been found to negatively impact teachers' intention for technology use (Joo et al., 2016; Verkijika, 2019). It also associates negatively with K-12 teachers' continued intention to use online teaching after the emergent remote teaching experience during the COVID-19 pandemic period (Chou & Chou, 2021). Techno-stress also negatively moderates the link between perceived usefulness and teachers' satisfaction with and continued intention for digital textbook adoption (Verkijika, 2019).

Current research has identified five sources of techno-stress: techno-invasion, techno-overload, techno-complexity, techno-insecurity and techno-uncertainty. Techno-invasion refers to the perception of one's instructional spaces and personal life being invaded by technology, such as tight curriculum schedules and excessive time needed to keep updated with technology skills. Techno-overload refers to the perception of being driven to work faster and longer due to increased work demands associated with ICT. Techno-complexity refers to work difficulty and challenges because of the complexity of ICT. Techno-insecurity is the fear of being replaced by technologies or other people who have higher ICT capacities. And techno-uncertainty refers to the feeling of ambiguous work requirements and expectations in relation to technology integration. Jena (2015) examined how one source of techno-stress, techno-invasion, influenced university teachers' job performance. Techno-invasion associated negatively with job satisfaction, organizational commitment and less technology enabled performance, and positively with negative affectivity. Li and Wang (2020) examined the other four sources of techno-stress and found that techno-complexity and techno-insecurity had significant negative associations with university teachers' work performance.

Researchers have found that the level of teachers' knowledge of technology use and teachers' perception of school technical support and peer support on the use of technology associated negatively with techno-stress (Joo et al. 2016; Özgür, 2020). Potential school support includes clear documentation of school expectations on technology use, rewarding mechanisms for using new technologies, help desk that is responsive to end-user requests, consultations with teachers before introducing new technologies, and teamwork in dealing with technology-related problems (Jena, 2015). Dong et al. (2020) examined how school support (administrative support and collegial support), computer self-efficacy and teachers' knowledge in technology integration for teaching interacted with one another to influence techno-stress. They found that computer self-efficacy and teachers' knowledge about technology integration negatively predicted techno-stress. Collegial support was a significant positive determinant of both computer self-efficacy and knowledge about technology integration, whereas administrative support predicted computer self-efficacy only. The researchers thus stressed the importance of strengthening long-term co-design between and mutual collaboration among colleagues to help mediate teachers' techno-stress. Syvänen et al. (2016) further found that, in addition to ICT competence and school support for ICT use, perceived alignment of ICT with one's teaching style and attitudes toward the educational use of technology were also significant predictors of techno-stress. The researchers thus recommended pedagogical enhancement related to different technologies as a means of enhancing teachers' awareness of diversified use of technology and boost positive appraisal of the alignment of technology with their teaching styles. Li and Wang (2021) examined the effects of three types of techno-stress inhibitors on techno-stress and work performance among university teachers. The three types of techno-stress inhibitors include: literacy facilitation (i.e., enhancing knowledge and skills), technical support provision (i.e., providing technical assistance), and involvement facilitation (i.e., involving teachers in decision-making throughout the process of ICT implementation). They found that involvement facilitation had a significant negative association with techno-overload, techno-complexity and techno-insecurity, and technical support provision was also negatively associated with techno-overload. Literacy facilitation and involvement facilitation had a positive direct association with teachers' work performance. The researchers concluded that involvement facilitation played the most important role in curbing techno-stress and promoting work performance.

Perceived enjoyment and playfulness

Perceived enjoyment refers to the extent to which the use of technology is perceived as fun in its own right. Perceived enjoyment has been reported to be a significant determinant of teachers' intention to adopt various technologies (Teo & Noyes, 2011). Perceived enjoyment also influences technology integration intention via perceived usefulness and perceived ease of use (Lee et al., 2019; Huang et al., 2020). An associated concept is perceived playfulness, which also has a significant positive association with attitudes toward technology (Chung & Tan, 2004).

Perceived enjoyment and playfulness are often derived from a person's interaction with environmental factors. Existing research has revealed that some personal factors, such as personal innovativeness in information technology, and some environmental factors, such as the extent that the technological experience promotes shared identity and social interaction, are significant antecedents to perceived enjoyment (Alalwan et al., 2018; Wang et al., 2012).

Thus, not only cognitive variables, such as beliefs, knowledge, and skills, but also emotional variables, such as anxiety, stress and enjoyment, are at play in shaping teachers' autonomous engagement with technology.

The dispositional dimension

In addition to cognitive and emotional factors, teachers' dispositional factors may also influence their autonomous action with technology. Liu and Geertshuis (2016) underscored a few psychological orientations that serve to guide teacher behavior, among which are personal innovativeness and openness to change.

Personal innovativeness

Personal innovativeness refers to "the willingness of an individual to try out any new information technology" (Agarwal & Prasad, 1998, p. 206). Innovative people have stronger risk-taking inclination and are more likely to perceive the compatibility of an innovation with their objectives (Jackson et al., 2013). Personal innovativeness is a significant antecedent to individuals' technology acceptance (Granić & Marangunić, 2019). Mazman Akar (2019) found that personal innovativeness was a significant predictor of Turkey K-12 teachers' perceived usefulness, perceived ease of use and subjective norm of technology integration for teaching. Similar findings have been reported on university educators. Lee and Jung (2021) pooled together a series of individual, institutional, and course design factors to examine their relative influence on the degree to which Korean university teachers used technology for instructional changes during the COVID-19 pandemic period. The researchers found that individual factors, particularly innovation propensity, were the strongest predictor of teachers' use of technology for instructional changes. In addition, personal innovativeness is also found to significantly moderate the associations of the quality and perceive enjoyment of the big data platforms with university academia's acceptance of big data platforms for teaching (Aldholayet al., 2022). Similarly, López-Pérez et al. (2019) found that personal innovativeness positively predicted Chile primary school teachers' performance expectancy, effort expectancy, perceived social influence, and facilitating conditions of classroom technology integration. Moreover, teachers with higher personal innovativeness are more likely to adopt new technology regardless of its complexity, whereas teachers with lower personal innovativeness are less likely to adopt new technology and more likely to abandon the adoption at certain points (Aldunate & Nussbaum, 2013).

Attitude toward change

Teachers' willingness to take risks and experiment with different teaching approaches is central to significant changes at school (Howard & Mozejko, 2015). Resistance to change is reflected in having difficulty changing the normal routine or having stress when faced with a change, and can manifest at the cognitive, affective, and behavioral levels. Resistance to change is one of the main reasons for the failure of education reforms (Fullan & Hargreaves, 1996). Alanoglu et al. (2022) examined the relation of Turkish primary school teachers' educational philosophy beliefs with their digital literacy levels. They found that resistance to change played a significant mediating role in the association between contemporary educational philosophy beliefs and teachers' digital literacy levels. That is, the greater contemporary educational beliefs one holds, the less likely he/she is to resist change, and the higher level his/her digital literacy might be.

On the contrary, openness to change is often associated with appreciation of new experiences and tolerance of uncertainty (Bano et al. 2019). Openness to change is a significant predictor of teacher technology competency and technology integration. Teachers who have a high level of openness to change are more likely to believe that ICT may enhance student learning (Bano et al., 2019). Research has identified a few critical conditions for the development of openness to change: 1) building a school culture that encourages teachers to experiment with new tools, approaches and teaching strategies without fear of negative impact; 2) actively involving teachers in the decision-making process about technology-related changes; and 3) providing teachers the time to learn, plan and collaborate on technology-enhanced curriculum (Howard & Mozejko, 2015).

Teacher external factors

Perrotta (2017) argued that culture, both at the local and macro level, filters or mediates factors for individual choices and behaviors. The macro level culture are discourses and ideologies reflected in national policies and institutional values, and the local level culture is the intra-group norms and support.

Macro-level factors

Policy pressure

Policy conveys a shared vision that guides and binds individual actions. For teachers, policy pressure comes from both national education policies and school policies. Positive associations between policy pressure and teacher technology integration have been reported in the existing literature. For instance, Huang and Teo (2020) found that perceived importance of technology-related school policies positively predicted Chinese university teachers' behavioral intention in relation to technology integration and their perceived usefulness of the behavior.

However, existing research also reveals that the association between policy and teacher technology integration might be a relative and dynamic one. For instance, Salinas et al. (2017) examined levels of technology integration among teachers across three Latin American countries that vary in public policy emphasis on technology integration. They found that when national policy stressed integrating ICT into the curriculum, teachers showed higher levels of technology adoption. More importantly, they identified that the association was not linear as expected. Instead, both teachers who reported feeling the least pressure and those who felt the most pressure display high levels of ICT adoption. Thus, the influence of national policy on individuals' intention for technology integration is dependent on individual teachers' motivation and degree of autonomy for action. Similarly, Zheng et al. (2019) found that the influence of the policy pressure was short term and varied in different stages of e-textbook adoption. For teachers who had limited intention for e-textbook adoption, policy pressure had a positive and significant effect on teachers. However, this effect was insignificant for teachers in the moderate and intensive intention states. Thus, although the policy may drive initial intention for technology integration, once teachers started to use technology, they became insensitive to pressure from policy.

School culture

Maslowski (2001) defined school culture as "the basic assumptions, norms and values, and cultural artefacts that are shared by school members" (p. 8-9). Organizational culture is a multifaceted concept. Zhu (2015) identified six dimensions of organizational culture. One dimension is goal-orientation, namely, the extent to which the school has clearly formulated visions that are shared among members. The second dimension is innovation orientation, which is the extent to which school members have open attitudes toward change. The third dimension is leadership, i.e., the extent to which members perceive clear expectations from school leaders for change and the extent to which activities organized at school are well structured. The fourth dimension is formal relationships, namely professional and nonprofessional ties among teachers. The fifth dimension is participative decision making, that is, the level of teacher involvement in decision making at school. The last dimension is shared vision, in other words, the extent to which the school has a powerful blueprint for the future and shared understanding among members.

Organizational culture shapes how individuals set personal and professional goals, perform tasks, and utilize resources to achieve goals (Lok & Crawford, 2004). Examining the association of different categories of organization culture with Chinese university teachers' intention for technology integration, Huang and Teo (2020) found a significant positive overall association between the two. Thus, the more the school culture is characterized by strong goal orientation, innovation orientation and shared visions towards technology use, supportive and instructive leadership, a high level of involvement of teachers in school decision making and strong relationships among school members, the more likely teachers are to integrate technology in instruction. They further reported that school culture also positively predicted teachers' perceived importance of technology-related school policy. The researchers hence advocated strengthening school culture to influence teachers' perceptions. Lai, Wang, and Huang (2022b) examined the influence of school culture together with other significant barrier factors to teacher technology adoption (belief systems, TPACK and professional development) on in-service university EFL teachers' different approaches to technology adoption. They found that when other important first-order and second-order barriers were controlled, school culture showed up to be a significant direct predictor of the use of technology for content delivery and the use of technology to transform teaching and learning to foster self-directed learning. The influence of school culture on technology integration is most significant among EFL teachers' collectivist-culture backgrounds, who are more likely to internalize external pressure and requirement and perceive these expectations as congruent with their self-concept (Huang et al., 2019).

Tondeur et al. (2008) further explored how different dimensions of school culture relate to teacher technology adoption. They examined four types of school culture factors: aspects of school culture (goal orientedness and school innovativeness), school leadership, ICT school policy (ICT school policy, teachers' perceptions of ICT school policy; content ICT plan), and ICT support (ICT-related support and training). They found that teachers' perceptions of school policy were the most significant determinant of the use of computers to develop computer skills and as a learning tool. Similarly, Xie et al. (2021) found that perception of shared school visions on technology integration was positively associated with beliefs in favor of technology integration and actual engagement in technology use. Thus, helping teachers develop a shared vision on the value of technology is essential. Teachers are more likely to integrate technology when they perceive supportive school culture, such as a shared vision of technology use, encouragement and recognition, and resources and technical support (Atman Uslu & Usluel, 2019; Tondeur et al., 2008). Language teachers regard the technical infrastructure and support at school, encouragement from the leadership team, and positive appraisal from colleagues as significant determinants of technology adoption inside the language classroom (Huang et al., 2019; Raygan & Moradkhani, 2020). Moreover, school openness to change was a significant predictor of the use of computer as a learning tool. Teachers at schools with an open culture to innovation are more likely to move forward with ICT integration.

Local-level factors

Subjective norms

Subjective norms refers to "a person's perception that most people who are important to him or her think he or she would or should not perform the behavior in question" (Fishbein & Ajzen, 1975, p. 302). Significant others that influence teacher technology adoption might be school leaders, colleagues, and students (Huang et al., 2019). Subjective norms are conceptualized as a direct determinant of individuals' behavioral intention in the Theory of Planned Behavior (Ajzen, 1985). Thus, it is included in major technology adoption models, such as TAM2 and UTAUT, as a major antecedent to intention to technology adoption (Venkatesh & Davis, 2000; Venkatesh et al., 2003). Meta-analysis studies on antecedents of technology adoption have attested to its significant predictive power on perceived usefulness and behavioral intention for technology integration (Feng et al., 2021; Zhao et al., 2021). Focusing on teachers' technology adoption in instruction, Scherer et al.'s (2019) meta-analysis study of 114 studies revealed that subjective norm has an overall small effect size on teachers' perceived usefulness of technology integration ($\beta = 0.28$) and a smaller effect size on teachers' perceived ease of use ($\beta = 0.09$). Researchers have further revealed that the association between subjective norm and behavioral intention was stronger for teachers who perceived a lower level of voluntariness in technology integration, who reported lower perceived competence in conducting the behavior, and who are in the collectivistic culture (Huang & Teo, 2021; La Barbera & Ajzen, 2020; Zhao et al., 2021).

Facilitating conditions

Facilitating conditions refer to individuals' perceptions of supporting organizational and technical infrastructure for technology integration. Supportive infrastructure manifests in both technical and pedagogical support, and assumes various forms, such as leadership encouragement, teacher evaluation and awarding systems, technical support, and colleague enthusiasm. Facilitating conditions are conceptualized as a direct driver of actual technology use and is found to be an important determinant of teachers' technology adoption (Huang et al., 2019; Lai, Wang & Huang, 2022b). Atman Uslu and Usluel (2019) found that encouragement from school on ICT use was a strong determinant of teachers' in-class technology integration. Perceived support from school associates positively with teachers' TPACK and is a significant predictor of attitudes toward technology integration (Huang et al., 2019; Raygan & Moradkhani, 2020). Insufficient technical infrastructure, lack of professional ICT trainings and lack of time are the oft-reported barriers to technology adoption among teachers. Lai, Wang, and Huang (2022b) found that school support is one of the strongest determinants of Chinese K-12 English language teachers' technology adoption after controlling for the influence of beliefs, knowledge and skills. In Scherer et al.'s meta-analysis, facilitating conditions were found to have significant effects on both perceived ease of use ($\beta =0.30$) and perceive usefulness ($\beta =0.12$), with a greater effect on the former.

Professional development opportunities

Teachers' participation in professional learning is a significant predictor of technology use for both lower-order and higher-order classroom tasks (Bowman et al., 2020; Han et al., 2018; Petko et al, 2015). Participation in professional learning may also influence technology use indirectly via teachers' knowledge and skills and via value beliefs about technology use (Bowman et al., 2020; Xie et al., 2017). Teachers are more likely to develop positive beliefs in favor of technology integration and sustain technology-enhanced teaching activities, when they have access to professional development (Xie et al., 2021).

Professional learning can take place both formally through organized training events and informally through self-initiated professional learning or peer discussion and collaboration (Han et al., 2018, Petko et al., 2015). Lai, Wang, and Huang (2022b) found that the contribution of formal and informal professional learning remained a significant predictor of teacher technology use, regardless of whether the use of technology was for content delivery, for learning enrichment, or for the transformation of teaching and learning. Moreover, Huang et al. (2022) found that informal professional learning contributed significantly to teachers' intention for technology adoption. The contribution of different types of informal professional learning varied: Among different sources of informal professional learning, the inner source of learning, i.e., learning through reflection, and the non-interactive social source of learning, i.e., learning through media, were the strongest determinants of teacher technology adoption. The effect of learning through student interaction was mediated equally by perceived usefulness and self-efficacy beliefs, while the effect of learning through colleague interaction was mediated only by perceived usefulness. Learning through stakeholder interaction was not a significant determinant of teacher technology adoption at all. Examining the short-time and long-term impact of different interventions on teachers' sustained use of e-textbooks, Zheng et al. (2019) further found that compulsory professional development led to immediate usage increase, but peer demonstration and experience-sharing sessions brought long-term impact. They thus advocated a dynamic approach for understanding the influences of different types of professional learning on teacher technology adoption. Moreover, Gamage, and Tanwar (2018) found that when teacher training is followed up with facilitating conditions such as on-site coaching, the effect size on technology integration increased by 0.48 and reached 1.31.

Moderating factors

So far, I have identified a set of core internal and external factors that have been reported in the existing literature as significant predictors of teacher technology integration. However, the associations of these core influencing factors with technology integration are rather relative, and the strength of the associations depends on individual characteristics (Venkatesh et al., 2003). Research on teacher technology integration has identified a few factors that moderate the relationship of these core factors with teacher technology integration. Some of the oft-cited moderating factors include teaching and learning experience, gender, and school level.

Experience

Experience refers to prior teaching and learning experience. Teaching and learning experience is strongly associated with teachers' conceptions of teaching and learning and their receptivity to innovative practices, and hence is expected to play a role in teachers' technology use intention (Teo & Zhou, 2017). Güneş and Bahçivan (2018) found that pre-service teachers' previous learning experience positively impacted both their epistemological beliefs and digital literacy skills. They reported cases where, despite holding naïve epistemological beliefs, teachers reported constructivist conceptions of teaching and learning, because they had personal experience of constructivist ways of teaching when attending high school. Thus, the more central beliefs about teaching and learning overrides the more peripheral belief about the nature of the subject, contributing to greater digital literacy skills. Contrasting the associations in the TAM model between pre-service teachers and in-service teachers, Scherer and Teo (2019b) found that existing literature suggests a significantly stronger link between perceived ease of use and attitudes towards technology use among pre-service teachers. Existing literature also reveals that perceived usefulness, perceived ease of use and attitudes toward technology use account for a greater variation of technology integration intention and actual technology use among in-service teachers (Scherer et al., 2019). Moreover, Cheng and Xie (2018) found that years of teaching negatively predicted teachers' technological knowledge, technological pedagogical knowledge, and technological pedagogical content knowledge. Syvänen and colleagues (2016) further found that technostress varied in response to teaching experience. Teachers with 16–30 years of working experience felt more stressed than teachers with 0–15 years of experience when using technology. Moreover, professional development initiatives on knowledge and skills had a greater effect in reducing the techno-overload and techno-complexity of more experienced teachers than of teachers with less than ten years' working experience (Li & Wang, 2021).

Gender

Gender is another factor that moderates the associations of core influencing factors and teacher technology adoption. For instance, Sharma and Srivastava (2019) further found that, although gender did not moderate the relation between self-efficacy belief and behavioral intentions, gender did significantly moderate the associations of value beliefs, perceived ease of use and subjective norm with Indian university teachers' intentions for technology integration. The researchers hence called for designing differential motivational plans and strategies to promote technology integration among male and female teachers. Specifically, Scherer and Teo's (2019) meta-analysis study revealed that the link between perceived usefulness and behavioral intention was stronger for male than for female teachers. Cheng and Xie (2018) also found that value beliefs mattered more for male than female teachers in enhancing technological knowledge and technological content knowledge. Similarly, Yuen and Ma (2002) found that the link between perceived ease of use and intention to computer use was significant for female teachers, but not significant for male teachers. For male teachers, perceived ease of use influenced intention to computer use primarily through perceived usefulness. Thus, male teachers might be driven more by productivity-related factors such as usefulness, and thus more time needs to be allocated to developing a positive perception of usefulness among male teachers.

Research further reveals that emotions have a greater impact on female than on male teachers. Syvänen and colleagues (2016) found that female teachers were more likely to suffer from technostress than male teachers. Guillén-Gámez and Rodríguez-Fernández (2022) conducted a meta-analysis study on studies that examined gender differences in teachers' attitudes towards ICT and identified a small to medium significant effect size of gender on teachers' emotional attitudes (anxiety or fun) towards ICT, favoring female teachers. That is, female teachers had stronger emotional response to ICT, either positive or negative. In contrast, male teachers reported significantly more favorable affective, cognitive, and behavioral beliefs of ICT and self-efficacy towards technology. These researchers further found that gender difference manifests differently in different sociocultural contexts. Gender difference in self-efficacy was significant in Asia and USA, but not in Africa. In contrast, gender difference in emotional attitudes was significant only in the Asian context, and gender difference in beliefs was only significant in the European context. They further found that gender differences in emotional attitudes and self-efficacy were significant for both K-12 teachers and university teachers, whereas gender difference in beliefs was significant only for K-12 teachers.

School level

Teaching different school levels implies different possibilities for innovation, given that school levels vary in the level of curriculum freedom, the characteristics of students, and the nature of educational responsibilities. Kelly (2014) examined teachers' perception of open education resources and found that elementary and secondary school teachers reported greater perceived usefulness than teachers working in the higher education contexts. Moreover, elementary school teachers reported lower self-efficacy in making use of open education resources, and secondary school teachers reported significantly higher self-efficacy than their counterparts in the elementary school sector and university education sector. However, secondary school teachers may also have greater techno-stress than primary school teachers (Syvänen et al., 2016). Similarly, Jung et al. (2019) found that teacher-related variables—TPACK, pedagogical beliefs, self-efficacy about using technology and perceived motivational support at school—associated differently with teacher technology adoption among Korean teachers working at different school levels. They found that although TPACK, self-efficacy and perceived motivational support were consistently the significant predictors of classroom technology use across both elementary school and secondary school teachers, the magnitude of the effects varied across the two groups. Perceived motivational support (e.g., school policy, administrators' support) was the most significant predictor for elementary school teachers, whereas TPACK was the factor with the largest effect for secondary school teachers. The researchers thus advocated adopting differential approaches in supporting technology integration among teachers at different school levels. Similarly, focusing on teachers' adoption of smart education, Kim and Kim (2013) found that the associations of attitudes, teacher efficacy towards smart education, and teachers' resistance to school change with intention for technology use were significantly greater for elementary school teachers than for secondary school teachers. In contrast, for secondary school teachers, the predictive powers of subjective

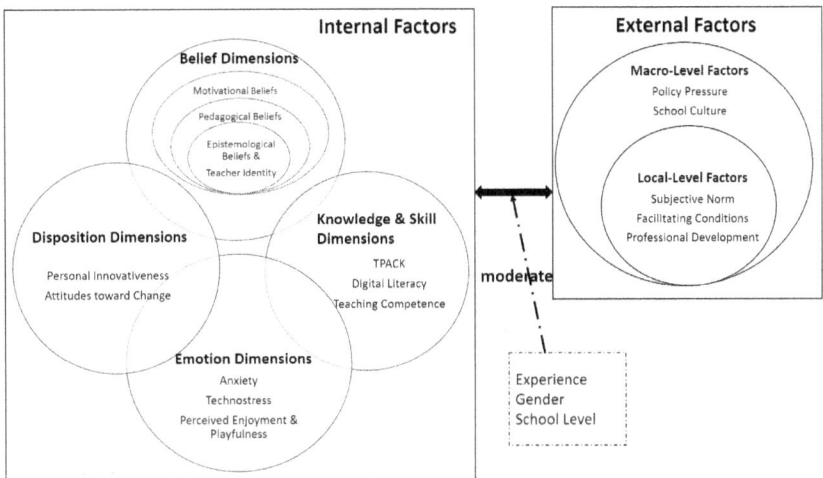

Figure 7 *Factors that influence teacher autonomy with technology in professional work*

norm and organization citizenship behavior (i.e., tendency towards voluntary behaviors for the overall good of the organization) were significantly higher. The researchers thus concluded that to promote elementary school teachers' use of smart education, interventions may focus on raising positive attitudes and efficacy towards smart education and reducing teaching pressure towards smart education. However, in the secondary school sector, the emphasis may need to put more on increasing the subjective norm, organizational citizenship behavior and teachers' efficacy. Thus, current literature suggests the importance of attitudes and motivational support for elementary school teachers, and the significance of skills and subjective norm for secondary school teachers.

Figure 7 summarizes the list of factors that may play significant roles in influencing teachers' autonomous engagement with technology for instruction and hence need to be attended to when fostering teacher autonomy with technology in professional work. Different dimensions of internal factors (belief, knowledge and skills, emotion, and disposition) and different levels of external factors (macro-level and local-level) interacted with one another to influence teacher technology adoption. Each dimension contains a set of core factors. The core factors of the belief dimension of internal factor are illustrated in circles to signify the central-peripheral continuum, where factors in the inner circles are more central to one's belief system and influence the factors in the outer circles. The core factors of the external factors are depicted as nested circles to indicate that local-level factors are situated in specific sociocultural and school contexts and are subject to the influence of these macro-level factors. The interaction of internal factors and external factors is moderated by a set of moderating factors, including experience, gender, and school level.

These core factors and their interactions need to be considered when developing interventions to boost teacher technology integration. Given that some personal and sociocultural factors may moderate the associations, a differentiated approach towards interventions is needed when effecting positive behavior intention towards technology adoption among different teacher populations.

Factors that influence teacher professional learning with technology

Teacher professional learning may originate in both inner sources and social sources, interactive and non-interactive. Learning with technology can assume different forms, such as attending webinars, taking MOOC courses, joining twitter groups, searching websites, and watching videos. These forms vary in the level of interactivity. Regardless of the level of interactivity involved, these online technology-enhanced learning activities contain both individual and social component. As Lantz-Andersson et al. (2018) put it, "While many of these resources can be engaged with on an individual, self-directed basis, these remain essentially social technologies." In this section, I examine factors that influence the individual and the social aspects of professional learning with technology.

Factors that influence the individual aspects of learning online

Lee et al. (2021) did a synthetic review and meta-analysis on factors that influence individuals' participation in online professional learning, and identified three categories of influences: individual, system, and environmental influences. Individual influences are learner characteristics, beliefs, and perceptions of themselves. System influences are the learning platform and course components, such as design, ease of use, and content quality. Environmental influences are the context learners are situated in, such as organizational support, time for training and the (non) presence of facilitators.

Individual factors

Individual factors are the most salient influence on professionals' engagement in online professional learning (Lee et al., 2021). Current literature has identified teacher beliefs, dispositional preferences and self-positioning as influential individual factors. Teacher self-efficacy and their perception of the usefulness of a particular learning experience are underscored in existing literature as the two significant determinants of teachers' participation in online professional learning (Lee et al., 2021; Zhang & Liu, 2019). For instance, Lee and colleagues (2021) revealed that technological efficacy and perceived usefulness of the learning experience were significantly and positively associated with professional workers' intentions to engage in online professional learning and their satisfaction with the learning experience. Zhang and Liu (2019) further revealed that self-efficacy and perceived usefulness interacted with each other. They documented a group of K-12 teachers' participation in an online professional development initiative that engaged them in watching video cases, taking part in online discussion, and submitting reflective diaries. They found that perceived value of online learning to enhance teaching practices, self-efficacy and motivational regulation significantly predicted these teachers' engagement in this online space. Moreover, teachers' motivational regulation mediated the path from perceived task value and learning engagement, and self-efficacy moderated the association between perceived task value and motivational regulation. Thus, when teachers perceive the learning tasks to be relevant and of value, they might exhibit higher interest and enthusiasm for online learning and are more likely to use motivational regulation strategies to heighten their learning engagement. The indirect association of perceived task value with learning engagement via motivational regulation is stronger for teachers with higher self-efficacy. Similarly, Gao and Li (2019) found that perceived usefulness and perceived fit of learning on Twitter with their professional tasks significantly predicted a group of teachers' adoption of Twitter for professional learning.

Teachers' dispositional traits and preferences are also found to influence their voluntary participation in online professional learning initiatives. Prestridge (2019) identified that teachers' curiosity towards innovations beyond the school grounds may drive teachers' self-initiation towards professional learning. A curious disposition includes perceived necessity to learning, to persistent, to find new ideas and ICT tools, and to use these new ideas and tools in the classroom. Another dispositional preference that shapes teachers' initiatives in self-directed professional learning is the degree of professional competitiveness, such as the urge to seek and develop novel ideas to make oneself unique. Moreover, the dispositional preference towards independent learning is also associated with a greater likelihood of using and completing online professional learning courses (Lee et al., 2021). Tsai et al. (2011) further found that a group of Taiwan elementary and junior high school teachers' epistemological beliefs in relation to the Internet shaped their online learning experience. They revealed that when teachers held sophisticated, constructivist epistemological beliefs about the Internet environments, they were more likely to exhibit greater ability to judge the web information, demonstrate more favorable web search strategies, and obtained better search outcomes. Sophisticated epistemological beliefs about the Internet manifest in preferences for online learning environments that provide authentic contents that bear resemblance to real-life situations, that contain rich information sources and interpretations that are challenging but helpful in problem solving, and that provide opportunities for communication and inquiry learning supported by timely guidance, self-reflection, and guided practices on information and source evaluation.

Moreover, teachers' self- and social-positioning is also an essential factor. Prestridge (2019) found that teachers' conceptualization of professional learning online and how they position themselves in relation to others shaped the type of actions teachers display in online spaces like social media. Prestridge identified four types of actions for learning through social media. The first type is info-consumer, who seeks new knowledge, ideas, and resources from the online spaces to fulfill self-driven needs and follows like-minded colleagues. To them, online spaces are venues to follow others for content to consume in order to build knowledge and expertise. The second type is info-networker, who also focuses on consuming new ideas and resources online but for the purpose of sharing the information with other colleagues. The third type is self-seeking contributor, who posts their knowledge, ideas, or curriculum materials to ask for feedback on or validation of their materials and to seek out answers to questions of personal interests. The fourth category is vocationalist, whose participation in online spaces is to contribute to knowledge building in the teaching field. Vocationalists pursue self-realization through actively trialing new ideas in their teaching contexts, leading discussions on the ideas and feeding back to the community with reflective cycles. Prestridge argued that the four different types of professional learning actions were driven by teachers' social reasoning (e.g., to fulfill self-driven needs vs. to focus on others' needs vs. to engage as a member of a community of learners) and interactivity reasoning (e.g., to consume content vs. to contribute content vs. to facilitate the development of new knowledge in the field). Gao and Li (2019) pointed out that what drove teachers' use of Twitter for professional learning was the teacher-defined purpose of Twitter usage for communication, resource sharing, and collaboration. They suggested that it is important to help teachers understand what Twitter can do for their professional learning and guide them to set specific plans on how to use Twitter to serve their own professional learning purposes. Harper-Hill, Beamish, Hay, Whelan, Kerr, Zelenko, and Villalba (2022) further found that teachers' recognition of and empathic response to student needs, their self-positioning as change agents and their self-efficacy drove them to engage in professional learning to change their teaching practice. The researchers further found that although these internal factors were drivers of self-initiated online professional learning, these factors interacted with external factors to shape teachers' successful engagement in professional learning opportunities.

System/experience factors

Design features that boost teachers' willingness to participate in online professional learning is an essential system factor. Bragg et al. (2021) synthesized a few design features of successful online professional programs. Among the features, embedding practical, hands-on activities and real-life observations and encouraging teachers to apply the acquired knowledge and skills to their teaching context are important to enhance perceived task value and stimulate teacher agency in self-directed learning. The inclusion of authentic contexts and realistic examples in the professional programs and materials that cater to current and future needs of their students and their instructional goals are also essential to enhance perceived credibility and relevance of the resources, and hence increase teachers' engagement with the program (Beach, 2017; Powell & Bodur, 2019). Relevance of the learning experience to one's professional practices and the alignment of the content to one's career goals are determinants of professionals' likelihood of participating in online professional learning courses (Lee et al., 2021). Moreover, Harper-Hill and colleagues (2022) found that the flexibility and adaptability of digital resources influenced teachers' engagement in online professional learning. Teachers preferred resources that were flexible, not time-consuming, and responsive to changing classroom needs. In addition, the navigation design of the platforms is equally important. In Lee and colleagues' (2021) synthetic study, perceived ease of use of the online learning platform was a significant predictor of individuals' intentions or continued intentions to engage in online professional learning, satisfaction with and persistence in the learning experience. To teachers, a logical, structured layout for intuitive navigation determines the ease of use of a platform.

Design features that support teachers' self-directed learning process are also essential. According to Bragg et al. (2021), providing differentiated activities (e.g., readings, observing, discussions) and varied applications (e.g., online resources, videos) that cater to individual differences in learning styles, interests and learning needs, and allowing teachers to choose the learning content and study at their own paces are important features that support self-directed learning process. Including goal-oriented content and activities and providing constant teacher reflections to enhance self-regulation of the learning process are equally important. In addition, regular structured supports help enhance program satisfaction and reduce attrition. The support could be navigation support, such as orientation sessions, syllabus information and technical support, and could also be adaptive support, such as evaluation reports, action plan and AI agents that provide subject-specific support. Lee and colleagues (2021) further found that well-timed release of the content and well-structured content encouraged learners' participation and completion of online courses.

Design features that support social connectedness also enhance teachers' sustained engagement in online professional learning. Having access to peers and facilitators can make learners feel less isolated and is important in increasing learners' persistence and sustaining their engagement in online professional learning (Bragg et al., 2021; Burns, 2013). Existing literature has generated a list of design features that support social connectedness. Bragg et al. (2021) suggested fostering social interaction, collaboration, and resource sharing to enhance learning engagement. System features that contain mechanisms for relationship building and enable teachers to view how others make use of the online learning platform give teachers the sense that they are not studying alone, and hence make them more likely to persist in learning (Burns, 2013; Lee et al., 2021).

In addition to these system design factors, characteristics of the learning experience also matter. Harper-Hill and colleagues (2022) revealed that characteristics of the professional learning, that is, whether the learning was prompted by the urge to meet students' needs and whether the professional learning was ongoing, also determined teachers' engagement in online professional learning. Moreover, their perceived level of expertise in both the content and the providers of the content was deemed crucial. To teachers, everyday practices that were supported by scientific evidence and lived experience signify expertise. Harper-Hill and colleagues found that perceived credibility (scientific evidence-based) and authenticity (facilitating solutions to workplace problems) of the learning experience mediated the influence of internal and external factors on teachers' engagement in online professional learning. That is, whether internal and external factors could boost professional learning depends on teachers' perception of the credibility and authenticity of the experience. The researchers hence called for careful consideration of the nature of learning experience that determines teacher agency in professional learning.

Environmental factors

Environmental factors include environmental support and facilitating situations (Lee et al., 2021). Environmental support may come from organization, administrators, or peers. Rewards and incentives from the organization, such as continuing education credit, may encourage teachers to use and complete online courses. Lee and colleagues (2021) found that managerial and peer support significantly and positively predicted intentions to use online professional learning. Similarly, Harper-Hill and colleagues (2022) found that teachers' willingness to engage in online professional learning was influenced by whether teachers perceived that their professional learning was recognized by administrators and colleagues formally or informally. They further found that the extent to which teachers felt that their professional learning was supported by like-minded peers with a range of expertise and capabilities was a significant determinant of teachers' engagement in online professional learning. Tayag and Ayuyao (2020) revealed that learning-centered leadership (i.e., building a learning vision, providing learning support, managing the learning program and modeling) did not directly influence teacher professional learning, but rather indirectly via teacher agency (i.e., the confidence teachers have towards their own capacity and desire for professional growth) and teacher trust (i.e., the confidence teachers have towards the school, school principal and colleagues). They hence argued that, to promote teachers' participation in professional learning for the sake of improving skills rather than just a form of compliance, school culture and support need to be directed towards boosting teacher agency and teacher trust. Moreover, facilitating conditions, such as the availability of time, resources and assistance, have also been found to significantly predicted professionals' persistence in online professional learning (Lee et al., 2021).

Factors that influence the social aspects of learning online

Social learning, both formally organized and informally developed, leads to the collective construction of professional knowledge. For social learning to emerge and sustain, sociality and leadership are essential to such communities (Lantz-Andersson et al., 2018).

Sociality factors

Sociality depends on shared values, common goals, and mutual trust and respect (Webster-Wright, 2009). Teachers' participation in online communities is influenced by various social factors, such as trust between community members, sense of community, social ability, and altruism (Macià & García, 2016). Trust between community peers is strengthened when community interaction is structured around work-related problems, where teachers perceive professional benefits (Booth, 2012; Matzat, 2013). Strengthening offline relations and providing opportunities for face-to-face contact may ameliorate the problems of lack of trust and free riding (Matzat, 2010). Pro-social attitudes and efficacy in knowledge sharing are equally important (Tseng & Kuo, 2014). Teachers with pro-social attitudes are more likely to share knowledge with other members. Teachers who feel confident in their abilities to share content may benefit more from the knowledge shared in the community. Tseng and Kuo (2014) further found that tie strength in the community (i.e., close connections among the members) significantly predicted teachers' knowledge sharing self-efficacy and their pro-social commitment. The researchers hence concluded that it is essential to develop online and offline social relationships among community members. Hur and Hara (2007) also concurred with the importance of providing online and offline interaction, identifying it as a facilitative condition for teachers' sustained engagement in the online professional community. They further uncovered an additional set of factors that are essential for sustained engagement in professional learning, including the autonomy of the community independent of external governance and the acknowledgement of the value of social participation.

Sociality is also shaped by discourse in the online community, which influences teachers' commitment to the learning communities. Xing and Gao (2018) examined how discourse features on Twitter influenced teachers' likelihood of sustaining their participation in Twitter professional communities. They classified three types of tweets: cognitive tweets, interactive tweets, and social tweets. Cognitive tweets refer to tweets that share personal ideas, opinions or experiences in a general way, and tweets that initiate conversations on a new topic. Interactive tweets refer to tweets that engage with others' tweets by expressing agreement, building upon an existing comment by elaboration or clarification, or offering complementary or alternative ways. Social tweets refer to tweets for social purposes, such as greetings, being courteous and expressing appreciation, or establishing rapport. They found that the more teachers were exposed to cognitive tweets and interactive tweets, the more likely they were to stay in the community. Tweets in the interactive dimension had a slightly stronger influence than tweets in the cognitive dimension, while exposure to excessive social tweets was associated with teachers' likelihood of dropping out of the community. The researchers hence concluded that the experience of contributing to collaborative problem-solving sustains teachers' sustained engagement in online communities. Thus, having moderators or automatic agents that promote more cognitive and interactive discussions on online communities is essential.

Moreover, since the affordances and constraints of technological platforms further shape the nature of what is being shared and how the sharing is presented to others, the selection and coordination of different technological tools in a professional learning environment may also affect sociality in online professional communities. For instance, instant messaging apps support immediate exchanges and frequent sharing of ideas, asynchronous blogging supports less immediate and interactive forms of reflection on personal experiences, whereas discussion forums support the co-construction of repositories of shared resources and extenuated practice-oriented discussions over time (Lantz-Andersson et al., 2018). Moreover, the asynchronous mode and the written medium may stimulate greater reflection and self-analysis of professional practice (Choi & Morrison, 2014). Liu (2013) suggested that, to enhance teacher engagement in online learning communities, the selection of communication tools should center on clearly explicated goals that have organic connections with the real-world practice of teachers.

Leadership factors

Leadership features group dynamics, supportive and shared leadership, and a climate of openness (Booth, 2012; Macià & García, 2016). Sustained "structured conversations" moderated by key coordinating individuals are essential to cultivating and sustaining knowledge sharing within the community (Booth, 2012, p. 19; Lantz-Andersson et al., 2018). To build a strong sense of ownership among the community members, Hur and Hara (2007) suggested inviting members on a yearly basis to serve as voluntary community moderators who are charged with the responsibility of welcoming new members, commenting on peers' messages and recommending good posts. The assignment of moderators is particularly important in the early stage of community building (Macià & García, 2016). Moderators play an important role in inspiring member engagement through seeding and facilitating specific discussion questions, initiating knowledge sharing, and promoting quality discussions (Goodyear et al., 2019; Xing & Gao, 2018). Similarly, Liu (2013) advocated building participant structure that encourages collaborative inquiries and shared leadership. The technological platform should allow for smaller subgroups to collaborate and self-initiate sharing and support the sharing and discussion of collective experience and/or curricular interests. In addition, clearly specified participant responsibilities (i.e., goals and core activities) need to be assigned to teachers when they first join the community. It needs to be fostered among the community members that every member has ideas and strengths valuable for the community and has the responsibility of co-developing the community. Members should be given the freedom to both select how they are to contribute to the community and create new ways to contribute and engage with others.

In addition, supportive leadership is essential. Alwafi et al. (2019) conducted an experimental study to understand the role of experienced practitioners in pre-service teachers' engagement in an online professional learning community. The experimental group's discussion on Facebook was around teacher-assigned topics related to technology integration and was facilitated by experienced school practitioners. The control group's discussion was non-facilitated. The facilitation was done through providing authentic examples of classroom technology integration, prompting questions and reflections, helping exchanges and collaborative knowledge construction. Experimental group exhibited a significantly greater increase in cognitive engagement and the occurrence of higher-level cognitive discourse, faster and greater levels of growth in the size of knowledge-sharing and knowledge-building networks, and greater collaboration across departments. The researchers thus recommended using school practitioners as a pedagogical tool to enhance pre-service teachers' engagement in online learning communities.

Figure 8 summarizes the factors that influence the individual and social aspects of teacher autonomous professional learning with technology. Some of these factors shape whether and how teacher exercise autonomy with technology in professional work and professional learning, and thus need to be intervened in supporting teacher autonomy with technology.

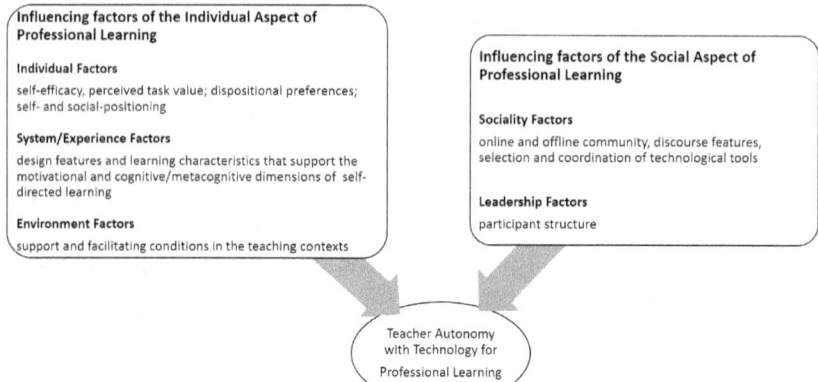

Figure 8 *Factors that influence teacher autonomy with technology for professional learning*

Other factors contribute to the variation in teacher autonomy with technology and suggest directions for differentiation in support.

9
Fostering Teacher Autonomy with Technology – The How

Key principles of adult learning

According to Bragg et al. (2021), two theoretical pillars of adult learning theory–andragogy or self-directed learning, and heutagogy or self-determined learning–are important considerations when devising effective models of teacher professional development and learning. The andragogical aspect highlights fostering and supporting teacher responsibility for their own practices and learning, and the heutagogical aspect underscores helping teachers develop the competencies and capabilities to acquire new knowledge and skills and apply them to novel and unfamiliar situations. To develop interventions to foster teacher autonomy with technology in professional work and professional learning, these two components need to be considered in parallel.

Andragogy focuses on activating and supporting adults' intrinsic motivation for learning. It contains a set of principles that characterize the cognitive process of adult learning. Principle 1 states that adult learning needs to respect and support learners' self-concept as an independent and self-directed learner. Principle 2 underscores the role of experience, stressing that experience defines an adult and hence needs to be the basis of adult learning. Principle 3 stresses that adults have an inherent readiness to learn what they believe they need to know. Principle 4 emphasizes that adult learning is oriented towards addressing problems and tasks of personal relevance. Principle 5 highlights that adults are more internally than externally motivated. Principle 6 emphasizes that adults need to know why they need to learn something (Knowles, 1980). Accordingly, andragogical adult learning programs feature a few characteristics. First, the program should facilitate equitable relationships, and build a trusting environment that respects adult interests and needs. Second, learning activities should connect to the wealth of adult experiences, cater to diversified interests and needs, and feature co-exploration and experiential learning. Moreover, learning programs should provide a full spectrum of clearly identified objectives and associated learning experience. The learning experience should be driven by relevant problems in teaching contexts, the solution to which can enhance job performance. In all, andragogical approaches feature problem-centered, self-directed active learning and collaboration (Carpenter & Linton, 2016; Tsuda et al., 2019).

Heutagogy focuses on enabling learners to determine their own learning and developing lifelong learning in response to the ever-changing environment. Heutagogy targets both learners' competencies (abilities to acquire knowledge and skills) and learners' capabilities (abilities to apply and reproduce knowledge and skills in novel and unfamiliar situations) (Hase & Kenyon, 2000). Heutagogical approaches feature double-loop learning with self-reflection. Double-loop learning includes 1) the process of problem solving and associated acquisition of knowledge and skills, and 2) reflection on the problem-solving process and concomitant changes in beliefs and actions (Kenyon & Hase, 2010). To Blaschke (2012), heutagogy emphasizes supporting learning how to learn. Blaschke elaborated that a heutagogical approach highlights learner-centeredness (learner-defined learning paths, learner-generated learning contexts and content, and learner-designed flexible curriculum), reflective practice (documentation of learning journey, experimentation with real-world scenarios, and personalized feedback to support reflective practice), and collaborative learning (shared meaning making in collaborative spaces and co-construction of the understanding of the learning process and of how people learn).

Facilitating formal professional learning

The andragogical and heutagogical theoretical pillars suggest four critical characteristics of professional learning experience that may facilitate teacher autonomy with technology: job-embeddedness, authenticity, collaborative and reflective. These four features correspond with the critical conditions of effective professional development espoused in existing literature: to be "relevant to teachers' professional learning needs," to "promote social aspects of learning," to "include content that is readily transferred to classroom environments," and to "encourage self-reflection" (Bragg et al., 2021, p. 2). Evidences from review studies on teacher professional development and learning also suggest that high-quality teacher professional learning needs to respond to the local context and national standards, connect with classroom practices, involve collaboration and feedback, and sustain over time (Desimone, 2009; Wei et al., 2009). These four features also reflect the essential characteristics of effective professional development for technology adoption identified by Ottenbreit-Leftwich and colleagues (2020): sustained over a period of time; situated in the teaching context; personalized learning content; modeling and in-class support; authentic and hands-on activities; and learning community support. Synthesizing the above literature, I will elaborate on these four key principles in developing formal professional development initiatives to support teacher autonomy with technology in professional work and professional learning.

Interest-driven job-embedded learning

Interest-driven learning

Researchers have pointed out that regardless of formal or informal professional learning, effective professional development needs to be interest-driven and cater to different needs (Darling-Hammond, 2005).

Interest-driven learning ensures that what is acquired is related to one's professional needs and helps solve actual problems. Hence, the acquired knowledge and skills would be deemed useful. Bragg et al. (2021) found that when professional development activities and associated resources take into consideration individual teachers' life experience and cater to their interests and self-identified needs, teachers show greater satisfaction with the training experience, and are more likely to integrate the training content into their instructional practices. Interest-driven design also increases teachers' likelihood of internalizing new information (Lutrick & Szabo, 2012). Elliott (2017) listed interest-driven as an essential quality of effective online professional development and argued that professional development offering should provide opportunities for choice making that align with learners' learning preferences and interests.

Interest-driven learning can be achieved through a respect for individuals' personal interests and using these interests to drive learning. Azevedo (2013) conceptualized that, to develop interest-based participation, instructional design needs to be open to tailoring that is "radical enough to include very many different topics/domains, concerns, values and modes of expression that might extend much beyond the immediate curricular targets" (p. 499) and is supported with rich and diversified resources. Moreover, the design also needs to realize the boundary-extending nature of interest-based practice participation, encouraging and supporting interest-driven pursuits beyond physical and temporal constraints into other realms of people's life. Azevedo further acknowledged that interests fluctuate and may flail. The dynamic changes need to be honored in instructional design, through providing people with multiple roles and responsibilities for maintaining the value and life in the bigger community and giving people freedom and choice over learning content and means of production. Such a design would enable people to "develop multiple and parallel lines of practice" (p. 500) and move freely in between these lines of practice over time.

A focus on interest in instructional design can also be realized through consciously developing individuals' interest in something. Acknowledging that interest is the driving force of enjoyable and effective learning journeys, Chan and colleagues (2018) introduced an interest-driven creator theory that comprises a cycle of three phases. The first phase is triggering, i.e., use precursor activities to induce interest for the target activity, such as using examples of gamification in daily life to arouse teachers' interest in developing an educational board game. The second phase is immersing, where teachers are fully immersed in the creation activity, supported by eye-opening and idea-invoking information and resources. The third phase is extending, i.e., design post-activities that involve the application of newly constructed knowledge in a similar or different context. The interest-driven creator theory has been utilized successfully in various studies to enhance student teachers' understanding of educational technology and computational thinking skills (Khambari & Nadi, 2019; Uzumcu & Bay, 2021). This approach has been found to instill innovativeness among teachers, which helps sustain interests, puts them in an autonomous position in learning, and enhances the transferability of acquired knowledge and skills in daily and professional life (Khambari & Nadi, 2019; Uzumcu & Bay, 2021). These researchers thus highlight the importance of piquing teachers' interest before the start of the training.

Arguing that existing teacher technology integration programs have focused too narrowly on didactic instruction on skills, Lohnes Watulak (2018) borrowed Ito and colleagues' (2013) connectedness learning framework to make space for teacher voice and choice in their learning journey on technology integration, and foster teacher agency in technology integration. They engaged a group of American pre-service teachers in a digital storytelling project, where teachers were charged with creating a digital storytelling artifact and generating a tip list for their future fellow teachers on the use of digital storytelling for instruction. The principles of connected learning, production-centered, open networked, interest-driven and peer-supported learning were integrated into the project design. Teachers were allowed to pursue their interests and make choices on both the artifact they would produce and the technology tools they could use to create the artifact. The researcher found that the connected learning approach helped develop competent and self-directed teachers in technology integration in teaching.

Job-embedded learning

Teachers learn by testing knowledge in their own teaching contexts. High quality professional development activities need to be connected with day-to-day teaching and coherent with other learning activities taking place concurrently in the teaching context (Garet et al., 2001). Powell and Bodur (2019) argued that teacher professional development, online or face-to-face, needs to be job-embedded, because it promotes continuous learning within teams, departments, schools, and districts.

Job-embedded learning supports the acquisition of knowledge for, in and of practice, and makes sure that professional learning covers the various dimensions of the teaching practice (content, pedagogy, student, teaching context). Job-embedded learning provides opportunities to observe, practice, collaborate, and receive feedback, and enhances the likelihood that learning is personalized and caters to teachers' ongoing needs (Powell & Bodur, 2019; Liao et al., 2017). Bragg et al. (2021) conducted a synthetic review of the design and delivery of online professional development and identified a few essential characteristics of learning design that contributes to teachers' pedagogical content knowledge, beliefs about teaching, self-efficacy and instructional practices. Embedded practical learning activities and the application of the acquired knowledge and skills in practice associated highly with changes in instructional practices and teachers' satisfaction with the training. Encouraging teachers to adapt and make localized adjustments to teaching techniques is an important characteristic of professional learning that enhances teachers' appropriation of training (Longhurst et al., 2021). With regard to teacher technology integration, Skoretz and Childress (2013) found that K-12 teachers who underwent a one-year job-embedded learning showed significantly higher efficacy in technology integration than those who did not go through the learning experience. Taking part in job-embedded learning was found to be particularly beneficial for experienced teachers who had more than 25 years of teaching experiences, for middle school teachers, and for teachers who taught a single subject.

Job-embedded learning can assume many forms. It could be realized through situating training in one's workplace. On-site mentoring and coaching are representative forms of this type of job-embedded learning. Liao et al. (2021) examined the effects of on-site coaching and mentoring on a group of elementary school teachers' technology integration. The coaching included activities such as on-site meetings on goal-setting, activity planning and reflection, in-class modeling, resource sharing and ongoing communication through emails or text messages. The trainee teachers appreciated the individualized goal-setting and learning support and the applicability of the learning content to their existing teaching practices. They also felt that in-class modeling made them switch in-between the role of teacher and learner in an authentic classroom context and allowed for immediate implementation for trial and error. Teachers who received on-site coaching demonstrated growth in pedagogical knowledge and skills, but the development was subject to teachers' existing technology dispositions and teaching practices. The researchers thus underscored the importance of understanding teachers' existing pedagogical viewpoints and the perceived value of technology use. They advocated incorporating this understanding in guiding personalized goal setting and reflections, and helping teachers embrace the mindset of pedagogy/learning before introducing relevant technology.

Job-embedded learning can also be realized through connecting the training to teaching practices and teaching artifacts. For instance, when discussing defining elements of effective online professional development communities, Quinn et al. (2019) identified relevance as a key element. By relevance, they emphasized that professional learning activities need to be practical and authentic and connect clearly with the culture and priorities of schools, i.e., job-embedded in essence. They further provided examples of how to make these activities job-embedded. One example they proposed is to engage teachers in videotaping, sharing and discussing students' working process with community members.

Moreover, different forms of job-embedded learning need to be used concurrently to stimulate changes in technology integration. Wilson (2021) conducted a meta-analysis of studies that examined effects of teacher education programs on pre-service teachers' attitudes and beliefs. He found that core course features in effective teacher education programs were mostly job-embedded in the form of mentoring/coaching, field experience, goal setting, observation, hands-on learning, and work sample analysis. He found that these job-embedded teacher education programs had a positive effect on pre-service teachers' pedagogical beliefs (ß=0.30) and a large effect on their attitudes toward technology integration (ß=0.65). More importantly, He found that no single course feature significantly improved teacher attitudes or beliefs. He thus concluded that it is important to combine different strategies of job-embeddedness when designing professional development initiatives. The necessity of combining different job-embedded learning elements is also corroborated in another meta-analytical study on the relation between teacher educational program and pre-service teachers' knowledge development (Wilson et al., 2020).

Sustained authentic experience-focused learning

Sustained learning

It has been widely acknowledged that one-time professional development workshops do not induce teacher change in practice (Desimone, 2009). Scholars have argued that professional development needs to evolve from standalone workshops to sustained learning that facilitates teachers' ongoing needs for the integration of technology in teaching (Prestridge & Tondeur, 2015).

Synthetic reviews of the effects of teacher professional development programs have consistently identified sustained learning as a key element. Gerard et al. (2011) conducted a meta-analysis of 360 studies on technology-enhanced professional development and found that effective professional development programs need to be long term (i.e., more than 1 year) and constructivist oriented, and allow teachers to reflect on and refine their pedagogical approaches. Zinger et al. (2017) further revealed that PD programs with longer duration (over two years) showed promising outcomes in teacher technology integration, whereas PD programs with duration of one year or less showed mixed findings.

Empirical studies on sustained professional learning have also generated convincing findings. Blanchard and colleagues (2016) conducted a three-year professional development program. The program consisted of week-long workshops with inquiry-based learning and lesson design activities every summer, which were supported by subsequent implementation of technology-focused lessons in their own classrooms and monthly online sessions with the PD facilitators. The researchers found that teachers exhibited a shift towards more student-centered pedagogical beliefs and became more comfortable using technologies. Longhurst et al. (2021) further pointed out that in order to enhance teachers' appropriation of training, both sustained engagement in the construction of conceptual ideas (e.g., monthly meetings to engage in dialogues around the concepts; writing responses to prompts) and sustained engagement in practical application of techniques are essential.

Authentic experience-focused learning

Active participation and engagement in task-oriented learning by teachers during professional learning is another important element of effective professional development experience (Yurtseven Avci et al., 2020). To effect changes in teachers and enhance the applicability of training materials, the tasks need to be authentic and connected to teaching practices and key teaching artifacts. When professional development activities are directly connected to teachers' content area, teachers are more likely to engage in student-centered use of technology (e.g., Twining et al., 2013). Teachers perceive learning that revolves around authentic tasks and authentic problem solving as more relevant, useful, and readily transferrable to new contexts (Reeves & Pedulla, 2013).

Authentic experience-focused learning frequently takes the form of various hands-on activities, such as problem-based learning, learning by doing, learning by design, inquiry-based learning, analysis of one's own and others' teaching cases, and write-up of personal teaching cases (Kharade & Peese, 2014; Jiménez Raya et al., 2017). In their pre-service language teacher training program, Kharade and Peese (2014) adopted a problem-based learning approach, where pre-service teachers were charged with coming up with technological solutions to authentic classroom teaching problems. They observed modeling practices of exemplary teachers, explored strategies, and reflected on outcomes. Pre-service teachers who undertook the training demonstrated improvement in their TPACK scores. Similarly, Tai (2015) utilized a learning-by-doing approach on computer-assisted language learning. The training program consisted of five steps: modeling, analyzing, demonstrating, applying, and reflecting. Pre-service teacher participants in the study showed an increase in their CALL competence. Ansyari (2015) adopted a learning-by-design model to engage pre-service English teachers in designing and implementing lesson plans and reflecting on outcomes. The participants also showed a significant increase in their technological pedagogical content knowledge. In addition, classroom research is also deemed a hands-on, experiential way to improve teaching quality, and has been shown to support teachers' internalization of innovative teaching practices and boost professional learning (van Katwijk et al., 2021; Yuan & Lee, 2015).

Another important dimension of authentic learning is modeling from teacher educators and experienced teachers. Observing the modeling of skillful intersection of technology, pedagogy and content enhances teachers' TPACK competence (Wang et al., 2018). Tondeur and colleagues (2012) developed a conceptual framework, SQD (Synthesis of Qualitative Evidence), that features authentic design tasks in fostering pre-service teachers' acquisition of TPACK. This framework consists of six key phases. The initial phase is role modeling, which involves the observation of prototypical examples of effective strategies of technology integration. The second phase is instructional design, where teachers engage in guided design-based practices with decreasing instructional support. The third phase is practice-oriented authentic experiences through micro-teaching. The fourth phase is collaborative discussion and analysis of successful and less successful ways of technology integration. The fifth phase is critical reflections on the role of educational technologies and one's learning process. And the last phase is formative feedback on students' design-based practices. Lachner and colleagues (2021) adopted this model with a group of German pre-service teachers. They found that the group who went through this design-focused training reported higher TPACK knowledge and perceived support and exhibited greater self-efficacy in technology integration than those who did not. Similarly, O'Hara and colleagues (2013) implemented a professional development program that consisted of several authentic learning activities. These activities included observing the modeling of experts on teaching with technology, designing their own technology-enhanced curriculum, and rehearsing technology-enhanced instruction to receive feedback and support from experts and peers during PD. The researchers found that these authentic learning experiences fostered a significant increase in these elementary school teachers' knowledge and skills in technology integration and teaching practices. Acknowledging the importance of authentic tasks for teacher professional learning, scholars advocate involving teachers in designing professional development activities to make the learning experience align better with their authentic experience at the workplace (Tonduer et al. 2017; Vrasidas & Zembylas, 2004).

Collaborative learning

Access to multiple supportive and collaborative experiences enhances teachers' appropriation of training (Longhurst et al., 2021). Teacher collaboration generates greater motivation, higher morale, greater efficiency, increased communication, improved technological skills, and more student-centered instructional strategies among teachers. It also contributes to school cultures that support innovation and intellectual enquiry (Vangrieken et al., 2015). Kennedy (2014) synthesized existing models of continuing professional development into a spectrum of CPD models that vary in the extent of transformation. In his taxonomy of CPD models, the more collaborative training models, such as collaborative professional inquiry models, community of practice models, coaching/mentoring models, fall into the more transformative or malleable categories that provide increasing capacity for professional autonomy and teacher agency. He further highlighted that focusing on the collective unit, rather than individuals, and adopting social constructivist stance for teacher learning contribute to democracy in professionalism. Synthesizing existing TPACK interventions for language teachers, Tseng and colleagues (2020) identified three essential conditions of effective interventions: to enhance language teachers' understanding of the TPACK framework; to provide modeling from expert teachers and teacher educators; and to engage teachers in collaborative lesson design. The observed positive effect of collaborative design of technology integration on language teachers' TPACK is consistent with findings from other review studies (Quinn et al., 2019; Voogt et al., 2013; Wang et al., 2018).

Collaboration can be strengthened by identifying and providing trusted connection to a community and supportive peers for teachers. It could also be achieved through providing opportunities for peer observation and feedback on each other's practice, providing access to experts, coaching, mentoring and reflection, and fostering cross-institution collaboration (Quinn et al. 2019). Collaboration can also take place in other forms, such as sharing ideas, materials and practices; forming teacher study group; engaging in team teaching, lesson study and classroom observations; arranging peer coaching and peer mentoring; performing joint work around a shared task; forming learning-oriented professional learning communities with shared values and visions; and conducting collaborative inquiry and shared practices of curricular and pedagogical strategies (Hargreaves, 2019; Vangrieken et al., 2015). An increasing volume of studies has attested to the positive effects of collaboration on teacher autonomy with technology. For instance, Tseng and colleagues (2016) introduced a teacher support group model, where a group of Chinese language teachers formed groups to support each other on web-conferencing technology integration. Team support consists of four stages: co-constructing understanding of the TPACK framework; observing each other's classes; adjusting instructions based on peer feedback; and co-reflecting on enhanced teaching. The authors found that the support group helped enhance teachers' understanding of the affordances and constraints of web-conferencing technology and boosted their TPACK in classroom integration of this technology.

Collaboration can also take place between in-service and pre-service teachers. Baya'a, Daher and Anabousy (2019) built a community of practice, consisting of in-service and pre-service teacher pairs. In-service teachers were instructed to watch and analyze video clips of technology integration in mathematics lessons by past years' pre-service teachers, and then design ICT-based math lessons together with pre-service teachers. They co-taught ICT-enhanced math lessons with pre-service teachers, which gradually progressed to semi-independent and independent teaching with ICT. The researchers found that the experience strengthened these in-service teachers' positive beliefs about technology integration, and enhanced their knowledge and skills in technology integration, which sparked off new goals and decisions related to active integration of ICT in teaching.

Collaboration could also be between teachers and experts. Scholars advocate establishing research-practice partnership between schools and universities as a way to sustain contextualized coaching that is informed by and at the same time inform research (Blanchard et al., 2016; Coburn & Penuel, 2016). Ottenbreit-Leftwich and colleagues (2020) reported a year-long study that involved local university researchers serving as coaches for K-6 teachers to examine how a research-based coaching model can support change in teacher technology integration practices. This coaching model emphasized personalizing coaching activities to individual needs, conducting needs analysis on teachers' dispositions, knowledge, and skills of technology integration, and working with teachers to identify teaching and learning goals that were of interest to them. The intervention included bi-weekly school-wide workshops and weekly coaching meetings that consisted of resource sharing, modeling, co-teaching, and teaching observations. Monthly co-reflection sessions were also arranged to revisit teaching needs and goals and make adjustments. Salient changes in teachers' abilities to implement technology integration practices were observed.

Teacher collaboration is influenced by a multitude of factors at different levels. Supporting the process of collaboration is essential to facilitate teacher collaboration, and the process can be supported by actions like setting up task interdependence, assigning clear roles for members, and setting a defined focus for collaboration. In addition, teacher collaboration can be facilitated by providing structural support, such as providing individual and common planning time, fostering shared and transformational leadership, creating a culture of mutual trust, and monitoring of collaboration. At the same time, effective collaboration also depends on the removal of potential hindering factors through fostering teachers' and groups' buy-in of collaboration and bolstering openness to collaboration (Vangrieken et al., 2015). Hargreaves (2019) further pointed out that giving time per se is not sufficient. Leaderships needs to "encourage, engage and empower teachers in the collaborative quest" (p. 618). He argued that it is important to foster professional capital in enhancing learning through collaboration. Professional capital consists of human capital (the competence, knowledge, qualifications, and commitment of individual members), decisional or decision-making capital (teachers' professional judgement and its development through personal experience, coaching and professional learning over time), and social capital (the collective group capital through networks of learning, mutual support, firm trust and shared professional development). To boost professional capital, Paulus et al. (2020) identified three essential conditions for effective professional learning communities that foster technology integration. First, it is important to guide teachers to create a shared vision with specific goals and performance outcomes that are situated in grade-level content standards and based on the realities of and resource availability in daily classroom instruction. Second, it is essential to sustain community dynamics for ongoing support, such as idea sharing, resource sharing, and constructive criticism. Third, it is equally important to build mechanisms that foster ongoing peer mentoring relationships.

Reflective learning

Reflection is a necessary condition for teacher professional development, as professional expertise is "the ability to construct experiential knowledge on the basis of a reflection on experience" (Mortari, 2012, p. 526). Reflection is considered essential to a teacher's thinking. Reflection is regarded as an integral component of teacher professional development (Avalos, 2011; Beauchamp, 2015). Bragg and colleagues' (2021) review study of online professional development revealed that reflection is an important design element that influences teachers' beliefs about teaching and their satisfaction with the training experience. Reflection can be realized through narrative inquiry, critical incident analysis, coaching and case analysis (Kaya & Adiguzel, 2021).

Reflective activities have been widely integrated into professional development programs to support technology integration. For instance, Hutchison and Woodward (2018) shared a year-long technology integration professional development project that prioritizes goal setting and reflection. The project adopted the Technology Integration Planning Cycle (TIPC) Model. The model included whole-group PD sessions that adopted the TIPC cycle (the set-up of instructional goals and associated instructional approaches, the selection of relevant tools, and critical analysis of potential contribution of the tool to the instruction and potential constraints of implementation), which were followed up with weekly emails on digital tool recommendations and lesson plans. In addition, the professional development program also included long-range planning of instructional goals and related technology integration, daily diary check-ins on actual technology implementation for the first week of each month, guided individual reflection based on class observations, and weekly collective reflection and discussions in the professional learning community. Participating teachers felt that the daily diaries engaged them in reflecting on the types of technologies they were using, which challenged them to try new technologies. The fact that the program was situated in their teaching contexts stimulated teachers' voluntary reflection on their instructional decisions. Collective reflections in the professional learning communities and with the instructional coach enhanced heightened understanding of their own skills and pedagogical use of technology. They further found that the TIPC provided a concrete model that enhanced the depth of individual and collective reflection. Kaya and Adiguzel (2021) examined how technology-enhanced evidence-based multimodal reflective professional training enhance in-service teachers' technology integration. They argued that reflection informed by data might be more sophisticated. Multimodal reflections, in the form of video recordings, video annotations and digital portfolios, allow for rich and thick descriptions, support connection building across different parts of a lesson, and cultivate self-regulated growth. Kaya and Adiguzel designed a professional training program for a group of English language teachers to feature evidence-based multimodal reflection. The reflection interventions included using video annotations to give feedback on specific parts of the lessons taught by oneself and by peers and creating short video clips to present multimodal reflection. The researchers documented increased understanding, knowledge, and skills in instructional technology integration among the participating teachers. The teachers also exhibited more sophisticated use of technology, such as focusing on language learning objectives in technology use and using technology to increase variety in interaction patterns and demonstrated increased depth of reflection over time.

At the same time, scholars have been concerned about the lack of depth in perfunctory reflections, which undermines the potential of reflection in stimulating deep thinking (Galea, 2012). To enhance the quality of reflection, educators need to be aware that there are four levels of reflection of increasing sophistication: descriptive statements of what happened; justification of the rationale behind actions and beliefs; critical evaluation of the situation and rationale; and discussion about alternative ideas and solutions to make changes (Leijen et al., 2012). Thompson and Pascal (2012) highlighted that quality reflection demands both depth and breadth: depth in the sense of "looking beneath the surface of a situation to see what assumptions are being made, what thoughts, feelings and values are being drawn upon," and breath in the sense of considering "the broader sociological context and include(ing) such factors as power relations, discrimination and oppression" (p. 321). Scholars further caution against treating reflection as a mere intellectual exercise and draw attention to a holistic approach to reflection. This approach highlights the emotional dimension of reflection (i.e., the issue of power and identity in the teaching contexts), and underscores nurturing personal and professional identify development as an aspect of reflection (Akbari,

2007). Thus, the commonly used retrospective reflection may not be sufficient. Instead, future-oriented reflection that directs teachers to imagine a professional identity that they aspire to would be helpful (Urzúa & Vásquez, 2008). Quinn and colleagues (2019) also advocated future-focused professional learning experience that features agentic inquiry into teaching and reflective practices, that focuses on developing high-level adaptive skills, challenging existing praxis and growing skills and methods to innovate in schooling context. According to them, future-focused professional learning can adopt various approaches to stimulate reflections that lead to fundamental changes in one's thinking about teaching and learning, such as immersive approach (provision of immersive experiences that enable a reorientation of fundamental values) and design-led approach (co-design and big data analytics). Moreover, there is a growing acknowledgement of the value of collective reflection and interactional reflective practices, where peers' and mentors' guidance and modeling on reflection are promoted to enhance the quality of reflection (Poom-Valickis & Mathews, 2013). In addition, giving teachers control over reflections, on areas like the focus of reflection, the target competence for reflection, the process of reflection and the format of reflection, leads to deeper and more critical reflection (Beauchamp, 2015).

Facilitating informal professional learning

The above four features are important aspects to consider when designing formal professional development programs, online or face-to-face, to promote teacher autonomy with technology in professional practices and professional learning. However, as elaborated earlier, teacher professional learning takes places both formally and informally. To promote teacher self-directed professional learning with technology in informal contexts, teacher autonomy and agency are key.

School cultures that support informal learning

Autonomy and agency manifest in individuals' interaction with the structure. Thus, to boost teacher autonomy and agency in informal learning, a facilitative school culture is essential.

First, a school culture that encourages looking for new ideas outside of one's workplace and supports continuing professional learning is essential to promote teacher self-direction (Vaessen et al., 2014). In addition to fostering an open culture for learning and a culture for collective enquiry, schools also need to make conscious efforts to create social learning mechanisms and spaces that stimulates informal sharing and dialogues around problems and solutions, and to organize network activities to promote the exchange of knowledge (Vaessen et al., 2014).

Second, feeling being trusted as a professional amplifies teacher agency. Liu and colleagues (2016) found that the sense of being trusted at school positively mediated the effect of school leadership on teachers' professional learning. The level of perceived trust was positively associated with teacher agency. Feeling being trusted as a professional boosted teacher agency in taking initiatives in professional practices, and enhanced teacher engagement in professional learning. The sense of being trusted can be bolstered through involving teachers in school decision making, developing a sense of collective responsibilities, establishing open authority structures, encouraging the use of out-of-school informal networks and resources, promoting distributed leadership where individual expertise is valued and actively sought after, and respecting teachers' workplace autonomy (Vaessen et al., 2014). Similarly, Barbosa and Borges-Andrade (2021) found that perceived workplace autonomy and opportunities to interact with colleague significantly predicted informal learning in the workplace. In addition, it is essential to help teachers identify with their role as active researchers and developers (Hökkä & Eteläpelto, 2014).

Professional development programs that encourage informal learning

Formal learning experience may influence teachers' mindset and capacity towards informal learning. Vaessen and colleauges (2014) argued for adopting a model of networked learning to build an expansive culture of learning, where "formal learning procedures can be augmented, complemented and informed by informal networked learning" (p. 66). They advocated making existing informal networks visible and strengthening these networks by giving them a place in formal learning programs.

Professional development programs that are open and deliberately extend learning beyond the training platforms to teachers' daily life spaces, such as social media, online media, online interest groups and communities, may also increase teachers' likelihood of accessing these spaces for professional learning on their own. Such experience may raise teachers' awareness of the value of these entertainment and socialization spaces for professional learning. It is equally important to help teachers see eye to eye with the value of networked learning across boundaries, identify and value informal learning venues and resources, and actively build relations and look for connections for venues of networked learning so as to develop their networking skills to make better use of these online social spaces for learning (Hanraets et al., 2011).

Moreover, formal professional learning experience that helps establish a mentality for lifelong learning is essential. Jiménez Raya et al. (2017) proposed that engaging teachers in experiential learning may encourage and sustain self-directed professional learning. Experiential learning can be in the form of enquiry (asking questions about and seeking information related to one's own teaching practices), regular self-appraisal of one's strengths, weaknesses and learning needs related to teaching practices, personal teaching experience with technology that may stimulate

Chapter 9

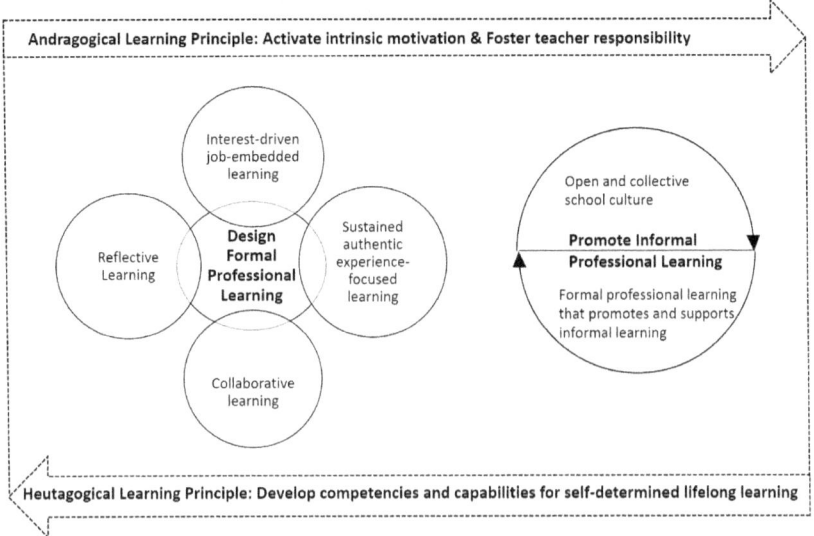

Figure 9 *Facilitating mechanisms of professional learning in support of teacher autonomy with technology*

learning needs, and regular practice of goal setting, planning and managing one's learning process. Brennan (2021) shared a professional learning program, where the school built a culture that encouraged learning and provided dedicated time, resources and managerial support, and teachers were asked to set and pursue personal professional learning goals. The researcher found that the program enhanced teachers' self-directed professional learning, which directly and indirectly impacted teachers' instructional practices. Richards and Farrell (2005) further listed some teacher development activities that may meet experiential pedagogy characteristics: self-monitoring, journal writing, critical incidents, critical friendships, case studies, teaching portfolios, action research, team teaching, support groups. Thus, incorporating some of these experiential pedagogy components in professional development programs may also facilitate teachers' self-directed professional learning with technology.

Mechanisms for promoting teacher autonomy with technology

Figure 9 synthesizes the mechanisms for professional learning in support of teacher autonomy with technology.

To support teacher autonomy with technology, teacher educators need to design formal professional learning that provides sustained, interest-driven, authentic, job-embedded experience that is supported by collaboration and reflection. Teacher educators need also to promote informal professional learning through building open and collective school culture and developing formal learning experience that extends learning to and supports learning in the informal learning contexts. The andragogical and heutagogical learning principles are the two key principles that guide the development of the formal and informal learning experience in support of teacher autonomy with technology.

Conclusion: Critical and Holistic Perspectives

At the beginning of this book, I highlight two premises in understanding the relationship between autonomy and technology: 1) a critical view towards the dialectical interaction between the two, and 2) a holistic view towards their interaction in situ. These two lenses guide the discussion of the relationship between autonomy and technology throughout the book and provide an elaborated look into the nature of the interaction. I argue that these two views should inform future research on technology and autonomy, and guide the development of interventions in facilitating reciprocal interactions between the two.

A critical perspective of the relationship

This book elaborates on how technology broadens our conceptualization of autonomy, and how technology, while amplifying and boosting autonomy, carries unintended and hidden consequences that may deter autonomy. In a similar fashion, autonomy may augment the educational potential of technology, but may also drive individuals away from technology, since teacher and students' decision makings are often pragmatics-driven and freedom in action may work in favor or against volitional use of technology for teaching and learning. The room for autonomy and the levels of capacity for relevant action may lead to the use of technology for better or for worse. Thus, both technology and autonomy are not neutral and may both benefit and constrain each other.

Figure 10 depicts this critical relationship between technology and autonomy. The circular interaction between technology and autonomy can be both positive and negative. More importantly, the boundary between the positive and negative effects is permeable, as indicated by the dotted lines at the boundary. Affordances in one context may very well be constraints in another context, and vice versa. For instance, advocacy of utilizing the affordance of technology to democratize learning may amplify autonomy in resource-rich contexts but may stifle autonomy in resource-deprived contexts. Thus, the relationship may be positive or negative, depending on the context and the learners. Moreover, affordances at one developmental stage may turn into constraints at another developmental

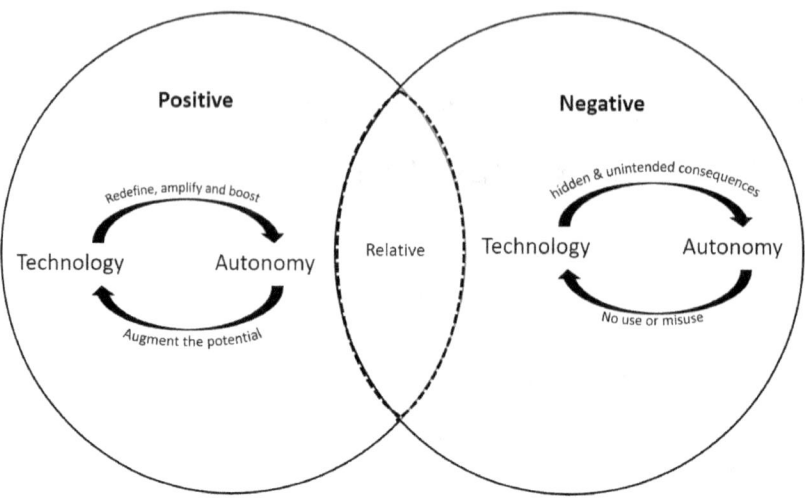

Figure 10 *A critical view of the relationship between technology and autonomy*

stage, and vice versa. For instance, structured technological resources may boost autonomy when learners' self-regulation skills are still developing. But as learners gain self-regulation skills over time, the same design feature of technological resources may become a hindrance to learner autonomy. Thus, the relationship between technology and autonomy is relative across situations and over time. This critical view of the relationship between autonomy and technology is essential to understanding learner and teacher autonomy in technological environments and with technology.

This critical view has implications for research. First of all, researchers need to view the concepts of autonomy and technology critically. Both autonomy and technology are not fixed entities, but rather shaped by the context of use. Researchers need to critically conceptualize the dimensions of autonomy in technological environments and be aware of how technology might have reshaped the nature of autonomy. Researchers also need to be wary that affordances and constraints of a particular technological tool or resource are not predetermined, but rather are constantly redefined by how learners perceive and position it and how learners put it into use. Second, the relationship between autonomy and technology also needs to be viewed critically. Researchers need to ward off a technology determinism stance, and always be alert to the unintended and hidden negative consequences of the use of technology in language learning and teaching. At the same time, a context-dependent view and a longitudinal approach need to be taken to examine how the relationship may be relative to contexts and learners and evolve over time.

Conclusion 237

   This critical view suggests a context-sensitive lens in defining the dimensions of autonomy that need to be fostered in driving autonomous action with technology. It also calls for greater attention to learner belief and positioning regarding technological resources when developing and implementing interventions that promote autonomous engagement with technology. This critical view further reminds educators to consciously consider the potential unintended and hidden consequences of technology use, and introduce mechanisms to ward off these negative consequences, when designing interventions to enhance learner and teacher autonomy with technology. Moreover, a differential approach needs to be taken when designing learning environments that facilitate positive reciprocal interaction between technology and autonomy in different contexts, for different types of learners and at different stages of development.

A holistic perspective of the relationship

A holistic view needs to be taken regarding factors that shape the interaction of technology and autonomy. This book has shown that the relationship between technology and autonomy is situated in the nexus of interaction among a set of individual, structural, social, and cultural factors. The situatedness demands a relative and systemic view towards researching the relationship of the two across situations. This relative and systemic view is also needed when developing interventions to facilitate autonomous engagement with technology in different contexts.

   A holistic view needs to be taken about the learning environments. Formal and informal learning are learning environments with unique parameters, which shape the distinct nature and manifestation of the interaction between technology and autonomy in each environment. The distinctiveness shapes different research foci and methods in these two contexts. Moreover, these two types of learning often intertwine, and are perpetually shaping and reshaping each other. Research work needs to consider the interaction of the two and examine how autonomy with technology in the formal learning context influences autonomy in the informal learning context, and vice versa. Research work should also adopt a holistic view to understand how different learning contexts in formal and informal environments interact with one another, exerting a mutual influence on one another. Dialogues between the two research communities need to be fostered. Similarly, developmental work needs to make a deliberate effort to connect the two to build an expansive network of learning. When designing learning experience for teachers and students, considerations need to be given on how to actively utilize teachers and learners' technology-mediated autonomous learning in informal learning contexts to enhance learner autonomy in formal contexts. Equal considerations also need to be given on how to use technology in ways that could spark off and facilitate teachers and learners' au-

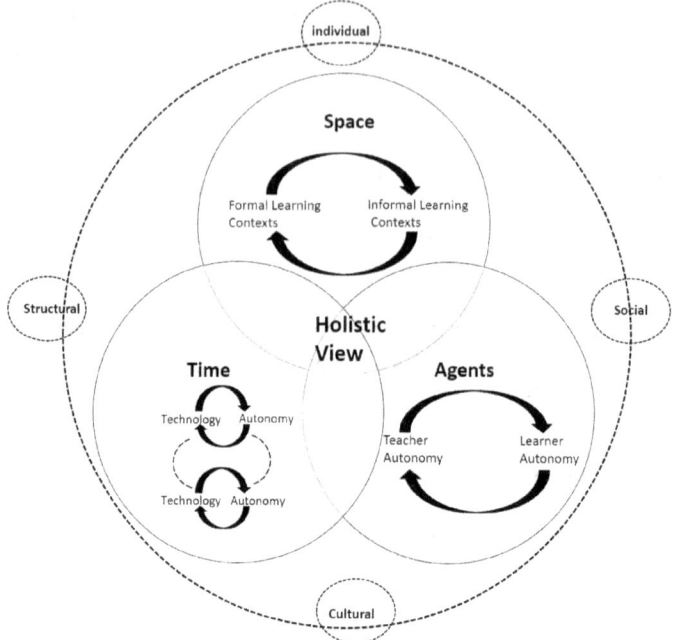

Figure 11 *A holistic view of the relationship between technology and autonomy*

tonomous use of technology in informal learning contexts.

A holistic view also needs to be taken when considering the agents of autonomy. Teacher autonomy and learner autonomy intertwine with each other. Teacher autonomy shapes the amount of and the nature of support learners may receive from teachers. Learner autonomy with technology may stimulate teachers' autonomous action with technology. A holistic view of the relationship demands research into the intersection of teacher and learner autonomy with technology, understanding how the nature of teacher autonomy and learner autonomy with technology may influence each other across formal and informal learning environments. Developmental work may actively utilize the potential mutual influences of the two to facilitate autonomy with technology in teaching and learning: strengthening teacher autonomy support to augment learner autonomy in formal and informal learning and featuring learner autonomy in teacher professional development initiatives to raise teachers' awareness and boost their autonomy with technology in professional practices and professional learning.

Moreover, a holistic view needs to take into consideration the temporal dimension of the relationship. Technology and autonomy interact with

Conclusion

each other in a two-way dialectical fashion over time. Thus, a longitudinal approach needs to be adopted to examine the dynamic interaction between the two over time. A longitudinal approach is also needed when examining the interplay between technology and learner autonomy across informal and formal learning environments over time. Similarly, it is worth exploring how the interplay between teacher autonomy and learner autonomy shapes the interaction between technology and autonomy over time. Dynamic interactions should be capitalized on to boost a positive reciprocal relationship between technology and autonomy over time.

Figure 11 summarizes a holistic view of the interaction between technology and autonomy across the space, agent, and time dimensions. The multiple layers of interaction are situated in the nexus of relationships across individual, social, cultural, and structural factors.

Concluding remarks

The relationship between autonomy and technology involves many dimensions. It is not only a psychological issue, but an educational, a social, a cultural and a political issue. Research and practice on autonomy and technology in language teaching and learning is indispensable and will surely benefit from insights from different disciplinary fields. This book draws on literature and research findings from various research fields, including educational technology, educational psychology, adult learning, and workplace learning, with the hope of enriching our understanding of and practices in relation to autonomy and technology in the language education fields. Future research and development work on autonomy and technology needs to actively seek the theoretical basis, practical tools, and research methods and tools from different disciplinary and research fields to advance scholarship in this field.

References

Abadi, E. A. M., & Baradaran, A. (2013). The relationship between learner autonomy and vocabulary learning strategies in Iranian EFL learners with different language proficiency level. *International Journal of Applied Linguistics and English Literature, 2*(3), 176–185.

Albion, P. R., & Tondeur, J. (2018). Section introduction: Professional learning and development of teachers. In J. Voogt, G. Knezek, R. Christensen, & K.-W. Lai (Eds.), *Second handbook of information technology in primary and secondary education* (pp. 377–379). Springer.

Abraham, L. B. (2008). Computer-mediated glosses in second language reading comprehension and vocabulary learning: A meta-analysis. *Computer Assisted Language Learning, 21*(3), 199–226.

Admiraal, W., Kruiter, J., Lockhorst, D., Schenke, W., Sligte, H., Smit, B., Tigelaar, D., & de Wit, W. (2016). Affordances of teacher professional learning in secondary schools. *Studies in Continuing Education, 38*(3), 281–298.

Agarwal, R., & Prasad, J. (1998). A conceptual and operational definition of personal innovativeness in the domain of informational technology. *Information Systems Research, 9*(2), 204–215.

Agbatogun, A. (2010). Self-concept, computer anxiety, gender and attitude towards interactive computer technologies: A predictive study among Nigerian teachers. *International Journal of Education and Development Using ICT, 6*(2), 55–68.

Ajzen, I. (1985). From intentions to actions: A theory of planned behavior. In K. Kuhl & J. Beckham (Eds.), *Action control* (pp. 11–39). Springer.

Akçayır, G., & Akçayır, M. (2018). The flipped classroom: A review of its advantages and challenges. *Computers & Education, 126*, 334–345.

Akbari, E., Pilot, A., & Simons, P. R. J. (2015). Autonomy, competence, and relatedness in foreign language learning through Facebook. *Computers in Human Behavior, 48*, 126–134.

Akbari, R. (2007). Reflections on reflection: A critical appraisal of reflective practices in L2 teacher education. *System, 35*(2), 192–207.

Akkerman, S. F., & Bakker, A. (2019). Persons pursuing multiple objects of interest in multiple contexts. *European Journal of Psychology of Education, 34*(1), 1–24.

Alalwan, A. A., Baabdullah, A. M., Rana, N. P., Tamilmani, K., & Dwivedi, Y. K. (2018). Examining adoption of mobile internet in Saudi Arabia: Extending TAM with perceived enjoyment, innovativeness and trust. *Technology in Society, 55*, 100–110.

Alanoglu, M., Aslan, S., & Karabatak, S. (2022). Do teachers' educational philosophies affect their digital literacy? The mediating effect of resistance to change. *Education and Information Technologies, 27*(3), 3447–3466.

Albero, B. (2003). Autoformation et contextes institutionnels d'éducation et de formation : Une approche socio-historique. In Dans B. Albero (Ed.), *Autoformation et enseignement supérieur* (p. 37–67). Hermès Science/Lavoisier.

Albion, P. R., & Tondeur, J. (2018). Section introduction: Professional learning and development of teachers. In J. Voogt, G. Knezek, R. Christensen & K.-

W. Lai (Eds.), *Second handbook of information technology in primary and secondary education* (pp. 377–379). Springer

Al-Busaidi, K. A., & Al-Shihi, H. (2012). Key factors to instructors' satisfaction of learning management systems in blended learning. *Journal of Computing in Higher Education, 24*(1), 18–39.

Aldholay, A., Isaac, O., Jalal, A. N., Anor, F. A., & Mutahar, A. M. (2021, June). Factors that Accelerate the Rise of Acceptance of Big Data Platforms for Academic Teaching: Personal Innovativeness as Moderating Variable. In M. Al-Emran, M. A. Al-Sharafi, M. N. Al-Kabi, & K. Shaalan (Eds.), *Proceedings of the International Conference on Emerging Technologies and Intelligent Systems* (pp. 227–243). Springer.

Allwright, D. (1990). *Autonomy in language pedagogy: CRILE Working Paper, 6*. University of Lancaster.

Alm, A. (2006). CALL for autonomy, competence and relatedness: Motivating language learning environments in Web 2.0. *The JALT CALL Journal, 2*(3), 29–38.

Almerich, G., Orellana, N., Suárez-Rodríguez, J., & Díaz-García, I. (2016). Teachers' information and communication technology competences: A structural approach. *Computers & Education, 100*, 110–125.

Alonso-Mencía, M. E., Alario-Hoyos, C., Maldonado-Mahauad, J., Estévez-Ayres, I., Pérez-Sanagustín, M., & Delgado Kloos, C. (2020). Self-regulated learning in MOOCs: Lessons learned from a literature review. *Educational Review, 72*(3), 319–345.

Alshammari, S. H., Ali, M. B., & Rosli, M. S. (2016). The influences of technical support, self efficacy and instructional design on the usage and acceptance of LMS: A comprehensive review. *Turkish Online Journal of Educational Technology-TOJET, 15*(2), 116–125.

Alwafi, E. M., Downey, C., & Kinchin, G. (2020). Promoting pre-service teachers' engagement in an online professional learning community: Support from practitioners. *Journal of Professional Capital and Community, 5*(2), 129–146.

AlZoubi, D., Kelley, J., Baran, E., Gilbert, S. B., Jiang, S., & Karabulut-Ilgu, A. (2021, January). Designing the TEACHActive feedback dashboard: A human centered approach. In *Companion Proceedings 11th International Conference on Learning Analytics & Knowledge (LAK21)* (pp. 124–126). Society for Learning Analytics Research. https://www.solaresearch.org/wp-content/uploads/2021/04/LAK21_CompanionProceedings.pdf

Amory, A. (2007). It's not about the tool, it's about the ideology. *South African Journal of Higher Education, 21*(6), 655–671.

Amory, A. (2012). Instructivist ideology: Education technology embracing the past? *Interactive Learning Environments, 20*(1), 41–55.

An, P., Bakker, S., Ordanovski, S., Paffen, C. L., Taconis, R., & Eggen, B. (2020, April). Dandelion diagram: aggregating positioning and orientation data in the visualization of classroom proxemics. In *Extended Abstracts of the 2020 CHI Conference on Human Factors in Computing Systems* (pp. 1–8).

An, Z., Wang, C., Li, S., Gan, Z., & Li, H. (2021). Technology-assisted self-regulated English language learning: Associations with English language self-efficacy, English enjoyment, and learning outcomes. *Frontiers in Psychology*, 3763.

Andrade, M. S., & Bunker, E. (2010). Self-regulated learning activities for an English language course. In *the 26th annual conference on distance teaching and learn-*

ing: 2010 proceedings and resources (pp. 430–434).

Ansyari, M. F. (2015). Designing and evaluating a professional development programme for basic technology integration in English as a foreign language (EFL) classrooms. *Australasian Journal of Educational Technology*, *31*(6), 699–712.

Anwaruddin, S. M. (2015). ICTs in language and literacy education in Bangladesh: A critical review. *Current Issues in Education*, *18*(1).

Aoki, N. (2000). Aspects of teacher autonomy: Capacity, freedom and responsibility. Paper presented at *2000 Hong Kong University of Science and Technology Language Centre Conference*.

Aragon, C., & Davis, K. (2019). *Writers in the secret garden: Fanfiction, youth, and new forms of mentoring*. MIT Press.

Ardasheva, Y., Wang, Z., Adesope, O. O., & Valentine, J. C. (2017). Exploring effectiveness and moderators of language learning strategy instruction on second language and self-regulated learning outcomes. *Review of Educational Research*, *87*(3), 544–582.

Asfar, N., & Zainuddin, Z. (2015). Secondary students' perceptions of information, communication and technology (ICT) use in promoting self directed learning in Malaysia. *The Online Journal of Distance Education and E-Learning*, *3*(4), 67–82.

Atman Uslu, N., & Usluel, Y. K. (2019). Predicting technology integration based on a conceptual framework for ICT use in education. *Technology, Pedagogy and Education*, *28*(5), 517–531.

Avalos, B. (2011). Teacher professional development in teaching and teacher education over ten years. *Teaching and teacher education*, *27*(1), 10–20.

Azevedo, F. S. (2013). The tailored practice of hobbies and its implication for the design of interest-driven learning environments. *Journal of the Learning Sciences*, *22*(3), 462–510.

Azevedo, R., & Hadwin, A. F. (2005). Scaffolding self-regulated learning and metacognition–Implications for the design of computer-based scaffolds. *Instructional Science*, *33*(5/6), 367–379.

Azevedo, R. (2014). Issues in dealing with sequential and temporal characteristics of self-and socially-regulated learning. *Metacognition and Learning*, *9*(2), 217–228.

Azevedo, R., & Witherspoon, A. M. (2009). Self-regulated learning with hypermedia. In D. J. Hacker, J. Dunlosky & A. C. Graesser (Eds.), *Handbook of metacognition in education* (p. 319–339). Routledge.

Azevedo, R., Mudrick, N. V., Taub, M., & Bradbury, A. E. (2019). Self-regulation in computer-assisted learning systems. In J. Dunlosky & K. A. Rawson (Eds.), *The Cambridge handbook of cognition and education* (pp. 587–618). Cambridge University Press

Bachmair, B., & Pachler, N. (2014). A cultural ecological frame for mobility and learning. *MedienPädagogik: Zeitschrift für Theorie und Praxis der Medienbildung*, *24*, 53–74.

Backfisch, I., Scherer, R., Siddiq, F., Lachner, A., & Scheiter, K. (2021). Teachers' technology use for teaching: Comparing two explanatory mechanisms. *Teaching and Teacher Education*, *104*, 103390.

Bahcivan, E., Gurer, M. D., Yavuzalp, N., & Akayoglu, S. (2019). Investigating the relations among pre-service teachers' teaching/learning beliefs and educational technology integration competencies: A structural equation modeling study. *Journal of Science Education and Technology*, *28*(5), 579–588.

Bai, B., & Wang, J. (2020). The role of growth mindset, self-efficacy and intrinsic value in self-regulated learning and English language learning achievements. *Language Teaching Research*, 1362168820933190. https://doi.org/10.1177/1362168820933190

Baki, R., Birgoren, B., & Aktepe, A. (2018). A meta analysis of factors affecting perceived usefulness and perceived ease of use in the adoption of e-learning systems. *Turkish Online Journal of Distance Education, 19*(4), 4–42.

Baker-Doyle, K. J. (2021). *Transformative teachers: Teacher leadership and learning in a connected world*. Harvard Education Press.

Bali, M. (2014). MOOC pedagogy: Gleaning good practice from existing MOOCs. *Journal of Online Learning and Teaching, 10*(1), 44–56.

Ball, S. J. (1998). Big policies/small world: An introduction to international perspectives in education policy. *Comparative education, 34*(2), 119–130.

Ballou, K. A. (1998). A concept analysis of autonomy. *Journal of Professional Nursing, 14*(2), 102–110.

Bandura, A. (1994). Self-efficacy. In V. S. Ramachaudran (Ed.), *Encyclopedia of human behavior* (Vol. 4, pp. 71–81). Academic Press.

Bandura, A. (1997). *Self-efficacy: The exercise of control*. W. H. Freeman and Company.

Bannert, M., Hildebrand, M., & Mengelkamp, C. (2009). Effects of a metacognitive support device in learning environments. *Computers in Human Behavior, 25*(4), 829–835.

Bannert, M., & Reimann, P. (2012). Supporting self-regulated hypermedia learning through prompts. *Instructional Science, 40*(1), 193–211.

Bano, S., Shah, U. U., & Ali, S. (2019). Personality and technology: Big five personality traits as descriptors of universal acceptance and usage of technology UTAUT. *Library Philosophy and Practice*, 2773. https://digitalcommons.unl.edu/libphilprac/2773

Bansal, A., Jain, S., Sharma, L., Sharma, N., Jain, C., & Madaan, M. (2020). Students' perception regarding pedagogy, andragogy, and heutagogy as teaching–learning methods in undergraduate medical education. *Journal of Education and Health Promotion, 9*, 301. https://doi.org/10.4103%2Fjehp.jehp_221_20

Banyard, P., Underwood, J., & Twiner, A. (2006). Do enhanced communication technologies inhibit or facilitate self‐regulated learning? *European Journal of Education, 41*(3‐4), 473–489.

Barbosa, F. L., & Borges-Andrade, J. E. (2021). Informal learning behaviors, interaction and workplace autonomy and readiness to learn. *Journal of Workplace Learning, 34*(4), 388–402.

Barbour, M. K. (2012). Teachers' perceptions of iPads in the classroom. *MACUL Journal, 32*(4), 24–25.

Barr, S., & Askell-Williams, H. (2020). Changes in teachers' epistemic cognition about self–regulated learning as they engaged in a researcher-facilitated professional learning community. *Asia-Pacific Journal of Teacher Education, 48*(2), 187–212.

Barron, B. (2006). Interest and self-sustained learning as catalysts of development: A learning ecology perspective. *Human Development, 49*(4), 193–224.

Barron, B., & Martin, C. K. (2016). Making matters: A framework for assessing digital media citizenship. In K. Peppler, E. R. Halverson & Y. B. Kafai (Eds.), *Makeology* (pp. 45–71). Routledge.

Barton, E. A., & Dexter, S. (2020). Sources of teachers' self-efficacy for technology integration from formal, informal, and independent professional learning. *Educational Technology Research and Development, 68*(1), 89–108.

Başar, H. (2003). *Classroom management* [in Turkish]. Anı Publishing.

Başaran, S., & Cabaroğlu N. (2014). The effect of language learning podcasts on English self-efficacy. *International Journal of Language Academy, 2*(2), 48–69.

Baya'a, N., Daher, W., & Anabousy, A. (2019). The development of in-service mathematics teachers' integration of ICT in a community of practice: Teaching-in-context theory. *International Journal of Emerging Technologies in Learning, 14*(1), 125–139.

Beach, P. (2017). Self-directed online learning: A theoretical model for understanding elementary teachers' online learning experiences. *Teaching and Teacher Education, 61*, 60–72.

Beach, P., Favret, E., & Minuk, A. (2021). Online teacher professional development in Canada: A review of the research. *Canadian Journal of Learning and Technology, 47*(2), 1–23. https://doi.org/10.21432/cjlt27948

Beauchamp, C. (2015). Reflection in teacher education: issues emerging from a review of current literature. *Reflective Practice, 16*(1), 123–141.

Beaudry, A., & Pinsonneault, A. (2010). The other side of acceptance: Studying the direct and indirect effects of emotions on information technology use. *MIS Quarterly*, 689–710.

Beaven, T. (2013). Use and Reuse of OER: professional conversations with language teachers. *Journal of E-Learning and Knowledge Society, 9*(1), 59–71.

Bechter, B. E., Dimmock, J. A., & Jackson, B. (2019). A cluster-randomized controlled trial to improve student experiences in physical education: Results of a student-centered learning intervention with high school teachers. *Psychology of Sport and Exercise, 45*, 101553.

Becker, H. J. (2000a). Who's wired and who's not: Children's access to and use of computer technology. *The Future of Children*, 44–75.

Becker H. J. (2000b). Findings from the teaching, learning and computing survey: Is Larry Cuban right? *Educational Policy Analysis Archives 8*, 1–32.

Beckers, J., Dolmans, D., & Van Merriënboer, J. (2016). e-Portfolios enhancing students' self-directed learning: A systematic review of influencing factors. *Australasian Journal of Educational Technology, 32*(2), 32–46. https://doi.org/10.14742/ajet.2528

Beckman, K., Bennett, S., & Lockyer, L. (2014). Understanding students' use and value of technology for learning. *Learning, Media and Technology, 39*(3), 346–367.

Beijaard, D., Verloop, N., & Vermunt, J. D. (2000). Teachers' perceptions of professional identity: An exploratory study from a personal knowledge perspective. *Teaching and Teacher Education, 16*(7), 749–764.

Belcher, D. D. (2017). On becoming facilitators of multimodal composing and digital design. *Journal of Second Language Writing, 38*, 80–85.

Bell, B. S. (2017). Strategies for supporting self-regulation during self-directed learning in the workplace. In J. E. Ellingson & R. A. Noe (Eds.), *Autonomous learning in the workplace* (pp. 117–134). Routledge.

Belz, J. A. (2002). Social dimensions of telecollaborative foreign language study. *Language Learning & Technology, 6*(1), 60–81.

Benali, M., Kaddouri, M., & Azzimani, T. (2018). Digital competence of Moroccan teachers of English. *International Journal of Education and Development using ICT, 14*(2), 99–120.

References

Bennett, L. (2014). Putting in more: emotional work in adopting online tools in teaching and learning practices. *Teaching in Higher Education, 19*(8), 919–930.

Bennett, S., & Maton, K. (2010). Beyond the 'digital natives' debate: Towards a more nuanced understanding of students' technology experiences. *Journal of Computer Assisted Learning, 26*(5), 321–331.

Benson, P. (1991). Autonomy and social interaction. *Teaching Philosophy, 14*(3), 329–332.

Benson, P. (1996). Concepts of autonomy in language learning. In R. Pemberton, E. S. L. Li, W. W. F. Or, & H. D. Pierson (Eds.), *Taking control: Autonomy in language learning* (pp. 27–34). Hong Kong University Press.

Benson, P. (1997). The philosophy and politics of learner autonomy. In P. Benson & P. Voller (Eds.), *Autonomy and independence in language learning* (pp. 18–34). Longman.

Benson, P. (2001). *Teaching and researching autonomy in language learning*. Longman.

Benson, P. (2009). Making sense of autonomy in language learning. In R. Pemberton, S. Toogood & A. Barfield (Eds.), *Maintaining control: Autonomy and language learning* (pp. 13–26). Hong Kong University Press.

Benson, P. (2010). Teacher education and teacher autonomy: Creating spaces for experimentation in secondary school English language teaching. *Language Teaching Research, 14*(3), 259–275.

Benson, P. (2016). Learner autonomy. In G. Hall (Ed.), *The Routledge handbook of English language teaching* (pp. 339–352). Routledge.

Benson, P., & Lamb, T. (2020). Autonomy in the Age of Multilingualism. In M. Jimenez Raya & F. Vieira (Eds.), *Autonomy in Language Education* (pp. 74–88). Routledge.

Ben-Eliyahu, A., & Bernacki, M. L. (2015). Addressing complexities in self-regulated learning: a focus on contextual factors, contingencies, and dynamic relations. *Metacognition and Learning, 10*(1), 1–13.

Benlahcene, A., Awang-Hashim, R., Kaur, A., & Wan-Din, W. Z. (2022). Perceived autonomy support and agentic engagement among Malaysian undergraduates: the mediatory role of personal best goals. *Journal of Further and Higher Education, 46*(1), 33–45.

Benson, P. (2011). Language learning and teaching beyond the classroom: An introduction to the field. In P. Benson & H. Reinders (Eds.), *Beyond the language classroom* (pp. 7–16). Palgrave Macmillan.

Benson, P. (2012) Learner-centered teaching. In A. Burns & Richards J. (Eds.), *The Cambridge guide to pedagogy and practice in second language teaching* (pp. 30–37). Cambridge University Press.

Benson, P. (2013). *Teaching and researching: Autonomy in language learning*. Routledge.

Benson, P. (2016). Learner autonomy. In G. Hall (Ed.), *The Routledge handbook of English language teaching* (pp. 339–352). Routledge.

Benson, P. (2022). Mapping language learning environments. In Reinders, H., Lai, C. & Sundqvist, P. (Eds.), *The Routledge handbook of language learning and teaching beyond the classroom* (pp. 24–35). Routledge.

Benson, P. & Lamb, T. (2020). Autonomy in the age of multilingualism. In M. J. Jiménez Raya & F. Vieira (Eds.) *Autonomy in language education: Theory, research and practice* (pp. 74–88). Routledge.

Bernacki, M. L., Aguilar, A. C., & Byrnes, J. P. (2011). Self-regulated learning and technology-enhanced learning environments: An opportunity-propensity analysis. In M. L. Bernacki, A. C. Aguilar & J. P. Byrnes (Eds.), *Fostering self-*

regulated learning through ICT (pp. 1–26). IGI Global.

Beynon, J., & Mackay, H. (1989). Information technology into education: Towards a critical perspective. *Journal of Education Policy*, *4*(3), 245–257.

Bhowmik, S. K., Hilman, B., & Roy, S. (2019). Peer collaborative writing in the EAP classroom: Insights from a Canadian postsecondary context. *TESOL Journal*, *10*(2), e00393.

Bhutada, G. (2021). *Visualizing the most used languages on the Internet*. https://www.visualcapitalist.com/the-most-used-languages-on-the-internet/

Biesta, G., Priestley, M., & Robinson, S. (2015). The role of beliefs in teacher agency. *Teachers and Teaching*, *21*(6), 624–640.

Bigum, C. (2012). Schools and computers: Tales of a digital romance. In L. Rowan & C. Bigum (Eds.), *Transformative Approaches to New Technologies and Student Diversity in Futures Oriented Classrooms* (pp. 15–28). Springer.

Bigum, C. Bulfin, S. & Johnson, N. F. (2015). Critical is something others (don't) do: Mapping the imaginative of educational technology. In S. Bulfin, N. Johnson and C. Bigum (Eds.), *Critical perspectives on technology and education* (pp. 1–14). Palgrave Macmillan.

Billett, S. (2018). Distinguishing lifelong learning from lifelong education. *Journal of Adult Learning, Knowledge and Innovation*, *2*(1), 1–7.

Bitner, N., & Bitner, J. O. E. (2002). Integrating technology into the classroom: Eight keys to success. *Journal of Technology and Teacher Education*, *10*(1), 95–100.

Bladergroen, M., Chigona, W., Bytheway, A., Cox, S., Dumas, C., & Van Zyl, I. (2012). Educator discourses on ICT in education: A critical analysis. *International Journal of Education and Development using ICT*, *8*(2), 107–119.

Black, R. W. (2006). Language, culture, and identity in online fanfiction. *E-learning and Digital Media*, *3*(2), 170–184.

Blake, R. (2016). Technology and the four skills. *Language Learning & Technology*, *20*(2), 129–142.

Blanchard, M. R., LePrevost, C. E., Tolin, A. D., & Gutierrez, K. S. (2016). Investigating technology-enhanced teacher professional development in rural, high-poverty middle schools. *Educational Researcher*, *45*(3), 207–220.

Blaschke, L. M. (2012). Heutagogy and lifelong learning: A review of heutagogical practice and self-determined learning. *The International Review of Research in Open and Distributed Learning*, *13*(1), 56–71.

Blaschke, L. M. (2019). The pedagogy–andragogy–heutagogy continuum and technology-supported personal learning environments. In I. Jung (Ed.), *Open and distance education theory revisited: Implications for the digital era* (pp. 75–84). Springer.

Blaschke, L. M., & Hase, S. (2016). Heutagogy: A holistic framework for creating twenty-first-century self-determined learners. In B. Gros & M. Maina (Eds.), *The future of ubiquitous learning: Learning designs for emerging pedagogies* (pp. 25–40). Springer.

Blattner, G., & Fiori, M. (2011). Virtual social network communities: An investigation of language learners' development of socio-pragmatic awareness and multiliteracy skills. *CALICO Journal*, *29*(1), 24–43.

Blau, I., & Shamir-Inbal, T. (2017). Re-designed flipped learning model in an academic course: The role of co-creation and co-regulation. *Computers & Education*, *115*, 69–81.

Blin, F. (2004). CALL and the development of learner autonomy: Towards an activity-theoretical perspective. *ReCALL*, *16*(2), 377–395.

Blin, F. (2010). Designing cybertasks for learner autonomy: Towards an activity theoretical pedagogical model. In M. J. Luzón, N. Ruiz-Madrid & M. L. Villanueva (Eds.), *Digital genres, new literacies and autonomy in language learning* (pp. 175–196). Cambridge Scholars Publishing.

Blitz, C. L. (2013). *Can online learning communities achieve the goals of traditional professional learning communities? What the literature says*. National Center for Education Evaluation and Regional Assistance. https://files.eric.ed.gov/fulltext/ED544210.pdf

Bloch, J. (2007). Abdullah's blogging: A generation 1.5 student enters the blogosphere. *Language Learning & Technology, 11*(2), 128–41.

Bock, G. W., Zmud, R. W., Kim, Y. G., & Lee, J. N. (2005). Behavioral intention formation in knowledge sharing: Examining the roles of extrinsic motivators, social-psychological forces, and organizational climate. *MIS Quarterly*, 87–111.

Bonney, C. R., Cortina, K. S., Smith-Darden, J. P., & Fiori, K. L. (2008). Understanding strategies in foreign language learning: Are integrative and intrinsic motives distinct predictors? *Learning and Individual Differences, 18*(1), 1–10.

Booth, D. (2012). *Development as a collective action problem: Africa Power and Politics Programme policy brief*. Africa Power and Politics Programme, Overseas Development Institute. https://cdn.odi.org/media/documents/appp-synthesis-report-development-as-a-collective-action-problem-david-booth-o_7un7DOu.pdf

Bouchard, P. (2009). Some factors to consider when designing semi-autonomous learning environments. *Electronic Journal of E-learning, 7*(2), 93–100.

Bouchard, P. (2011). Self-directed learning and learner autonomy. In S. Norbert (Ed.), *The Encyclopedia of the sciences of learning* (pp. 2997–3000). Springer.

Boulton, A., & Cobb, T. (2017). Corpus use in language learning: A meta-analysis. *Language Learning, 67*(2), 348–393.

Bower, M., & Sturman, D. (2015). What are the educational affordances of wearable technologies? *Computers & Education, 88*, 343–353.

Bowman, M. A., Vongkulluksn, V. W., Jiang, Z., & Xie, K. (2020). Teachers' exposure to professional development and the quality of their instructional technology use: The mediating role of teachers' value and ability beliefs. *Journal of Research on Technology in Education*, 1–17.

Bragg, L. A., Walsh, C., & Heyeres, M. (2021). Successful design and delivery of online professional development for teachers: A systematic review of the literature. *Computers & Education, 166*, 104158.

Breen, M. P., & Mann, S. J. (2014). Shooting arrows at the sun: Perspectives on a pedagogy for autonomy. In P. Benson & P. Voller (Eds.), *Autonomy and independence in language learning* (pp. 132–149). Routledge.

Brennan, A. R. (2021). *Reconceptualizing teacher professional development as professional learning: A qualitative case study of a school-supported self-directed professional learning model* [Unpublished doctoral dissertation]. Miami University.

Brevik, L. M. (2019). Gamers, surfers, social media users: Unpacking the role of interest in English. *Journal of Computer Assisted Learning, 35*(5), 595–606.

Broadbent, J., Panadero, E., & Fuller-Tyszkiewicz, M. (2020). Effects of mobile-app learning diaries vs online training on specific self-regulated learning components. *Educational Technology Research and Development, 68*(5), 2351–2372.

Brocca, N., Borowiec, E., & Masia, V. (2020). Didactics of pragmatics as a way to improve social media literacy. An experiment proposal with Polish and

Italian students in L1. *heiEDUCATION Journal. Transdisziplinäre Studien zur Lehrerbildung, 5*, 81–109.

Brookfield, S. (1993). Self-directed learning, political clarity, and the critical practice of adult education. *Adult Education Quarterly, 43*(4), 227–242.

Buchanan, R. (2015). Teacher identity and agency in an era of accountability. *Teachers and Teaching, 21*(6), 700–719.

Buchem, I., Tur, G., & Hölterhof, T. (2014). Learner control in personal learning environments: A crosscultural study. *Journal of Literacy and Technology, 15*(2), 14–53.

Burbules, N. C., & Callister Jr, T. A. (1999). The risky promises and promising risks of new information technologies for education. *Bulletin of Science, Technology & Society, 19*(2), 105–112.

Burch, P., & Miglani, N. (2018). Technocentrism and social fields in the Indian EdTech movement: formation, reproduction and resistance. *Journal of Education Policy, 33*(5), 590–616.

Burnette, J. L., O'boyle, E. H., VanEpps, E. M., Pollack, J. M., & Finkel, E. J. (2013). Mind-sets matter: a meta-analytic review of implicit theories and self-regulation. *Psychological Bulletin, 139*(3), 655–701.

Burns, M. (2013). The future of professional learning. *Learning & Leading with Technology, 40*(8), 14–18.

Burstein, J., Shore, J., Sabatini, J., Moulder, B., Lentini, J., Biggers, K., & Holtzman, S. (2014). From teacher professional development to the classroom: How NLP technology can enhance teachers' linguistic awareness to support curriculum development for English language learners. *Journal of Educational Computing Research, 51*(1), 119–144.

Buske, R. (2018). The principal as a key actor in promoting teachers' innovativeness–analyzing the innovativeness of teaching staff with variance-based partial least square modeling. *School Effectiveness and School Improvement, 29*(2), 262–284.

Butler, Y. G. (2014). Socioeconomic disparities and early English education: A case in Changzhou, China. In N. Murray & A. Scarino (Eds.), *Dynamic Ecologies* (pp. 95–115). Springer.

Cabot, M. (2014). *English as a foreign language and technological artefacts in school and out of school* (Unpublished master thesis). University College Stord.

Cai, Z., Fan, X., & Du, J. (2017). Gender and attitudes toward technology use: A meta-analysis. *Computers & Education, 105*, 1–13.

Campbell, R. J., Kyriakides, L., Muijs, R. D., & Robinson, W. (2003). Differential teacher effectiveness: Towards a model for research and teacher appraisal. *Oxford Review of Education, 29*(3), 347–362.

Canada, K. and Brusca, F. (1993). The technological gender gap: evidence and recommendations for educators and computer-based instruction designers. *Educational Technology Research and Development (39)*, 43–51.

Canagarajah, A. S. (1999). *Resisting linguistic imperialism in English teaching*. Oxford University Press.

Carhill-Poza, A. (2017). Re-examining English language teaching and learning for adolescents through technology. *System, 67*(7), 111–120.

Carpenter, J. P., Kimmons, R., Short, C. R., Clements, K., & Staples, M. E. (2019). Teacher identity and crossing the professional-personal divide on Twitter. *Teaching and Teacher Education, 81*, 1–12.

Carpenter, J. P., & Krutka, D. G. (2015). Social media in teacher education. In M. L. Niess & H. Gillow-Wiles (Eds.), *Handbook of research on teacher education in the digital age* (pp. 28–54). IGI Global.

Carpenter, J. P., & Linton, J. N. (2016). Edcamp unconferences: Educators' perspectives on an untraditional professional learning experience. *Teaching and Teacher Education, 57*, 97–108.

Carpenter, J. P., Morrison, S. A., Craft, M., & Lee, M. (2020). How and why are educators using Instagram? *Teaching and Teacher Education, 96*, 103149.

Carpenter, J. P., & Willet, K. B. S. (2021). The teachers' lounge and the debate hall: Anonymous self-directed learning in two teaching-related subreddits. *Teaching and Teacher Education, 104*, 103371.

Castaño-Muñoz, J., Punie, Y., & Inamorato dos Santos, A. (2016). *MOOCs in Europe: Evidence from pilot surveys with universities and MOOC learners.* European Commission. https://joint-research-centre.ec.europa.eu/system/files/2016-06/JRC%2520brief%2520MOOCs_JRC101956.pdf

Castellano, J., Mynard, J. & Rubesch, T. (2011). Student technology use in a self-access center. *Language Learning & Technology, 15*(3), 12–27.

Chai, C. S., Wong, L. H., & King, R. B. (2016). Surveying and modeling students' motivation and learning strategies for mobile-assisted seamless Chinese language learning. *Journal of Educational Technology & Society, 19*(3), 170–180.

Chan, H. W. (2016). Popular culture, English out-of-class activities, and learner autonomy among highly proficient secondary students in Hong kong. *Universal Journal of Educational Research, 4*(8), 1918–1923.

Chan, T. W., Looi, C. K., Chen, W., Wong, L. H., Chang, B., Liao, C. C., ... & Ogata, H. (2018). Interest-driven creator theory: towards a theory of learning design for Asia in the twenty-first century. *Journal of Computers in Education, 5*(4), 435–461.

Chang, C. C. (2018). Outdoor ubiquitous learning or indoor CAL? Achievement and different cognitive loads of college students. *Behaviour and Information Technology, 37*(1), 38–49.

Chang, M. M. (2010). Effects of self-monitoring on web-based language learner's performance and motivation. *CALICO Journal, 27*(2), 298–310.

Chemero, A. (2003). An outline of a theory of affordances. *Ecological Psychology, 15*, 181–195.

Chen, B., Fan, Y., Zhang, G., Liu, M., & Wang, Q. (2020). Teachers' networked professional learning with MOOCs. *PloS one, 15*(7), e0235170.

Chen, C. H., & Chiu, C. H. (2016). Collaboration scripts for enhancing metacognitive self-regulation and mathematics literacy. *International Journal of Science and Mathematics Education, 14*(2), 263–280.

Chen, C. M., & Huang, S. H. (2014). Web‐based reading annotation system with an attention‐based self‐regulated learning mechanism for promoting reading performance. *British Journal of Educational Technology, 45*(5), 959–980.

Chen, C. M., & Li, Y. L. (2010). Personalised context-aware ubiquitous learning system for supporting effective English vocabulary learning. *Interactive Learning Environments, 18*(4), 341–364.

Chen, C. M., Wang, J. Y., & Chen, Y. C. (2014). Facilitating English-language reading performance by a digital reading annotation system with self regulated learning mechanisms. *Journal of Educational Technology & Society, 17*(1), 102–114.

Chen, H. H. J., Yang, C. T. Y., & Lai, K. K. W. (2020). Investigating college EFL learners' perceptions toward the use of Google Assistant for foreign language learning. *Interactive Learning Environments*, 1–16.

Chen, G. (2020). A visual learning analytics (VLA) approach to video-based teacher professional development: Impact on teachers' beliefs, self-efficacy, and classroom talk practice. *Computers & Education, 144*, 103670.

Chen, G., & Chan, C. K. (2022). Visualization-and analytics-supported video-based professional development for promoting mathematics classroom discourse. *Learning, Culture and Social Interaction, 33*, 100609.

Chen, G., Clarke, S. N., & Resnick, L. B. (2015). Classroom discourse analyzer (CDA): A discourse analytic tool for teachers. *Technology, Instruction, Cognition and Learning, 10*(2), 85–105.

Chen, J., Lin, C. H., & Chen, G. (2021). A cross-cultural perspective on the relationships among social media use, self-regulated learning and adolescents' digital reading literacy. *Computers & Education, 175*, 104322.

Chen, J., Wang, M., Kirschner, P. A., & Tsai, C. C. (2018). The role of collaboration, computer use, learning environments, and supporting strategies in CSCL: A meta-analysis. *Review of Educational Research, 88*(6), 799–843.

Chen, P. Y. & Hwang, G. H. (2019). An IRS‐facilitated collective issue‐quest approach to enhancing students' learning achievement, self‐regulation and collective efficacy in flipped classrooms. *British Journal of Educational Technology, 50*(4), 1996–2013.

Chen, Y., Mayall, H. J., York, C. S., & Smith, T. J. (2019). Parental perception and English learners' mobile-assisted language learning: An ethnographic case study from a technology-based funds of knowledge approach. *Learning, Culture and Social Interaction, 22*, 100325. https://doi.org/10.1016/j.lcsi.2019.100325

Chen, Y. L., & Hsu, C. C. (2020). Self-regulated mobile game-based English learning in a virtual reality environment. *Computers & Education, 154*, 103910

Chen, Y., Zhang, P., & Huang, L. (2022). Translanguaging/trans-semiotizing in teacher-learner interactions on social media: Making learner agency visible and achievable. *System, 104*, 102686.

Chen, Z., Chen, W., Jia, J., & An, H. (2020). The effects of using mobile devices on language learning: a meta-analysis. *Educational Technology Research and Development, 68*(4), 1769–1789.

Chen Hsieh, J. S., Wu, W. C. V., & Marek, M. W. (2017). Using the flipped classroom to enhance EFL learning. *Computer Assisted Language Learning, 30*(1–2), 1–21.

Cheng, L. (2014). The use of web-based self-directed learning for Mandarin study. *Excellence in Education Journal, 3*(1), 46–94.

Cheng, A., & Lee, C. (2018). Factors affecting tertiary English learners' persistence in the self-directed language learning journey. *System, 76*, 170–182.

Cheng, S. L., Lu, L., Xie, K., & Vongkulluksn, V. W. (2020). Understanding teacher technology integration from expectancy-value perspectives. *Teaching and Teacher Education, 91*, 103062.

Cheng, S. L., & Xie, K. (2018). The relations among teacher value beliefs, personal characteristics, and TPACK in intervention and non-intervention settings. *Teaching and Teacher Education, 74*, 98–113.

Cheng, J., Sagaya Raj, G., & Tan Tjin Ai, J. (2018). The relationship among learning strategy, autonomy and language proficiency of Chinese EFL learners. *International Journal of Foreign Language Teaching and Research, 6*(23), 23–34.

Cheon, S. H., Reeve, J., & Vansteenkiste, M. (2020). When teachers learn how to provide classroom structure in an autonomy-supportive way: Benefits to teachers and their students. *Teaching and Teacher Education, 90*, 103004.

Chere-Masopha, J. (2018). Personal landscapes of teacher professional identities versus digital technology adoption and integration in Lesotho schools. *International Journal of Learning, Teaching and Educational Research, 17*(3), 28–42.

Chern, C.‐l. and Dooley, K. (2014). Learning English by walking down the street. *ELT Journal 68*(2): 113–123.

Chik, A. (2018). Beliefs and practices of foreign language learning: A visual analysis. *Applied Linguistics Review, 9*(2–3), 307–331.

Chik, A., & Ho, J. (2017). Learn a language for free: Recreational learning among adults. *System, 69*, 162–171.

Chikuni, P. R., Cox, G., & Czerniewicz, L. (2019). Exploring the Institutional OER Policy Landscape in South Africa: Dominant Discourses and Assumptions. *International Journal of Education and Development using Information and Communication Technology, 15*(4), 165–179.

Chiu, T. K. (2017). Introducing electronic textbooks as daily‐use technology in schools: A top‐down adoption process. *British Journal of Educational Technology, 48*(2), 524–537.

Chiu, T. K. (2022). School learning support for teacher technology integration from a self-determination theory perspective. *Educational Technology Research and Development*, 1–19.

Chiu, T. K., & Churchill, D. (2016). Adoption of mobile devices in teaching: Changes in teacher beliefs, attitudes and anxiety. *Interactive Learning Environments, 24*(2), 317–327.

Cho, K., Lee, S., Joo, M. H., & Becker, B. J. (2018). The effects of using mobile devices on student achievement in language learning: A meta-analysis. *Education Sciences, 8*(3), 105–121.

Choi, J., & Park, E. A. (2013). Epistemological beliefs and self-directedness in learning of South Korean middle school students. *The Asia-Pacific Education Researcher, 22*(4), 541–548.

Choi, D. S. Y., & Morrison, P. (2014). Learning to get it right: Understanding change processes in professional development for teachers of English learners. *Professional Development in Education, 40*(3), 416–435.

Chou, H. L., & Chou, C. (2021). A multigroup analysis of factors underlying teachers' technostress and their continuance intention toward online teaching. *Computers & Education, 175*, 104335.

Christiansen, M. S., & Koelzer, M. L. (2016). Digital storytelling: Using different technologies for EFL. *MexTESOL Journal, 40*(1), 1–14.

Chu, T. H., & Chen, Y. Y. (2016). With good we become good: Understanding e-learning adoption by theory of planned behavior and group influences. *Computers & Education, 92*, 37–52.

Chun, D., Kern, R., & Smith, B. (2016). Technology in language use, language teaching, and language learning. *The Modern Language Journal, 100*(S1), 64–80.

Chung, J., & Tan, F. B. (2004). Antecedents of perceived playfulness: an exploratory study on user acceptance of general information-searching websites. *Information & Management, 41*(7), 869–881.

Chylinski, R., & Hanewald, R. (2011). Creating supportive environments for CALL teacher autonomy. In I. Chen (Ed.), *Instructional Design: Concepts, Methodologies, Tools and Applications* (pp. 840–860). IGI Global.

Clarke, D., & Hollingsworth, H. (2002). Elaborating a model of teacher professional growth. *Teaching and Teacher Education, 18*(8), 947–967.

Clements, K. I., & Pawlowski, J. M. (2012). User‐oriented quality for OER:

Understanding teachers' views on re‑use, quality, and trust. *Journal of Computer Assisted Learning, 28*(1), 4–14.

Clinton, V. (2019). Reading from paper compared to screens: A systematic review and meta‑analysis. *Journal of Research in Reading, 42*(2), 288–325.

Coburn, C. E., Mata, W. S., & Choi, L. (2013). The embeddedness of teachers' social networks: Evidence from a study of mathematics reform. *Sociology of Education, 86*(4), 311–342.

Coburn, C. E., & Penuel, W. R. (2016). Research–practice partnerships in education: Outcomes, dynamics, and open questions. *Educational Researcher, 45*(1), 48–54.

Codreanu, T., & Combe, C. (2020). Vlogs, video publishing, and informal language learning. In M. Dressman & R. W. Sadler (Eds.), *The Handbook of Informal Language Learning* (pp. 153–168). John Wiley & Sons.

Cole, J., & Vanderplank, R. (2016). Comparing autonomous and class-based learners in Brazil: Evidence for the present-day advantages of informal, out-of-class learning. *System, 61*, 31–42.

Coleman, H. (2011). *Dreams and realities: Developing countries and the English language.* The British Council.

Conley, A. M., Pintrich, P. R., Vekiri, I., & Harrison, D. (2004). Changes in epistemological beliefs in elementary science students. *Contemporary Educational Psychology, 29*(2), 186–204.

Corbalan, G., van Merriënboer, J. J., & Kicken, W. (2010). Shared control over task selection: a Way out of the self-directed learning paradox? *Technology, Instruction, Cognition & Learning, 8*(2), 119–136.

Costa, A. L., & Kallick, B. (Eds.), (2008). *Learning and leading with habits of mind: 16 essential characteristics for success.* ASCD.

Credé, M., & Kuncel, N.R. (2008). Study habits, skills, and attitudes: the third pillar supporting collegiate academic performance. *Perspectives on Psychological Science, 3*(6), 425–453.

Cribb, A., & Gewirtz, S. (2007). Unpacking autonomy and control in education: Some conceptual and normative groundwork for a comparative analysis. *European Educational Research Journal, 6*(3), 203–213.

Cross, J. (2014). Promoting autonomous listening to podcasts: A case study. *Language Teaching Research, 18*(1), 8–32.

Cuban, L. (1986). *Teachers and machines: The classroom use of technology since 1920.* Teachers College Press.

Cuban, L. (1993). Computers meet classroom: Classroom wins. *Teachers College Record, 95*(2), 185–210.

Dabbagh, N., & Kitsantas, A. (2012). Personal Learning Environments, social media, and self-regulated learning: A natural formula for connecting formal and informal learning. *The Internet and Higher Education, 15*(1), 3–8.

Dalton, B. (2014). E-text and e-books are changing literacy landscape. *Phi Delta Kappan, 96*(3), 38–43.

Dam, L. (2008). How do we recognize an autonomous classroom? Revisited. In TESOL (Ed.), *A TESOL symposium: Learner autonomy: What does the future hold?* Conference proceedings, 2008 (pp. 13–32). TESOL.

Dam, L. (2013). How to engage learners in authentic target language use—Examples from an autonomy classroom. In A. Burkert, L. Dam, & C. Ludwig (Eds.), *The Answer is autonomy: Issues in language teaching and learning* (pp. 76–94). IATEFL.

Dam, L., Eriksson, R., Little, D., Milliander, J., & Trebbi, T. (1990). Towards a definition of autonomy. In T. Trebbi (Ed.), *Third Nordic workshop on developing autonomous learning in FL classroom* (pp. 102–103). University of Bergen. https://warwick.ac.uk/fac/soc/al/research/groups/llta/research/past_projects/dahla/archive/trebbi-1990.pdf

Dang, T. T. (2012). Learner autonomy: A synthesis of theory and practice. *The Internet Journal of Language, Culture and Society, 35,* 52–67.

Darling-Hammond, L. (2005). Teaching as a profession: Lessons in teacher preparation and professional development. *Phi Delta Kappan, 87*(3), 237–240.

Davis, F. D. (1989). Perceived usefulness, perceived ease of use, and user acceptance of information technology. *MIS Quarterly,* 319–340.

Davis, D., Chen, G., Jivet, I., Hauff, C., & Houben, G. J. (2016). Encouraging metacognition & self-regulation in MOOCs through increased learner feedback. In *Proceedings of the eighth international learning analytics & knowledge conference* (pp. 17–22). LAK'16, April, Edinburgh, Scotland.

Davis, D., Jivet, I., Kizilcec, R. F., Chen, G., Hauff, C., & Houben, G. J. (2017). Follow the successful crowd: raising MOOC completion rates through social comparison at scale. In *Proceedings of the seventh international learning analytics & knowledge conference* (pp. 454–463). LAK'17, March 13–17, Vancouver, Canada. http://dx.doi.org/10.1145/3027385.3027411

Davis, M. (2013). Beyond the classroom: The role of self-guided learning in second language listening and speaking practice. *Studies in Self-Access Learning Journal, 4*(2), 85–95.

Dawson, K. (2012). Using action research projects to examine teacher technology integration practices. *Journal of Digital Learning in Teacher Education, 28*(3), 117–123.

Dawson, S., Joksimović, S., Kovanović, V., Gašević, D., & Siemens, G. (2015). Recognising learner autonomy: Lessons and reflections from a joint x/c MOOC. *Proceedings of Higher Education Research and Development Society of Australia 2015.*

De Brabander, C. J., & Glastra, F. J. (2018). Testing a unified model of task-specific motivation: How teachers appraise three professional development activities. *Frontline Learning Research, 6*(1), 54–76.

De los Arcos, B., Farrow, R., Pitt, R., Weller, M., & McAndrew, P. (2016). Adapting the curriculum: How K-12 teachers perceive the role of open educational resources. *Journal of Online Learning Research, 2*(1), 23–40.

De Moraes Garcia, D. N., O'Connor, K., & Cappellini, M. (2017). A typology of metacognition: Examining autonomy in a collective blog compiled in a teletandem environment. In M. Cappellini, T. Lewis & A. Rivens Mompean (Eds.), *Learner autonomy and Web 2.0* (pp. 67–90). Equinox.

De Vos, J. F., Schriefers, H., Nivard, M. G., & Lemhöfer, K. (2018). A meta - analysis and meta - regression of incidental second language word learning from spoken input. *Language Learning, 68*(4), 906–941.

Deci, E. L., & Flaste, R. (1995). *Why we do what we do: The dynamics of personal autonomy.* G. P. Putnam's Sons.

Deci, E. L., & Ryan, R. M. (1985). The general causality orientations scale: Self-determination in personality. *Journal of Research in Personality, 19*(2), 109–134.

Deci, E. L., & Ryan, R. M. (1987). The support of autonomy and the control of behavior. *Journal of Personality and Social Psychology, 53*(6), 1024–1037.

Deci, E. L., & Ryan, R. M. (2002). Self-determination research: Reflections and future directions. In E. L. Deci & R. M. Ryan (Eds.), *Handbook of self-determination research* (pp. 431–441). University of Rochester Press.

De la Fuente, M. J. (2014). Learners' attention to input during focus on form listening tasks: The role of mobile technology in the second language classroom. *Computer Assisted Language Learning, 27*(3), 261–276.

Delgado, P., Vargas, C., Ackerman, R., & Salmerón, L. (2018). Don't throw away your printed books: A meta-analysis on the effects of reading media on reading comprehension. *Educational Research Review, 25*, 23–38.

Deniz, H. (2011). Examination of changes in prospective elementary teachers' epistemological beliefs in science and exploration of factors meditating that change. *Journal of Science Education and Technology, 20*(6), 750–760.

Deng, D. F. (2007). An exploration of the relationship between learner autonomy and English proficiency. *Asian EFL Journal.* Retrieved from http://www.asian-efl-journal.com/pta_Nov_07_dd.pdf

Deng, F., Chai, C. S., Tsai, C. C., & Lee, M. H. (2014). The relationships among Chinese practicing teachers' epistemic beliefs, pedagogical beliefs and their beliefs about the use of ICT. *Journal of Educational Technology & Society, 17*(2), 245–256.

Depaepe, F., De Corte, E., & Verschaffel, L. (2016). Mathematical epistemological beliefs. In J. A. Greene & W. A. Sandoval, I. Bråten (Eds.), *Handbook of epistemic cognition* (pp. 159–176). Routledge.

Desimone, L. M. (2009). Improving impact studies of teachers' professional development: Toward better conceptualizations and measures. *Educational Researcher, 38*(3), 181–199.

Devolder, A., van Braak, J., & Tondeur, J. (2012). Supporting self‐regulated learning in computer‐based learning environments: systematic review of effects of scaffolding in the domain of science education. *Journal of Computer Assisted Learning, 28*(6), 557–573.

Dexter, S. L., Anderson, R. E., & Becker, H. J. (1999). Teachers' views of computers as catalysts for changes in their teaching practice. *Journal of Research on Computing in Education, 31*(3), 221–239.

Dexter, S., Barton, E., Morgan, M. A., & Meyer, J. P. (2016, March). Relative uses, impact, and possibilities for teachers' uses of formal, informal, and independent learning to integrate technology. In *Society for Information Technology & Teacher Education International Conference* (pp. 1195–1202). Association for the Advancement of Computing in Education (AACE).

Digón-Regueiro, P., Gewerc-Barujel, A., & Pérez-Crego, C. (2021). Dilemmas in the integration of technologies in a Primary school classroom: the dialogue between teacher agency, curriculum and digital technologies. *Pedagogies: An International Journal*, 1–19.

Diamond, J. (1997). *Guns, germs, and steel.* WW Norton & Company.

Dickinson, L. (1987). *Self-instruction in language learning.* Cambridge University Press

Dickinson, L. (1995). Autonomy and motivation a literature review. *System, 23*(2), 165–174.

Dignath, C., & Büttner, G. (2008). Components of fostering self-regulated learning among students. A meta-analysis on intervention studies at primary and secondary school level. *Metacognition and Learning, 3*(3), 231–264.

Dignath-van Ewijk, C., Fabriz, S., & Büttner, G. (2015). Fostering self-regulated learning among students by means of an electronic learning diary: A training experiment. *Journal of Cognitive Education and Psychology, 14*(1), 77–97.

Dincer, A. (2020). Understanding the characteristics of English language learners' out-of-class language learning through digital practices. *IAFOR Journal of Education, 8*(2), 47–65.

Dong, Y., Xu, C., Chai, C. S., & Zhai, X. (2020). Exploring the structural relationship among teachers' technostress, technological pedagogical content knowledge (TPACK), computer self-efficacy and school support. *The Asia-Pacific Education Researcher, 29*(2), 147–157.

Dörnyei, Z. (2009). The L2 motivational self system. *Motivation, language identity and the L2 self, 36*(3), 9–11.

Drent, M., & Meelissen, M. (2008). Which factors obstruct or stimulate teacher educators to use ICT innovatively? *Computers & Education, 51*(1), 187–199.

Duckworth, A. L., Peterson, C., Matthews, M. D., & Kelly, D. R. (2007). Grit: perseverance and passion for long-term goals. *Journal of Personality and Social Psychology, 92*(6), 1087–1101.

Dvir, N., & Schatz-Oppenheimer, O. (2020). Novice teachers in a changing reality. *European Journal of Teacher Education, 43*(4), 639–656.

Dweck, C.S. (2006). *Mindset: The new psychology of success.* Random House.

Eccles, J. S., & Wigfield, A. (2002). Motivational beliefs, values, and goals. *Annual Review of Psychology, 53*(1), 109–132.

Edgar, A. (2005). *The philosophy of Habermas.* New York: Routledge

Ehrlinger, J., Johnson, K., Banner, M., Dunning, D., & Kruger, J. (2008). Why the unskilled are unaware: Further explorations of (absent) self-insight among the incompetent. *Organizational Behavior and Human Decision Processes, 105*(1), 98–121.

Elabdali, R. (2021). Are two heads really better than one? A meta-analysis of the L2 learning benefits of collaborative writing. *Journal of Second Language Writing, 52*, 100788.

Elliott, J. C. (2017). The evolution from traditional to online professional development: A review. *Journal of Digital Learning in Teacher Education, 33*(3), 114–125.

Elola, I., & Oskoz, A. (2017). Writing with 21st century social tools in the L2 classroom: New literacies, genres, and writing practices. *Journal of Second Language Writing, 36*, 52–60.

Emirbayer, M. & Mische, A. (1998). 'What is agency?' *The American Journal of Sociology, 103*, 962–1023.

Emo, W. (2015). Teachers' motivations for initiating innovations. *Journal of Educational Change, 16*(2), 171–195.

Enfield, J. (2013). Looking at the impact of the flipped classroom model of instruction on undergraduate multimedia students at CSUN. *TechTrends, 57*(6), 14–27.

Engen, B. (2019). Understanding social and cultural aspects of teachers' digital competencies. Comunicar. *Media Education Resarch Journal, 61*, 9–19. https://www.scipedia.com/public/Engen_2019a

Eraut, M. (2004). Informal learning in the workplace. *Studies in Continuing Education, 26*(2), 247–273.

Ertmer, P. A., & Ottenbreit-Leftwich, A. T. (2010). Teacher technology change: How knowledge, confidence, beliefs, and culture intersect. *Journal of Research on Technology in Education, 42*(3), 255–284.

Ertmer, P. A., Ottenbreit-Leftwich, A. T., Sadik, O., Sendurur, E., & Sendurur,

P. (2012). Teacher beliefs and technology integration practices: A critical relationship. *Computers & Education, 59*(2), 423–435.

Escueta, M., Nickow, A. J., Oreopoulos, P., & Quan, V. (2020). Upgrading education with technology: Insights from experimental research. *Journal of Economic Literature, 58*(4), 897–996.

Escueta, M., Quan, V., Nickow, A. J., & Oreopoulos, P. (2017). *Education technology: An evidence-based review*. NBER Working Paper No 23744.

Eskildsen, S. W., Pekarek Doehler, S., Piirainen-Marsh, A., & Hellermann, J. (2019). Introduction: On the complex ecology of language learning "in the wild." In Hellermann, S. W. Eskildsen, S. Pekarek Doehler, & A. Piirainen-Marsh (Eds.), *Conversation analytic research on learning-in-action* (pp. 1–21). Springer, Cham.

Everhard, C. J. (2016). What is this thing called autonomy? Finding a definition and a model. *Selected Papers on Theoretical and Applied Linguistics, 21*, 548–568.

Everhard-Theophilidou, C. J. (2012). *Degrees of autonomy in foreign language learning*. [Unpublished doctoral dissertation]. University of Thessaloniki, Greece. http://ikee.lib.auth.gr/record/128755/files/GRI-2012-8252.pdf

Evertson, C. M., & Weinstein, C. S. (2006). *Handbook of classroom management: Research, practice, and contemporary issues*. Lawrence Erlbaum Associates

Falloon, G. (2020). From digital literacy to digital competence: the teacher digital competency (TDC) framework. *Educational Technology Research and Development, 68*(5), 2449–2472.

Farjon, D., Smits, A., & Voogt, J. (2019). Technology integration of pre-service teachers explained by attitudes and beliefs, competency, access, and experience. *Computers & Education, 130*, 81–93.

Fathali, S., & Okada, T. (2017). A self-determination theory approach to technology-enhanced out-of-class language learning intention: A case of Japanese EFL learners. *International Journal of Research Studies in Language Learning, 6*(4), 53–64.

Fathali, S., & Okada, T. (2018). Technology acceptance model in technology-enhanced OCLL contexts: A self-determination theory approach. *Australasian Journal of Educational Technology, 34*(4), 138–154.

Fedorov, A., & Mikhaleva, G. (2020). Current trends in media and information literacy in research and scientific publications of the early 21st century. *International Journal of Media and Information Literacy, 5*(2), 153–163.

Feng, G. C., Su, X., Lin, Z., He, Y., Luo, N., & Zhang, Y. (2021). Determinants of technology acceptance: Two model-based meta-analytic reviews. *Journalism & Mass Communication Quarterly, 98*(1), 83–104.

Fini, A. (2009). The technological dimension of a massive open online course: The case of the CCK08 course tools. *International Review of Research in Open and Distributed Learning, 10*(5). https://doi.org/10.19173/irrodl.v10i5.643

Fırat, M., Kılınç, H., & Yüzer, T. V. (2018). Level of intrinsic motivation of distance education students in e‑learning environments. *Journal of Computer Assisted Learning, 34*(1), 63–70.

Fishbein, M., & Ajzen, I. (1975). *Belief, attitude, intention and behavior: An introduction to theory and research*. Addison-Wesley.

Fisher, L., Evans, M., Forbes, K., Gayton, A., & Liu, Y. (2020). Participative multilingual identity construction in the languages classroom: A multi-theoretical conceptualisation. *International Journal of Multilingualism, 17*(4), 448–466.

Fishman, E. J. (2014). With great control comes great responsibility: The relationship between perceived academic control, student responsibility, and self‐regulation. *British Journal of Educational Psychology*, *84*(4), 685–702.

Flowers, S., Kelsen, B., & Cvitkovic, B. (2019). Learner autonomy versus guided reflection: How different methodologies affect intercultural development in online intercultural exchange. *ReCALL*, *31*(3), 221–237.

Flunger, B., Hollmann, L., Hornstra, L., & Murayama, K. (2022). It's more about a lesson than a domain: Lesson-specific autonomy support, motivation, and engagement in math and a second language. *Learning and Instruction*, *77*, 101500.

Forbes, K., Evans, M., Fisher, L., Gayton, A., Liu, Y., & Rutgers, D. (2021). Developing a multilingual identity in the languages classroom: The influence of an identity-based pedagogical intervention. *The Language Learning Journal*, *49*(4), 433-451.

Fox, A., & Bird, T. (2017). The challenge to professionals of using social media: Teachers in England negotiating personal-professional identities. *Education and Information Technologies*, *22*(2), 647-675.

Frambach, J. M., Driessen, E. W., Chan, L. C., & van der Vleuten, C. P. (2012). Rethinking the globalisation of problem‐based learning: how culture challenges self‐directed learning. *Medical Education*, *46*(8), 738-747.

Friesen, N. (2008). Critical theory: Ideology critique and the myths of E-learning. *Ubiquity*, *9*(22). http://2017s.pbworks.com/w/file/fetch/120805056/15-Myths%20of%20E-Learning.pdf

Frostenson, M. (2015). Three forms of professional autonomy: De-professionalisation of teachers in a new light. *Nordic Journal of Studies in Educational Policy*, *2015*(2), 28464.

Fuchs, C. (2014). *Social media: A critical introduction*. Sage.

Fuchs, C., Hauck, M., & Müller-Hartmann, A. (2012). Promoting learner autonomy through multiliteracy skills development in cross-institutional exchanges. *Language Learning & Technology*, *16*(3), 82–102.

Fukuda, S. T., Sakata, H., & Pope, C. J. (2019). Developing self-coaching skills in university EFL classrooms to encourage out-of-class study time. *Innovation in Language Learning and Teaching*, *13*(2), 118–132.

Fullan, M., & Hargreaves, A. (1996). *What's worth fighting for in your school?* (Rev. ed). Teachers College Press.

Galea, S. (2012). Reflecting reflective practice. *Educational Philosophy and Theory*, *44*(3), 245–258.

Galvin, S., & Greenhow, C. (2020). Educational networking: A novel discipline for improved K-12 learning based on social networks. In S. Hargadon (Ed.), *Educational networking* (pp. 3–41). Springer.

Gamage, S. N., & Tanwar, T. (2018). Systematic reviews (SRs) | factors affecting the use of ICTs in the classroom by teachers: A systematic review of the literature. *Information Technologies & International Development*, *14*, 105–115.

Gao, F., & Li, L. (2019). Predicting educators' use of Twitter for professional learning and development. *Education and Information Technologies*, *24*(4), 2311–2327.

Gao, X. (2010). *Strategic language learning: The roles of agency and context* (Vol. 49). Multilingual Matters.

Gao, X. (2018). Language teacher autonomy and social censure. In A. Chik, N. Aoki, & R. Smith (Eds.), *Autonomy in language learning and teaching* (pp. 29–49).

Palgrave Pivot.

García Botero, G., Questier, F., & Zhu, C. (2019). Self-directed language learning in a mobile-assisted, out-of-class context: Do students walk the talk? *Computer Assisted Language Learning, 32*(1–2), 71–97.

García Botero, G., Botero Restrepo, M. A., Zhu, C., & Questier, F. (2021). Complementing in-class language learning with voluntary out-of-class MALL. Does training in self-regulation and scaffolding make a difference? *Computer Assisted Language Learning, 34*(8), 1013–1039.

Garet, M. S., Porter, A. C., Desimone, L., Birman, B. F., & Yoon, K. S. (2001). What makes professional development effective? Results from a national sample of teachers. *American Educational Research Journal, 38*(4), 915–945.

Garner, J. K., & Kaplan, A. (2019). A complex dynamic systems perspective on teacher learning and identity formation: an instrumental case. *Teachers and Teaching, 25*(1), 7–33.

Garrido, M., Koepke, L., Anderson, S., Felipe Mena, A., Macapagal, M., & Dalvit, L. (2016). *The advancing MOOCs for development initiative: An examination of MOOC usage for professional workforce development outcomes in Colombia, the Philippines, & South Africa.* Technology & Social Change Group.

Gagen-Lanning, K. (2015). *The effects of metacognitive strategy training on ESL learners' self-directed use of TED Talk videos for second language listening* [Doctoral dissertation, Iowa State University]. Semantic Scholar. https://doi.org/10.31274/ETD-180810-3906

Garrison, D. R. (1997). Self-directed learning: Toward a comprehensive model. *Adult Education Quarterly, 48*, 18–33.

Garzón, J., Baldiris, S., Gutiérrez, J., & Pavón, J. (2020). How do pedagogical approaches affect the impact of augmented reality on education? A meta-analysis and research synthesis. *Educational Research Review, 31*, 100334.

Gerard, L. F., Varma, K., Corliss, S. B., & Linn, M. C. (2011). Professional development for technology-enhanced inquiry science. *Review of Educational Research, 81*(3), 408–448.

Germain, C., & Netten, J. (2004). Facteurs de développement de l'autonomie langagière en FLE/FLS. *Alsic. Apprentissage des Langues et Systèmes d'Information et de Communication, 7*, 55–69.

Ghomi, M., & Redecker, C. (2019). Digital competence of educators (DigCompEdu): Development and evaluation of a self-assessment instrument for teachers' digital competence. In *Proceedings of the 11th International Conference on Computer Supported Education (CSEDU)* (pp. 541–548). Science and Technology Publications.

Ghorbandordinejad, F., & Ahmadabad, R. M. (2016). Examination of the relationship between autonomy and English achievement as mediated by foreign language classroom anxiety. *Journal of Psycholinguistic Research, 45*(3), 739–752.

Ghorbani, M. R., & Golparvar, S. E. (2020). Modeling the relationship between socioeconomic status, self-initiated, technology-enhanced language learning, and language outcome. *Computer Assisted Language Learning, 33*(5–6), 607–627.

Gieve, S., & Clark, R. (2005). 'The Chinese approach to learning': Cultural trait or situated response? The case of a self-directed learning programme. *System, 33*(2), 261–276.

Gill, M. G., Ashton, P. T., & Algina, J. (2004). Changing preservice teachers' epistemological beliefs about teaching and learning in mathematics: An intervention study. *Contemporary Educational Psychology, 29*(2), 164–185.

Gobel, P., & Kano, M. (2014). Implementing a year-long reading while listening program for Japanese University EFL students. *Computer Assisted Language Learning, 27*(4), 279–293.

Godwin-Jones, R. (2016). Augmented reality and language learning: From annotated vocabulary to place-based mobile games. *Language Learning & Technology, 20*(3), 9–19.

Godwin-Jones, R. (2018). Chasing the butterfly effect: Informal language learning online as a complex system. *Language Learning & Technology, 22*(2), 8–27.

Godwin-Jones, R. (2019). Riding the digital wilds: Learner autonomy and informal language learning. *Language Learning & Technology, 23*(1), 8–25.

Godwin-Jones, R. (2020). Building the porous classroom: An expanded model for blended language learning. *Language Learning & Technology, 24*(3), 1–18.

Goh, T. T., Seet, B. C., & Chen, N. S. (2012). The impact of persuasive SMS on students' self‐regulated learning. *British Journal of Educational Technology, 43*(4), 624–640.

Gokcearslan, S. (2017). Perspectives of students on acceptance of tablets and self-directed learning with technology. *Contemporary Educational Technology, 8*(1), 40–55.

Golonka, E. M., Bowles, A. R., Frank, V. M., Richardson, D. L., & Freynik, S. (2014). Technologies for foreign language learning: A review of technology types and their effectiveness. *Computer Assisted Language Learning, 27*(1), 70–105.

Goode, J. (2010). The digital identity divide: how technology knowledge impacts college students. *New Media & Society, 12*(3), 497–513.

Goodyear, P. (2021). Navigating difficult waters in a digital era: Technology, uncertainty and the objects of informal lifelong learning. *British Journal of Educational Technology, 52*(4), 1594–1611.

Goodyear, V. A., Casey, A., & Kirk, D. (2014). Tweet me, message me, like me: Using social media to facilitate pedagogical change within an emerging community of practice. *Sport, Education and Society, 19*(7), 927–943.

Goodyear, V. A., Parker, M., & Casey, A. (2019). Social media and teacher professional learning communities. *Physical Education and Sport Pedagogy, 24*(5), 421–433.

Gong, Y., & Lai, C. (2018). Technology integration into the language classroom: Developmental trajectory of beginning teachers. *Frontiers of Education in China, 13*(1), 1–27.

Granger, B. P., & Levine, E. L. (2010). The perplexing role of learner control in e‐learning: will learning and transfer benefit or suffer? *International Journal of Training and Development, 14*(3), 180–197.

Granić, A., & Marangunić, N. (2019). Technology acceptance model in educational context: A systematic literature review. *British Journal of Educational Technology, 50*(5), 2572–2593.

Green, D. P., Shapiro, I., & Shapiro, I. (1994). *Pathologies of rational choice theory: A critique of applications in political science.* Yale University Press.

Greene, J. A., & Azevedo, R. (2007). A theoretical review of Winne and Hadwin's model of self-regulated learning: New perspectives and directions. *Review of Educational Research, 77*(3), 334–372.

Greenhalgh, S., Krutka, D. G., & Oltmann, S. M. (2021). Gab, Parler, and (Mis)educational Technologies: Reconsidering Informal Learning on Social Media Platforms. *The Journal of Applied Instructional Design, 10*(3).

Greenhow, C., Galvin, S. M., Brandon, D. L., & Askari, E. (2020). A decade of research on K–12 teaching and teacher learning with social media: Insights on the state of the field. *Teachers College Record, 122*(6), 1–72.

Greenhow, C., & Lewin, C. (2016). Social media and education: Reconceptualizing the boundaries of formal and informal learning. *Learning, Media and Technology, 41*(1), 6–30.

Greenhow, C., & Robelia, B. (2009). Old communication, new literacies: Social network sites as social learning resources. *Journal of Computer-Mediated Communication, 14*(4), 1130–1161.

Grover, S. & Hannegan, L. D. (2005). Not just for Listening: Integrating Audio Books into the Curriculum. *Book Links, 14*(5), 16–19.

Gu, M. M., & Lai, C. (2019). An ethical analysis of how ESL teachers construct their professional identities through the use of information technology in teaching. *British Educational Research Journal, 45*(5), 918–937.

Guillén-Gámez, F. D., & Rodríguez-Fernández, R. (2021). Meta-analysis on the attitudes of active teachers about the use of educational technology according to gender. *Contemporary Educational Technology, 14*(1), ep339.

Guglielmino, P. J., & Guglielmino, L. M. (2006). Culture, self-directed learning readiness, and per capita income in five countries. *SAM Advanced Management Journal, 71*(2), 21–28.

Gui, M., & Argentin, G. (2011). Digital skills of internet natives: Different forms of digital literacy in a random sample of northern Italian high school students. *New Media & Society, 13*(6), 963–980.

Guikema, J. P. (2014). *Digital literacies in foreign and second language education*. In J. P. Guikema & L. Williams (Eds.), *CALICO monograph series, vol. 12* (pp. 1–8). CALICO.

Güneş, E., & Bahçivan, E. (2018). A mixed research-based model for pre-service science teachers' digital literacy: Responses to "which beliefs" and "how and why they interact" questions. *Computers & Education, 118*, 96–106.

Guth, S., & Helm, F. (2012). Developing multiliteracies in ELT through telecollaboration. *ELT Journal, 66*(1), 42–51.

Guzman, A., & Nussbaum, M. (2009). Teaching competencies for technology integration in the classroom. *Journal of Computer Assisted Learning, 25*(5), 453–469.

Guzzetti, B. J., Snyder, T. E., Glass, G. V., & Gamas, W. S. (1993). Promoting conceptual change in science: A comparative meta-analysis of instructional interventions from reading education and science education. *Reading Research Quarterly*, 117–159.

Habowski, T., & Mouza, C. (2014). Pre-service teachers' development of technological pedagogical content knowledge (TPACK) in the context of a secondary science teacher education program. *Journal of Technology and Teacher Education, 22*(4), 471–495.

Hackman, J. R., & Oldham, G. R. (1975). Development of the job diagnostic survey. *Journal of Applied Psychology, 60*(2), 159.

Hadwin, A., & Oshige, M. (2011). Self-regulation, coregulation, and socially shared regulation: Exploring perspectives of social in self-regulated learning theory. *Teachers College Record, 113*(2), 240–264.

Hafner, C. A. (2015). Remix culture and English language teaching: The expression of learner voice in digital multimodal compositions. *TESOL Quarterly, 49*(3), 486–509.

Hafner, C. A., Chik, A., & Jones, R. (2015). Digital literacies and language learning. *Language Learning & Technology, 19*(3), 1–7.

Hafner, C. A., & Miller, L. (2011). Fostering learner autonomy in English for science: A collaborative digital video project in a technological learning environment. *Language Learning & Technology, 15*(3), 68–86.

Hager, P. (2012). Informal learning: a vital component of lifelong learning. In D. N. Aspin, J. Chapman, K. Evans & R. Bagnall (Eds.), *Second international handbook of lifelong learning* (pp. 773–785). Springer.

Hamid, S., Waycott, J., Kurnia, S., & Chang, S. (2015). Understanding students' perceptions of the benefits of online social networking use for teaching and learning. *The Internet and higher education, 26*, 1–9.

Hamilton, M. (2013). *Autonomy and foreign language learning in a virtual learning environment*. A&C Black.

Hannafin, M., Land, S., & Oliver, K. (1999). Open learning environments: Foundations, methods, and models. *Instructional-design theories and models: A new paradigm of instructional theory, 2*, 115–140.

Hansen, J. D., & Reich, J. (2015). Democratizing education? Examining access and usage patterns in massive open online courses. *Science, 350*(6265), 1245–1248.

Halupa, C. M. (2015). Pedagogy, andragogy, and heutagogy. In C. Halupa (Ed.), *Transformative curriculum design in health sciences education* (pp. 143–158). IGI Global.

Hämäläinen, R., Nissinen, K., Mannonen, J., Lämsä, J., Leino, K., & Taajamo, M. (2021). Understanding teaching professionals' digital competence: What do PIAAC and TALIS reveal about technology-related skills, attitudes, and knowledge? *Computers in Human Behavior, 117*, 106672.

Han, I., Byun, S. Y., & Shin, W. S. (2018). A comparative study of factors associated with technology-enabled learning between the United States and South Korea. *Educational Technology Research and Development, 66*(5), 1303–1320.

Hannafin, M. J., & Land, S. M. (1997). The foundations and assumptions of technology-enhanced student-centered learning environments. *Instructional Science, 25*(3), 167–202.

Hannafin, M. J., Land, S. M., & Oliver, K. (1999). Open learning environments: Foundation, methods, and models. In C. Reigeluth (Ed.), *Instructional-design theories and models: A new paradigm of instructional theory* (Vol. II, pp. 115–140). Mahwah, NJ: Erlbaum.

Hanraets, I., Hulsebosch, J., & de Laat, M. (2011). Experiences of pioneers facilitating teacher networks for professional development. *Educational Media International, 48*(2), 85–99.

Hargreaves, A. (2019). Teacher collaboration: 30 years of research on its nature, forms, limitations and effects. *Teachers and Teaching, 25*(5), 603–621.

Harper-Hill, K., Beamish, W., Hay, S., Whelan, M., Kerr, J., Zelenko, O., & Villalba, C. (2022). Teacher engagement in professional learning: what makes the difference to teacher practice?. *Studies in Continuing Education, 44*(1), 105–118.

Hase, S., & Kenyon, C. (2000). From andragogy to heutagogy. *UltiBASE In Site*.

Hawi, N. S., & Samaha, M. (2016). To excel or not to excel: Strong evidence on the adverse effect of smartphone addiction on academic performance. *Computers & Education, 98*, 81–89.

Hazenberg, S., & Hulstijn, J. H. (1996). Defining a minimal receptive second-language vocabulary for non-native university students: An empirical investigation. *Applied Linguistics, 17*(2), 145–163.

Hazzan, O. (2003). How students attempt to reduce abstraction in the learning of mathematics and in the learning of computer science. *Computer Science Education, 13*(2), 95–122.

He, T., & Zhu, C. (2017). Digital informal learning among Chinese university students: the effects of digital competence and personal factors. *International Journal of Educational Technology in Higher Education, 14*(1), 1–19.

Hedberg, J. G. (2011). Towards a disruptive pedagogy: Changing classroom practice with technologies and digital content. *Educational Media International, 48*(1), 1–16.

Henderson, J., & Corry, M. (2021). Teacher anxiety and technology change: a review of the literature. *Technology, Pedagogy and Education, 30*(4), 573–587.

Hennis, T., de Vries, P. & Veen, W. (2017). Engaging at-risk youth through self-directed learning. *Italian Journal of Educational Technology, 25*(1), 18–30.

Henriksen, D., Cain, W., & Mishra, P. (2018). Everyone designs: Learner autonomy through creative, reflective, and iterative practice mindsets. *Journal of Formative Design in Learning, 2*(2), 69–81.

Henry, A. (2017). L2 motivation and multilingual identities. *The Modern Language Journal, 101*(3), 548–565.

Hershkovitz, A., Elhija, M. A., & Zedan, D. (2019). WhatsApp is the message: Out-of-class communication, student-teacher relationship, and classroom environment. *Journal of Information Technology Education, 18*.

Hester, J. R. (2002). *The influence of select variables on the instructional use of computers in Shelby County School District*. The University of Memphis.

Hew, K. F., & Brush, T. (2007). Integrating technology into K-12 teaching and learning: Current knowledge gaps and recommendations for future research. *Educational Technology Research and Development, 55*(3), 223–252.

Ho, W. Y. J., & Tai, K. W. (2021). Translanguaging in digital learning: the making of translanguaging spaces in online English teaching videos. *International Journal of Bilingual Education and Bilingualism*, 1–22.

Hobbs, R. (2011). The state of media literacy: A response to Potter. *Journal of Broadcasting & Electronic Media, 55*(3), 419–430.

Hobbs, R., & Coiro, J. (2019). Design features of a professional development program in digital literacy. *Journal of Adolescent & Adult Literacy, 62*(4), 401–409.

Hofer, B. K., & Pintrich, P. R. (1997). The development of epistemological theories: Beliefs about knowledge and knowing and their relation to learning. *Review of Educational Research, 67*(1), 88–140.

Hoi, V. N., & Mu, G. M. (2021). Perceived teacher support and students' acceptance of mobile - assisted language learning: Evidence from Vietnamese higher education context. *British Journal of Educational Technology, 52*(2), 879–898.

Hökkä, P., & Eteläpelto, A. (2014). Seeking new perspectives on the development of teacher education: A study of the Finnish context. *Journal of Teacher Education, 65*(1), 39–52.

Holden, C. L., & Sykes, J. M. (2011). Leveraging mobile games for place-based language learning. *International Journal of Game-Based Learning (IJGBL), 1*(2), 1–18.

Holec, H. (1981). *Autonomy in foreign language learning*. Pergamon.

Honarzad, R., & Rassaei, E. (2019). The role of EFL learners' autonomy, motivation and self-efficacy in using technology-based out-of-class language learning activities. *The JALT CALL Journal*, *15*(3), 23–42.

Hospel, V., & Galand, B. (2016). Are both classroom autonomy support and structure equally important for students' engagement? A multilevel analysis. *Learning and Instruction*, *41*, 1–10.

Howard, S. K. (2013). Risk-aversion: Understanding teachers' resistance to technology integration. *Technology, Pedagogy and Education*, *22*(3), 357–372.

Howard, S., Curwood, J., & McGraw, K. (2018). Leaders fostering teachers' learning environments for technology integration. In J. Voogt, G. Knezek, R. Christensen, & K.-W. Lai (Eds.), *Second handbook of information technology in primary and secondary education* (pp. 515–533). Springer.

Howard, S. K., & Mozejko, A. (2015). Teachers: Technology, change and resistance. In M. J. Henderson & G. Romeo (Eds.), *Teaching and digital technologies: Big issues and critical questions* (pp. 307–317). Cambridge University Press.

Hromalik, C. D., & Koszalka, T. A. (2018). Self-regulation of the use of digital resources in an online language learning course improves learning outcomes. *Distance Education*, *39*(4), 528–547.

Hsu, C. Y., Liang, J. C., Chuang, T. Y., Chai, C. S., & Tsai, C. C. (2021). Probing in-service elementary school teachers' perceptions of TPACK for games, attitudes towards games, and actual teaching usage: a study of their structural models and teaching experiences. *Educational Studies*, *47*(6), 734–750.

Hsu, L. (2016). Examining EFL teachers' technological pedagogical content knowledge and the adoption of mobile-assisted language learning: a partial least square approach. *Computer Assisted Language Learning*, *29*(8), 1287–1297.

Hu, D., Yuan, B., Luo, J., & Wang, M. (2021). A review of empirical research on ICT applications in teacher professional development and teaching practice. *Knowledge Management & E-Learning: An International Journal*, *13*(1), 1–20.

Huang, F., Teo, T., & Zhou, M. (2020). Chinese students' intentions to use the Internet-based technology for learning. *Educational Technology Research and Development*, *68*(1), 575–591.

Huang, J. (2005). Teacher autonomy in language learning: A review of the research. *Research Studies in Education*, *3*, 203–218.

Huang, R. T. (2014). Exploring the moderating role of self-management of learning in mobile English learning. *Journal of Educational Technology & Society*, *17*(4), 255–267.

Huang, R. T., Jang, S. J., Machtmes, K., & Deggs, D. (2012). Investigating the roles of perceived playfulness, resistance to change and self‐management of learning in mobile English learning outcome. *British Journal of Educational Technology*, *43*(6), 1004–1015.

Huang, F., & Teo, T. (2020). Influence of teacher-perceived organisational culture and school policy on Chinese teachers' intention to use technology: An extension of technology acceptance model. *Educational Technology Research and Development*, *68*(3), 1547–1567.

Huang, F., & Teo, T. (2021). Examining the role of technology‐related policy and constructivist teaching belief on English teachers' technology acceptance: A study in Chinese universities. *British Journal of Educational Technology*, *52*(1), 441–460.

Huang, F., Teo, T., & Scherer, R. (2020). Investigating the antecedents of university students' perceived ease of using the Internet for learning. *Interactive Learning Environments*, 1–17.

Huang, F., Teo, T., & Zhou, M. (2019). Factors affecting Chinese English as a foreign language teachers' technology acceptance: A qualitative study. *Journal of Educational Computing Research, 57*(1), 83–105.

Huang, R. T., Yu, C. L., Tang, T. W., & Chang, S. C. (2021). A study of the use of mobile learning technology in Taiwan for language learning. *Innovations in Education and Teaching International, 58*(1), 59–71.

Huang, X. (2021). Striving for better teaching and student creativity development: Linking informal workplace learning and teaching for creativity. *Thinking Skills and Creativity, 41*, 100889.

Hubbard, P. (2004). Learner training for effective use of CALL. In S. Fotos & C. M. Browne (Eds.), *New perspectives on CALL for second language classrooms* (pp. 45–68). Lawrence Erlbaum Associates.

Huggins, A. (2012). Autonomy supportive curriculum design: A salient factor in promoting law students' wellbeing. *UnsWlJ, 35,* 683–716.

Hur, J. W., & Hara, N. (2007). Factors cultivating sustainable online communities for K-12 teacher professional development. *Journal of Educational Computing Research, 36*(3), 245–268.

Husband, R. E., & Short, P. M. (1994). Interdisciplinary teams lead to greater teacher empowerment. *Middle School Journal, 26*(2), 58–60.

Hutchison, A. C., & Woodward, L. (2018). Examining the technology integration planning cycle model of professional development to support teachers' instructional practices. *Teachers College Record, 120*(10), 1–44.

Illés, É. (2012). Learner autonomy revisited. *ELT Journal, 66*(4), 505–513.

Illich, I. (1971). *Deschooling society.* https://globalintelhub.com/wp-content/uploads/2013/07/DeschoolingSociety.pdf

Inaba, M. (2020). How do social networks facilitate out-of-class L2 learning activities? In A. Carhill-Poza & N. Kurata (Eds.), *Social networks in language learning and language teaching* (pp. 138–158). Bloomsbury.

Idros, S. N. S., Mohamed, A. R., Esa, N., Samsudin, M. A., & Daud, K. A. M. (2010). Enhancing self-directed learning skills through e-SOLMS for Malaysian learners. *Procedia-Social and Behavioral Sciences, 2,* 698–706.

Islam, A. A., Gu, X., Crook, C., & Spector, J. M. (2020). Assessment of ICT in Tertiary Education Applying Structural Equation Modeling and Rasch Model. *SAGE Open, 10*(4), 2158244020975409.

Ito M. (2013). *Hanging out, messing around, and geeking out: Kids living and learning with new media.* The MIT Press.

Ito, M., Arum, R., Conley, D., Gutiérrez, K., Kirshner, B., Livingstone, S., Michalchik, V., Penuel, W., Peppler, K., Pinkard, N., Rhodes, J., Tekinbaş, K. S., Schor, J., Sefton-Green, J., & Watkins, S. C. (2020). *The connected learning research network: Reflections on a decade of engaged scholarship.* Irvine, CA: Connected Learning Alliance.

Ito, M., Gutiérrez, K., Livingstone, S., Penuel, B., Rhodes, J., Salen, K., Schor, J., Sefton-Green, J., & Watkins, S. C. (2013). *Connected learning: An agenda for research and design.* Digital Media and Learning Research Hub.

Jackson, N. J. (2013). Learning ecology narratives. In N. Jackson & B. Cooper (Eds.), *Lifewide learning, education and personal development.* Lifewide Education.

Jackson, J. D., Mun, Y. Y., & Park, J. S. (2013). An empirical test of three mediation models for the relationship between personal innovativeness and user acceptance of technology. *Information & Management, 50*(4), 154–161.

Jang, H., Reeve, J., & Deci, E. L. (2010). Engaging students in learning activities: It is not autonomy support or structure but autonomy support and structure. *Journal of Educational Psychology, 102*(3), 588–600.

Jansen, R. S., Van Leeuwen, A., Janssen, J., Jak, S., & Kester, L. (2019). Self-regulated learning partially mediates the effect of self-regulated learning interventions on achievement in higher education: A meta-analysis. *Educational Research Review, 28*, 100292.

Jena, R. K. (2015). Technostress in ICT enabled collaborative learning environment: An empirical study among Indian academician. *Computers in Human Behavior, 51*, 1116–1123. https://doi.org/10.1016/j.chb.2015.03.020

Jenkins, H., Purushota, R., Clinton, K., Weigel, M., & Robinson, A. (2006). *Confronting the challenges of participatory culture: Media education for the 21st century*. Chicago: MacArthur Foundation.

Jiang, L. (2018). Digital multimodal composing and investment change in learners' writing in English as a foreign language. *Journal of Second Language Writing, 40*, 60–72.

Jiang, L., & Luk, J. (2016). Multimodal composing as a learning activity in English classrooms: Inquiring into the sources of its motivational capacity. *System, 59*, 1–11.

Jiang, L., Yang, M., & Yu, S. (2020). Chinese ethnic minority students' investment in English learning empowered by digital multimodal composing. *TESOL Quarterly, 54*(4), 954–979.

Jiménez Raya, M. J., & Fernández, J. M. P. (2002). Learner autonomy and new technologies. *Educational Media International, 39*(1), 61–68.

Jiménez Raya, M. J., Lamb, T., & Vieira, F. (2017). *Mapping autonomy in language education: A framework for learner and teacher development*. Peter Lang.

Jiménez Raya, M., & Vieira, F. (2011). *Understanding and exploring pedagogy for autonomy in language education–A case-based approach*. Authentik.

Johnson, M. L., Vaughn, A. R., & Taasoobshirazi, G. (2021). Common misconceptions and challenges in the teaching of motivation principles. In D. K. Meyer & A. Emery (Eds.), *Teaching motivation for student engagement* (pp. 57–78). Information Age Publishing.

Johnson, N. F. (2015). The work of theory in ed-tech research. In S. Bulfin, N. F. Johnson, & C. Bigum (Eds.), *Critical perspectives on technology and education* (pp. 35–50). Palgrave Macmillan.

Jones, R., & Hafner, C. (2012). *Understanding digital literacies: A practical introduction*. Routledge.

Joo, Y. J., Lim, K. Y., & Kim, N. H. (2016). The effects of secondary teachers' technostress on the intention to use technology in South Korea. *Computers & Education, 95*, 114–122.

Jung, Y. J., Cho, K., & Shin, W. S. (2019). Revisiting critical factors on teachers' technology integration: the differences between elementary and secondary teachers. *Asia Pacific Journal of Education, 39*(4), 548–561.

Kachru, B. B. (1988). The sacred cows of English. *English today, 4*(4), 3–8.

Kagan, D. M. (1992). Implication of research on teacher belief. *Educational Psychologist, 27*(1), 65–90.

Kaplan, A., & Garner, J. K. (2017). A complex dynamic systems perspective on identity and its development: The dynamic systems model of role identity. *Developmental Psychology, 53*(11), 2036–2051.

Kara, M. (2022). Revisiting online learner engagement: exploring the role of learner characteristics in an emergency period. *Journal of Research on Technology in Education, 54*(sup1), S236–S252.

Karaoğlan Yılmaz, F. G., Olpak, Y. Z., & Yılmaz, R. (2018). The effect of the metacognitive support via pedagogical agent on self-regulation skills. *Journal of Educational Computing Research*, *56*(2), 159–180.

Karatas, K., & Arpaci, I. (2021). The role of self-directed learning, metacognition, and 21st century skills predicting the readiness for online learning. *Contemporary Educational Technology*, *13*(3), ep300. https://doi.org/10.30935/cedtech/10786

Karatza, Z. (2019). Information and communication technology (ICT) as a tool of differentiated instruction: An informative intervention and a comparative study on educators' views and extent of ICT use. *International Journal of Information and Education Technology*, *9*(1), 8–15.

Kartal, T., Kiziltepe, I. S., & Kartal, B. (2022). Extending technology acceptance model with scientific epistemological and Science teaching efficacy beliefs: A study with preservice teachers. *Journal of Education in Science, Environment and Health*, *8*(1), 1–16.

Karimi, S. (2016). Do learners' characteristics matter? An exploration of mobile-learning adoption in self-directed learning. *Computers in Human Behavior*, *63*, 769–776.

Karlsson, L. (2012). Sharing stories: Autobiographical narratives in advising. In J. Mynard & L. Carson (Eds.), *Advising in language learning: Dialogue, tools and context* (pp.185–204). Routledge.

Kashiwa, M., & Benson, P. (2018). A road and a forest: Conceptions of in-class and out-of-class learning in the transition to study abroad. *TESOL Quarterly*, *52*(4), 725–747.

Kasinathan, G. (2018). *Domination and emancipation: a framework for assessing ICT and education programs*. https://idl-bnc-idrc.dspacedirect.org/bitstream/handle/10625/56846/56892.pdf?sequence=1

Kato, S., & Mynard, J. (2016). *Reflective dialogue: Advising in language learning*. Routledge.

Kay, R., Jovanovic, P., & Hughes, J. (2020). Exploring the benefits and challenges of using wearable technologies for K-12 teachers: A review of the literature. *EdMedia + innovate learning* (pp. 229–236). Association for the Advancement of Computing in Education.

Kaya, M. H., & Adiguzel, T. (2021). Technology integration through evidence-based multimodal reflective professional training. *Contemporary Educational Technology*, *13*(4), ep323.

Keengwe, J., Kidd, T., & Kyei-Blankson, L. (2009). Faculty and technology: Implications for faculty training and technology leadership. *Journal of Science Education and Technology*, *18*(1), 23–28.

Kelly, H. (2014). A path analysis of educator perceptions of open educational resources using the technology acceptance model. *International Review of Research in Open and Distributed Learning*, *15*(2), 26–42.

Kemp, A., Preston, J., Page, C., Harper, R., Dillard, B., Flynn, J., & Yamaguchi, M. (2015). Technology and teaching: A conversation among faculty regarding the pros and cons of technology. *Qualitative Report*, *19*(3), 1–23.

Kennedy, A. (2014). Understanding continuing professional development: the need for theory to impact on policy and practice. *Professional Development in Education*, *40*(5), 688–697.

Kennedy, D. M., & Fox, R. (2013). "Digital natives": An Asian perspective for using learning technologies. *International Journal of Education and Development using*

ICT, 9(1), 65–79.

Kennedy, G., Judd, T., Dalgarno, B., & Waycott, J. (2010). Beyond natives and immigrants: exploring types of net generation students. *Journal of Computer Assisted Learning, 26*(5), 332–343.

Kenyon, C., & Hase, S. (2010). Andragogy and heutagogy in postgraduate work. In T. Kerry (Ed.), *Meeting the challenges of change in postgraduate education* (pp. 165–177). Continuum Press.

Kern, R. (2021). Twenty-five years of digital literacies in CALL. *Language Learning & Technology, 25*(3), 132–150.

Khambari, M., & Nida, M. (2019). Instilling innovativeness, building character, and enforcing camaraderie through interest-driven challenge-based learning approach. *Research and Practice in Technology Enhanced Learning, 14*(1), 1–19.

Kharade, K., & Peese, H. (2014). Problem-based learning: A promising pathway for empowering pre-service teachers for ICT-mediated language teaching. *Policy Futures in Education, 12*(2), 262–272.

Kicken, W., Brand‐Gruwel, S., & Van Merriënboer, J. J. (2008). Scaffolding advice on task selection: a safe path toward self‐directed learning in on‐demand education. *Journal of Vocational Education and Training, 60*(3), 223–239.

Kicken, W., Brand-Gruwel, S., Van Merriënboer, J., & Slot, W. (2009). Design and evaluation of a development portfolio: how to improve students' self-directed learning skills. *Instructional Science, 37*(5), 453–473.

Kienhues, D., Bromme, R., & Stahl, E. (2008). Changing epistemological beliefs: The unexpected impact of a short-term intervention. *British Journal of Educational Psychology, 78*, 545–565.

Kim, C., Kim, M. K., Lee, C., Spector, J. M., & DeMeester, K. (2013). Teacher beliefs and technology integration. *Teaching and Teacher Education, 29*, 76–85.

Kim, D. H., Wang, C., Ahn, H. S., & Bong, M. (2015). English language learners' self-efficacy profiles and relationship with self-regulated learning strategies. *Learning and Individual Differences, 38*, 136–142.

Kim, S. (2018). "It was kind of a given that we were all multilingual": Transnational youth identity work in digital translanguaging. *Linguistics and Education, 43*, 39–52.

Kim, S. Y., & Kim, M. R. (2013). Comparison of Perception toward the Adoption and Intention to Use Smart Education between Elementary and Secondary School Teachers. *Turkish Online Journal of Educational Technology-TOJET, 12*(2), 63–76.

Kirschner, P. A., & De Bruyckere, P. (2017). The myths of the digital native and the multitasker. *Teaching and Teacher Education, 67*, 135–142.

Kizilcec, R. F., Pérez-Sanagustín, M., & Maldonado, J. J. (2017). Self-regulated learning strategies predict learner behavior and goal attainment in Massive Open Online Courses. *Computers & Education, 104*, 18–33.

Kizilcec, R. F., Saltarelli, A., J., Reich, J., & Cohen, G. L. (2017). Closing global achievement gaps in MOOCs. *Science, 355*(6322), 251–252.

Klein, H. K., & Kleinman, D. L. (2002). The social construction of technology: Structural considerations. *Science, Technology, & Human Values, 27*(1), 28–52.

Kling, R., & Courtright, C. (2003). Group behavior and learning in electronic forums: A sociotechnical approach. *The Information Society, 19*(3), 221–235.

Ko, M., Yang, S., Lee, J., Heizmann, C., Jeong, J., Lee, U., Shin, D., Yatani, K., Song, J., & Chung, K. M. (2015). NUGU: A group-based intervention app for improving self-regulation of limiting smartphone use. In *Proceedings of the 18th*

ACM conference on computer supported cooperative work & social computing (pp. 1235–1245). Association for Computing Machinery.

Kohonen, V. (1992). Experiential language learning: Second language learning as cooperative learning. In D. Nunan (Ed.), *Collaborative language learning and teaching* (pp. 14–39). Cambridge University Press.

Kooken, J. W., Zaini, R., & Arroyo, I. (2021). Simulating the dynamics of self-regulation, emotion, grit, and student performance in cyber-learning environments. *Metacognition and Learning, 16*(2), 367–405.

Kopcha, T. J. (2012). Teachers' perceptions of the barriers to technology integration and practices with technology under situated professional development. *Computers & Education, 59*(4), 1109–1121.

Kopcha, T. J., Neumann, K. L., Ottenbreit-Leftwich, A., & Pitman, E. (2020). Process over product: The next evolution of our quest for technology integration. *Educational Technology Research and Development, 68*(2), 729–749.

Kopecký, K., & Szotkowski, R. (2017). Cyberbullying, cyber aggression and their impact on the victim–The teacher. *Telematics and Informatics, 34*(2), 506–517.

Kormos, J., & Csizér, K. (2014). The interaction of motivation, self-regulatory strategies, and autonomous learning behavior in different learner groups. *TESOL Quarterly, 48*(2), 275–299.

Kormos, J., & Kiddle, T. (2013). The role of socio-economic factors in motivation to learn English as a foreign language: The case of Chile. *System, 41*(2), 399–412.

Koutsogiannis, D. (2007). A political multi-layered approach to researching children's digital literacy practices. *Language and Education, 21*(3), 216–231.

Koutsogiannis, D. (2015). Translocalization in digital writing, orders of literacy, and schooled literacy. In S. Bulfin, N. F. Johnson & C. Bigum (Eds.), *Critical perspectives on technology and education* (pp. 183–201). Palgrave Macmillan.

Koutsodimou, K., & Jimoyiannis, A. (2015, November). MOOCs for teacher professional development: investigating views and perceptions of the participants. In *Proceedings of the 8th International Conference of Education, Research and Innovation–ICERI 2015* (pp. 6968–6977).

Koukis, N., & Jimoyiannis, A. (2019). MOOCS for teacher professional development: exploring teachers' perceptions and achievements. *Interactive Technology and Smart Education*.

Knezek, G., & Christensen, R. (2016). Extending the will, skill, tool model of technology integration: Adding pedagogy as a new model construct. *Journal of Computing in Higher Education, 28*(3), 307–325.

Knight, S. W., Marean, L., & Sykes, J. M. (2019). Gaming and informal language learning. In M. Dressman & R. W. Sadler (Eds.), *The Handbook of Informal Language Learning* (pp. 101–115). John Wiley & Sons.

Knowles, J. R. (1980). Enzyme-catalyzed phosphoryl transfer reactions. *Annual review of biochemistry, 49*(1), 877–919.

Kress, G. (2000). Multimodality. In B. Cope & M. Kalantzis (Eds.), *Multiliteracies: Literacy learning and the design of social futures* (pp. 182–202). Routledge.

Kress, G. (2003). *Literacy in the new media age*. Routledge.

Kress, G. (2010). *Multimodality: A Social Semiotic Approach to Contemporary Communication*. New York: Routledge

Kukulska-Hulme, A., Gaved, M., Jones, A., Norris, L., & Peasgood, A. (2017). Mobile language learning experiences for migrants beyond the classroom. In *Council of Europe Symposium* (pp. 219–224). De Gruyter Mouton.

Kukulska-Hulme, A. (2005). Mobile usability and user experience. In A. Kukulska-Hulme & J. Traxler (Eds.), *Mobile Learning: A handbook for educators and trainers* (pp. 45–56). Routledge.

Kumar, P. C., Vitak, J., Chetty, M., & Clegg, T. L. (2019). The platformization of the classroom: Teachers as surveillant consumers. *Surveillance & Society*, *17*(1/2), 145–152.

Kuo, F. W., Cheng, W., & Yang, S. C. (2017). A study of friending willingness on SNSs: Secondary school teachers' perspectives. *Computers & Education*, *108*, 30–42.

Kuznetsova, N., & Soomro, K. A. (2019). Students' out-of-class Web 2.0 practices in foreign language learning. *Journal of Education and Educational Development*, *6*(1), 78–94.

Kwakman, K. (2003). Factors affecting teachers' participation in professional learning activities. *Teaching and Teacher Education*, *19*(2), 149–170.

Kwangsawad, T. (2016). Examining EFL pre-service teachers' TPACK trough self-report, lesson plans and actual practice. *Journal of Education and Learning*, *10*(2), 103–108.

Kyndt, E., Gijbels, D., Grosemans, I., & Donche, V. (2016). Teachers' everyday professional development: Mapping informal learning activities, antecedents, and learning outcomes. *Review of Educational Research*, *86*(4), 1111–1150.

Kyriacou, C., & Zuin, A. (2016). Cyberbullying of teachers by students on YouTube: challenging the image of teacher authority in the digital age. *Research Papers in Education*, *31*(3), 255–273.

La Barbera, F., & Ajzen, I. (2020). Understanding support for European integration across generations: A study guided by the theory of planned behavior. *Europe's Journal of Psychology*, *16*(3), 437–457.

Lachner, A., Fabian, A., Franke, U., Preiß, J., Jacob, L., Führer, C., Küchler, U., Paravicini, W., Randler, C., & Thomas, P. (2021). Fostering pre-service teachers' technological pedagogical content knowledge (TPACK): A quasi-experimental field study. *Computers & Education*, *174*(8), 104304.

Lai, C. (2013). A framework for developing self-directed technology use for language learning. *Language Learning & Technology*, *17*(2), 100–122.

Lai, C. (2015a). Perceiving and traversing in-class and out-of-class learning: accounts from foreign language learners in Hong Kong. *Innovation in Language Learning and Teaching*, *9*(3), 265–284.

Lai, C. (2015b). Modeling teachers' influence on learners' self-directed use of technology for language learning outside the classroom. *Computers & Education*, *82*, 74–83.

Lai, C. (2018). *Autonomous language learning with technology: Beyond the classroom*. Bloomsbury Publishing.

Lai, C. (2019a). Learning beliefs and autonomous language learning with technology beyond the classroom. *Language Awareness*, *28*(4), 291–309.

Lai, C. (2019b). The influence of extramural access to mainstream culture social media on ethnic minority students' motivation for language learning. *British Journal of Educational Technology*, *50*(4), 1929–1941.

Lai, C., & Gu, M. (2011). Self-regulated out-of-class language learning with technology. *Computer Assisted Language Learning*, *24*(4), 317–335.

Lai, C., Gu, M., Gao, F., & Yung, J. W. S. (2020). Motivational mechanisms of ethnic minorities' social media engagement with mainstream culture. *Journal of Multilingual and Multicultural Development*, *43*(5), 387–403.

Lai, C., Hu, X., & Lyu, B. (2018). Understanding the nature of learners' out-of-class language learning experience with technology. *Computer Assisted Language Learning, 31*(1–2), 114–143.

Lai, C., & Jin, T. (2021). Teacher professional identity and the nature of technology integration. *Computers & Education, 175*, 104314.

Lai, C., Liu ,Y., Hu, J. J., Benson, P. & Lyu, B. N. (2022). Association between the Characteristics of out-of-class technology-mediated language experience and L2 vocabulary knowledge. *Language Learning & Technology, 26*(1), 1–24.

Lai, C., Shum, M., & Tian, Y. (2016). Enhancing learners' self-directed use of technology for language learning: the effectiveness of an online training platform. *Computer Assisted Language Learning, 29*(1), 40–60.

Lai, C., Wang, Q., Li, X., & Hu, X. (2016a). The influence of individual espoused cultural values on self-directed use of technology for language learning beyond the classroom. *Computers in Human Behavior, 62*, 676–688.

Lai, C., Wang, Q., & Lei, J. (2012). What factors predict undergraduate students' use of technology for learning? A case from Hong Kong. *Computers & Education, 59*(2), 569–579.

Lai, C., Wang, Q., & Huang, X. (2022a). The evolution of the association between teacher technology integration and its influencing factors over time. *Journal of Research on Technology in Education*, 1–21. Advance online publication. https://doi.org/10.1080/15391523.2022.2030266

Lai, C., Wang, Q., & Huang, X. (2022b). The differential interplay of TPACK, teacher beliefs, school culture and professional development with the nature of in‑service EFL teachers' technology adoption. *British Journal of Educational Technology, 53*(5), 1389–1411.

Lai, C., Yeung, Y., & Hu, J. (2016b). University student and teacher perceptions of teacher roles in promoting autonomous language learning with technology outside the classroom. *Computer Assisted Language Learning, 29*(4), 703–723.

Lai, C., & Zheng, D. (2018). Self-directed use of mobile devices for language learning beyond the classroom. *ReCALL, 30*(3), 299–318.

Lai, C., Zhu, W., & Gong, G. (2015). Understanding the quality of out‑of‑class English learning. *TESOL Quarterly, 49*(2), 278–308.

Lai, Y., Saab, N., & Admiraal, W. (2022). University students' use of mobile technology in self-directed language learning: Using the integrative model of behavior prediction. *Computers & Education, 179*, 104413.

Lam, W. S. E. (2000). L2 literacy and the design of the self: A case study of a teenager writing on the Internet. *TESOL Quarterly, 34*(3), 457–482.

Lam, Y. (2000). Technophilia vs. technophobia: A preliminary look at why second-language teachers do or do not use technology in their classrooms. *Canadian Modern Language Review, 56*(3), 389–420.

Lamb, M (2011) A Matthew Effect in English language education in a developing country context. In H. Coleman (Ed.), *Dreams and realities: Developing countries and the English language* (pp. 186–206). The British Council.

Lamb, M. (2013, April). Blackberries in the forest: Technology and autonomous learning in rural areas. *IATEFL Learner Autonomy Special Interest Group Pre-Conference Event, IATEFL 47th Annual Conference and Exhibition.* April 8, 2013, Liverpool ACC, UK.

Lamb, M. (2013). "Your mum and dad can't teach you!": Constraints on agency among rural learners of English in the developing world. *Journal of Multilingual and Multicultural Development, 34*(1), 14–29.

Lamb, M., & Arisandy, F. E. (2020). The impact of online use of English on motivation to learn. *Computer Assisted Language Learning*, *33*(1–2), 85–108.

Lamb, T. (2008). Learner autonomy and teacher autonomy: Synthesising an agenda. In T. Lamb & H. Reinders (Eds.), *Learner and teacher autonomy: Concepts, realities, and responses* (pp. 269–284). John Benjamins Publishing Company.

Lamb, T. (2011). Fragile identities: Exploring learner identity, learner autonomy and motivation through young learners' voices. *Canadian Journal of Applied Linguistics*, *14*(2), 68–85.

Lamb, T., & Murray, G. (2018). Space, place and autonomy in language learning: An introduction. In G. Murray & T. Lamb (Eds.), *Space, place and autonomy in language learning* (pp. 1–6). Routledge.

Lamb, T. & Vodicka, G. (2018). Collective autonomy and multilingual spaces in super-diverse urban contexts: Interdisciplinary perspectives. In G. Murray & T. Lamb (Eds.), *Space, place and autonomy in language learning* (pp. 9–28). Routledge.

Lamy, M. N. (2013). We don't have to always post stuff to help us learn: Informal learning through social networking in a beginners' Chinese group. In C. Meskill (Ed.), *Online teaching and learning: Sociocultural perspectives* (pp. 219–238). Bloomsbury.

Lan, Y. J. (2018). Technology enhanced learner ownership and learner autonomy through creation. *Educational Technology Research and Development*, *66*(4), 859–862.

Lantz-Andersson, A., Lundin, M., & Selwyn, N. (2018). Twenty years of online teacher communities: A systematic review of formally-organized and informally-developed professional learning groups. *Teaching and Teacher Education*, *75*, 302–315.

Larsen–Freeman, D. (2019). On language learner agency: A complex dynamic systems theory perspective. *The Modern Language Journal*, *103*, 61–79.

Larsen-Freeman, D., & Anderson, M. (2013). *Techniques and principles in language teaching* (3rd ed.). Oxford University Press.

Lau, B. T., & Sim, C. H. (2008). Exploring the extent of ICT adoption among secondary school teachers in Malaysia. *International Journal of Computing and ICT research*, *2*(2), 19–36.

Laurillard, D. (2016). The educational problem that MOOCs could solve: professional development for teachers of disadvantaged students. *Research in Learning Technology*, *24*. https://doi.org/10.3402/rlt.v24.29369

Lawrence, G. (2013). A working model for intercultural learning and engagement in collaborative online language learning environments. *Intercultural Education*, *24*, 303–314.

Lecat, A., Raemdonck, I., Beausaert, S., & März, V. (2019). The what and why of primary and secondary school teachers' informal learning activities. *International Journal of Educational Research*, *96*, 100–110.

Lee, C., Yeung, A. S., & Ip, T. (2016). Use of computer technology for English language learning: do learning styles, gender, and age matter? *Computer Assisted Language Learning*, *29*(5), 1035–1051.

Lee, J. S., & Lee, K. (2020). Affective factors, virtual intercultural experiences, and L2 willingness to communicate in in-class, out-of-class, and digital settings. *Language Teaching Research*, *24*(6), 813–833.

Lee, L. (2011). Blogging: Promoting learner autonomy and intercultural competence through study abroad. *Language Learning & Technology*, *15*(3), 87–109.

Lee, L. (2016). Autonomous learning through task-based instruction in fully online language courses. *Language Learning & Technology, 20*(2), 81–97.

Lee, J. S. (2019). Informal digital learning of English and second language vocabulary outcomes: Can quantity conquer quality? *British Journal of Educational Technology, 50*(2), 767–778.

Lee, J. H., & Kim, H. (2016). Implementation of SMART teaching 3.0: Mobile-based self-directed EFL teacher professional development. *Journal of Asia TEFL, 13*(4), 331–346.

Lee, J., Kim, J., & Choi, J. Y. (2019). The adoption of virtual reality devices: The technology acceptance model integrating enjoyment, social interaction, and strength of the social ties. *Telematics and Informatics, 39*, 37–48.

Lee, J., & Jung, I. (2021). Instructional changes instigated by university faculty during the COVID-19 pandemic: the effect of individual, course and institutional factors. *International Journal of Educational Technology in Higher Education, 18*(1), 1–19.

Lee, J., Sanders, T., Antczak, D., Parker, R., Noetel, M., Parker, P., & Lonsdale, C. (2021). Influences on user engagement in online professional learning: a narrative synthesis and meta-analysis. *Review of Educational Research, 91*(4), 518–576.

Lee, M. K., Cheung, C. M., & Chen, Z. (2005). Acceptance of Internet-based learning medium: the role of extrinsic and intrinsic motivation. *Information & Management, 42*(8), 1095–1104.

Lee, Y., Lee, J., & Hwang, Y. (2015). Relating motivation to information and communication technology acceptance: Self-determination theory perspective. *Computers in Human Behavior, 51*, 418–428.

Leidner, D. E., & Kayworth, T. (2006). A review of culture in information systems research: Toward a theory of information technology culture conflict. *MIS Quarterly*, 357–399.

Leijen, Ä., Valtna, K., Leijen, D. A., & Pedaste, M. (2012). How to determine the quality of students' reflections? *Studies in Higher Education, 37*(2), 203–217.

Lenkaitis, C. A. (2020). Technology as a mediating tool: videoconferencing, L2 learning, and learner autonomy. *Computer Assisted Language Learning, 33*(5–6), 483–509.

Lennert da Silva, A. L., & Mølstad, C. E. (2020). Teacher autonomy and teacher agency: A comparative study in Brazilian and Norwegian lower secondary education. *The Curriculum Journal, 31*(1), 115–131.

Leona, N. L., van Koert, M. J., van der Molen, M. W., Rispens, J. E., Tijms, J., & Snellings, P. (2021). Explaining individual differences in young English language learners' vocabulary knowledge: The role of Extramural English Exposure and motivation. *System, 96*, 102402.

Leuven, E., Lindahl, M., Oosterbeek, H., & Webbink, D. (2007). The effect of extra funding for disadvantaged pupils on achievement. *The Review of Economics and Statistics, 89*(4), 721–36.

Levin, T., & Wadmany, R. (2005). Changes in educational beliefs and classroom practices of teachers and students in rich technology-based classrooms. *Technology, Pedagogy and Education, 14*(3), 281–307.

Levine, D. N. (1981). Rationality and freedom: Weber and beyond. *Sociological Inquiry, 51*(1), 5–25.

Lewis, T. (2013). Between the social and the selfish: Learner autonomy in online environments. *Innovation in Language Learning and Teaching, 7*(3), 198–212.

Lewis, T. (2014). Learner autonomy and the theory of sociality. In G. Murray

(Ed.), *Social dimensions of autonomy in language learning* (pp. 37–59). Palgrave Macmillan.

Lewis, T., Cappellini, M. & Rivens Mompean, A. (2017). Introduction. In M. Cappellini, T. Lewis, & A. Rivens Mompean, A. (Eds). *Learner Autonomy and Web 2.0* (pp. 1-11). Bristol, CT: Equinox.

Li, H., Majumdar, R., Chen, M. R. A., & Ogata, H. (2021). Goal-oriented active learning (GOAL) system to promote reading engagement, self-directed learning behavior, and motivation in extensive reading. *Computers & Education, 171,* 104239.

Li, L., & Wang, X. (2021). Technostress inhibitors and creators and their impacts on university teachers' work performance in higher education. *Cognition, Technology & Work, 23*(2), 315-330.

Li, N., & Kirkup, G. (2007). Gender and cultural differences in Internet use: A study of China and the UK. *Computers & Education, 48*(2), 301-317.

Li, S., & Zheng, J. (2018). The relationship between self-efficacy and self-regulated learning in one-to-one computing environment: the mediated role of task values. *The Asia-Pacific Education Researcher, 27*(6), 455–463.

Li, Y., Chen, K., Su, Y., & Yue, X. (2021). Do social regulation strategies predict learning engagement and learning outcomes? A study of English language learners in wiki-supported literature circles activities. *Educational Technology Research and Development, 69*(2), 917–943.

Li, Y., Garza, V., Keicher, A., & Popov, V. (2019). Predicting high school teacher use of technology: Pedagogical beliefs, technological beliefs and attitudes, and teacher training. *Technology, Knowledge and Learning, 24*(3), 501–518.

Li, W. (2011). Moment analysis and translanguaging space: Discursive construction of identities by multilingual Chinese youth in Britain. *Journal of Pragmatics, 43*(5), 1222–1235.

Li, W. (2018). Translanguaging as a practical theory of language. *Applied Linguistics, 39*(1), 9–30.

Li, W. & Lin, A. M. (2019). Translanguaging classroom discourse: Pushing limits, breaking boundaries. *Classroom Discourse, 10*(3–4), 209–215.

Li, Y., Chen, K., Su, Y., & Yue, X. (2021). Do social regulation strategies predict learning engagement and learning outcomes? A study of English language learners in wiki-supported literature circles activities. *Educational Technology Research and Development, 69*(2), 917–943.

Li, Z., & Hegelheimer, V. (2013). Mobile-assisted grammar exercises: Effects on self-editing in L2 writing. *Language Learning & Technology, 17*(3), 135–156.

Liao, Y. C., Ottenbreit-Leftwich, A., Karlin, M., Glazewski, K., & Brush, T. (2017). Supporting change in teacher practice: Examining shifts of teachers' professional development preferences and needs for technology integration. *Contemporary Issues in Technology and Teacher Education, 17*(4), 522–548.

Liao, Y. C., Ottenbreit-Leftwich, A., Glazewski, K., & Karlin, M. (2021). Coaching to support teacher technology integration in elementary classrooms: A multiple case study. *Teaching and Teacher Education, 104,* 103384.

Liem, A. D., Lau, S., & Nie, Y. (2008). The role of self-efficacy, task value, and achievement goals in predicting learning strategies, task disengagement, peer relationship, and achievement outcome. *Contemporary Educational Psychology, 33* (4), 486–512.

Lier, L. V. (2007). Action-based teaching, autonomy and identity. *International Journal of Innovation in Language Learning and Teaching, 1*(1), 46–65.

Ligas, G. C. (2021). Democratic language education against educational failure and for social inclusion: The perception of "democracy" in learning/teaching processes. In *Proceedings of the 2nd International Conference on the Journal Scuola Democratica "Reinventing Education," Volume 1, Citizenship, Work and the Global Age* (pp. 49–60). Associazione "Per Scuola Democratica." https://www.scuolademocratica-conference.net/proceedings-2/

Lim, J., & Newby, T. J. (2021). Preservice teachers' attitudes toward Web 2.0 personal learning environments (PLEs): Considering the impact of self-regulation and digital literacy. *Education and Information Technologies, 26*(4), 3699–3720.

Lim, C. P., Pek, M. S., & Chai, C. S. (2005). Classroom management issues in ICT-mediated learning environments: Back to the basics. *Journal of Educational Multimedia and Hypermedia, 14*(4), 391–414.

Lin, C.-H., Warschauer, M., & Blake, R. (2016). Language learning through social networks: Perceptions and reality. *Language Learning and Technology, 20*(1), 124–147.

Lin, J. J., & Lin, H. (2019). Mobile-assisted ESL/EFL vocabulary learning: A systematic review and meta-analysis. *Computer Assisted Language Learning, 32*(8), 878–919.

Lin, J. W., Lai, Y. C., Lai, Y. C., & Chang, L. C. (2016). Fostering self‐regulated learning in a blended environment using group awareness and peer assistance as external scaffolds. *Journal of Computer Assisted Learning, 32*(1), 77–93.

Little, D. (1991). *Learner autonomy 1: definitions, issues and problems.* Authentik.

Little, D. (1995). Learning as dialogue: The dependence of learner autonomy on teacher autonomy. *System, 23*(2), 175–181.

Little, D. (2007). Language learner autonomy: Some fundamental considerations revisited. *International Journal of Innovation in Language Learning and Teaching, 1*(1), 14–29.

Little, D. (2013). Learner autonomy as discourse. The role of the target language. In Burkert, A., L. Dam, & C. Ludwig (Eds.), *The Answer is Autonomy: Issues in Language Teaching and Learning* (pp. 26-39). IATEFL.

Little, D., & Dam, L. (1998). Learner autonomy: What and why? *Language Teacher: Kyoto JALT, 22,* 7–8.

Little, D., Dam, L., & Legenhausen, L. (2017). *Language learner autonomy: Theory, practice and research.* Multilingual Matters.

Little, D. & Thorne, S. L. (2017). From learner autonomy to rewilding: A discussion. In M. Cappellini, T. Lewis & A. Rivens Mompean (Eds), *Learner autonomy and web 2.0* (pp. 12–35). Equinox.

Littlejohn, A., Hood, N., Milligan, C., & Mustain, P. (2016). Learning in MOOCs: Motivations and self-regulated learning in MOOCs. *The Internet and Higher Education, 29,* 40–48.

Littlemore, J. (2001). Learner autonomy, self-instruction and new technologies in language. In A. Chambers & G. Davis (Eds.), *ICT and language learning: A European perspective* (pp. 39–52). Swets and Zeitlinger Publishers.

Littlewood, W. (1997). Self-access work and curriculum ideologies. In P. Benson & P. Voller (Eds.), *Autonomy and independence in language learning* (pp. 181–191). London: Longman.

Littlewood, W. (2004). The task-based approach: Some questions and suggestions. *ELT Journal, 58*(4), 319–326.

Liu, C. Y., & Yu, C. P. (2013). Can Facebook use induce wellbeing? *Cyberpsychology, Behavior, and Social Networking, 16*(9), 674–678.

Liu, H., Lin, C. H., & Zhang, D. (2017). Pedagogical beliefs and attitudes toward information and communication technology: a survey of teachers of English as a foreign language in China. *Computer Assisted Language Learning, 30*(8), 745–765.

Liu, M. C., Huang, Y. M., & Xu, Y. H. (2018). Effects of individual versus group work on learner autonomy and emotion in digital storytelling. *Educational Technology Research and Development, 66*(4), 1009–1028.

Liu, Q., & Geertshuis, S. (2016). Professional identity and teachers' learning technology adoption: a review of adopter-related antecedents. In S. Barker, S. Dawson, A. Pardo, & C. Colvin (Eds.), *Show me the learning* (pp. 365–374). ASCILITE.

Liu, Q., & Geertshuis, S. (2021). Professional identity and the adoption of learning management systems. *Studies in Higher Education, 46*(3), 624–637.

Liu, S. H. (2013). Teacher professional development for technology integration in a primary school learning community. *Technology, Pedagogy and Education, 22*(1), 37–54.

Liu, S., Hallinger, P., & Feng, D. (2016). Learning-centered leadership and teacher learning in China: Does trust matter? *Journal of Educational Administration, 54*(6), 661–682.

Livingstone, D. W. (2006). Informal learning: Conceptual distinctions and preliminary findings. *Counterpoints, 249*, 203–227.

Ljubin-Golub, T., Rijavec, M., & Olčar, D. (2020). Student flow and burnout: The role of teacher autonomy support and student autonomous motivation. *Psychological Studies, 65*(2), 145–156.

Lodewyk, K. R., Winne, P. H., & Jamieson‐Noel, D. L. (2009). Implications of task structure on self‐regulated learning and achievement. *Educational Psychology, 29*(1), 1–25.

Löfström, E., & Poom-Valickis, K. (2013). Beliefs about teaching: Persistent or malleable? A longitudinal study of prospective student teachers' beliefs. *Teaching and Teacher Education, 35*, 104–113.

Lohnes Watulak, S. (2018). Making space for preservice teacher agency through connected learning in preservice educational technology courses. *Journal of Digital Learning in Teacher Education, 34*(3), 166–178.

Lok, P., & Crawford, J. (2004). The effect of organisational culture and leadership style on job satisfaction and organisational commitment: A cross‐national comparison. *Journal of Management Development, 23*(4), 321–338.

Long, M. H. (2020). Optimal input for language learning: Genuine, simplified, elaborated, or modified elaborated?. *Language Teaching, 53*(2), 169–182.

Longhurst, M. L., Jones, S. H., & Campbell, T. (2021). Mediating influences in professional learning: Factors that lead to appropriation & principled adaptation. *Professional Development in Education*, 1–17.

Lopez-Perez, V. A., Ramirez-Correa, P. E., & Grandon, E. E. (2019). Innovativeness and factors that affect the information technology adoption in the classroom by primary teachers in Chile. *Informatics in Education, 18*(1), 165–181.

Lou, N. M., Chaffee, K. E., Lascano, D. I. V., Dincer, A., & Noels, K. A. (2018). Complementary perspectives on autonomy in self-determination theory and language learner autonomy. *TESOL Quarterly, 52*(1), 210–220.

Louws, M. L., Meirink, J. A., van Veen, K., & van Driel, J. H. (2017). Teachers' self-directed learning and teaching experience: What, how, and why teachers want to learn. *Teaching and Teacher Education, 66,* 171–183.

Loyens, S. M., Magda, J., & Rikers, R. M. (2008). Self-directed learning in problem-based learning and its relationships with self-regulated learning. *Educational Psychology Review, 20*(4), 411–427.

Lucas, M., Bem-Haja, P., Siddiq, F., Moreira, A., & Redecker, C. (2021). The relation between in-service teachers' digital competence and personal and contextual factors: What matters most? *Computers & Education, 160,* 104052.

Luckin, R. (2010). *Re-designing learning contexts: Technology-rich, learner-centred ecologies.* Routledge.

Luef, E. M., Ghebru, B., & Ilon, L. (2019). Language proficiency and smartphone-aided second language learning: A look at English, German, Swahili, Hausa and Zulu. *Electronic Journal of e-Learning, 17*(1), 25–37.

Luke, A. (2004). On the material consequences of literacy. *Language and Education, 18*(4), 331–335.

Luo, B. (2020). The influence of teaching learning techniques on students' long-term learning behavior. *Computer Assisted Language Learning, 33*(4), 388–412.

Lutrick, E., & Szabo, S. (2012). Instructional leaders' beliefs about effective professional development. *Delta Kappa Gamma Bulletin, 78*(3), 6–12.

Lynch, J. (2015). Researching with heart in ed-tech: What opportunities does the socially indeterminate character of technological artifacts open up for affirming emergent and marginalized practices? In S. Bulfin, N. Johnson, & C. Bigum (Eds.), *Critical perspectives on technology and education* (pp. 141–161). Palgrave Macmillan.

Lyu, B., & Lai, C. (2022a). Analysing learner engagement with native speaker feedback on an educational social networking site: an ecological perspective. *Computer Assisted Language Learning.* Advance online publication. https://doi.org/10.1080/09588221.2022.2030364

Lyu, B., & Lai, C. (2022b). Learners' engagement on a social networking platform: An ecological analysis. *Language Learning & Technology, 26*(1), 1–22.

Ma, Q. (2017). A multi-case study of university students' language-learning experience mediated by mobile technologies: A socio-cultural perspective. *Computer Assisted Language Learning, 30*(3–4), 183–203.

Ma, W., Adesope, O. O., Nesbit, J. C., & Liu, Q. (2014). Intelligent tutoring systems and learning outcomes: A meta-analysis. *Journal of Educational Psychology, 106*(4), 901–919.

Macaro, E. (1997). *Target language, collaborative learning and autonomy* (Vol. 5). Multilingual Matters.

Macaro, E. (2008). The shifting dimensions of language learner autonomy. In T. Lamb & H. Reinders (Eds.) *Learner and teacher autonomy: Concepts, realities, and responses* (pp. 47–62). John Benjamins Publishing Company.

Macaro, E., Handley, Z., & Walter, C. (2012). A systematic review of CALL in English as a second language: Focus on primary and secondary education. *Language Teaching, 45*(1), 1–43.

Macià, M., & García, I. (2016). Informal online communities and networks as a source of teacher professional development: A review. *Teaching and Teacher Education, 55,* 291–307.

Major, C., & McDonald, E. (2021). Developing Instructor TPACK: A Research Review and Narrative Synthesis. *Journal of Higher Education Policy And Leadership Studies, 2*(2), 51–67.

Major, L., Warwick, P., Rasmussen, I., Ludvigsen, S., & Cook, V. (2018). Classroom dialogue and digital technologies: A scoping review. *Education and Information Technologies, 23*(5), 1995–2028.

Malamud, O. & Pop-Eleches, C. (2011). Home Computer Use and the Development of Human Capital. *The Quarterly Journal of Economics, 126(2)*, 987–1027.

Manca, S., & Ranieri, M. (2016). Facebook and the others. Potentials and obstacles of social media for teaching in higher education. *Computers & Education, 95*, 216–230.

Mansfield, C. F., & Volet, S. E. (2010). Developing beliefs about classroom motivation: Journeys of preservice teachers. *Teaching and Teacher Education, 26*(7), 1404–1415.

Manzano Vázquez, B. (2018). Teacher development for autonomy: An exploratory review of language teacher education for learner and teacher autonomy. *Innovation in Language Learning and Teaching, 12*(4), 387–398.

Margaryan, A., Littlejohn, A., & Vojt, G. (2011). Are digital natives a myth or reality? University students' use of digital technologies. *Computers & Education, 56*(2), 429–440.

Markauskaite, L., & Goodyear, P. (2017). *Epistemic fluency and professional education: Innovation, knowledgeable action and actionable knowledge.* Springer

Markus, H. R., & Kitayama, S. (1991). Culture and the self: Implications for cognition, emotion, and motivation. *Psychological Review, 98*(2), 224–253.

Martin, A. (2006). A European framework for digital literacy. *Nordic Journal of Digital Literacy, 1*(2), 151–161.

Martin, S., & Vallance, M. (2008). The impact of synchronous inter-networked teacher training in Information and Communication Technology integration. *Computers & Education, 51*(1), 34–53.

Martinovic, D., & Zhang, Z. (2012). Situating ICT in the teacher education program: Overcoming challenges, fulfilling expectations. *Teaching and Teacher Education, 28*(3), 461–469.

Maslowski, R. (2001). *School culture and school performance.* Doctoral Thesis Twente University Press

Mason, S. L., & Kimmons, R. (2018). Effects of open textbook adoption on teachers' open practices. *International Review of Research in Open and Distributed Learning, 19*(3). https://doi.org/10.19173/irrodl.v19i3.3517

Matzat, U. (2010). Reducing problems of sociability in online communities: Integrating online communication with offline interaction. *American Behavioral Scientist, 53*(8), 1170–1193.

Matzat, U. (2013). Do blended virtual learning communities enhance teachers' professional development more than purely virtual ones? A large scale empirical comparison. *Computers & Education, 60*(1), 40–51.

Matuk, C. F., Linn, M. C., & Eylon, B. S. (2015). Technology to support teachers using evidence from student work to customize technology-enhanced inquiry units. *Instructional Science, 43*(2), 229–257.

Mausethagen, S., & Mølstad, C. E. (2015). Shifts in curriculum control: contesting ideas of teacher autonomy. *Nordic Journal of Studies in Educational Policy, 2015*(2), 28520.

Mayer, R. E. (2011). Towards a science of motivated learning in technology-supported environments. *Educational Technology Research and Development, 59*, 301–308.

Mayer, R. E. (2014). Cognitive theory of multimedia learning. In R. E. Mayer (Ed.), *The Cambridge handbook of multimedia learning* (2nd ed., pp. 43–71). Cambridge University Press.

Mazman Akar, S. G. (2019). Does it matter being innovative: Teachers' technology acceptance. *Education and Information Technologies*, *24*(6), 3415–3432.

McGrath, I. (2000). Teacher autonomy. In B. Sinclair, I. McGrath & T. Lamb (Eds.), *Learner autonomy, teacher autonomy: Future directions* (pp. 100–110). Harlow, England: Pearson Education.

Mei, B., Brown, G. T., & Teo, T. (2018). Toward an understanding of preservice English as a Foreign Language teachers' acceptance of computer-assisted language learning 2.0 in the People's Republic of China. *Journal of Educational Computing Research*, *56*(1), 74-104.

Mercer, S. (2011). Understanding learner agency as a complex dynamic system. *System*, *39*(4), 427-436.

Merriam, S. B. (2001). Andragogy and self-directed learning: Pillars of adult learning theory. *New Directions for Adult and Continuing Education*, *2001*(89), 3-14.

McConnell, M., Montplaisir, L., & Offerdahl, E. G. (2020). A model of peer effects on instructor innovation adoption. *International Journal of STEM Education*, *7*(1), 1-11.

Mishra, P., & Koehler, M. J. (2006). Technological pedagogical content knowledge: A framework for teacher knowledge. *Teachers College Record*, *108*(6), 1017–1054.

Mitchell, C., Friedrich, L., & Appleget, C. (2019). Preservice teachers' blogging: collaboration across universities for meaningful technology integration. *Teaching Education*, *30*(4), 356–372.

Mitra, S. (2013). *Beyond the hole in the wall: Discover the power of self-organized learning*. Ted Conferences.

Mohamed, H., & Lamia, M. (2018). Implementing flipped classroom that used an intelligent tutoring system into learning process. *Computers & Education*, *124*, 62–76.

Moltó Egea, O. (2014). Neoliberalism, education and the integration of ICT in schools. A critical reading. *Technology, Pedagogy and Education*, *23*(2), 267–283.

Moos, D. C., & Azevedo, R. (2008). Self-regulated learning with hypermedia: The role of prior domain knowledge. *Contemporary Educational Psychology*, *33*(2), 270-298.

Moreno, R., Mayer, R. E., Spires, A. H., & Lester, J. C. (2001). The case for social agency in computer-based teaching: Do students learn more deeply when they interact with animated pedagogical agents? *Cognition and Instruction*, *79*(2), 177–213.

Morris, T. H. (2019). Self-directed learning: A fundamental competence in a rapidly changing world. *International Review of Education*, *65*(4), 633–653.

Morrison, D., & McCutheon, J. (2019). Empowering older adults' informal, self-directed learning: harnessing the potential of online personal learning networks. *Research and Practice in Technology Enhanced Learning*, *14*(1), 1-16.

Mortari, L. (2012). Learning thoughtful reflection in teacher education. *Teachers and Teaching*, *18*(5), 525-545.

Moxnes, P. (Ed.), (2000). *Læring og ressursutvikling i arbeidsmiljøet* [Learning and resource development in the work environment]. P. Moxnes.

Mozzon-McPherson, M., & Tassinari, M. G. (2020). From language teachers to language learning advisors: A journey map. *Philologia Hispalensis*, *34*(1), 121–139.

Munezane, Y. (2013). Motivation, ideal L2 self and valuing of global English. In

M. T. Apple, D. D. Silva & T. Fellner (Eds.), *Language learning motivation in Japan* (pp. 152–168). Multilingual Matters.

Muñoz, C. (2020). Boys like games and girls like movies: Age and gender differences in out-of-school contact with English. *Revista Española de Lingüística Aplicada/Spanish Journal of Applied Linguistics, 33*(1), 171–201.

Muñoz, C., & Cadierno, T. (2021). How do differences in exposure affect English language learning? A comparison of teenagers in two learning environments. *Studies in Second Language Learning and Teaching, 11*(2), 185–212.

Munro, M. (2018). The complicity of digital technologies in the marketisation of UK higher education: exploring the implications of a critical discourse analysis of thirteen national digital teaching and learning strategies. *International Journal of Educational Technology in Higher Education, 15*(1), 1–20.

Murray, G. L. (1999). Autonomy and language learning in a simulated environment. *System, 27*(3), 295–308.

Murray, G. (2014). The social dimensions of learner autonomy and self-regulated learning. *Studies in Self-Access Learning Journal, 5*(4), 320–341.

Murray, G. (2017). Autonomy in the time of complexity: Lessons from beyond the classroom. *Studies in Self-Access Learning Journal, 8*(2), 116–134.

Murray, G., Fujishima, N., & Uzuka, M. (2014). The semiotics of place: Autonomy and space. In *Social dimensions of autonomy in language learning* (pp. 81–99). Palgrave Macmillan.

Myartawan, I. P. N. W., Latief, M. A., & Suharmanto, S. (2013). The correlation between learner autonomy and English proficiency of Indonesian EFL college learners. *TEFLIN Journal, 24*(1), 63–81.

Mynard, J. (2020). Advising for language learner autonomy: Theory, practice, and future directions. In M. J. Raya & F. Vieira (Eds.), *Autonomy in language education* (pp. 46–62). Routledge.

Mynard, J. & Kato, S. (2022). Enhancing language learning beyond the classroom through advising. In H. Reinders, C. Lai & P. Sundqvist (Eds.), *The Routledge handbook of language learning and teaching beyond the classroom* (pp. 244–257). Routledge.

Nascimbeni, F. (2018). Rethinking digital literacy for teachers in open and participatory societies. *International Journal of Digital Literacy and Digital Competence (IJDLDC), 9*(3), 1–11.

Nation, P. (2015). Principles guiding vocabulary learning through extensive reading. *Reading in a Foreign Language, 27*(1), 136–145.

Navarro, D., & Thornton, K. (2011). Investigating the relationship between belief and action in self-directed language learning. *System, 39*(3), 290–301.

Nawrot, I., & Doucet, A. (2014, April). Building engagement for MOOC students: introducing support for time management on online learning platforms. In *Proceedings of the 23rd International Conference on world wide web* (pp. 1077–1082).

Näykki, P., Isohätälä, J., Järvelä, S., Pöysä-Tarhonen, J., & Häkkinen, P. (2017). Facilitating socio-cognitive and socio-emotional monitoring in collaborative learning with a regulation macro script–an exploratory study. *International Journal of Computer-Supported Collaborative Learning, 12*(3), 251–279.

Neufeld, P., & Delcore, H. (2018). Situatedness and variations in student adoption of technology practices: towards a critical techno-pedagogy. *Journal of Information Technology Education: Research, 17*(1), 1–38.

Nguyen, D., Pietsch, M., & Gümüş, S. (2021). Collective teacher innovativeness in 48 countries: Effects of teacher autonomy, collaborative culture, and professional learning. *Teaching and Teacher Education, 106*, 103463.

Nikolopoulou, K. (2020). Secondary education teachers' perceptions of mobile phone and tablet use in classrooms: benefits, constraints and concerns. *Journal of Computers in Education, 7*(2), 257–275.

Niemiec, C. P., & Ryan, R. M. (2009). Autonomy, competence, and relatedness in the classroom: Applying self-determination theory to educational practice. *Theory and Research in Education, 7*(2), 133–144.

Niesz, T., & D'Amato, R. (2021). Social media connections between educators and advocacy networks. In M. M. Griffin & C. Zinskie (Eds). *Social Media: Influences on Education* (pp. 299–336). Information Age Publishing.

Nikolopoulou, K. (2020). Secondary education teachers' perceptions of mobile phone and tablet use in classrooms: benefits, constraints and concerns. *Journal of Computers in Education, 7*(2), 257–275.

Nikoopour, J., & Khoshroudi, M. S. (2021). EFL learners' learning styles and self-regulated learning: Do gender and proficiency level matter? *Journal of Language Teaching and Research, 12*(4), 616–623.

Nikou, S. A., & Economides, A. A. (2017). Mobile-based assessment: Integrating acceptance and motivational factors into a combined model of self-determination theory and technology acceptance. *Computers in Human Behavior, 68*, 83–95.

Noe, R. A., Tews, M. J., & Marand, A. D. (2013). Individual differences and informal learning in the workplace. *Journal of Vocational Behavior, 83*(3), 327–335.

Nunan, D. (1996). *Towards autonomous learning: some theoretical, empirical and practical issues* (pp. 13-26). In R. Pemberton, E. S. L. Li, W. W. F. Or, & H. D. Pierson (Eds.), *Taking control: Autonomy in language learning* (pp. 13–26). Hong Kong University Press.

Odden, A., Archibald, S., Fermanich, M., & Gallagher, H. A. (2002). A cost framework for professional development. *Journal of Education Finance, 28*(1), 51–74.

Ogata, H., & Yano, Y. (2004, March). Context-aware support for computer-supported ubiquitous learning. In *The 2nd IEEE International Workshop on Wireless and Mobile Technologies in Education, 2004. Proceedings.* (pp. 27–34). IEEE.

Oga‐Baldwin, W. L. Q., & Nakata, Y. (2015). Structure also supports autonomy: Measuring and defining autonomy‐supportive teaching in Japanese elementary foreign language classes. *Japanese Psychological Research, 57*(3), 167–179.

O'Hara, S., Pritchard, R., Huang, C., & Pella, S. (2013). Learning to integrate new technologies into teaching and learning through a design-based model of professional development. *Journal of Technology and Teacher Education, 21*(2), 203–223.

Okada, R. (2018). Effects of teachers' autonomy support: A meta-analysis. *Memoirs of the Faculty of Education, Kagawa University. Part I, 150,* 31–50.

Okada, R. (2021). *Effects of perceived autonomy support on academic achievement and motivation among higher education students: A meta‐analysis.* Japanese Psychological Research. https://doi.org/10.1111/jpr.12380

O'Keefe, P. A., & Linnenbrink-Garcia, L. (2014). The role of interest in optimizing performance and self-regulation. *Journal of Experimental Social Psychology, 53,* 70–78.

O'Leary, C. (2014). Developing autonomous language learners in HE: A social constructivist perspective. In G. Murray (Ed.), *Social dimensions of autonomy in language learning* (pp. 15–36). Palgrave Macmillan.

Oliver, R., & Nguyen, B. (2017). Translanguaging on Facebook: Exploring Australian Aboriginal multilingual competence in technology-enhanced environments and its pedagogical implications. *Canadian Modern Language Review, 73*(4), 463–487.

Opfer, V. D., Kaufman, J. H., & Thompson, L. E. (2016). *Implementation of K-12 state standards for mathematics and English language arts and literacy: Findings from the American teacher panel*. RAND Corporation. http://www.rand.org/t/RR1529

Ortega, L. (2019). SLA and the study of equitable multilingualism. *The Modern Language Journal, 103*, 23–38.

Osei, C. D., Larbi, E., & Osei-Boadu, Y. (2014). Multidimensional barriers to information and communication technology adoption among senior high school teachers in Ghana. *International Journal of Education and Research, 2*(12), 389–396.

Ottenbreit-Leftwich, A., Liao, Y. C., Karlin, M., Lu, Y. H., Ding, A. C. E., & Guo, M. (2020). Year-long implementation of a research-based technology integration professional development coaching model in an elementary school. *Journal of Digital Learning in Teacher Education, 36*(4), 206–220.

Oxford, R. L. (2008). Hero with a thousand faces: Learner autonomy, learning strategies and learning tactics in independent language learning. In S. Hurd & T. Lewis (Eds.), *Language learning strategies in independent settings* (pp. 41–67). Multilingual Matters.

Oxford, R. (2015). Emotion as the amplifier and the primary motive: Some theories of emotion with relevance to language learning. *Studies in Second Language Learning and Teaching*, (3), 371–393.

Oyserman, D. (2009). Identity-based motivation: Implications for action-readiness, procedural-readiness, and consumer behavior. *Journal of Consumer Psychology, 19*(3), 250–260.

Özgür, H. (2020). Relationships between teachers' technostress, technological pedagogical content knowledge (TPACK), school support and demographic variables: A structural equation modeling. *Computers in Human Behavior, 112*, 106468.

Pacheco, M., Smith, B., & Carr, S. (2019). Sounding funny" and making sense: Multimodal codemeshing as a culturally sustaining pedagogy in an Englishcentric classroom. In K. M. Brinegar, L. M. Harrison & E. Hurd (Eds.), *Equity and cultural responsiveness in the middle grades* (pp. 93–112). Information Age Publishing

Pajares, M. F. (1992). Teachers' beliefs and educational research: Cleaning up a messy construct. *Review of Educational Research, 62*(3), 307–332.

Palfreyman, D. M. (2014). The ecology of learner autonomy. In G. Murray (Ed.), *Social dimensions of autonomy in language learning* (pp. 175–191). Palgrave Macmillan.

Pan, S. C., & Franklin, T. (2011). In-service teachers' self-efficacy, professional development, and Web 2.0 tools for integration. *New Horizons in Education, 59* (3), 28–40.

Pan, X. (2020). Technology acceptance, technological self-efficacy, and attitude toward technology-based self-directed learning: learning motivation as a mediator. *Frontiers in Psychology*, 2791. https://doi.org/10.3389/fpsyg.2020.564294

Panadero, E., Jonsson, A., & Botella, J. (2017). Effects of self-assessment on self-regulated learning and self-efficacy: Four meta-analyses. *Educational Research*

Review, 22, 74–98.

Park, M., & Sung, Y. K. (2013). Teachers' perceptions of the recent curriculum reforms and their implementation: what can we learn from the case of Korean elementary teachers? *Asia Pacific Journal of Education, 33*(1), 15–33.

Parker, G. (2015). Teachers' autonomy. *Research in Education, 93*(1), 19–33.

Pasha-Zaidi, N., Afari, E., Sevi, B., Urganci, B., & Durham, J. (2019). Responsibility of learning: A cross-cultural examination of the relationship of grit, motivational belief and self-regulation among college students in the US, UAE and Turkey. *Learning Environments Research, 22*(1), 83–100.

Paulsen, M. B., & Feldman, K. A. (2005). The conditional and interaction effects of epistemological beliefs on the self-regulated learning of college students: Motivational strategies. *Research in Higher Education, 46*(7), 731–768.

Paulus, M. T., Villegas, S. G., & Howze-Owens, J. (2020). Professional learning communities: Bridging the technology integration gap through effective professional development. *Peabody Journal of Education, 95*(2), 193–202.

Pearson, L. C., & Moomaw, W. (2006). Continuing validation of the teaching autonomy scale. *The Journal of Educational Research, 100*(1), 44–51.

Peeters, W., & Ludwig, C. (2017). Old concepts in new spaces'?–A model for developing learner autonomy in social networking spaces. In M. Cappellini, T. Lewis & A. Rivens Mompean (Eds.), *Learner autonomy and Web 2.0* (pp. 117–142). Equinox.

Perera Muthupoltotage, U., & Gardner, L. (2018). Analysing the relationships between digital literacy and self-regulated learning of undergraduates—a preliminary investigation. In N. Paspallis, M. Raspopoulos, C. Barry, M. Lang, H. Linger, & C. Schneider (Eds.), *Advances in information systems development* (pp. 1–16). Springer.

Perrotta, C. (2017). Beyond rational choice: How teacher engagement with technology is mediated by culture and emotions. *Education and Information Technologies, 22*(3), 789–804.

Peters, E. (2018). The effect of out-of-class exposure to English language media on learners' vocabulary knowledge. *ITL-International Journal of Applied Linguistics, 169*(1), 142–168.

Peters, E., Noreillie, A. S., Heylen, K., Bulté, B., & Desmet, P. (2019). The impact of instruction and out‐of‐school exposure to foreign language input on learners' vocabulary knowledge in two languages. *Language Learning, 69*(3), 747–782.

Peters, E., & Webb, S. (2018). Incidental vocabulary acquisition through viewing L2 television and factors that affect learning. *Studies in Second Language Acquisition, 40*(3), 551–577.

Petko, D., Egger, N., Cantieni, A., & Wespi, B. (2015). Digital media adoption in schools: Bottom-up, topdown, complementary or optional? *Computers & Education, 84*, 49–61.

Phelps, R., Graham, A., & Watts, T. (2011). Acknowledging the complexity and diversity of historical and cultural ICT professional learning practices in schools. *Asia-Pacific Journal of Teacher Education, 39*(1), 47–63.

Pill, T. J. H. (2001). *Adult learners' perceptions of out-of-class access to English* [Unpublished doctoral dissertation]. The University of Hong Kong, Hong Kong.

Pintrich, P. R. (2000). The role of goal orientation in self-regulated learning. In M. Boekaerts, P. R. Pintrich & M. Zeidner (Eds.), *Handbook of self-*

regulation (pp. 451–502). Academic Press.

Pintrich, P. R., & Schunk, D. H. (1996). *Motivation in education: Theory, research, and applications*. Merrill.

Pirbhai‐Illich, F. (2010). Aboriginal students engaging and struggling with critical multiliteracies. *Journal of Adolescent & Adult Literacy, 54*(4), 257–266.

Plonsky, L., & Ziegler, N. (2016). The CALL-SLA interface: Insights from a second-order synthesis. *Language Learning & Technology, 20*(2), 17–37.

Polio, C. (2019). Keeping the language in second language writing classes. *Journal of Second Language Writing, 46*, 100675.

Poom-Valickis, K., & Mathews, S. (2013). Reflecting others and own practice: an analysis of novice teachers' reflection skills. *Reflective Practice, 14*(3), 420–434.

Powell, C. G., & Bodur, Y. (2019). Teachers' perceptions of an online professional development experience: Implications for a design and implementation framework. *Teaching and Teacher Education, 77*, 19–30.

Priestley, M., Biesta, G. J. J., Philippou, S., & Robinson, S. (2015). *The teacher and the curriculum: Exploring teacher agency* (Vol. 27). London: SAGE Publications Ltd.

Prensky, M. (2001). Fun, play and games: What makes games engaging. *Digital game-based learning, 5*(1), 5–31.

Prestridge, S. (2017). Conceptualising self-generating online teacher professional development. *Technology, Pedagogy and Education, 26*(1), 85–104.

Prestridge, S. (2019). Categorising teachers' use of social media for their professional learning: A self-generating professional learning paradigm. *Computers & Education, 129*, 143–158.

Prestridge, S., & Main, K. (2018). Teachers as drivers of their professional learning through design teams, communities, and networks. In J. Voogt, G. Knezek, R. Christensen & K. W. Lai (Eds.), *Second handbook of information technology in primary and secondary education* (pp. 433–447). Springer.

Prestridge, S., & Tondeur, J. (2015). Exploring elements that support teachers engagement in online professional development. *Education Sciences, 5*(3), 199–219.

Prichard, C. (2013). Training L2 learners to use SNSs appropriately and effectively. *CALICO Journal, 30*, 204–225.

Puebla, C., Fievet, T., Tsopanidi, M., & Clahsen, H. (2022). Mobile-assisted language learning in older adults: Chances and challenges. *ReCALL, 34*(2), 169–184.

Quinn, F., Charteris, J., Adlington, R., Rizk, N., Fletcher, P., Reyes, V., & Parkes, M. (2019). Developing, situating and evaluating effective online professional learning and development: a review of some theoretical and policy frameworks. *The Australian Educational Researcher, 46*(3), 405–424.

Rasheed, R. A., Kamsin, A., & Abdullah, N. A. (2020). Challenges in the online component of blended learning: A systematic review. *Computers & Education, 144*, 103701

Rasheed, R. A., Kamsin, A., Abdullah, N. A., Kakudi, H. A., Ali, A. S., Musa, A. S., & Yahaya, A. S. (2020). Self-regulated learning in flipped classrooms: A systematic literature review. *International Journal of Information and Education Technology, 10*(11), 848–853.

Rasi, P., Vuojärvi, H., & Ruokamo, H. (2019). Media literacy education for all ages. *Journal of Media Literacy Education, 11*(2), 1–19.

Rashid, S., Howard, J., Cunningham, U., & Watson, K. (2021). Learner training in MALL: a Pakistani case study. *Innovation in Language Learning and Teaching, 15*(2), 181–194.

Rashid, T., & Asghar, H. M. (2016). Technology use, self-directed learning, student engagement and academic performance: Examining the interrelations. *Computers in Human Behavior, 63,* 604–612.

Rasmussen, I., & Hagen, Å. (2015). Facilitating students' individual and collective knowledge construction through microblogs. *International Journal of Educational Research, 72,* 149–161.

Ratner, H., Andersen, B. L., & Madsen, S. R. (2019). Configuring the teacher as data user: public-private sector mediations of national test data. *Learning, Media and Technology, 44*(1), 22–35.

Raygan, A., & Moradkhani, S. (2020). Factors influencing technology integration in an EFL context: investigating EFL teachers' attitudes, TPACK level, and educational climate. *Computer Assisted Language Learning, 35*(8), 1789–1810.

Reeve, J. (2016). Autonomy-supportive teaching: What it is, how to do it. In W. C. Liu, J. C. K. Wang & R. M. Ryan (Eds.), *Building autonomous learners* (pp. 129–152). Springer.

Reeve, J., & Cheon, S. H. (2021). Autonomy-supportive teaching: Its malleability, benefits, and potential to improve educational practice. *Educational Psychologist, 56*(1), 54–77.

Reeve, J., & Jang, H. (2006). What teachers say and do to support students' autonomy during a learning activity. *Journal of Educational Psychology, 98*(1), 209–218.

Reeves, J. L., Karp, J., Mendez, G. A., Alemany, J., McDermott, M., Borror, J., Hayes Capo, B., & Schlosser, C. A. (2015). Building an online learning community for technology integration in education. *FDLA Journal, 2*(1), 3, 1–1 3.

Reeves, T. D., & Pedulla, J. J. (2013). Bolstering the impact of online professional development for teachers. *Journal of Educational Research & Policy Studies, 13*(1), 50–66.

Reinhardt, J. (2019). Social media in second and foreign language teaching and learning: Blogs, wikis, and social networking. *Language Teaching, 52*(1), 1–39.

Reinders, H. (2020). A framework for learning beyond the classroom. In M. J. Jiménez Raya & F. Vieira (Eds.), *Autonomy in language education: Theory, research and practice* (pp. 63–73). Routledge.

Reinders, H., & Hubbard, P. (2013). CALL and learner autonomy: Affordances and constraints. In M. Thomas (Ed.), *Contemporary computer assisted language learning* (pp. 359–375). Bloomsbury.

Reinders, H., & White, C. (2010). The theory and practice of technology in materials development and task design. In N. Harwood (Ed.), *Materials in ELT: Theory and practice* (pp. 58–80). Cambridge University Press.

Reinders, H., & White, C. (2016). 20 years of autonomy and technology: How far have we come and where to next? *Language Learning & Technology, 20*(2), 143–154.

Reinhardt, J. (2019). Social media in second and foreign language teaching and learning: Blogs, wikis, and social networking. *Language Teaching, 52*(1), 1–39.

Renninger, K. A., & Hidi, S. E. (2015). *The power of interest for motivation and engagement.* Routledge.

Renninger, K. A., & Hidi, S. E. (2019). Interest development and learning. In K. A. Renninger & S. E. Hidi (Eds.), *The Cambridge handbook of motivation and learning* (pp. 265–290). Cambridge University Press. https://

doi.org/10.1017/9781316823279.013

Richards, J. C. (2015). The changing face of language learning: Learning beyond the classroom. *RELC Journal*, *46*(1), 5–22.

Richter, D., Kunter, M., Lüdtke, O., Klusmann, U., & Baumert, J. (2011). Soziale Unterstützung beim Berufseinstieg ins Lehramt. *Zeitschrift für Erziehungswissenschaft*, *14*(1), 35–59.

Riley, A. & Burke, P.J. (1995). Identities and self-verification in the small group. *Social Psychology Quarterly 58*(2), 61–73.

Richards, J. C., & Farrell, T. S. (2005). *Professional development for language teachers: Strategies for teacher learning.* Cambridge University Press.

Rokeach, M. (1968). A theory of organization and change within value-attitude systems. *Journal of Social Issues*, *24*(1), 13–33. https://doi.org/10.1111/j.1540-4560.1968.tb01466.x

Romeo, K., & Hubbard, P. (2011). Pervasive CALL learner training for improving listening proficiency. In M. Levy, F. Blin, C. B. Siskin & O. Takeuchi (Eds.), *WorldCALL: International perspectives on computer-assisted language learning* (pp. 228–242). Routledge.

Rogers, E. (1995). *Diffusion of innovations.* The Free Press.

Rogoff, B., Callanan, M., Gutiérrez, K. D., & Erickson, F. (2016). The organization of informal learning. *Review of Research in Education*, *40*(1), 356–401.

Rosell-Aguilar, F. (2018). Autonomous language learning through a mobile application: a user evaluation of the busuu app. *Computer Assisted Language Learning*, *31*(8), 854–881.

Rosen, L. (2010). *Rewired: Understanding the iGeneration and the Way They Learn.* New York: Palgrave Macmillan.

Rosenberg, L., Pade, M., Reizis, H., & Bar, M. A. (2019). Associations between meaning of everyday activities and participation among children. *The American Journal of Occupational Therapy*, *73*(6), 1–10. https://doi.org/10.5014/ajot.2019.032508

Roth, G., Assor, A., Kanat-Maymon, Y., & Kaplan, H. (2007). Autonomous motivation for teaching: how self-determined teaching may lead to self-determined learning. *Journal of Educational Psychology*, *99*(4), 761–774.

Roth, G., & Weinstock, M. (2013). Teachers' epistemological beliefs as an antecedent of autonomy-supportive teaching. *Motivation and Emotion*, *37*(3), 402–412.

Roussinos, D., & Jimoyiannis, A. (2019). Examining primary education teachers' perceptions of TPACK and the related educational context factors. *Journal of Research on Technology in Education*, *51*(4), 377–397.

Rubin, J. (1975). What the "good language learner" can teach us. *TESOL Quarterly*, *9*(1), 41–51.

Ryan, R. M., & Deci, E. L. (2000). Intrinsic and extrinsic motivations: Classic definitions and new directions. *Contemporary Educational Psychology*, *25*(1), 54–67.

Saadatmand, M., & Kumpulainen, K. (2012). Emerging technologies and new learning ecologies: Learners' perceptions of learning in open and networked environments. In V. Hodgson, C. Jones, M. de Laat, D. McConnell, T. Ryberg, & P. Sloep (Eds.), *Proceedings of the 8th International Conference on Networked Learning* (pp. 266-275). Lancaster University.

Şakrak-Ekin, G., & Balcikanli, C. (2019). Does autonomy really matter in language Learning? *Journal of Language and Education*, *5*(4), 98–111.

Saks, K., & Leijen, Ä. (2014). Distinguishing self-directed and self-regulated learning and measuring them in the e-learning context. *Procedia-Social and Behavioral Sciences, 112*, 190–198.

Salinas, Á., Nussbaum, M., Herrera, O., Solarte, M., & Aldunate, R. (2017). Factors affecting the adoption of information and communication technologies in teaching. *Education and Information Technologies, 22*(5), 2175–2196.

Salmela-Aro, K., Upadyaya, K., Hakkarainen, K., Lonka, K., & Alho, K. (2017). The dark side of internet use: Two longitudinal studies of excessive internet use, depressive symptoms, school burnout and engagement among Finnish early and late adolescents. *Journal of Youth and Adolescence, 46*(2), 343–357.

Salomon, G. & Almog, T. (1998). Educational psychology and technology: A matter of reciprocal relations. *Teachers College Record, 100*(1), 222–241.

Samruayruen, B., Enriquez, J., Natakuatoong, O., & Samruayruen, K. (2013). Self-regulated learning: A key of a successful learner in online learning environments in Thailand. *Journal of Educational Computing Research, 48*(1), 45–69.

Sangrà, A., Raffaghelli, J. E., & Veletsianos, G. (2019). Lifelong learning Ecologies: Linking formal and informal contexts of learning in the digital era. *British Journal of Educational Technology, 50*(4), 1615–1618.

Sato, M. (2020). Metacognitive instruction for collaborative interaction: The process and product of self-regulated learning in the Chilean EFL context. In C. Lambert & R. Oliver (Eds.), *Using tasks in second language teaching: Practice in diverse contexts*. Clevedon, UK: Multilingual Matters.

Sauro, S. (2019). Fan fiction and informal language learning. In M. Dressman & R. W. Sadler (Eds.), *The handbook of informal language learning* (pp. 139–151). John Wiley & Sons.

Savaskan, I. (2017). Does foreign language classroom anxiety mitigate learner autonomy development. *Psychology Research, 7*(8), 436–444.

Sawyer, A., Dick, L., Shapiro, E., & Wismer, T. (2019). The top 500 mathematics pins: An analysis of elementary mathematics activities on Pinterest. *Journal of Technology and Teacher Education, 27*(2), 235–263.

Schweder, S., & Raufelder, D. (2019). Positive emotions, learning behavior and teacher support in self-directed learning during adolescence: Do age and gender matter? *Journal of Adolescence, 73*, 73–84.

Seifert, T. L., & O'Keefe, B. A. (2001). The relationship of work avoidance and learning goals to perceived competence, externality and meaning. *British Journal of Educational Psychology, 71*(1), 81–92.

Selwyn, N. (2007). The use of computer technology in university teaching and learning: a critical perspective. *Journal of computer assisted learning, 23*(2), 83–94.

Selwyn, N. (2011). *Education and technology: Key issues and debates*. London: Continuum International Publishing.

Selwyn, N. (2012). Making sense of young people, education and digital technology: The role of sociological theory. *Oxford Review of Education, 38*(1), 81–96.

Selwyn, N. (2015). Technology and education – Why it's crucial to be critical. In S. Bulfin, N. Johnson and C. Bigum (Eds.), *Critical perspectives on technology and education* (pp. 245–255). Palgrave Macmillan.

Selwyn, N. (2016). Digital downsides: Exploring university students' negative engagements with digital technology. *Teaching in Higher Education, 21*(8), 1006–1021.

Serdyukov, P. (2017). Innovation in education: what works, what doesn't, and what to do about it?. *Journal of Research in Innovative Teaching & Learning, (10)*, 4–

33.

Serin, H., & Bozdag, F. (2020). Relationship between Teachers' Attitudes towards Technology Use in Education and Autonomy Behaviors. *Turkish Online Journal of Educational Technology-TOJET, 19*(3), 60–69.

Scheiter, K., & Gerjets, P. (2007). Learner control in hypermedia environments. *Educational Psychology Review, 19*(3), 285–307.

Scherer, R., Siddiq, F., & Teo, T. (2015). Becoming more specific: Measuring and modeling teachers' perceived usefulness of ICT in the context of teaching and learning. *Computers & Education, 88*, 202–214.

Scherer, R., Siddiq, F., & Tondeur, J. (2019). The technology acceptance model (TAM): A meta-analytic structural equation modeling approach to explaining teachers' adoption of digital technology in education. *Computers & Education, 128*, 13–35.

Scherer, R., & Teo, T. (2019). Editorial to the special section—Technology acceptance models: What we know and what we (still) do not know. *British Journal of Educational Technology, 50*(5), 2387–2393.

Scherer, R., & Teo, T. (2019b). Unpacking teachers' intentions to integrate technology: A meta-analysis. *Educational Research Review, 27*, 90–109.

Schmenk, B. (2005). Globalizing learner autonomy. *TESOL Quarterly, 39*(1), 107–118.

Schmid, R., & Petko, D. (2019). Does the use of educational technology in personalized learning environments correlate with self-reported digital skills and beliefs of secondary-school students? *Computers & Education, 136*, 75–86.

Schmitt, N. (2014). Size and depth of vocabulary knowledge: What the research shows. *Language Learning, 64*(4), 913–951.

Schweder, S., & Raufelder, D. (2021). Examining positive emotions, autonomy support and learning strategies: Self-directed versus teacher-directed learning environments. *Learning Environments Research, 25*(3), 507–522.

Scott, T., & Husain, F. N. (2021). Textbook reliance: Traditional curriculum dependence is symptomatic of a larger educational problem. *Journal of Educational Issues, 7*(1), 233–248.

Sfard, A. (1998). On two metaphors for learning and the dangers of choosing just one. *Educational Researcher, 27*(2), 4–13.

Shadiev, R., & Yang, M. (2020). Review of studies on technology-enhanced language learning and teaching. *Sustainability, 12*(2), 524, 1–22. https://doi.org/10.3390/su12020524

Shamir, H., Pocklington, D., Feehan, K., & Yoder, E. (2020, April). Using CAI with fidelity: Impacts on literacy skills of kindergarten students across demographics. In *Proceedings of the Society for Information Technology & Teacher Education international conference* (pp. 832–837). Association for the Advancement of Computing in Education (AACE).

Sharma, L., & Srivastava, M. (2019). Teachers' motivation to adopt technology in higher education. *Journal of Applied Research in Higher Education, 12*(4), 673–692.

Shelton-Strong, S. J. (2018). Fostering the development of language learner autonomy through peer and self-assessment. *RELAY Journal, 1*(1), 21–46.

Shirrell, M., Hopkins, M., & Spillane, J. P. (2019). Educational infrastructure, professional learning, and changes in teachers' instructional practices and beliefs. *Professional Development in Education, 45*(4), 599–613.

Silva, J. C. S., Zambom, E., Rodrigues, R. L., Ramos, J. L. C., & de Souza, F. D.

F. (2018). Effects of learning analytics on students' self-regulated learning in flipped classroom. *International Journal of Information and Communication Technology Education*, *14*(3), 91–107.

Silvia, P. J. (2008). Interest—The curious emotion. *Current directions in psychological science*, *17*(1), 57–60.

Simons, K. D., & Klein, J. D. (2007). The impact of scaffolding and student achievement levels in a problem-based learning environment. *Instructional Science*, *35*, 41–72.

Simonson, M., Schlosser, C., & Orellana, A. (2011). Distance education research: A review of the literature. *Journal of Computing in Higher Education*, *23*(2), 124–142.

Skoretz, Y., & Childress, R. (2013). An evaluation of a school-based, job-embedded professional development program on teachers' efficacy for technology integration: Findings from an initial study. *Journal of Technology and Teacher Education*, *21*(4), 461–484.

Slater, C. E., Cusick, A., & Louie, J. C. (2017). Explaining variance in self-directed learning readiness of first year students in health professional programs. *BMC Medical Education*, *17*(1), 1–10.

Smit, E. S., Zeidler, C., Resnicow, K., & de Vries, H. (2019). Identifying the most autonomy-supportive message frame in digital health communication: a 2x2 between-subjects experiment. *Journal of Medical Internet Research*, *21*(10), e14074.

Smith, R.C. (2000) Starting with ourselves: Teacher-learner autonomy in language learning. In B. Sinclair, I. McGrath and T. Lamb (eds.) *Learner autonomy, teacher autonomy: Future directions*. London: Longman. 89–99.

Smith, R. C. (2003). Teacher education for teacher-learner autonomy. In *Symposium for Language Teacher Educators: Papers from Three IALS Symposia (CD-ROM). Edinburgh: IALS, University of Edinburgh*. http://www.warwick.ac.uk/~elsdr/Teacher_autonomy.pdf

Smith, R., Erdoğan, S. (2008). Teacher-learner autonomy. In T. Lamb & H. Reinders (Eds.), *Learner and teacher autonomy: Concepts, realities, and responses* (pp. 83–102). John Benjamins Publishing Company.

Smith, R., Kuchah, K., & Lamb, M. (2018). Learner autonomy in developing countries. In A. Chik, N. Aoki & R. Smith (Eds.), *Autonomy in language learning and teaching* (pp. 7–27). Palgrave.

Sockett, G., & Toffoli, D. (2012). Beyond learner autonomy: A dynamic systems view of the informal learning of English in virtual online communities. *ReCALL*, *24*(2), 138–151.

Sockett, G. & Toffoli, D. (2020). Last words: Naming, framing and challenging the field. In M. Dressman & R. W. Sadler (Eds.), *The handbook of informal language learning* (pp. 471–488). John Wiley & Sons.

Song, H. S., Kalet, A. L., & Plass, J. L. (2016). Interplay of prior knowledge, self‐regulation and motivation in complex multimedia learning environments. *Journal of Computer Assisted Learning*, *32*(1), 31–50.

Song, L., & Hill, J. R. (2007). A conceptual model for understanding self-directed learning in online environments. *Journal of Interactive Online Learning*, *6*(1), 27–42.

Sorgenfrei, C., & Smolnik, S. (2016). The effectiveness of e‐learning systems: A review of the empirical literature on learner control. *Decision Sciences Journal of Innovative Education*, *14*(2), 154–184.

Southerland, S. A., Sowell, S., & Enderle, P. (2011). Science teachers' pedagogical discontentment: Its sources and potential for change. *Journal of Science Teacher Education*, *22*(5), 437–457.

Sparrius, M. (2020). Exploring the relevance of information security policies within UK schools: A practitioner perspective. In P. Bednar, A. Nolte, M. Rajanen, H. V. Hult, A. S. Islind, & F. Pigni (Eds.), *Proceedings of the 6th International Workshop on Socio-Technical Perspective in IS Development (STIPIS 2020)* (pp. 84-90). CEUR-WS.

Sproull, L., & Kiesler, S. (1991). *Connections: New ways of working in the networked organization*. MIT Press.

Steel, C. H., & Levy, M. (2013). Language students and their technologies: Charting the evolution 2006–2011. *ReCALL*, *25*(3), 306–320.

Steenekamp, K., van der Merwe, M., & Mehmedova, A. S. (2018). Enabling the development of student teacher professional identity through vicarious learning during an educational excursion. *South African Journal of Education*, *38*(1), 1–8.

Stefanou, C. R., Perencevich, K. C., DiCintio, M., & Turner, J. C. (2004). Supporting autonomy in the classroom: Ways teachers encourage student decision making and ownership. *Educational Psychologist*, *39*(2), 97–110

Stockwell, G. (2007). Vocabulary on the move: Investigating an intelligent mobile phone-based vocabulary tutor. *Computer Assisted Language Learning*, *20*(4), 365–383.

Stockwell, G. (2008). Investigating learner preparedness for and usage patterns of mobile learning. *ReCALL*, *20*(3), 253–270.

Stockwell, G. (2010). Using mobile phones for vocabulary activities: Examining the effect of platform. *Language Learning & Technology*, *14*(2), 95–110.

Stockwell, G., & Hubbard, P. (2013). Some emerging principles for mobile-assisted language learning. *The International Research Foundation for English Language Education*, 1–15.

Storch, N. (2019). Collaborative writing. *Language Teaching*, *52*(1), 40–59.

Su, Y. L., & Reeve, J. (2011). A meta-analysis of the effectiveness of intervention programs designed to support autonomy. *Educational Psychology Review*, *23*(1), 159–188.

Suárez-Rodríguez, J., Almerich, G., Orellana, N., & Díaz-García, I. (2018). A basic model of integration of ICT by teachers: competence and use. *Educational Technology Research and Development*, *66*(5), 1165–1187.

Subekti, A. S. (2022). L2 learning online: Self-directed learning and gender influence in Indonesian university students. *JEES (Journal of English Educators Society)*, *7*(1), 10–17.

Sultana, S., & Dovchin, S. (2021). Relocalization in digital language practices of university students in Asian peripheries: Critical awareness in a language classroom. *Linguistics and Education*, *62*, 100752.

Šumak, B., Polancic, G., & Hericko, M. (2010, February). An empirical study of virtual learning environment adoption using UTAUT. In *2010 Second international conference on mobile, hybrid, and on-line learning* (pp. 17–22). IEEE.

Šumak, B., Heričko, M., & Pušnik, M. (2011). A meta-analysis of e-learning technology acceptance: The role of user types and e-learning technology types. *Computers in Human Behavior*, *27*(6), 2067–2071.

Sumuer, E. (2018). Factors related to college students' self-directed learning with technology. *Australasian Journal of Educational Technology*, *34*(4), 29–43.

Sun, Y. C., & Chang, Y. J. (2012). Blogging to learn: Becoming EFL academic writers through collaborative dialogues. *Language Learning & Technology*, *16*(1), 43–61.

Sundqvist, P. (2019). Commercial-off-the-shelf games in the digital wild and L2 learner vocabulary. *Language Learning & Technology*, *23*(1), 87–113.

Sundqvist, P., & Sylvén, L. K. (2014). Language-related computer use: Focus on young L2 English learners in Sweden. *ReCALL*, *26*(1), 3–20.

Sundqvist, P., & Sylvén, L. K. (2016). *Extramural English in teaching and learning: From theory and research to practice*. Springer.

Sundqvist, P., & Wikström, P. (2015). Out-of-school digital gameplay and in-school L2 English vocabulary outcomes. *System*, *51*, 65–76.

Sung, Y. T., Chang, K. E., & Yang, J. M. (2015). How effective are mobile devices for language learning? A meta-analysis. *Educational Research Review*, *16*, 68–84.

Sutherland, R., Armstrong, V., Barnes, S., Brawn, R., Breeze, N., Gall, M., Matthewman, S., Olivero, F., Taylor, A., Triggs, P., Wishart, J., & John, P. (2004). Transforming teaching and learning: embedding ICT into everyday classroom practices. *Journal of Computer Assisted Learning*, *20*(6), 413–425.

Sullivan, R., Neu, V., & Yang, F. (2018). Faculty development to promote effective instructional technology integration: A qualitative examination of reflections in an online community. *Online Learning*, *22*(4), 341–359.

Sykes, J., Oskoz, A., & Thorne, S. L. (2008). Web 2.0, synthetic immersive environments, and the future of language education. *CALICO Journal*, *25*, 528–546.

Sykes, J. M., Reinhardt, J., & Thorne, S. L. (2010). Multiuser digital games as sites for research and practice. In F. M. Hult (Ed.), *Directions and prospects for educational linguistics* (pp. 117–135). Dordrecht.

Sylvén, L. K., & Sundqvist, P. (2012). Gaming as extramural English L2 learning and L2 proficiency among young learners. *ReCALL*, *24*(3), 302–321.

Syvänen, A., Mäkiniemi, J. P., Syrjä, S., Heikkilä-Tammi, K., & Viteli, J. (2016). When does the educational use of ICT become a source of technostress for Finnish teachers? *Seminar.net*, *12*(2), 95–109. https://doi.org/10.7577/seminar.2281

Taghizadeh, M., & Hasani Yourdshahi, Z. (2020). Integrating technology into young learners' classes: language teachers' perceptions. *Computer Assisted Language Learning*, *33*(8), 982–1006.

Tai, S. J. D. (2015). From TPACK-in-action workshops to classrooms: CALL competency developed and integrated. *Language Learning & Technology*, *19*(1), 139–164.

Taibi, D., Fulantelli, G., Monteleone, V., Schicchi, D., & Scifo, L. (2021, October). An innovative platform to promote social media literacy in school contexts. In *Proceedings of the ECEL 2021 20th European Conference on e-Learning* (p. 460–470). Academic Conferences International limited.

Taimalu, M., & Luik, P. (2019). The impact of beliefs and knowledge on the integration of technology among teacher educators: A path analysis. *Teaching and Teacher Education*, *79*, 101–110.

Tarhini, A., Hone, K., Liu, X., & Tarhini, T. (2017). Examining the moderating effect of individual-level cultural values on users' acceptance of e-learning in developing countries: A structural equation modeling of an extended technology acceptance model. *Interactive Learning Environments*, *25*(3), 306–328.

Tarling, I., & Ng'ambi, D. (2016). Teachers pedagogical change framework: a diagnostic tool for changing teachers' uses of emerging technologies. *British Journal of Educational Technology*, *47*(3), 554–572.

Tayag, J., & Ayuyao, N. (2020). Exploring the relationship between school leadership and teacher professional learning through structural equation modeling. *International Journal of Educational Management*. 34(8), 1237–1251.

Tchounikine, P. (2019). Learners' agency and CSCL technologies: towards an emancipatory perspective. *International Journal of Computer-Supported Collaborative Learning*, *14*(2), 237–250.

Teo, T., & Noyes, J. (2011). An assessment of the influence of perceived enjoyment and attitude on the intention to use technology among pre-service teachers: A structural equation modeling approach. *Computers & Education*, *57*(2), 1645–1653.

Teo, T., & Zhou, M. (2017). The influence of teachers' conceptions of teaching and learning on their technology acceptance. *Interactive Learning Environments*, *25*(4), 513–527.

Theobald, M. (2021). Self-regulated learning training programs enhance university students' academic performance, self-regulated learning strategies, and motivation: A meta-analysis. *Contemporary Educational Psychology*, *66*, 101976.

Thorne SL, Hellermann J, Jones A, Lester D (2015) Interactional practices and artifact orientation in mobile augmented reality game play. PsychNology J 13(2–3), 259–286.

Tillberg-Webb, H., & Strobel, J. (2013). Ideologies in the Conceptualization and use of Educational Technology. In M. P. Clough, J. K. Olson, & D. S. Niederhauser (Eds.), *The Nature of technology: Implications for learning and teaching* (pp. 329–344). Sense Publishers.

Thillmann, H., Künsting, J., Wirth, J., & Leutner, D. (2009). Is it merely a question of "what" to prompt or also "when" to prompt? The role of point of presentation time of prompts in self-regulated learning. *Zeitschrift für Pädagogische Psychologie*, *23*(2), 105–115.

Theophilou, E., Amarasinghe, I., Hernández Leo, D., Lobo, R., & Crespi, F. (2021). Towards socially shared regulation within CSCL scripts: Mirroring group participation in PyramidApp. In A. Hernández-García, D. Hernández-Leo, M. Caeiro-Rodríguez, & T. Sancho-Vinuesa (Eds.), *Proceedings of the Learning Analytics Summer Institute Spain 2021: Learning analytics in times of COVID-19: Opportunity from crisis (LASI-SPAIN 2021)* (pp. 73–80). CEUR-WS.

Thompson, P. (2013). The digital natives as learners: Technology use patterns and approaches to learning. *Computers & Education*, *65*, 12–33.

Thompson, L., & Ku, H. Y. (2005). Chinese graduate students' experiences and attitudes toward online learning. *Educational Media International*, *42*(1), 33–47.

Thompson, N., & Pascal, J. (2012). Developing critically reflective practice. *Reflective Practice*, *13*(2), 311–325.

Thorne, S. L., & Black, R. W. (2007). Language and literacy development in computer-mediated contexts and communities. *Annual Review of Applied Linguistics*, *27*, 133–160.

Thorne, S. L., & Reinhardt, J. (2008). "Bridging activities," new media literacies, and advanced foreign language proficiency. *CALICO Journal*, *25*(3), 558–572.

Toffoli, D., & Perrot, L. (2017). Autonomy, the online informal learning of english (OILE) and learning resource centers (LRCs): The relationships between learner autonomy, L2 proficiency, L2 autonomy and digital literacy. In M.

Cappellini, T. Lewis & A. R. Mompean (Eds.), *Learner autonomy and Web 2.0* (pp. 198–228). Equinox.

Tomlinson, M. (2020). Teaching is a Political Profession: Stepping into the Arena. In M. Soski (Ed.), *Flip the System US: How teachers can transform education and save democracy* (pp. 131–138). Eye on Education.

Tondeur, J. (2020). Teachers' pedagogical beliefs and technology use. In M. A. Peters (Ed.), *Encyclopedia of teacher education* (pp. 1–5). Springer. https://doi.org/10.1007/978-981-13-1179-6_111-1

Tondeur, J., Pareja Roblin, N., van Braak, J., Voogt, J., & Prestridge, S. (2017). Preparing beginning teachers for technology integration in education: Ready for take-off? *Technology, Pedagogy and Education*, *26*(2), 157–177.

Tondeur, J., Scherer, R., Siddiq, F., & Baran, E. (2020). Enhancing pre-service teachers' technological pedagogical content knowledge (TPACK): A mixed-method study. *Educational Technology Research and Development*, *68*(1), 319–343.

Tondeur, J., Valcke, M., & Van Braak, J. (2008). A multidimensional approach to determinants of computer use in primary education: Teacher and school characteristics. *Journal of Computer Assisted Learning*, *24*(6), 494–506.

Tondeur, J., Van Braak, J., Ertmer, P. A., & Ottenbreit-Leftwich, A. (2017). Understanding the relationship between teachers' pedagogical beliefs and technology use in education: a systematic review of qualitative evidence. *Educational Technology Research and Development*, *65*(3), 555–575.

Tondeur, J., Van Braak, J., Sang, G., Voogt, J., Fisser, P., & Ottenbreit-Leftwich, A. (2012). Preparing pre-service teachers to integrate technology in education: A synthesis of qualitative evidence. *Computers & Education*, *59*(1), 134–144.

Tondeur, J., Van Keer, H., Van Braak, J., & Valcke, M. (2008). ICT integration in the classroom: Challenging the potential of a school policy. *Computers & Education*, *51*(1), 212–223.

Tort-Moloney, D. (1997). *Teacher autonomy: A Vygotskian theoretical framework*. CLCS Occasional Paper No. 48. Trinity College CLCS.

Tough, A. (1971). *The adult's learning projects. A fresh approach to theory and practice in adult learning*. The Ontario Institute for Studies in Education.

Trebbi, T. (2008). Freedom–a prerequisite for learner autonomy? Classroom innovation and language teacher education. In T. Lamb & H. Reinders (Eds.), *Learner and teacher autonomy: Concepts, realities, and responses* (pp. 33–46). John Benjamins Publishing Company.

Trinder, R. (2017). Informal and deliberate learning with new technologies. *ELT Journal*, *71*(4), 401–412.

Tripathi, R., Cervone, D., & Savani, K. (2018). Are the motivational effects of autonomy-supportive conditions universal? Contrasting results among Indians and Americans. *Personality and Social Psychology Bulletin*, *44*(9), 1287–1301.

Trust, T., & Prestridge, S. (2021). The interplay of five elements of influence on educators' PLN actions. *Teaching and Teacher Education*, *97*, 103195.

Tseng, F. C., & Kuo, F. Y. (2014). A study of social participation and knowledge sharing in the teachers' online professional community of practice. *Computers & Education*, *72*, 37–47.

Tseng, J. J., Chai, C. S., Tan, L., & Park, M. (2020). A critical review of research on technological pedagogical and content knowledge (TPACK) in language teaching. *Computer Assisted Language Learning*, *35*(4), 948–971.

Tseng, W. T., Cheng, H. F., & Hsiao, T. Y. (2019). Validating a motivational process model for mobile-assisted language learning. *English Teaching & Learn-*

ing, 43(4), 369–388.

Tseng, W. T., Liou, H. J., & Chu, H. C. (2020). Vocabulary learning in virtual environments: Learner autonomy and collaboration. *System, 88*, 102190.

Tsai, P. S., Tsai, C. C., & Hwang, G. J. (2011). The correlates of Taiwan teachers' epistemological beliefs concerning Internet environments, online search strategies, and search outcomes. *The Internet and Higher Education, 14*(1), 54–63.

Tsai, Y. R. (2021). Promotion of learner autonomy within the framework of a flipped EFL instructional model: perception and perspectives. *Computer Assisted Language Learning, 34*(7), 979–1011.

Tseng, F. C., & Kuo, F. Y. (2014). A study of social participation and knowledge sharing in the teachers' online professional community of practice. *Computers & Education, 72*, 37–47.

Tsuda, E., Sato, T., Wyant, J. D., & Hasegawa, E. (2019). Japanese elementary teachers' experiences of physical education professional development in depopulated rural school districts. *Curriculum Studies in Health and Physical Education, 10*(3), 262–276.

Turan, Z., & Akdag-Cimen, B. (2020). Flipped classroom in English language teaching: a systematic review. *Computer Assisted Language Learning, 33*(5–6), 590–606.

Tveit, Å. K., & Mangen, A. (2014). A Joker in the class: Teenage readers' attitudes and preferences to reading on different devices. *Library & Information Science Research, 36*(3–4), 179–184. http://dx.doi.org/10.1016/j.lisr.2014.08.001

Twining, P., Raffaghelli, J., Albion, P., & Knezek, D. (2013). Moving education into the digital age: the contribution of teachers' professional development. *Journal of Computer Assisted Learning, 29*(5), 426–437.

Ünal, S., Çeliköz, N., & Sari, I. (2017). EFL Proficiency in Language Learning and Learner Autonomy Perceptions of Turkish Learners. *Journal of Education and Practice, 8*(11), 117–122.

Urzúa, A., & Vásquez, C. (2008). Reflection and professional identity in teachers' future-oriented discourse. *Teaching and Teacher Education, 24*(7), 1935–1946.

Ushioda, E. (2011). Language learning motivation, self and identity: Current theoretical perspectives. *Computer Assisted Language Learning, 24*(3), 199–210.

Uzumcu, O., & Bay, E. (2021). The effect of computational thinking skill program design developed according to interest driven creator theory on prospective teachers. *Education and Information Technologies, 26*(1), 565–583.

Vaessen, M., Van Den Beemt, A., & De Laat, M. (2014). Networked Professional Learning: Relating the Formal and the Informal. *Frontline Learning Research, 2*(2), 56–71.

Vahedi, V. S., Ghonsooly, B., & Pishghadam, R. (2016). Vocabulary glossing: A meta-analysis of the relative effectiveness of different gloss types on L2 vocabulary acquisition. *Teaching English with Technology, 16*(1), 3–25.

Valero-Porras, M. J., & Cassany, D. (2015). Multimodality and language learning in a scanlation community. *Procedia-Social and Behavioral Sciences, 212*, 9–15.

van Bommel, J., Randahl, A. C., Liljekvist, Y., & Ruthven, K. (2020). Tracing teachers' transformation of knowledge in social media. *Teaching and Teacher Education, 87*, 102958.

Van Dijk, J. A. G. M. (2005). *The deepening divide: Inequality in the information society*. Los Angeles: Sage Publications.

Van Dijk, J. A. G. M. (2012). The evolution of the digital divide-the digital divide turns to inequality of skills and usage. In J. Bus, M. Crompton, M. Hildebrandt & G. Metakides (Eds.), *Digital enlightenment yearbook 2012* (pp. 57–75). IOS Press.

Van Katwijk, L., Jansen, E., & van Veen, K. (2021). Pre-service teacher research: a way to futureproof teachers? *European Journal of Teacher Education*. Advance online publication. https://doi.org/10.1080/02619768.2021.1928070

Van Loon, A. M., Ros, A., & Martens, R. (2012). Motivated learning with digital learning tasks: what about autonomy and structure? *Educational Technology Research and Development*, *60*(6), 1015–1032.

Van Raaij, E. M., & Schepers, J. J. (2008). The acceptance and use of a virtual learning environment in China. *Computers & Education*, *50*(3), 838–852.

Vanderlinde, R., Van Braak, J., & Dexter, S. (2012). ICT policy planning in a context of curriculum reform: Disentanglement of ICT policy domains and artifacts. *Computers & Education*, *58*(4), 1339–1350.

Vangrieken, K., Dochy, F., Raes, E., & Kyndt, E. (2015). Teacher collaboration: A systematic review. *Educational Research Review*, *15*, 17–40.

Vangrieken, K., Grosemans, I., Dochy, F., & Kyndt, E. (2017). Teacher autonomy and collaboration: A paradox? Conceptualising and measuring teachers' autonomy and collaborative attitude. *Teaching and Teacher Education*, *67*, 302–315.

Vangrieken, K., Meredith, C., Packer, T., & Kyndt, E. (2017). Teacher communities as a context for professional development: A systematic review. *Teaching and Teacher Education*, *61*, 47–59.

Vansteenkiste, M., Simons, J., Lens, W., Sheldon, K. M., & Deci, E. L. (2004). Motivating learning, performance, and persistence: the synergistic effects of intrinsic goal contents and autonomy-supportive contexts. *Journal of Personality and Social Psychology*, *87*(2), 246–260.

Vanwynsberghe, H., Vanderlinde, R., Georges, A., & Verdegem, P. (2015). The librarian 2.0: Identifying a typology of librarians' social media literacy. *Journal of Librarianship and Information Science*, *47*(4), 283–293.

Varank, I., & Ilhan, S. (2013). The Effects of Teachers' Educational Technology Skills on Their Classroom Management Skills. *Online Submission*, *3*(4), 138–146.

Vázquez Cano, E., Parra González, M. E., Segura Robles, A., & López Meneses, E. (2022). The Negative Effects of Technology on Education: A Bibliometric and Topic Modeling Mapping Analysis (2008–2019). *International Journal of Instruction*, *15*(2), 37–60.

Venkatesh, V., & Davis, F. D. (2000). A theoretical extension of the technology acceptance model: Four longitudinal field studies. *Management Science*, *46*(2), 186–204.

Venkatesh, V., Morris, M. G., Davis, G. B., & Davis, F. D. (2003). User acceptance of information technology: Toward a unified view. *MIS Quarterly*, 425–478.

Verkijika, S. F. (2019). Digital textbooks are useful but not everyone wants them: The role of technostress. *Computers & Education*, *140*, 103591.

Veronis, L., Tabler, Z., & Ahmed, R. (2018). Syrian refugee youth use social media: Building transcultural spaces and connections for resettlement in Ottawa, Canada. *Canadian Ethnic Studies*, *50*(2), 79–99.

Viberg, O., & Grönlund, Å. (2013). Cross-cultural analysis of users' attitudes toward the use of mobile devices in second and foreign language learning in higher education: A case from Sweden and China. *Computers & Education*, *69*, 169–180.

Vieira, F. (1997). Pedagogy for autonomy: Exploratory answers to questions any teacher should ask. In M. Miller-Verweyen (Ed.), *Neues Lernen, Selbstgesteuert, Autonom* (pp. 53–72). Goethe Institut.

Vieira, F. (2020). Language teacher education for autonomy: The role of inquiry in practicum experiences. In M. J. Jiménez Raya & F. Vieira (Eds.) *Autonomy in language education: Theory, research and practice* (pp. 227–248). Routledge.

Vitta, J. P., & Al-Hoorie, A. H. (2020). The flipped classroom in second language learning: A meta-analysis. *Language Teaching Research*. Advance online publication. https://doi.org/10.1177/1362168820981403

Vogel, F., Wecker, C., Kollar, I., & Fischer, F. (2017). Socio-cognitive scaffolding with computer-supported collaboration scripts: A meta-analysis. *Educational Psychology Review, 29*(3), 477–511.

Vongkulluksn, V. W., Xie, K., & Bowman, M. A. (2018). The role of value on teachers' internalization of external barriers and externalization of personal beliefs for classroom technology integration. *Computers & Education, 118*, 70–81.

Voogt, J., Fisser, P., Pareja Roblin, N., Tondeur, J., & van Braak, J. (2013). Technological pedagogical content knowledge—a review of the literature. *Journal of Computer Assisted Learning, 29*(2), 109–121.

Vrasidas, C., & Zembylas, M. (2004). Online professional development: Lessons from the field. *Education + Training, 46*, 326–334.

Vuorikari, R., Punie, Y., Gomez, S. C., & Van Den Brande, G. (2016). *DigComp 2.0: The digital competence framework for citizens. Update phase 1: The conceptual reference model* (No. JRC101254). Joint Research Centre (Seville site).

Wagner, J. (2015). Designing for language learning in the wild: Creating social infrastructures for second language learning. In T. Cadierno & S. W. Eskildsen (Eds.), *Usage-based perspectives on second language learning* (pp. 75–101). De Gruyter Mouton.

Wagner, J. (2019). Towards an epistemology of second language learning in the wild. In J. Hellerman, S. W. Eskildsen, S. P. Doehler, & A. Piirainen-Marsh (Eds.), *Conversation analytic research on learning-in-action* (pp. 251–271). Springer.

Warner, C., & Dupuy, B. (2018). Moving toward multiliteracies in foreign language teaching: Past and present perspectives… and beyond. *Foreign Language Annals, 51*(1), 116–128.

Wang, L., Ertmer, P. A., & Newby, T. J. (2004). Increasing preservice teachers' self-efficacy beliefs for technology integration. *Journal of Research on Technology in Education, 36*(3), 231–250.

Wang, A., Yu, S., Wang, M., & Chen, L. (2019). Effects of a visualization-based group awareness tool on in-service teachers' interaction behaviors and performance in a lesson study. *Interactive Learning Environments, 27*(5–6), 670–684.

Wang, W., & Jiang, L. (2021). Writing on WeChat moments: impact on writing performance and learner autonomy. *Computer Assisted Language Learning*, 1–29.

Wang, X., Li, Z., Ouyang, Z., & Xu, Y. (2021). The Achilles Heel of technology: How does technostress affect university students' wellbeing and technology-enhanced Learning. *International Journal of Environmental Research and Public Health, 18*(23), 12322.

Wang, S., & Vásquez, C. (2012). Web 2.0 and second language learning: What does the research tell us? *CALICO Journal, 29*(3), 412–430.

Wang, Q., & Zhang, H. (2014). Promoting teacher autonomy through university–school collaborative research. *Language Teaching Research, 18*(2), 222–241.

Wang, S., Tlili, A., Zhu, L., & Yang, J. (2021). Do playfulness and university support facilitate the adoption of online education in a crisis? COVID-19 as a case study based on the technology acceptance model. *Sustainability*, *13*(16), 9104.

Wang, W., Schmidt-Crawford, D., & Jin, Y. (2018). Preservice teachers' TPACK development: A review of literature. *Journal of Digital Learning in Teacher Education*, *34*(4), 234–258.

Wang, Y. S., Lin, H. H., & Liao, Y. W. (2012). Investigating the individual difference antecedents of perceived enjoyment in students' use of blogging. *British Journal of Educational Technology*, *43*(1), 139–152.

Warschauer, M., Knobel, M., & Stone, L. (2004). Technology and equity in schooling: Deconstructing the digital divide. *Educational Policy*, *18*(4), 562–588.

Wasserman, S., & Faust, K. (1994). *Social network analysis: Methods and applications*. Cambridge University Press.

Webb, S., & Nation, P. (2012). Teaching vocabulary. In C. A. Chapelle (Ed.), *The encyclopedia of applied linguistics* (pp.1–5). Wiley Online Library. https://doi.org/10.1002/9781405198431.wbeal1177

Webb, S., & Nation, P. (2017). *How vocabulary is learned*. Oxford University Press.

Webster-Wright, A. (2009). Reframing professional development through understanding authentic professional learning. *Review of Educational Research*, *79*(2), 702–739.

Wei, R. C., Darling-Hammond, L., Andree, A., Richardson, N., & Orphanos, S. (2009). Professional Learning in the Learning Profession: A Status Report on Teacher Development in the US and Abroad. Technical Report. *National Staff Development Council*.

Wermke, W. (2011). Continuing professional development in context: teachers' continuing professional development culture in Germany and Sweden. *Professional Development in Education*, *37*(5), 665–683.

Wermke, W., & Höstfält, G. (2014). Contextualizing teacher autonomy in time and space: A model for comparing various forms of governing the teaching profession. *Journal of Curriculum Studies*, *46*(1), 58–80.

Wermke, W., Olason Rick, S., & Salokangas, M. (2019). Decision-making and control: Perceived autonomy of teachers in Germany and Sweden. *Journal of Curriculum Studies, 51*(3), 306–325.

Wermke, W., & Salokangas, M. (2021). *The autonomy paradox: Teachers' perceptions of self-governance across Europe*. Springer International Publishing.

White, C., & Bown, J. (2020). Encouraging learners to become better-informed consumers of L2 learning opportunities. *Language Teaching Research Quarterly*, *19*, 5–18.

Wigfield, A. i Eccles, JS (2000). Expectancy-value theory of motivation. *Contemporary Educational Psychology*, *25*, 68–81.

Wilches, J. U. (2007). Teacher autonomy: A critical review of the research and concept beyond applied linguistics. *Íkala, Revista de Lenguaje y Cultura*, *12*(18), 245–275.

Wilcox, K., & Stephen, A. T. (2013). Are close friends the enemy? Online social networks, self-esteem, and self-control. *Journal of Consumer Research*, *40*(1), 90–103.

Williams, R., & Edge, D. (1996). The social shaping of technology. *Research Policy (25)*, 865–899.

Willis, J., Weiser, B., & Smith, D. (2016). Increasing teacher confidence in teaching and technology use through vicarious experiences within an environmental education context. *Applied Environmental Education & Communication, 15*(3), 199–213.

Wilmer, H. H., Sherman, L. E., & Chein, J. M. (2017). Smartphones and cognition: A review of research exploring the links between mobile technology habits and cognitive functioning. *Frontiers in Psychology, 8*, 605. https://doi.org/10.3389/fpsyg.2017.00605

Wilson, M. L. (2021). The impact of technology integration courses on preservice teacher attitudes and beliefs: A meta-analysis of teacher education research from 2007–2017. *Journal of Research on Technology in Education.* Advance online publication. https://doi.org/10.1080/15391523.2021.1950085

Wilson, M. L., Ritzhaupt, A. D., & Cheng, L. (2020). The impact of teacher education courses for technology integration on pre-service teacher knowledge: A meta-analysis study. *Computers & Education, 156.* Advance online publication. https://doi.org/10.1016/j.compedu.2020.103941

Wolters, C. A., & Hussain, M. (2015). Investigating grit and its relations with college students' self-regulated learning and academic achievement. *Metacognition and Learning, 10*(3), 293–311.

Wong, J., Baars, M., Davis, D., Van Der Zee, T., Houben, G. J., & Paas, F. (2019). Supporting self-regulated learning in online learning environments and MOOCs: A systematic review. *International Journal of Human–Computer Interaction, 35*(4–5), 356–373.

Wood, S. G., Moxley, J. H., Tighe, E. L., & Wagner, R. K. (2018). Does use of text-to-speech and related read-aloud tools improve reading comprehension for students with reading disabilities? A meta-analysis. *Journal of Learning Disabilities, 51*(1), 73–84.

Wu, Y. T., Chai, C. S., & Wang, L. J. (2022). Exploring secondary school teachers' TPACK for video-based flipped learning: the role of pedagogical beliefs. *Education and Information Technologies, 27*, 8793–8819.

Wu, Y., & Wu, F. (2018). The relationship between teacher autonomy and ICT competency of pre-service teachers. In *2018 Seventh International Conference of Educational Innovation through Technology (EITT)* (pp. 11–15). IEEE.

Xie, K., Kim, M. K., Cheng, S. L., & Luthy, N. C. (2017). Teacher professional development through digital content evaluation. *Educational Technology Research and Development, 65*(4), 1067–1103.

Xie, K., Nelson, M. J., Cheng, S. L., & Jiang, Z. (2021). Examining changes in teachers' perceptions of external and internal barriers in their integration of educational digital resources in K-12 classrooms. *Journal of Research on Technology in Education.* Advance online publication. https://doi.org/10.1080/15391523.2021.1951404

Xing, W., & Gao, F. (2018). Exploring the relationship between online discourse and commitment in Twitter professional learning communities. *Computers & Education, 126*, 388–398.

Yamashita, H. (2015). Affect and the development of learner autonomy through advising. *Studies in Self-Access Learning Journal, 6*(1), 62–85.

Yeh, E., & Swinehart, N. (2020). Social media literacy in L2 environments: Navigating anonymous user-generated content. *Computer Assisted Language Learning, 38*(8), 1731–1753.

Yeh, H. C. (2018). Exploring the perceived benefits of the process of multimodal video making in developing multiliteracies. *Language Learning & Technolo-*

gy, 22(2), 28–37.

Yeh, Y. F., Chen, M. C., Hung, P. H., & Hwang, G. J. (2010). Optimal self-explanation prompt design in dynamic multi-representational learning environments. *Computers & Education, 54*(4), 1089–1100.

Yeh, Y. L., & Lan, Y. J. (2018). Fostering student autonomy in English learning through creations in a 3D virtual world. *Educational Technology Research and Development, 66*(3), 693–708.

Yelland, N., & Masters, J. (2007). Rethinking scaffolding in the information age. *Computers & Education, 48*(3), 362–382.

Yen, C. J., Tu, C. H., Sujo-Montes, L. E., Armfield, S. W., & Chan, J. Y. (2016). The Relationship between self-regulated learning and PLE management. In M. Raisinghani (Ed.), *Revolutionizing education through web-based instruction* (pp. 253–280). IGI Global.

Yen, M. H., Chen, S., Wang, C. Y., Chen, H. L., Hsu, Y. S., & Liu, T. C. (2018). A framework for self‑regulated digital learning (SRDL). *Journal of Computer Assisted Learning, 34*(5), 580–589.

Yildiz, A. (2021). The relationship between secondary education students' digital addiction. *Research in Pedagogy, 11*(1), 151–164.

Yokoyama, M., & Miwa, K. (2018). Relationship between goal orientation, conception of learning and learning behavior. *Proceedings of 15th international conference of cognition and exploratory learning in digital age (CELDA 2018)* (pp. 233–240). International Association for the Development of the Information Society. http://files.eric.ed.gov/fulltext/ED600599.pdf

You, J. W., & Kang, M. (2014). The role of academic emotions in the relationship between perceived academic control and self-regulated learning in online learning. *Computers & Education, 77*, 125–133.

Yuan, R. & Lee, I. (2015). Action research facilitated by university–school collaboration. *ELT Journal, 69*(1), 1–10. https://doi.org/10.1093/elt/ccu031

Yudintseva, A. (2015). Synthesis of research on video games for the four second language skills and vocabulary practice. *Open Journal of Social Sciences, 3*(11), 81–98.

Yuen, A. H., & Ma, W. W. (2002). Gender differences in teacher computer acceptance. *Journal of Technology and Teacher Education, 10*(3), 365–382.

Yurtseven Avci, Z., O'Dwyer, L. M., & Lawson, J. (2020). Designing effective professional development for technology integration in schools. *Journal of Computer Assisted Learning, 36*(2), 160–177.

Zainuddin, Z., & Halili, S. H. (2016). Flipped classroom research and trends from different fields of study. *International Review of Research in Open and Distributed Learning, 17*(3), 313–340.

Zhan, Y., & Andrews, S. (2014). Washback effects from a high-stakes examination on out-of-class English learning: Insights from possible self theories. *Assessment in Education: Principles, Policy & Practice, 21*(1), 71–89.

Zhang, S., & Liu, Q. (2019). Investigating the relationships among teachers' motivational beliefs, motivational regulation, and their learning engagement in online professional learning communities. *Computers & Education, 134*, 145–155. https://doi.org/10.1016/j.compedu.2019.02.013

Zhang, S., Liu, Q., Chen, W., Wang, Q., & Huang, Z. (2017). Interactive networks and social knowledge construction behavioral patterns in primary school teachers' online collaborative learning activities. *Computers & Education, 104*, 1–17. https://doi.org/10.1016/j.compedu.2016.10.011

Zhao, Y., Wang, N., Li, Y., Zhou, R., & Li, S. (2021). Do cultural differences affect users' e‐learning adoption? A meta‐analysis. *British Journal of Educational Technology*, *52*(1), 20–41.

Zheng, L. (2016). The effectiveness of self-regulated learning scaffolds on academic performance in computer-based learning environments: A meta-analysis. *Asia Pacific Education Review*, *17*(2), 187–202. https://doi.org/10.1080/10494820.2019.1610457

Zheng, L., Gibson, D., & Gu, X. (2019). Understanding the process of teachers' technology adoption with a dynamic analytical model. *Interactive Learning Environments*, *27*(5–6), 726–739. https://doi.org/10.1080/10494820.2019.1610457

Zheng, L., Li, X., & Chen, F. (2018). Effects of a mobile self-regulated learning approach on students' learning achievements and self-regulated learning skills. *Innovations in Education and Teaching International*, *55*(6), 616–624.

Zheng, C., Liang, J. C., Li, M., & Tsai, C. C. (2018). The relationship between English language learners' motivation and online self-regulation: A structural equation modelling approach. *System*, *76*, 144–157.

Zheng, C., Liang, J. C., Yang, Y. F., & Tsai, C. C. (2016). The relationship between Chinese university students' conceptions of language learning and their online self-regulation. *System*, *57*, 66–78.

Zhou, M. (2016). Chinese university students' acceptance of MOOCs: A self-determination perspective. *Computers & Education*, *92*, 194–203. https://doi.org/10.1016/j.compedu.2015.10.012

Zhou, X., Chai, C. S., Jong, M. S. Y., & Xiong, X. B. (2021). Does relatedness matter for online self-regulated learning to promote perceived learning gains and satisfaction? *The Asia-Pacific Education Researcher*, *30*(3), 205–215.

Zhu, C. (2015). Organisational culture and technology-enhanced innovation in higher education. *Technology, Pedagogy and Education*, *24*(1), 65–79.

Zhu, G. (2021). Is flipping effective? A meta-analysis of the effect of flipped instruction on K-12 students' academic achievement. *Educational Technology Research and Development*, *69*(2), 733–761.

Zimmerman, B. J. (1990). Self-regulated learning and academic achievement: An overview. *Educational Psychologist*, *25*(1), 3–17.

Zimmerman, B. J., & Bandura, A. (1994). Impact of self-regulatory influences on writing course attainment. *American Educational Research Journal*, *31*(4), 845–862.

Zimmerman, B. J., & Kitsantas, A. (2005). Homework practices and academic achievement: The mediating role of self-efficacy and perceived responsibility beliefs. *Contemporary Educational Psychology*, *30*(4), 397–417.

Zimmerman, B. J., & Schunk, D. H. (2011). Self-regulated learning and performance: An introduction and an overview. In B. J. Zimmerman & D. H. Schunk (Eds.), *Handbook of self-regulation of learning and performance* (pp. 1–12). Routledge.

Zinger, D., Tate, T., & Warschauer, M. (2017). Learning and teaching with technology: Technological pedagogy and teacher practice. In D. J. Candinin & J. Husu (Eds.), *The SAGE handbook of research on teacher education* (pp. 577–593). Sage.

Index

addiction, digital *see* digital addiction
agency, *see* learner agency
andragogy, 24–25, 96, 115, 219
anxiety, 83, 93, 96, 100, 122, 128, 197–198, 207
augmented reality (AR), 29–30
autonomy
   amplifying, 18, 109, 114, 117, 119, 130, 141,
   as language learner, 17, 19, 123
   as language user, 17, 19, 27, 123, 132, *see also* autonomy as communicator
   as person, 17, 19, 123, 135–136
   language, *see* language autonomy
   learner, *see* learner autonomy
   personal, *see* personal autonomy
   professional, *see* professional autonomy
   situational freedom of, *see* situational freedom of autonomy
   supportive pedagogy, 24, 117, 120
   teacher, *see* teacher autonomy
   autonomous motivation, *see* motivation, autonomous

bridging activity, 41, 110, 113 see also connect in–class and out–of–class learning

collective autonomy, 14, 26, 31–32, 41, 88
connected learning, 33, 139, 222
context–aware, 29, 98
context–sensitive lens, 237
coordination and supplementation approach, 111
critical perspective, 50, 71, 235
cultural belief, 61–62, 103
cultural value, 68–69, 101–102

culturally shaped technological practice, 101–103

democratize learning, 235
digital
   addiction, 60
   divide, 64–66, 67
   habits, 53–55
   literacy, 65, 72, 88, 90, 193, 195 196, 201, 206
   wild, 29, 33–35, 40, 113
discursive resource, 103–104, 122

e-portfolio, *see* portfolio
education governance, 162
epistemological belief, 75, 185–187, 206, 211
ethnographic approach, 113
expectancy value theory, 80–81
extramural activity, 38

facilitating condition, 183, 201, 204, 215
formal professional learning, 148
   facilitate, 220
framework of barriers to teacher technology integration, 184

goal of autonomy, 17
goal orientation, 82
grit, 83–84
growth mindset, 84

heutagogical approaches, 40, 96, 115, 219–220
holistic perspective, 237

identity–oriented pedagogy, 138

Index

in-class learning, 5, 24, 30, 32–33, 37, 39–41, 67, 104–105, 110–111
independent learning, 6, 111, 149, 156, 222
informal learning, 8, 20, 31, 33–35, 37, 39–40, 42, 66, 77, 94–95, 106, 112–113, 132
informal professional learning, 148–150, 156, 169, 172, 175, 231–232
  facilitate, 231–232
  sources, 150
informed consumer approach, 138
instructional support, 97–100, 108, 164, 226
interest-driven learning, 221
interest, 35, 95, 118, 139–140

job-embedded learning, 222

L2 motivational self-system, 81
language advising, 127
language autonomy, 16
learner
  agency, *see* learner agency
  autonomy, *see* learner autonomy
  choice, 3, 21, 25, 33, 46, 59, 92, 94, 112, 117–118, 120, *see also* student choice
  control, 8–9, 25, 59, 74, 95–96, 100
  empowerment, 175–176
  training, 122–123, 141
learner agency, 18, 45, 47–48, 60, 62, 115
learner autonomy, 13–16, 20–21, 136
  approaches, 19
  aspects, 15–16
  definition, 1
  dimensions, 1, 20, 23, 123
  goals, 17
  purposes, 16
  technical aspect of *see* technical aspect of learner autonomy
learning
  belief, 46, 76, 116
  ecology perspective, 39
  vicarious, *see* vicarious learning
linguistic power, 66

literacy
  digital, *see* digital literacy
  practice, 13, 22, 63, 72, 112, 195
macro-level, 177, 202, 209
mastery experience, 164
media and information literacy, 53, 133, 185
meso-level, 177, 179
micro-level, 177, 181
motivation, 2, 5, 9, 21, 28, 29, 31, 32, 39, 74, 75, 76, 77, 84, 87, 89, 90, 93, 95, 104
  autonomous, 24, 84
  factors, 78-82
  intrinsic, 46
  learning, 26, 27, 41, 65
  personal, 21
  regulation of, 87
  self-, 43
  to use digital technologies, 66
multilingual identity, 137–138
multimodal project, 5, 27–28, 36

neoliberalism, 70–71

out-of-class learning, 4, 34, 39, 41, 63, 77, 80, 89, 110–112, 122

pedagogical agent, 44, 99, 126
pedagogical belief, 153, 185, 187–188, 225
perceived playfulness, 77, 96, 200
personal autonomy, 1, 14, 16, 123, 155
personal innovativeness, 84, 200–201
personal learning context, 19, 123, 138–139
personalized language learning ecology, 37, 40, 138
political aspects of learner autonomy, 1, 16, 23, 46, 152
portfolio, 128, 130, 136, 139, 165, 170, 205, 230, 233
positioning, 3, 5, 110, 114, 162, 210, 212, 237
post-technocratic view of technology, 51

professional autonomy, 145
psychological aspect of learner autonomy, 1, 16, 23, 42

rewilding, 19, 110

school culture, 60, 64, 151, 180, 194, 201–204, 231
self-access center, 19, 21
self-determination theory, 24, 43, 79, 121
self-directed learning, 19, 74–75, 81, 85, 88, 90, 92, 94, 99, 100, 102–103, 105, 120–121, 213, 151, 155, 171, 175, 189, 203, 213, 219
self-direction, 74, 79, 94, 101, 136, 145
self-regulated learning, 31 89–91, 94, 96, 123–125, 130, 186
self-regulation skills, 44, 53, 63, 65, 79, 89–90, 122, 130, 141, 245
self-regulation training, 9, 123–124
  cooperative learning, 130
  prompts, 9, 125
  protocols, 128
situational freedom of autonomy, 9, 15, 23
social media literacy, 134
societal censure, 177–179
structured unpredictability, 18, 35, 110
structuredness, 94, 112, 119, 236
student choice, 25, *see also* learner choice
subjective norm, 80, 102, 104, 154, 192, 200, 204, 207, 209
sustained learning, 224

TAM, *see* Technology Acceptance Model
teacher autonomy, 145–147
  development, 153
  in professional learning, 148
  in professional work, 146–147
  support, 154–155
teacher
  autonomy, *see* teacher autonomy
  identity, 191
  support, 88, 105–106, 136, 227

technical aspect of learner autonomy, 1, 23, 42
techno-stress, 60, 197, 207–209
Technology Acceptance Model, 184, 204, 206
Technology, Pedagogy And Content Knowledge, *see* TPACK
TPACK, 193–195, 203, 205, 209, 225–227
training, learner *see* learner training
translanguaging and trans–semiotizing practices, 4, 47–48, 135, 137

UNESCO Media and Information Literacy Curriculum, 133
UTAUT. 183, 204
ubiquitous learning, 5, 29, 57, 98,
unintended consequence, 50, 59–60, 173,
usage–based experiential pedagogies, 40, 113

vicarious learning, 149, 164–166

Will, Skill, Tool and Pedagogy Model, 184

Index

www.ingramcontent.com/pod-product-compliance
Lightning Source LLC
Chambersburg PA
CBHW050207130526
44590CB00043B/3053